The Metamorphoses by Ovid

Books VIII-XV

Literally Translated into English Prose by Henry Thomas Riley

Publius Ovidius Naso but better known to us as simply Ovid was born on 20th March 43 BC in Sulmo (modern day Sulmona) in Italy.

He was educated in rhetoric in Rome in preparation for the practice of Law. Accounts of his character say that he was emotional and not able to stay within the argumentative boundaries of rhetoric discipline. After the early death of his brother, Ovid ceased his law studies and travelled to Athens, Asia Minor, and Sicily. He held a number of minor public posts but, around 29-25 BC began to pursue poetry, a decision that brought with it his father's disapproval.

Ovid's first recitation occurred when he was eighteen (around 25 BC). He was part of the circle centered on the patron Marcus Valerius Messalla Corvinus, and appears to have been a friend of poets in the circle of Maecenas.

He married three times and divorced twice by the time he was thirty years old. He fathered a daughter, who eventually bore him grandchildren. His last wife was connected to the influential gens Fabia (an ancient Roman patrician family) and would help him during his later exile.

The first decades of Ovid's literary career were mostly spent writing poetry with erotic themes. The chronology of these early works cannot, however, be relied upon.

His earliest extant work is thought to be the 'Heroides', letters of mythological heroines to absent lovers, which is believed to have been published in 19 BC.

The first five-book collection of the 'Amores', erotic poems addressed to a lover, Corinna, is believed to have been published in 16–15 BC. The surviving three book version appears to have been published c. 8–3 BC.

Between these two editions of the 'Amores' his tragedy 'Medea', which was much admired in antiquity but is no longer extant, was performed.

Ovid buoyed by his glowing reputation now increased the tempo of his writing. 'Medicamina Faciei', was followed by the 'Ars Amatoria, the Art of Love' and immediately followed by 'Remedia Amoris'. This body of elegiac, erotic poetry saw Ovid cited as the equal of the Roman elegists Gallus, Tibullus, and Propertius.

By AD 8, he had completed his most ambitious work, the 'Metamorphoses', a 15-book hexameter epic poem. It catalogued Greek and Roman mythology, from the emergence of the universe to the apotheosis of Julius Caesar.

Concurrent with this, he worked on the 'Fasti', planned as 12-books but only 6 volumes (January to June were completed) in elegiac couplets on the calendar of Roman festivals and astronomy were completed. The remaining six books were interrupted by Ovid's sentence to exile.

In AD 8, Ovid was banished to Tomis, on the Black Sea, by the Emperor Augustus. This event shadowed his life and shaped his remaining poetic output. Ovid wrote that his exile was for carmen et error – "a poem and a mistake", claiming his crime was worse than murder, more harmful than poetry.

Ovid was also a contemporary of the older Virgil and Horace, with whom he is often ranked as one of the three canonical poets of Latin literature. The Imperial scholar Quintilian considered him the last of the Latin love elegists.

His poetry was much imitated during Late Antiquity and the Middle Ages, and greatly influenced Western art and literature. The Metamorphoses remains one of the most important sources of classical mythology.

In exile, Ovid wrote 'Tristia' and 'Epistulae ex Ponto', pointedly focused on his sadness and desolation. He was far from Rome and his beloved third wife.

The five books of the elegiac Tristia, a series of poems expressing the poet's despair in exile and advocating his return to Rome, are dated to AD 9–12.

'The Ibis', an elegiac curse poem attacking an adversary at home is also dated to this period. 'The Epistulae ex Ponto', a series of letters to friends in Rome asking them to effect his return, are thought to be his last compositions.

Ovid died at Tomis in AD 17 or 18. It is thought that the Fasti, which he spent time revising, were published posthumously.

Index of Contents

FABLE VIII
HENRY THOMAS RILEY (TRANSLATOR)

INTRODUCTION

The Metamorphoses of Ovid are a compendium of the Mythological narratives of ancient Greece and Rome, so ingeniously framed, as to embrace a large amount of information upon almost every subject connected with the learning, traditions, manners, and customs of antiquity, and have afforded a fertile field of investigation to the learned of the civilized world. To present to the public a faithful translation of a work, universally esteemed, not only for its varied information, but as being the masterpiece of one of the greatest Poets of ancient Rome, is the object of the present volume.

To render the work, which, from its nature and design, must, of necessity, be replete with matter of obscure meaning, more inviting to the scholar, and more intelligible to those who are unversed in Classical literature, the translation is accompanied with Notes and Explanations, which, it is believed, will be found to throw considerable light upon the origin and meaning of some of the traditions of heathen Mythology.

In the translation, the text of the Delphin edition has been generally adopted; and no deviation has been made from it, except in a few instances, where the reason for such a step is stated in the notes; at the same time, the texts of Burmann and Gierig have throughout been carefully consulted. The several editions vary materially in respect to punctuation; the Translator has consequently used his own discretion in adopting that which seemed to him the most fully to convey in each passage the intended meaning of the writer.

The Metamorphoses of Ovid have been frequently translated into the English language. On referring to Mr. Bohn's excellent Catalogue of the Greek and Latin Classics and their Translations, we find that the whole of the work has been twice translated into English Prose, while five translations in Verse are there enumerated. A prose version of the Metamorphoses was published by Joseph Davidson, about the middle of the last century, which professes to be "as near the original as the different idioms of the Latin and English will allow;" and to be "printed for the use of schools, as well as of private gentlemen." A few moments' perusal of this work will satisfy the reader that it has not the slightest pretension to be considered a literal translation, while, by its departure from the strict letter of the author, it has gained nothing in elegance of diction. It is accompanied by "critical, historical, geographical, and classical notes in English, from the best Commentators, both ancient and modern, beside a great number of notes, entirely new;" but notwithstanding this announcement, these annotations will be found to be but few in number, and, with some exceptions in the early part of the volume, to throw very little light on the obscurities of the text. A fifth edition of this translation was published so recently as 1822, but without any improvement, beyond the furbishing up of the old-fashioned language of the original preface. A far more literal translation of the Metamorphoses is that by John Clarke, which was first published about the year 1735, and had attained to a seventh edition in 1779. Although this version may be pronounced very nearly to fulfil the promise set forth in its title page, of being "as literal as possible," still, from the singular inelegance of its style, and the fact of its being couched in the conversational language of the early part of the last century, and being unaccompanied by any attempt at explanation, it may safely be pronounced to be ill adapted to the requirements of the present age. Indeed, it would not, perhaps, be too much to assert, that, although the translator may, in his own words, "have done an acceptable service to such gentlemen as are desirous of regaining or improving the skill they acquired at school," he has, in many instances, burlesqued rather than translated his author. Some of the curiosities of his version will be found set forth in the notes; but, for the purpose of the more readily justifying this assertion, a few of them are adduced: the word "nitidus" is always rendered "neat," whether applied to a fish, a cow, a chariot, a laurel, the steps of a temple, or the art of wrestling. He renders "horridus," "in a rude pickle;" "virgo" is generally translated "the young lady;" "vir" is "a gentleman;" "senex" and "senior" are indifferently "the old blade," "the old fellow," or "the old gentleman;" while "summa arx" is "the very tip-top." "Misera" is "poor soul;" "exsilio" means "to bounce forth;" "pellex" is "a miss;" "lumina" are "the peepers;" "turbatum fugere" is "to scower off in a mighty bustle;" "confundor" is "to be jumbled;" and "squalidus" is "in a sorry pickle." "Importuna" is "a plaguy baggage;" "adulterium" is rendered "her pranks;" "ambages" becomes either "a long rabble of words," "a long-winded detail," or "a tale of a tub;" "miserabile carmen" is "a dismal ditty;" "increpare hos" is "to rattle these blades;" "penetralia" means "the parlour;" while "accingere," more literally than elegantly, is translated "buckle to." "Situs" is "nasty stuff;" "oscula jungere" is "to tip him a kiss;" "pingue ingenium" is a circumlocution for "a blockhead;" "anilia instrumenta" are "his old woman's accoutrements;" and "repetito munere Bacchi" is conveyed to the sense of the reader as, "they return again to their bottle, and take the other glass." These are but a specimen of the blemishes which disfigure the most literal of the English translations of the Metamorphoses.

In the year 1656, a little volume was published, by John Bulloker, entitled "Ovid's Metamorphosis, translated grammatically, and, according to the propriety of our English tongue, so far as grammar and the verse will bear, written chiefly for the use of schools, to be used according to the directions in the preface to the painfull schoolmaster, and more fully in the book called, 'Ludus Literarius, or the Grammar school, chap. 8.'" Notwithstanding a title so pretentious, it contains a translation of no more than the first 567 lines of the first Book, executed in a fanciful and pedantic manner; and its rarity is now the only merit of the volume. A literal interlinear translation of the first Book "on the plan recommended by Mr. Locke," was published in 1839, which had been already preceded by "a selection from the Metamorphoses of Ovid, adapted to the Hamiltonian system, by a literal and interlineal translation," published by James Hamilton, the author of the Hamiltonian system. This work contains selections only from the first six books, and consequently embraces but a very small portion of the entire work.

For the better elucidation of the different fabulous narratives and allusions, explanations have been added, which are principally derived from the writings of Herodotus, Apollodorus, Pausanias, Dio Cassius, Dionysius of Halicarnassus, Strabo, Hyginus, Nonnus, and others of the historians, philosophers, and mythologists of antiquity. A great number of these illustrations are collected in the elaborate edition of Ovid, published by the Abbé Banier, one of the most learned scholars of the last century; who has, therein, and in his "Explanations of the Fables of Antiquity," with indefatigable labour and research, culled from the works of ancient authors, all such information as he considered likely to throw any light upon the Mythology and history of Greece and Rome.

This course has been adopted, because it was considered that a statement of the opinions of contemporary authors would be the most likely to enable the reader to form his own ideas upon the various subjects presented to his notice. Indeed, except in two or three instances, space has been found too limited to allow of more than an occasional reference to the opinions of modern scholars. Such being the object of the explanations, the reader will not be surprised at the absence of critical and lengthened discussions on many of those moot points of Mythology and early history which have occupied, with no very positive result, the attention of Niebuhr, Lobeck, Müller, Buttmann, and many other scholars of profound learning.

A SYNOPTICAL VIEW OF THE PRINCIPAL TRANSFORMATIONS MENTIONED IN THE METAMORPHOSES

BOOK VIII

In the mean time Minos besieges Megara. Scylla, becoming enamoured of him, betrays her country, the safety of which depends upon the purple lock of her father Nisu. Being afterwards rejected by Minos, she clings to his ship, and is changed into a bird, while her father becomes a sea eagle. Minos returns to Crete, and having erected the Labyrinth with the assistance of Dædalus, he there encloses the Minotaur, the disgrace of his family, and feeds it with his Athenian captives. Theseus being one of these, slays the monster: and having escaped from the Labyrinth by the aid of Ariadne, he takes her with him, but deserts her in the isle of Dia, where Bacchus meets with her, and places her crown among the Constellations. Dædalus being unable to escape from the island of Crete, invents wings and flies away; while Icarus, accompanying his father, is drowned. The partridge beholds the father celebrating his funeral rites, and testifies his joy: Perdix, or Talus, who had been envied by Minos for his ingenuity, and had been thrown by him from the temple of Minerva, having been transformed into that bird. Theseus, having now become celebrated, is invited to the chase of the Calydonian boar, which Atalanta is the first to wound. Meleager slays the monster; and his death is accelerated by his mother Althæa, who places in the fire the fatal billet. Returning from the expedition, Theseus comes to Acheloüs, and sees the islands called the Echinades, into which the Naiads have been transformed. Pirithoüs denies the possibility of this; but Lelex quotes, as an example, the case of Baucis and Philemon, who were changed into trees, while their house became a temple, and the neighbouring country a pool of water. Acheloüs then tells the story of the transformations of Proteus and of Metra, and how Metra supported her father Erisicthon, while afflicted with violent hunger.

BOOK IX

Acheloüs then relates his own transformations, when he was contending with Hercules for the hand of Deïanira. Hercules wins her, and Nessus attempts to carry her off: on which Hercules pierces him with one of his arrows that has been dipped in the blood of the Hydra. In revenge, Nessus, as he is dying, gives to Deïanira his garment stained with his blood. She, distrusting her husband's affection, sends him the garment; he puts it on, and his vitals are consumed by the venom. As he is dying, he hurls his attendant Lychas into the sea, where he becomes a rock. Hercules is conveyed to heaven, and is enrolled in the number of the Deities. Alcmena, his mother, goes to her daughter-in-law Iole, and tells her how Galanthis was changed into a weasel; while she, in her turn, tells the story of the transformation of her sister Dryope into the lotus. In the meantime Iolaüs comes, whose youth has been restored by Hebe. Jupiter shows, by the example of his sons Æacus and Minos, that all are not so blessed. Miletus, flying from Minos, arrives in Asia, and becomes the father of Byblis and Caunus. Byblis falls in love with her brother, and is transformed into a fountain. This would have appeared more surprising to all, if Iphis had not a short time before, on the day of her nuptials, been changed into a man.

BOOK X

Hymenæus attends these nuptials, and then goes to those of Orpheus; but with a bad omen, as Eurydice dies soon after, and cannot be brought to life. In his sorrow, Orpheus repairs to the solitudes of the mountains, where the trees flock around him at the sound of his lyre; and, among others, the pine, into which Atys has been changed; and the cypress, produced from the transformation of Cyparissus. Orpheus sings of the rape of Ganymede; of the change of Hyacinthus, who was beloved and slain by Apollo, into a flower; of the transformation of the Cerastæ into bulls; of the Propœtides, who were changed into stones; and of the statue of Pygmalion, which was changed into a living woman, who became the mother of Paphos. He then sings, how Myrrha, for her incestuous intercourse with her father, was changed into the myrrh tree; and how Adonis (to whom Venus relates the transformation of Hippomenes and Atalanta into lions) was transformed into an anemone.

BOOK XI

Orpheus is torn to pieces by the Thracian women; on which, a serpent, which attacks his face, is changed into stone. The women are transformed into trees by Bacchus, who deserts Thrace, and betakes himself to Phrygia; where Midas, for his care of Silenus, receives the power of making gold. He loathes this gift; and bathing in the river Pactolus, its sands become golden. For his stupidity, his ears are changed by Apollo into those of an ass. After this, that God goes to Troy, and aids Laomedon in building its walls. Hercules rescues his daughter Hesione, when fastened to a rock, and his companion Telamon receives her as his wife; while his brother Peleus marries the sea Goddess, Thetis. Going to visit Ceyx, he learns how Dædalion has been changed into a hawk, and sees a wolf changed into a rock. Ceyx goes to consult the oracle of Claros, and perishes by shipwreck. On this, Morpheus appears to Halcyone, in the form of her husband, and she is changed into a kingfisher; into which bird Ceyx is also transformed. Persons who observe them, as they fly, call to mind how Æsacus, the son of Priam, was changed into a sea bird, called the didapper.

BOOK XII

Priam performs the obsequies for Æsacus, believing him to be dead. The children of Priam attend, with the exception of Paris, who, having gone to Greece, carries off Helen, the wife of Menelaüs. The Greeks pursue Paris, but are detained at Aulis, where they see a serpent changed into stone, and prepare to sacrifice Iphigenia to Diana; but a hind is substituted for her. The Trojans hearing of the approach of the Greeks, in arms await their arrival. At the first onset, Cygnus, dashed by Achilles against a stone, is changed by Neptune into the swan, a bird of the same name, he having been vulnerable by no weapon. At the banquet of the chiefs, Nestor calls to mind Cæneus, who was also invulnerable; and who having been changed from a woman into a man, on being buried under a heap of trees, was transformed into a bird. This Cæneus was one of the Lapithæ, at the battle of whom with the Centaurs, Nestor was present. Nestor also tells how his brother, Periclymenus, was changed into an eagle. Meanwhile, Neptune laments the death of Cygnus, and entreats Apollo to direct the arrow of Paris against the heel of Achilles, which is done, and that hero is slain.

BOOK XIII

Ajax Telamon and Ulysses contend for the arms of Achilles. Ihe former slays himself, on which a hyacinth springs up from his blood. Troy being taken, Hecuba is carried to Thrace, where she tears out the eyes of Polymnestor, and is afterwards changed into a bitch. While the Gods deplore her misfortunes, Aurora is occupied with grief for the death of her son Memnon, from whose ashes the birds called Memnonides arise. Æneas flying from Troy, visits Anius, whose daughters have been changed into doves; and after touching at other places, remarkable for various transformations, he arrives in Sicily, where is the maiden Scylla, to whom Galatea relates how Polyphemus courted her, and how he slew Acis. On this, Glaucus, who has been changed into a sea Deity, makes his appearance.

BOOK THE EIGHTH

FABLE I [VIII.1-151]

Minos commences the war with the siege of Megara. The preservation of the city depends on a lock of the hair of its king, Nisus. His daughter, Scylla, falling in love with Minos, cuts off the fatal lock, and gives it to him. Minos makes himself master of the place; and, abhorring Scylla and the crime she has been guilty of, he takes his departure. In despair, she throws herself into the sea, and follows his fleet. Nisus, being transformed into a sea eagle, attacks her in revenge, and she is changed into a bird called Ciris.

Now, Lucifer unveiling the day and dispelling the season of night, the East wind[1] fell, and the moist vapours arose. The favourable South winds gave a passage to the sons of Æacus,[2] and Cephalus returning; with which, being prosperously impelled, they made the port they were bound for, before it was expected.

In the meantime Minos is laying waste the Lelegeian coasts,[3] and previously tries the strength of his arms against the city Alcathoë, which Nisus had; among whose honoured hoary hairs a lock, distinguished by its purple colour, descended from the middle of his crown, the safeguard of his powerful kingdom. The sixth horns of the rising Phœbe were now growing again, and the fortune of the war was still in suspense, and for a long time did victory hover between them both with uncertain wings. There was a regal tower built with vocal walls, on which the son of Latona[4] is reported to have laid his golden harp; and its sound adhered to the stone. The daughter of Nisus was wont often to go up thither, and to strike the resounding stones with a little pebble, when it was a time of peace. She used, likewise, often to view the fight, and the contests of the hardy warfare, from that tower. And now, by the continuance of the hostilities, she had become acquainted with both the names of the chiefs, their arms, their horses, their dresses, and the Cydonean[5] quivers.

Before the rest, she had observed the face of the chieftain, the son of Europa; even better than was enough for merely knowing him. In her opinion, Minos, whether it was that he had enclosed his head in a helm crested with feathers, was beauteous in a helmet; or whether he had taken up a shield shining with gold, it became him to assume that shield. Drawing his arm back, did he hurl the slender javelin; the maiden commended his skill, joined with strength. Did he bend the wide bow with the arrow laid upon it; she used to swear that thus Phœbus stood, when assuming his arrows. But when he exposed his face, by taking off the brazen helmet, and, arrayed in purple, pressed the back of a white horse, beauteous with embroidered housings, and guided his foaming mouth; the virgin daughter of Nisus was hardly mistress of herself, hardly able to control a sound mind. She used to call the javelin happy which he touched, and the reins happy which he was pressing with his hand. She had an impulse (were it only possible) to direct her virgin footsteps through the hostile ranks; she had an impulse to cast her body from the top of the towers into the Gnossian camp, or to open the gates, strengthened with brass, to the enemy; or, indeed, anything else, if Minos should wish it. And as she was sitting, looking at the white tents of the Dictæan king, she said, "I am in doubt whether I should rejoice, or whether I should grieve, that this mournful war is carried on. I grieve that Minos is the enemy of the person who loves him; but unless there had been a war, would he have been known to me? yet, taking me for a hostage, he might cease the war, and have me for his companion, me as a pledge of peace. If, most beauteous of beings, she who bore thee, was such as thou art thyself, with reason was the God Jupiter inflamed with love for her. Oh! thrice happy were I, if, moving upon wings through the air, I could light upon the camp of the Gnossian king, and, owning myself and my flame, could ask him with what dowry he could wish to be purchased; provided only, that he did not ask the city of my father. For, perish rather the desired alliance, than that I should prevail by treason; although the clemency of a merciful conqueror has often made it of advantage to many, to be conquered. He certainly carries on a just war for his slain son,[6] and is strong both in his cause, and in the arms that defend his cause.

"We shall be conquered, as I suppose. If this fate awaits this city, why should his own arms, and not my love, open the walls to him? It will be better for him to conquer without slaughter and delay, and the expense of his own blood. How much, indeed, do I dread, Minos, lest any one should unknowingly wound thy breast! for who is so hardened as to dare, unless unknowingly, to direct his cruel lance against thee? The design pleases me; and my determination is to deliver up my country as a dowry, together with myself, and so to put an end to the war. But to be willing, is too little; a guard watches the approaches, and my father keeps the keys of the gates. Him alone, in my wretchedness, do I dread; he alone obstructs my desires. Would that the Gods would grant I might be without a father! Every one, indeed, is a God to himself. Fortune is an enemy to idle prayers. Another woman, inflamed with a passion so great, would long since have taken a pleasure in destroying whatever stood in the way of her love. And why should any one be bolder than myself? I could dare to go through flames, and amid swords. But in this case there is no occasion for any flames or any swords; I only want the lock of my father. That purple lock is more precious to me than gold; it will make me happy, and mistress of my own wish."

As she is saying such things, the night draws on, the greatest nurse of cares, and with the darkness her boldness increases. The first slumbers are now come, in which sleep takes possession of the breast wearied with the cares of the day. She silently enters the chamber of her father, and (O abominable crime!) the daughter despoils the father of his fatal lock, and having got the prize of crime, carries with her the spoil of her impiety; and issuing forth by the gate, she goes through the midst of the enemy, (so great is her confidence in her deserts) to the king, whom, in astonishment, she thus addresses: "'Twas love that urged the deed. I am Scylla, the royal issue of Nisus; to thee do I deliver the fortunes of my country and my own, as well; I ask for no reward, but thyself. Take this purple lock, as a pledge of my love; and do not consider that I am delivering to thee a lock of hair, but the life of my father." And then, in her right hand, she holds forth the infamous present. Minos refuses it, thus held out; and shocked at the thought of so unheard of a crime, he says, "May the Gods, O thou reproach of our age, banish thee from their universe; and may both earth and sea be denied to thee. At least, I will not allow so great a monster to come into Crete, the birth-place of Jupiter, which is my realm." He thus spoke;[7] and when, like a most just lawgiver, he had imposed conditions on the vanquished, he ordered the halsers of the fleet to be loosened, and the brazen beaked ships to be impelled with the oars. Scylla, when she beheld the launched ships sailing on the main, and saw that the prince did not give her the expected reward of her wickedness, having spent all her entreaties, fell into a violent rage, and holding up her hands, with her hair dishevelled, in her frenzy she exclaimed,

"Whither dost thou fly, the origin of thy achievements thus left behind, O thou preferred before my country, preferred before my father? Whither dost thou fly, barbarous man? whose victory is both my crime and my merit. Has neither the gift presented to thee, nor yet my passion, moved thee? nor yet the fact that all my hopes were centred in thee alone? For whither shall I return, forsaken by thee? To my country? Subdued, it is ruined. But suppose it were still safe; by my treachery, it is shut against me. To the face of my father, that I have placed in thy power. My fellow-citizens hate me deservedly; the neighbours dread my example. I have closed the whole world against me, that Crete alone might be open to me. And dost thou thus forbid me that as well? Is it thus, ungrateful one, that thou dost desert me? Europa was not thy mother, but the inhospitable Syrtis,[8] or Armenian[9] tigresses, or Charybdis disturbed by the South wind. Nor wast thou the son of Jupiter; nor was thy mother beguiled by the assumed form of a bull. That story of thy birth is false. He was both a fierce bull, and one charmed with the love of no heifer, that begot thee. Nisus, my father, take vengeance upon me. Thou city so lately betrayed, rejoice at my misfortunes; for I have deserved them, I confess, and I am worthy to perish. Yet let some one of those, whom I have impiously ruined, destroy me. Why dost thou, who hast conquered by means of my crime, chastise that crime? This, which was treason to my country and to my father, was an act of kindness to thee. She is truly worthy[10] of thee for a husband, who, adulterously enclosed in wood, deceived the fierce-looking bull, and bore in her womb an offspring of shape dissimilar to herself. And do my complaints reach thy ears? Or do the same winds bear away my fruitless words, and thy ships, ungrateful man? Now, ah! now, it is not to be wondered at that Pasiphaë preferred the bull to thee; thou didst have the more savage nature of the two. Wretch that I am! He joys in speeding onward, and the waves resound, cleaved by his oars. Together with myself, alas! my native land recedes from him. Nothing dost thou avail; oh thou! forgetful to no purpose of my deserts. In spite of thee, will I follow thee, and grasping thy crooked stern, I will be dragged through the long seas."

Scarce has she said this, when she leaps into the waves, and follows the ships, Cupid giving her strength, and she hangs, an unwelcome companion, to the Gnossian ship. When her father beholds her, (for now he is hovering in the air, and he has lately been made a sea eagle, with tawny wings), he is going to tear her in pieces with his crooked beak. Through fear she quits the stern; but the light air seems to support her as she is falling, that she may not touch the sea. It is feathers that support her. With feathers, being changed into a bird, she is called Ciris;[11] and this name does she obtain from cutting off the lock.

[Footnote 1: The East wind.—Ver. 2. Eurus, or the East wind, while blowing, would prevent the return of Cephalus from the island of Ægina to Athens.]

[Footnote 2: The sons of Æacus.—Ver. 4. 'Æacidis' may mean either the forces sent by Æacus, or his sons Telamon and Peleus, in command of those troops. It has been well observed, that 'redeuntibus,' 'returning,' is here somewhat improperly applied to the troops of Æacus, for they were not, strictly speaking, returning to Athens although Cephalus was.]

[Footnote 3: Lelegeian coasts.—Ver. 6. Of Megara, which is also called Alcathoë, from Alcathoüs, its restorer.]

[Footnote 4: Of Latona.—Ver. 15. The story was, that when Alcathoüs was rebuilding the walls of Megara, Apollo assisted him, and laying down his lyre among the stones, its tones were communicated to them.]

[Footnote 5: Cydonean.—Ver 22. From Cydon, a city of Crete.]

[Footnote 6: His slain son.—Ver. 58. Namely, his son Androgeus, who had been put to death, as already mentioned.]

[Footnote 7: He thus spoke.—Ver. 101. The poet omits the continuation of the siege by Minos, and how he took Megara by storm, as not pertaining to the developement of his story.]

[Footnote 8: Inhospitable Syrtis.—Ver. 120. There were two famous quicksands, or 'Syrtes,' in the Mediterranean Sea, near the coast of Africa; the former near Cyrene, and the latter near Byzacium, which were known by the name of 'Syrtis Major' and 'Syrtis Minor.' The inhabitants of the neighbouring coasts were savage and inhospitable, and subsisted by plundering the shipwrecked vessels.]

[Footnote 9: Armenian.—Ver. 121. Armenia was a country of Asia, lying between Mount Taurus and the Caucasian chain, and extending from Cappadocia to the Caspian Sea. It was divided into the greater and the less Armenia, the one to the East, the other to the West. Its tigers were noted for their extreme fierceness.]

[Footnote 10: She is truly worthy.—Ver. 131. Pasiphaë, who was the mother of the Minotaur.]

[Footnote 11: She is called Ciris.—Ver. 151. From the Greek word κείρω, 'to clip,' or 'cut.' According to Virgil, who, in his Ciris, describes this transformation, this bird was of variegated colours, with a purple breast, and legs of a reddish hue, and lived a solitary life in retired spots. It is uncertain what kind of bird it was; some think it was a hawk, some a lark, and others a partridge. It has been suggested that Ovid did not enter into the details of this transformation, because it had been so recently depicted in beautiful language by Virgil. Hyginus says that the 'Ciris' was a fish.]

EXPLANATION

Minos, having raised an army and received auxiliary troops from his allies, made war upon the Athenians, to revenge the death of his son, Androgeus. Having conquered Nisea, he laid siege to Megara, which was betrayed by the perfidy of Scylla, the daughter of its king, Nisus. Pausanias and other historians say that the story here related by the Poet is based on fact; and that Scylla held a secret correspondence with Minos during the siege of Megara, and, at length, introduced him into the town, by opening the gates to him with the keys which she had stolen from her father, while he was asleep. This is probably alluded to under the allegorical description of the fatal lock of hair, though why it should be depicted in that form especially, it is difficult to guess. The change of Scylla into a lark, or partridge, and of her father into a sea eagle, are poetical fictions based on the equivocal meanings of their names, the one Greek and the other Hebrew; for the name 'Ciris' resembles the Greek verb κείρω, which signifies 'to clip,' or 'cut short.' 'Nisus,' too, resembles the Hebrew word 'Netz,' which means a bird resembling the osprey, or sea eagle. Apollodorus says, that Minos ordered Scylla to be thrown into the sea; and Zenodotus, that he caused her to be hanged at the mainmast of his ship.

FABLE II [VIII.152-182]

Minos, having overcome the Athenians, obliges them to pay a tribute of youths and virgins of the best families, to be exposed to the Minotaur. The lot falls on Theseus, who, by the assistance of Ariadne, kills the monster, escapes from the labyrinth, which Dædalus made, and carries Ariadne to the island of Naxos, where he abandons her. Bacchus wooes her, and, to immortalize her name, he transforms the crown which he has given her into a Constellation.

Minos paid, as a vow to Jupiter, the bodies of a hundred bulls, as soon as, disembarking from his ships, he reached the land of the Curetes; and his palace was decorated with the spoils there hung up. The reproach of his family had now grown up, and the shameful adultery of his mother was notorious, from the unnatural shape of the two-formed monster. Minos resolves to remove the disgrace from his abode, and to enclose it in a habitation of many divisions, and an abode full of mazes. Dædalus, a man very famed for his skill in architecture, plans the work, and confounds the marks of distinction, and leads the eyes into mazy wanderings, by the intricacy of its various passages. No otherwise than as the limpid Mæander sports in the Phrygian fields, and flows backwards and forwards with its varying course, and, meeting itself, beholds its waters that are to follow, and fatigues its wandering current, now pointing to its source, and now to the open sea. Just so, Dædalus fills innumerable paths with windings; and scarcely can he himself return to the entrance, so great are the intricacies of the place. After he has shut up here the double figure of a bull and of a youth;[12] and the third supply, chosen by lot each nine years, has subdued the monster twice before gorged with Athenian blood; and when the difficult entrance, retraced by none of those who have entered it before, has been found by the aid of the maiden, by means of the thread gathered up again; immediately, the son of Ægeus, carrying away the daughter of Minos, sets sail for Dia,[13] and barbarously deserts his companion on those shores.

Her, thus deserted and greatly lamenting, Liber embraces and aids; and, that she may be famed by a lasting Constellation, he places in the heavens the crown taken from off her head. It flies through the yielding air, and, as it flies, its jewels are suddenly changed into fires, and they settle in their places, the shape of the crown still remaining; which is in the middle,[14] between the Constellation resting on his knee,[15] and that which holds the serpents.

[Footnote 12: Of a youth.—Ver. 169. Clarke translates this line, 'In which, after he had shut the double figure of a bull and a young fellow.']

[Footnote 13: Sets sail for Dia.—Ver. 174. Dia was another name of the island of Naxos, one of the Cyclades, where Theseus left Ariadne. Commentators have complained, with some justice, that Ovid has here omitted the story of Ariadne; but it should be remembered that he has given it at length in the third book of the Fasti, commencing at line 460.]

[Footnote 14: In the middle.—Ver. 182. The crown of Ariadne was made a Constellation between those of Hercules and Ophiuchus. Some writers say, that the crown was given by Bacchus to Ariadne as a marriage present; while others state that it was made by Vulcan of gold and Indian jewels, by the light of which Theseus was aided in his escape from the labyrinth, and that he afterwards presented it to Ariadne. Some authors, and Ovid himself, in the Fasti, represent Ariadne herself as becoming a Constellation.]

[Footnote 15: Resting on his knee.—Ver. 182. Hercules, as a Constellation, is represented in the attitude of kneeling, when about to slay the dragon that watched the gardens of the Hesperides.]

EXPLANATION

Oppressed with famine, and seeing the enemy at their gates, the Athenians went to consult the oracle at Delphi; and were answered, that to be delivered from their calamities, they must give satisfaction to Minos. They immediately sent ambassadors to him, humbly suing for peace, which he granted them, on condition that each year, according to Apollodorus and Diodorus Siculus, or every nine years, according to Plutarch and Ovid, they should send him seven young men and as many virgins. The severity of these conditions provoked the Athenians to render Minos as odious as possible; whereupon, they promulgated the story, that he destined the youths that were sent to him, to fight in the Labyrinth against the Minotaur, which was the fruit of an intrigue of his wife Pasiphaë with a white bull which Neptune had sent out of the sea. They added, that Dædalus favoured this extraordinary passion of the queen; and that Venus inspired Pasiphaë with it, to be revenged for having been surprised with Mars by Apollo, her father. Plato, Plutarch, and other writers acknowledge that these stories were invented from the hatred which the Greeks bore to the king of Crete.

As, however, these extravagant fables have generally some foundation in fact, we are informed by Servius, Tzetzes, and Zenobius, that, in the absence of Minos, Pasiphaë fell in love with a young noble of the Cretan court, named Taurus, who, according to Plutarch, was the commander of the fleet of Minos; that Dædalus, their confidant, allowed their assignations to take place in his house, and that the queen was afterwards delivered of twins, of which the one resembled Minos, and the other Taurus. This, according to those authors, was the foundation of the story as to the fate for which the young Athenians were said to be destined. Philochorus, quoted by Plutarch, says that Minos instituted funeral games in honour of his son Androgeus, and that those who were vanquished became the slaves of the conquerors. That author adds, that Taurus was the first who won all the prizes in these games, and that he used the unfortunate Athenians, who became his slaves, with great barbarity. Aristotle tells us that the tribute was paid three times by the Athenians, and that the lives of the captives were spent in the most dreadful servitude.

Dædalus, on returning into Crete, built a labyrinth there, in which, very probably, these games were celebrated. Palæphatus, however, says that Theseus fought in a cavern, where the son of Taurus had been confined. Plutarch and Catullus say, that Theseus voluntarily offered to go to Crete with the other Athenians, while Diodorus Siculus says that the lot fell on him to be of the number. His delivery by Ariadne, through her giving him the thread, is probably a poetical method of informing us that she gave her lover the plan of the labyrinth where he was confined, that he might know its windings and the passage out. Eustathius, indeed, says, that Ariadne received a thread from Dædalus; but he must mean a plan of the labyrinth, which he himself had designed. The story of Ariadne's intercourse with Bacchus is most probably founded on the fact, that on arriving at the Isle of Naxos, when she was deserted by Theseus, she became the wife of a priest of Bacchus.

FABLE III [VIII.183-259]

Dædalus, weary of his exile, finds means, by making himself wings, to escape out of Crete. His son Icarus, forgetting the advice of his father, and flying too high, the Sun melts his wings, and he perishes in the sea, which afterwards bore his name. The sister of Dædalus commits her son Perdix to his care, for the purpose of being educated. Dædalus, being jealous of the talent of his nephew, throws him from a tower, with the intention of killing him; but Minerva supports him in his fall, and transforms him into a partridge.

In the meantime, Dædalus, abhorring Crete and his prolonged exile,[16] and inflamed by the love of his native soil, was enclosed there by the sea. "Although Minos," said he, "may beset the land and the sea, still the skies, at least, are open. By that way will we go: let Minos possess everything besides: he does not sway the air." Thus he spoke; and he turned his thoughts to arts unknown till then; and varied the course of nature. For he arranges feathers in order, beginning from the least, the shorter one succeeding the longer; so that you might suppose they grew on an incline. Thus does the rustic pipe sometimes rise by degrees, with unequal straws. Then he binds those in the middle with thread, and the lowermost ones with wax; and, thus ranged, with a gentle curvature, he bends them, so as to imitate real wings of birds. His son Icarus stands together with him; and, ignorant that he is handling the source of danger to himself, with a smiling countenance, he sometimes catches at the feathers which the shifting breeze is ruffling; and, at other times, he softens the yellow wax with his thumb; and, by his playfulness, he retards the wondrous work of his father.

After the finishing hand was put to the work, the workman himself poised his own body upon the two wings, and hung suspended in the beaten air. He provided his son with them as well; and said to him, "Icarus, I recommend thee to keep the middle tract; lest, if thou shouldst go too low, the water should clog thy wings; if too high, the fire of the sun should scorch them. Fly between both; and I bid thee neither to look at Boötes, nor Helice,[17] nor the drawn sword of Orion. Under my guidance, take thy way." At the same time, he delivered him rules for flying, and fitted the untried wings to his shoulders. Amid his work and his admonitions, the cheeks of the old man were wet, and the hands of the father trembled. He gives kisses to his son, never again to be repeated; and, raised upon his wings, he flies before, and is concerned for his companion, just as the bird which has led forth her tender young from the lofty nest into the air. And he encourages him to follow, and instructs him in the fatal art, and both moves his own wings himself, and looks back on those of his son. A person while he is angling for fish with his quivering rod, or the shepherd leaning on his crook, or the ploughman on the plough tail, when he beholds them, is astonished, and believes them to be Divinities, who thus can cleave the air. And now Samos,[18] sacred to Juno, and Delos, and Paros, were left behind to the left hand. On the right were Lebynthus,[19] and Calymne,[20] fruitful in honey; when the boy began to be pleased with a bolder flight, and forsook his guide; and, touched with a desire of reaching heaven, pursued his course still higher. The vicinity of the scorching Sun softened the fragrant wax that fastened his wings. The wax was melted; he shook his naked arms, and, wanting his oar-like wings, he caught no more air. His face, too, as he called on the name of his father, was received in the azure water, which received its name[21] from him.

But the unhappy father, now no more a father, said, "Icarus, where art thou? In what spot shall I seek thee, Icarus?" did he say; when he beheld his wings in the waters, and then he cursed his own arts; and he buried his body in a tomb, and the land was called from the name of him buried there. As he was laying the body of his unfortunate son in the tomb, a prattling partridge beheld him from a branching holm-oak,[22] and, by its notes, testified its delight. 'Twas then but a single bird of its kind, and never seen in former years, and, lately made a bird, was a grievous reproof, Dædalus, to thee. For, ignorant of the decrees of fate, his sister had entrusted her son to be instructed by him, a boy who had passed twice six birthdays, with a mind eager for instruction. 'Twas he, too, who took the backbones observed in the middle of the fish, for an example, and cut a continued row of teeth in iron, with a sharp edge, and thus discovered the use of the saw.

He was the first, too, that bound two arms of iron to one centre, that, being divided and of equal length, the one part might stand fixed, and the other might describe a circle. Dædalus was envious, and threw him headlong from the sacred citadel of Minerva, falsely pretending that he had fallen by accident. But Pallas, who favours ingenuity, received him, and made him a bird; and, in the middle of the air, he flew upon wings. Yet the vigour of his genius, once so active, passed into his wings and into his feet; his name, too, remained the same as before. Yet this bird does not raise its body aloft, nor make its nest in the branches and the lofty tops of trees, but flies near the ground, and lays its eggs in hedges: and, mindful of its former fall, it dreads the higher regions.

[Footnote 16: His prolonged exile.—Ver. 184. Dædalus had been exiled for murdering one of his scholars in a fit of jealousy; probably Perdix, his nephew, whose story is related by Ovid.]

[Footnote 17: Helice.—Ver. 207. This was another name of the Constellation called the Greater Bear, into which Calisto had been changed.]

[Footnote 18: Samos.—Ver. 220. This island, off the coast of Caria in Asia Minor, was famous as the birth-place of Juno, and the spot where she was married to Jupiter. She had a famous temple there.]

[Footnote 19: Lebynthus.—Ver. 222. This island was one of the Cyclades, or, according to some writers, one of the Sporades, a group that lay between the Cyclades and Crete.]

[Footnote 20: Calymne.—Ver. 222. This island was near Rhodes. Its honey is praised by Strabo.]

[Footnote 21: Received its name.—Ver. 230. The island of Samos being near the spot where he fell, received the name of Icaria.]

[Footnote 22: Branching holm oak.—Ver. 237. Ovid here forgot that partridges do not perch in trees; a fact, which, however, he himself remarks in line 257.]

EXPLANATION

Dædalus was a talented Athenian, of the family of Erechtheus; and he was particularly famed for his skill in statuary and architecture. He became jealous of the talents of his nephew, Talos, whom Ovid here calls Perdix; and, envying his inventions of the saw, the compasses, and the art of turning, he killed him privately. Flying to Crete, he was favourably received by Minos, who was then at war with the Athenians. He there built the Labyrinth, as Pliny the Elder asserts, after the plan of that in Egypt, which is described by Herodotus, Diodorus Siculus, and Strabo. Philochorus, however, as quoted by Plutarch, says that it did not resemble the Labyrinth of Egypt, and that it was only a prison in which criminals were confined.

Minos, being informed that Dædalus had assisted Pasiphaë in carrying out her criminal designs, kept him in prison; but escaping thence, by the aid of Pasiphaë, he embarked in a ship which she had prepared for him. Using sails, which till then, according to Pausanias and Palæphatus, were unknown, he escaped from the galleys of Minos, which were provided with oars only. Icarus, either fell into the sea, or, overpowered with the fatigues of the voyage, died near an island in the Archipelago, which afterwards received his name. These facts have been disguised by the poets under the ingenious fiction of the wings, and the neglect of Icarus to follow his father's advice, as here related.

FABLE IV [VIII.260-546]

Diana, offended at the neglect of Œneus, king of Calydon, when performing his vows to the Gods, sends a wild boar to ravage his dominions; on which Œneus assembled the princes of the country for its pursuit. His son Meleager leads the chase, and, having killed the monster, presents its head to his mistress, Atalanta, the daughter of the king of Arcadia. He afterwards kills his two uncles, Plexippus and Toxeus, who would deprive her of this badge of his victory. Their sister Althæa, the mother of Meleager, filled with grief at their death, loads her son with execrations; and, remembering the torch which she received from the Fates at his birth, and on which the preservation of his life depends, she throws it into the fire. As soon as it is consumed, Meleager expires in the greatest torments. His sisters mourn over his body, until Diana changes them into birds.

And now the Ætnæan land received Dædalus in his fatigue; and Cocalus,[23] taking up arms for him as he entreated, was commended for his kindness. And now Athens has ceased to pay her mournful tribute, through the exploits of Theseus. The temples are decked with garlands, and they invoke warlike Minerva, with Jupiter and the other Gods, whom they adore with the blood of victims vowed, and with presents offered, and censers[24] of frankincense. Wandering Fame had spread the renown of Theseus throughout the Argive cities, and the nations which rich Achaia contained, implored his aid amid great dangers. Calydon, too, although it had Meleager,[25] suppliantly addressed him with anxious entreaties. The occasion of asking aid was a boar, the servant and the avenger of Diana in her wrath.

For they say that Œneus, for the blessings of a plenteous year, had offered the first fruits of the corn to Ceres, to Bacchus his wine, and the Palladian juice[26] of olives to the yellow-haired Minerva. These invidious honours commencing with the rural Deities, were continued to all the Gods above; they say that the altars of the daughter of Latona, who was omitted, were alone left without frankincense. Wrath affects even the Deities. "But this," says she, "I will not tamely put up with; and I, who am thus dishonoured, will not be said to be unrevenged as well:" and she sends a boar as an avenger throughout the lands of Œneus, than which not even does verdant Epirus[27] possess bulls of greater size; even the fields of Sicily have them of less magnitude. His eyes shine with blood and flames, his rough neck is stiff; bristles, too,[28] stand up, like spikes, thickly set; like palisades[29] do those bristles project, just like high spikes. Boiling foam, with a harsh noise, flows down his broad shoulders; his tusks rival the tusks of India. Thunders issue from his mouth; the foliage is burnt up with the blast. One while he tramples down the corn in the growing blade, and crops the expectations of the husbandman, doomed to lament, as yet unripe, and he intercepts the corn in the ear. In vain does the threshing floor, and in vain do the barns await the promised harvest. The heavy grapes, with the long branches of the vine, are scattered about, and the berries with the boughs of the ever-green olive. He vents his fury, too, upon the flocks. These, neither dogs nor shepherds can protect; not even the fierce bulls are able to defend the herds. The people fly in all directions, and do not consider themselves safe, but in the walls of a city, until Meleager, and, together with him, a choice body of youths, unite from a desire for fame.

The two sons of Tyndarus,[30] the one famous for boxing, the other for his skill in horsemanship; Jason, too, the builder of the first ship, and Theseus, with Pirithoüs,[31] happy unison, and the two sons of Thestius,[32] and Lynceus,[33] the son of Aphareus, and the swift Idas, and Cæneus,[34] now no longer a woman; and the valiant Leucippus,[35] and Acastus,[36] famous for the dart, and Hippothoüs,[37] and Dryas,[38] and Phœnix,[39] the son of Amyntor, and the two sons of Actor,[40] and Phyleus,[41] sent from Elis, are there. Nor is Telamon[42] absent; the father, too, of the great Achilles;[43] and with the son of Pheres,[44] and the Hyantian Iolaüs,[45] the active Eurytion,[46] and Echion,[47] invincible in the race, and the Narycian Lelex,[48] and Panopeus,[49] and Hyleus,[50] and bold Hippasus,[51] and Nestor,[52] now but in his early years. Those, too, whom Hippocoön[53] sent from ancient Amyclæ,[54] and the father-in-law of Penelope,[55] with the Parrhasian Ancæus,[56] and the sage son of Ampycus,[57] and the descendant of Œclus,[58] as yet safe from his wife, and Tegeæan[59] Atalanta, the glory of the Lycæan groves. A polished buckle fastened the top of her robe; her plain hair was gathered into a single knot. The ivory keeper of her weapons rattled, hanging from her left shoulder; her left hand, too, held a bow. Such was her dress, and her face such as you might say, with reason, was that of a maid in a boy, that of a boy in a maid. Her the Calydonian hero both beheld, and at the same moment sighed for her, against the will of the God; and he caught the latent flame, and said, "Oh, happy will he be, if she shall vouchsafe to make any one her husband." The occasion and propriety allow him to say no more; the greater deeds of the mighty contest now engage him.

A wood, thick with trees, which no age has cut down, rises from a plain, and looks down upon the fields below. After the heroes are come there, some extend the nets; some take the couples off the dogs, some follow close the traces of his feet, and are anxious to discover their own danger. There is a hollow channel, along which rivulets of rain water are wont to discharge themselves. The bending willows cover the lower parts of the cavity, and smooth sedges, and marshy rushes, and oziers, and thin reeds with their long stalks. Aroused from this spot, the boar rushes violently into the midst of the enemy, like lightning darted from the bursting clouds. In his onset the grove is laid level, and the wood, borne down, makes a crashing noise. The young men raise a shout, and with strong right hands hold their weapons extended before them, brandished with their broad points. Onward he rushes, and disperses the dogs, as any one of them opposes his career; and scatters them, as they bark at him, with sidelong wounds.

The spear that was first hurled by the arm of Echion, was unavailing, and made a slight incision in the trunk of a maple tree. The next, if it had not employed too much of the strength of him who threw it, seemed as if it would stick in the back it was aimed at: it went beyond. The owner of the weapon was the Pagasæan Jason. "Phœbus," said the son of Ampycus,[60] "if I have worshipped thee, and if I do worship thee, grant me the favour to reach what is now aimed at, with unerring weapon." The God consented to his prayer, so far as he could. The boar was struck by him, but without a wound; Diana took the steel head from off the flying weapon; the shaft reached him without the point. The rage of the monster was aroused, and not less violently was he inflamed than the lightnings; light darted from his eyes, and flame was breathed from his breast. As the stone flies, launched by the tightened rope, when it is aimed[61] at either walls, or towers filled with soldiers, with the like unerring onset is the destroying boar borne on among the youths, and lays upon the ground Eupalamus and Pelagon,[62] who guard the right wing. Thus prostrate, their companions bear them off. But Enæsimus, the son of Hippocoön, does not escape a deadly wound. The sinews of his knee, cut by the boar, fail him as he trembles, and prepares to turn his back.

Perhaps, too, the Pylian Nestor would have perished[63] before the times of the Trojan war: but taking a spring, by means of his lance, planted in the ground, he leaped into the branches of a tree that was standing close by, and, safe in his position, looked down upon the enemy which he had escaped. He, having whetted his tusk on the trunk of an oak, fiercely stood, ready for their destruction; and, trusting to his weapons newly pointed, gored the thigh of the great Othriades[64] with his crooked tusks. But the two brothers, not yet made Constellations of the heavens, distinguished from the rest, were borne upon horses whiter than the bleached snow; and both were brandishing the points of their lances, poised in the air, with a tremulous motion. They would have inflicted wounds, had not the bristly monster entered the shady wood, a place penetrable by neither weapons nor horses. Telamon pursues him; and, heedless in the heat of pursuit, falls headlong, tripped up by the root of a tree. While Peleus[65] is lifting him up, the Tegeæan damsel fits a swift arrow to the string, and, bending the bow, lets it fly. Fixed under the ear of the beast, the arrow razes the surface of the skin, and dyes the bristles red with a little blood. And not more joyful is she at the success of her aim than Meleager is.

He is supposed to have observed it first, and first to have pointed out the blood to his companions, and to have said, "Thou shalt receive due honour for thy bravery." The heroes blush in emulation; and they encourage one another, and raise their spirits with shouts, and discharge their weapons without any order. Their very multitude is a hindrance to those that are thrown, and it baffles the blow for which it is designed. Behold! the Arcadian,[66] wielding his battle-axe, rushing madly on to his fate, said, "Learn, O youths, how much the weapons of men excel those of women, and give way for my achievement. Though the daughter of Latona herself should protect him by her own arms, still, in spite of Diana, shall my right hand destroy him." Such words did he boastingly utter with self-confident lips; and lifting his double-edged axe with both hands, he stood erect upon tiptoe. The beast seized him thus bold, and, where there is the nearest way to death, directed his two tusks to the upper part of his groin. Ancæus fell; and his bowels, twisted, rush forth, falling with plenteous blood, and the earth was soaked with gore. Pirithoüs, the son of Ixion, was advancing straight against the enemy, shaking his spear in his powerful right hand. To him the son of Ægeus, at a distance, said, "O thou, dearer to me than myself; stop, thou better part of my soul; we may be valiant at a distance: his rash courage was the destruction of Ancæus." Thus he spoke, and he hurled his lance of cornel wood, heavy with its brazen point; which, well poised, and likely to fulfil his desires, a leafy branch of a beech-tree opposed.

The son of Æson, too, hurled his javelin, which unlucky chance turned away from the beast, to the destruction of an unoffending dog, and running through his entrails, it was pinned through those entrails into the earth. But the hand of the son of Œneus has different success; and of two discharged by him, the first spear is fastened in the earth, the second in the middle of his back. There is no delay; while he rages, while he is wheeling his body round, and pouring forth foam, hissing with the fresh blood, the giver of the wound comes up, and provokes his adversary to fury, and buries his shining hunting spear in his opposite shoulder. His companions attest their delight in an encouraging shout, and in their right hands endeavour to grasp the conquering right hand; and with wonder they behold the huge beast as he lies upon a large space of ground, and they do not deem it safe as yet to touch him; but yet they, each of them, stain their weapons with his blood. Jason himself, placing his foot upon it, presses his frightful head, and thus he says: "Receive, Nonacrian Nymph, the spoil that is my right; and let my glory be shared by thee." Immediately he gives her the skin as the spoil, thick with the stiffening bristles, and the head remarkable for the huge tusks. The giver of the present, as well as the present, is a source of pleasure to her. The others envy her, and there is a murmuring throughout the whole company. Of these, stretching out their arms, with a loud voice, the sons of Thestius cry out, "Come, lay them down, and do not thou, a woman, interfere with our honours; let not thy confidence in thy beauty deceive thee, and let the donor, seized with this passion for thee, keep at a distance." And then from her they take the present, and from him the right of disposing of the present.

The warlike[67] prince did not brook it, and, indignant with swelling rage, he said, "Learn, ye spoilers of the honour that belongs to another, how much deeds differ from threats;" and, with his cruel sword, he pierced the breast of Plexippus, dreading no such thing. Nor suffered he Toxeus, who was doubtful what to do, and both wishful to avenge his brother, and fearing his brother's fate, long to be in doubt; but a second time warmed his weapon, reeking with the former slaughter, in the blood of the brother.

Althæa was carrying gifts to the temples of the Gods, her son being victorious, when she beheld her slain brothers carried off from the field: uttering a shriek, she filled the city with her sad lamentations, and assumed black garments in exchange for her golden ones. But soon as the author of their death was made known, all grief vanished; and from tears it was turned to a thirst for vengeance. There was a billet, which, when the daughter of Thestius was lying in labour with her son, the three Sisters, the Fates, placed in the flames, and spinning the fatal threads, with their thumbs pressed upon them, they said, "We give to thee, O new-born babe, and to this wood, the same period of existence." Having uttered this charm, the Goddesses departed; and the mother snatched the flaming brand from the fire, and sprinkled it with flowing water. Long had it been concealed in her most retired apartment; and being thus preserved, had preserved, O youth, thy life. This billet the mother now brings forth, and orders torches to be heaped on broken pieces of wood; and when heaped, applies to them the hostile flames. Then four times essaying to lay the branch upon the flames, four times does she pause in the attempt. Both the mother and the sister struggle hard, and the two different titles influence her breast in different ways. Often is her countenance pale with apprehension of the impending crime; often does rage, glowing in her eyes, produce its red colour. And one while is her countenance like that of one making some cruel threat or other; at another moment, such as you could suppose to be full of compassion. And when the fierce heat of her feelings has dried up her tears, still are tears found to flow. Just as the ship, which the wind and a tide running contrary to the wind, seize, is sensible of the double assault, and unsteadily obeys them both; no otherwise does the daughter of Thestius fluctuate between two varying affections, and in turn lays by her anger, and rouses it again, when thus laid by. Still, the sister begins to get the better of the parent; and that, with blood she may appease the shades of her relations, in her unnatural conduct she proves affectionate.

For after the pernicious flames gained strength, she said, "Let this funeral pile consume my entrails." And as she was holding the fatal billet in her ruthless hand, she stood, in her wretchedness, before the sepulchral altars,[68] and said, "Ye Eumenides,[69] the three Goddesses of punishment, turn your faces towards these baleful rites; I am both avenging and am committing a crime. With death must death be expiated; crime must be added to crime, funeral to funeral; by accumulated calamities, let this unnatural race perish. Shall Œneus, in happiness, be blessed in his victorious son; and shall Thestius be childless? It is better that you both should mourn. Only do ye, ghosts of my brothers, phantoms newly made, regard this my act of affection, and receive this funeral offering,[70] provided at a cost so great, the guilty pledge of my womb. Ah, wretched me! Whither am I hurried away? Pardon, my brothers, the feelings of a mother. My hands fail me in my purpose, I confess that he deserves to die; but the author of his death is repugnant to me. Shall he then go unpunished? Alive and victorious, and flushed with his success, shall he possess the realms of Calydon? And shall you lie, a little heap of ashes, and as lifeless phantoms? For my part, I will not endure this. Let the guilty wretch perish, and let him carry along with him the hopes of his father,[71] and the ruin of his kingdom and country. But where are the feelings of a mother, where are the affectionate ties of the parent? Where, too, are the pangs which for twice five months[72] I have endured? Oh, that thou hadst been burnt, when an infant, in that first fire! And would that I had allowed it! By my aid hast thou lived; now, for thy own deserts, shalt thou die. Take the reward of thy deeds; and return to me that life which was twice given thee, first at thy birth, next when the billet was rescued; or else place me as well in the tomb of my brothers. I both desire to do it, and I am unable. What shall I do? one while the wounds of my brothers are before my eyes, and the form of a murder so dreadful; at another time, affection and the name of mother break my resolution. Wretch that I am! To my sorrow, brothers, will you prevail; but still prevail; so long as I myself shall follow the appeasing sacrifice that I shall give you, and you yourselves;" she thus said, and turning herself away, with trembling right hand she threw the fatal brand into the midst of the flames.

That billet either utters, or seems to utter, a groan, and, caught by the reluctant flames, it is consumed. Unsuspecting, and at a distance, Meleager is burned by that flame, and feels his entrails scorched by the secret fires; but with fortitude he supports the mighty pain. Still, he grieves that he dies by an inglorious death, and without shedding his blood, and says that the wounds of Ancæus were a happy lot. And while, with a sigh, he calls upon his aged father, and his brother, and his affectionate sisters, and with his last words the companion of his bed,[73] perhaps, too, his mother as well; the fire and his torments increase; and then again do they diminish. Both of them are extinguished together, and by degrees his spirit vanishes into the light air.

Lofty Calydon now lies prostrate. Young and old mourn, both people and nobles lament; and the Calydonian matrons of Evenus,[74] tearing their hair, bewail him. Lying along upon the ground, his father pollutes his white hair and his aged features with dust, and chides his prolonged existence. But her own hand, conscious to itself of the ruthless deed, exacted punishment of the mother, the sword piercing her entrails.[75] If a God had given me a mouth sounding with a hundred tongues, and an enlarged genius, and the whole of Helicon besides; still I could not enumerate the mournful expressions of his unhappy sisters. Regardless of shame, they beat their livid bosoms, and while the body still exists, they embrace it, and embrace it again; they give kisses to it, and they give kisses to the bier there set. After he is reduced to ashes, they pour them, when gathered up, to their breasts; and they lie prostrate around the tomb, and kissing his name cut out in the stone, they pour their tears upon his name. Them, the daughter of Latona, at length satiated with the calamities of the house of Parthaon,[76] bears aloft on wings springing from their bodies, except Gorge,[77] and the daughter-in-law of noble Alcmena; and she stretches long wings over their arms, and makes their mouths horny, and sends them, thus transformed, through the air.

[Footnote 23: Cocalus.—Ver. 261. He was the king of Sicily, who received Dædalus with hospitality.]

[Footnote 24: And censers.—Ver. 265. Acerris. The 'acerra' was properly a box used for holding incense for the purposes of sacrifice, which was taken from it, and placed on the burning altar. According to Festus, the word meant a small altar, which was placed before the dead, and on which perfumes were burnt. The Law of the Twelve Tables restricted the use of 'acerræ' at funerals.]

[Footnote 25: Meleager.—Ver. 270. He was the son of Œneus, king of Calydon, a city of Ætolia, who had offended Diana by neglecting her rites.]

[Footnote 26: Palladian juice.—Ver. 275. Oil, the extraction of which, from the olive, Minerva had taught to mortals.]

[Footnote 27: Epirus.—Ver. 283. This country, sometimes also called Chaonia, was on the north of Greece, between Macedonia, Thessaly, and the Ionian sea, comprising the greater part of what is now called Albania. It was famous for its oxen. According to Pliny the Elder, Pyrrhus, its king, paid particular attention to improving the breed.]

[Footnote 28: Bristles too.—Ver. 285. This line, or the following one, is clearly an interpolation, and ought to be omitted.]

[Footnote 29: Palisades.—Ver. 286. The word 'vallum' is found applied either to the whole, or a portion only, of the fortifications of a Roman camp. It is derived from 'vallus,' 'a stake;' and properly means the palisade which ran along the outer edge of the 'agger,' or 'mound:' but it frequently includes the 'agger' also. The 'vallum,' in the latter sense, together with the 'fossa,' or 'ditch,' which surrounded the camp outside of the 'vallum,' formed a complete fortification.]

[Footnote 30: Sons of Tyndarus.—Ver. 301. These were Castor and Pollux, the putative sons of Tyndarus, but really the sons of Jupiter, who seduced Leda under the form of a swan. According to some, however, Pollux only was the son of Jupiter. Castor was skilled in horsemanship, while Pollux excelled in the use of the cestus.]

[Footnote 31: Pirithoüs.—Ver. 303. He was the son of Ixion of Larissa, and the bosom friend of Theseus.]

[Footnote 32: Sons of Thestius.—Ver. 304. These were Toxeus and Plexippus, the uncles of Meleager, and the brothers of Althæa, who avenged their death in the manner afterwards described by Ovid. Pausanias calls them Prothoüs and Cometes. Lactantius adds a third, Agenor.]

[Footnote 33: Lynceus.—Ver. 304. Lynceus and Idas were the sons of Aphareus. From his skill in physical science, the former was said to be able to see into the interior of the earth.]

[Footnote 34: Cæneus.—Ver. 305. This person was originally a female, by name Cænis. At her request, she was changed by Neptune into a man, and was made invulnerable. Her story is related at length in the 12th book of the Metamorphoses.]

[Footnote 35: Leucippus.—Ver. 306. He was the son of Perieres, and the brother of Aphareus. His daughters were Elaira, or Ilaira, and Phœbe, whom Castor and Pollux attempted to carry off.]

[Footnote 36: Acastus.—Ver. 306. He was the son of Pelias, king of Thessaly.]

[Footnote 37: Hippothoüs.—Ver. 307. According to Hyginus, he was the son of Geryon, or rather, according to Pausanias, of Cercyon.]

[Footnote 38: Dryas.—Ver. 307. The son of Mars, or, according to some writers, of Iapetus.]

[Footnote 39: Phœnix.—Ver. 307. He was the son of Amyntor. Having engaged in an intrigue, by the contrivance of his mother, with his father's mistress, he fled to the court of Peleus, king of Thessaly, who entrusted to him the education of Achilles, and the command of the Dolopians. He attended his pupil to the Trojan war, and became blind in his latter years.]

[Footnote 40: Two sons of Actor.—Ver. 308. These were Eurytus and Cteatus, the sons of Actor, of Elis. They were afterwards slain by Hercules.]

[Footnote 41: Phyleus.—Ver. 308. He was the son of Augeas, king of Elis, whose stables were cleansed by Hercules.]

[Footnote 42: Telamon.—Ver. 309. He was the son of Æacus. Ajax Telamon was his son.]

[Footnote 43: Great Achilles.—Ver. 309. His father was Peleus, the brother of Ajax, and the son of Æacus and Ægina. Peleus was famed for his chastity.]

[Footnote 44: The son of Pheres.—Ver. 310. This was Admetus, the son of Pheres, of Pheræ, in Thessaly.]

[Footnote 45: Hyantian Iolaüs.—Ver. 310. Iolaüs, the Bœotian, the son of Iphiclus, aided Hercules in slaying the Hydra.]

[Footnote 46: Eurytion.—Ver. 311. He was the son of Irus, and attended the Argonautic expedition.]

[Footnote 47: Echion.—Ver. 311. He was an Arcadian, the son of Mercury and the Nymph Antianira, and was famous for his speed.]

[Footnote 48: Narycian Lelex.—Ver. 312. So called from Naryx, a city of the Locrians.]

[Footnote 49: Panopeus.—Ver. 312. He was the son of Phocus, who built the city of Panopæa, in Phocis, and was the father of Epytus, who constructed the Trojan horse.]

[Footnote 50: Hyleus.—Ver. 312. According to Callimachus, he was slain, together with Rhœtus, by Atalanta, for making an attempt upon her virtue.]

[Footnote 51: Hippasus.—Ver. 313. He was a son of Eurytus.]

[Footnote 52: Nestor.—Ver. 313. He was the son of Neleus and Chloris. He was king of Pylos, and went to the Trojan war in his ninetieth, or, as some writers say, in his two hundredth year.]

[Footnote 53: Hippocoön.—Ver. 314. He was the son of Amycus. He sent his four sons, Enæsimus, Alcon, Amycus, and Dexippus, to hunt the Calydonian boar. The first was killed by the monster, and the other three, with their father, were afterwards slain by Hercules.]

[Footnote 54: Amyclæ.—Ver. 314. This was an ancient city of Laconia, built by Amycla, the son of Lacedæmon.]

[Footnote 55: Of Penelope.—Ver. 315. This was Laërtes, the father of Ulysses, the husband of Penelope, and king of Ithaca.]

[Footnote 56: Ancæus.—Ver. 315. He was an Arcadian, the son of Lycurgus.]

[Footnote 57: Son of Ampycus.—Ver. 316. Ampycus was the son of Titanor, and the father of Mopsus, a famous soothsayer.]

[Footnote 58: Descendant Œclus.—Ver. 317. This was Amphiaraüs, who, having the gift of prophecy, foresaw that he would not live to return from the Theban war; and, therefore, hid himself, that he might not be obliged to join in the expedition. His wife, Eriphyle, being bribed by Adrastus with a gold necklace, betrayed his hiding-place; on which, proceeding to Thebes, he was swallowed up in the earth, together with his chariot. Ovid refers here to the treachery of his wife.]

[Footnote 59: Tegeæan.—Ver. 317. Atalanta was the daughter of Iasius, and was a native of Tegeæa, in Arcadia. She was the mother of Parthenopæus, by Meleager. She is thought, by some, to have been a different person from Atalanta, the daughter of Schœneus, famed for her swiftness in running, who is mentioned in the tenth book of the Metamorphoses.]

[Footnote 60: Son of Ampycus.—Ver. 350. Mopsus was a priest of Apollo.]

[Footnote 61: When it is aimed.—Ver. 357. When discharged from the 'balista,' or 'catapulta,' or other engine of war.]

[Footnote 62: Eupalamus and Pelagon.—Ver. 360. They are not previously named in the list of combatants; and nothing further is known of them.]

[Footnote 63: Would have perished.—Ver. 365. What is here told of Nestor, one of the Commentators on Homer attributes to Thersites, who, according to him, being the son of Agrius, the uncle of Meleager, was present on this occasion.]

[Footnote 64: Othriades.—Ver. 371. Nothing further is known of him.]

[Footnote 65: Peleus.—Ver. 375. According to Apollodorus, Peleus accidentally slew Eurytion on this occasion.]

[Footnote 66: The Arcadian.—Ver. 391. This was Ancæus, who is mentioned before, in line 215.]

[Footnote 67: Warlike.—Ver. 437. 'Mavortius' may possibly mean 'the son of Mars,' as, according to Hyginus, Mars was engaged in an intrigue with Althæa.]

[Footnote 68: Sepulchral altars.—Ver. 480. The 'sepulchralis ara' is the funeral pile, which was built in the form of an altar, with four equal sides. Ovid also calls it 'funeris ara,' in the Tristia, book iii. Elegy xiii. line 21.]

[Footnote 69: Eumenides.—Ver. 482. This name properly signifies 'the well-disposed,' or 'wellwishers,' and was applied to the Furies by way of euphemism, it being deemed unlucky to mention their names.]

[Footnote 70: Funeral offering.—Ver. 490. The 'inferiæ' were sacrifices offered to the shades of the dead. The Romans appear to have regarded the souls of the departed as Gods; for which reason they presented them wine, milk, and garlands, and offered them victims in sacrifice.]

[Footnote 71: Hopes of his father.—Ver. 498. Œneus had other sons besides Meleager, who were slain in the war that arose in consequence of the death of Plexippus and Toxeus. Nicander says they were five in number; Apollodorus names but three, Toxeus, Tyreus, and Clymenus.]

[Footnote 72: Twice five months.—Ver. 500. That is, lunar months.]

[Footnote 73: Of his bed.—Ver. 521. Antoninus Liberalis calls her Cleopatra, but Hyginus says that her name was Alcyone. Homer, however, reconciles this discrepancy, by saying that the original name of the wife of Meleager was Cleopatra, but that she was called Alcyone, because her mother had the same fate as Alcyone, or Halcyone.]

[Footnote 74: Evenus.—Ver. 527. Evenus was a river of Ætolia.]

[Footnote 75: Piercing her entrails.—Ver. 531. Hyginus says that she hanged herself.]

[Footnote 76: Parthaon.—Ver. 541. Parthaon was the grandfather of Meleager and his sisters, Œneus being his son.]

[Footnote 77: Gorge.—Ver. 542. Gorge married Andræmon, and Deïanira was the wife of Hercules, the son of Alcmena. The two sisters of Meleager who were changed into birds were Eurymede and Melanippe.]

EXPLANATION

It is generally supposed that the story of the chase of the Calydonian boar, though embracing much of the fabulous, is still based upon historical facts. Homer, in the 9th book of the Iliad, alludes to it, though in somewhat different terms from the account here given by Ovid; and from the ancient historians we learn, that Œneus, offering the first fruits to the Gods, forgot Diana in his sacrifices. A wild boar, the same year having ravaged some part of his dominions, and particularly a vineyard, on the cultivation of which he had bestowed much pains, these circumstances, combined, gave occasion for saying that the boar had been sent by Diana. As the wild beast had killed some country people, Meleager collected the neighbouring nobles, for the purpose of destroying it. Plexippus and Toxeus, having been killed, in the manner mentioned by the Poet, Althæa, their sister, in her grief, devoted her son to the Furies; and, perhaps, having used some magical incantations, the story of the fatal billet was invented.

Homer does not mention the death of Meleager; but, on the contrary, says that his mother, Althæa, was pacified. Some writers, however, think that he really was poisoned by his mother. The story of the change of the sisters of Meleager into birds is only the common poetical fiction, denoting the extent of their grief at the untimely death of their brother.

FABLE V [VIII.547-610]

Theseus, returning from the chase of the Calydonian boar, is stopped by an inundation of the river Acheloüs, and accepts of an invitation from the God of that river, to come to his grotto. After the repast, Acheloüs gives him the history of the five Naiads, who had been changed into the islands called Echinades, and an account of his own amour with the Nymph Perimele, whom, being thrown by her father into the sea, Neptune had transformed into an island.

In the meantime, Theseus having performed his part in the joint labour, was going to the Erecthean towers of Tritonis. But Acheloüs, swollen with rains, opposed his journey,[78] and caused him delay as he was going. "Come," said he, "famous Cecropian, beneath my roof; and do not trust thyself to the rapid floods. They are wont to bear away strong beams, and to roll down stones, as they lie across, with immense roaring. I have seen high folds, contiguous to my banks, swept away, together with the flocks; nor was it of any avail there for the herd to be strong, nor for the horses to be swift. Many bodies, too, of young men has this torrent overwhelmed in its whirling eddies, when the snows of the mountains dissolved. Rest is the safer for thee; until the river runs within its usual bounds, until its own channel receives the flowing waters."

To this the son of Ægeus agreed; and replied, "I will make use of thy dwelling and of thy advice, Acheloüs;" and both he did make use of. He entered an abode built of pumice stone with its many holes, and the sand-stone far from smooth. The floor was moist with soft moss, shells with alternate rows of murex arched the roof. And now, Hyperion having measured out two parts of the light, Theseus and the companions of his labours lay down upon couches; on the one side the son of Ixion,[79] on the other, Lelex, the hero of Trœzen, having his temples now covered with thin grey hairs; and some others whom the river of the Acarnanians, overjoyed with a guest so great, had graced with the like honour. Immediately, some Nymphs, barefoot, furnished with the banquet the tables that were set before them; and the dainties being removed, they served up wine in bowls adorned with gems. Then the mighty hero, surveying the seas that lay beneath his eyes, said, "What place is this?" and he pointed with his finger; "and inform me what name that island bears; although it does not seem to be one only?" In answer to these words, the River said, "It is not, indeed, one object that we see; five countries lie there; they deceive through their distance. And that thou mayst be the less surprised at the deeds of the despised Diana, these were Naiads; who, when they had slain twice five bullocks, and had invited the Gods of the country to a sacrifice, kept a joyous festival, regardless of me. At this I swelled, and I was as great as I ever am, in my course, when I am the fullest; and, redoubled both in rage and in flood, I tore away woods from woods, and fields from fields; and together with the spot, I hurled the Nymphs[80] into the sea, who then, at last, were mindful of me. My waves and those of the main divided the land, before continuous, and separated it into as many parts, as thou seest islands, called Echinades, in the midst of the waves.

"But yet, as thou thyself seest from afar, one island, see! was withdrawn far off from the rest, an island pleasing to me. The mariner calls it Perimele.[81] This beloved Nymph did I deprive of the name of a virgin. This her father, Hippodamas, took amiss, and pushed the body of his daughter, when about to bring forth, from a rock, into the sea. I received her; and bearing her up when swimming, I said, 'O thou bearer of the Trident, who hast obtained, by lot, next in rank to the heavens, the realms of the flowing waters, in which we sacred rivers end, and to which we run; come hither, Neptune, and graciously listen to me, as I pray. Her, whom I am bearing up, I have injured. If her father, Hippodamas, had been mild and reasonable, or if he had been less unnatural, he ought to have pitied her, and to have forgiven me. Give thy assistance; and grant a place, Neptune, I beseech thee, to her, plunged in the waters by the cruelty of her father; or allow her to become a place herself. Her, even, thus will I embrace.' The King of the ocean moved his head, and shook all the waters with his assent. The Nymph was afraid; but yet she swam. Her breast, as she was swimming, I myself touched, as it throbbed with a tremulous motion; and while I felt it, I perceived her whole body grow hard, and her breast become covered with earth growing over it. While I was speaking, fresh earth enclosed her floating limbs, and a heavy island grew upon her changed members."

[Footnote 78: Opposed his journey.—Ver. 548. It has been objected to this passage, that the river Acheloüs, which rises in Mount Pindus, and divides Acarnania from Ætolia, could not possibly lie in the road of Theseus, as he returned from Calydon to Athens.]

[Footnote 79: Son of Ixion.—Ver. 566. Pirithoüs lay on the one side, and Lelex on the other; the latter is called 'Trœzenius,' from the fact of his having lived with Pittheus, the king of Trœzen.]

[Footnote 80: I hurled the Nymphs.—Ver. 585. Clarke translates 'Nymphas in freta provolvi,' 'I tumbled the nymphs into the sea.']

[Footnote 81: Perimele.—Ver. 590. According to Apollodorus, the name of the wife of Acheloüs was Perimede; and she bore him two sons, Hippodamas and Orestes. The Echinades were five small islands in the Ionian Sea, near the coast of Acarnania, which are now called Curzolari.]

EXPLANATION

This story is simply based upon physical grounds. The river Acheloüs, running between Acarnania and Ætolia, and flowing into the Ionian Sea, carried with it a great quantity of sand and mud, which probably formed the islands at its mouth, called the Echinades. The same solution probably applies to the narrative of the fate of the Nymph Perimele.

FABLE VI [VIII.611-737]

Jupiter and Mercury, disguised in human shape, are received by Philemon and Baucis, after having been refused admittance by their neighbours. The Gods, in acknowledgment of their hospitality, transform their cottage into a temple, of which, at their own request, they are made the priest and priestess; and, after a long life, the worthy couple are changed into trees. The village where they live is laid under water, on account of the impiety of the inhabitants, and is turned into a lake. Acheloüs here relates the surprising changes of Proteus.

After these things the river was silent. The wondrous deed had astonished them all. The son of Ixion laughed at them,[82] believing the story; and as he was a despiser of the Gods, and of a haughty disposition, he said, "Acheloüs, thou dost relate a fiction, and dost deem the Gods more powerful than they are, if they both give and take away the form of things." At this all were amazed, and did not approve of such language; and before all, Lelex, ripe in understanding and age, spoke thus: "The power of heaven is immense, and has no limits; and whatever the Gods above will, 'tis done.

"And that thou mayst the less doubt of this, there is upon the Phrygian hills, an oak near to the lime tree, enclosed by a low wall.[83] I, myself, have seen the spot; for Pittheus sent me into the land of Pelops, once governed by his father, Pelops. Not far thence is a standing water, formerly habitable ground, but now frequented by cormorants and coots, that delight in fens. Jupiter came hither in the shape of a man, and together with his parent, the grandson of Atlas, Mercury, the bearer of the Caduceus, having laid aside his wings. To a thousand houses did they go, asking for lodging and for rest. A thousand houses did the bolts fasten against them. Yet one received them, a small one indeed, thatched with straw,[84] and the reeds of the marsh. But a pious old woman named Baucis, and Philemon of a like age, were united in their youthful years in that cottage, and in it, they grew old together; and by owning their poverty, they rendered it light, and not to be endured with discontented mind. It matters not, whether you ask for the masters there, or for the servants; the whole family are but two; the same persons both obey and command. When, therefore, the inhabitants of heaven reached this little abode, and, bending their necks, entered the humble door, the old man bade them rest their limbs on a bench set there; upon which the attentive Baucis threw a coarse cloth. Then she moves the warm embers on the hearth, and stirs up the fire they had had the day before, and supplies it with leaves and dry bark, and with her aged breath kindles it into a flame; and brings out of the house faggots split into many pieces, and dry bits of branches, and breaks them, and puts them beneath a small boiler. Some pot-herbs, too, which her husband has gathered in the well-watered garden, she strips of their leaves.

"With a two-pronged fork Philemon lifts down[85] a rusty side of bacon, that hangs from a black beam; and cuts off a small portion from the chine that has been kept so long; and when cut, softens it in boiling water. In the meantime, with discourse they beguile the intervening hours; and suffer not the length of time to be perceived. There is a beechen trough there, that hangs on a peg by its crooked handle; this is filled with warm water, and receives their limbs to refresh them. On the middle of the couch, its feet and frame[86] being made of willow, is placed a cushion of soft sedge. This they cover with cloths, which they have not been accustomed to place there but on festive occasions; but even these cloths are coarse and old, though not unfitting for a couch of willow. The Gods seat themselves. The old woman, wearing an apron, and shaking with palsy, sets the table before them. But the third leg of the table is too short; a potsherd, placed beneath, makes it equal. After this, being placed beneath, has taken away the inequality, green mint rubs down the table thus made level. Here are set the double-tinted berries[87] of the chaste Minerva, and cornel-berries, gathered in autumn, and preserved in a thin pickle; endive, too, and radishes, and a large piece of curdled milk, and eggs, that have been gently turned in the slow embers; all served in earthenware. After this, an embossed goblet of similar clay is placed there; cups, too, made of beech wood, varnished, where they are hollowed out, with yellow wax.

"There is now a short pause;[88] the fire then sends up the warm repast; and wine kept no long time, is again put on; and then, set aside for a little time, it gives place to the second course. Here are nuts, and here are dried figs mixed with wrinkled dates, plums too, and fragrant apples in wide baskets, and grapes gathered from the purple vines. In the middle there is white honey-comb. Above all, there are welcome looks, and no indifferent and niggardly feelings. In the meanwhile, as oft as Baucis and the alarmed Philemon behold the goblet, when drunk off, replenish itself of its own accord, and the wine increase of itself, astonished at this singular event, they are frightened, and, with hands held up, they offer their prayers, and entreat pardon for their entertainment, and their want of preparation. There was a single goose, the guardian of their little cottage, which its owners were preparing to kill for the Deities, their guests. Swift with its wings, it wearied them, rendered slow by age, and it escaped them a long time, and at length seemed to fly for safety to the Gods themselves. The immortals forbade it[89] to be killed, and said, 'We are Divinities, and this impious neighbourhood shall suffer deserved punishment. To you it will be allowed to be free from this calamity; only leave your habitation, and attend our steps, and go together to the summit of the mountain.'

"They both obeyed; and, supported by staffs, they endeavoured to place their feet on the top of the high hill. They were now as far from the top, as an arrow discharged can go at once, when they turned their eyes, and beheld the other parts sinking in a morass, and their own abode alone remaining. While they were wondering at these things, and while they were bewailing the fate of their fellow countrymen, that old cottage of theirs, too little for even two owners, was changed into a temple. Columns took the place of forked stakes, the thatch grew yellow, and the earth was covered with marble; the doors appeared carved, and the roof to be of gold. Then, the son of Saturn uttered such words as these with benign lips: 'Tell us, good old man, and thou, wife, worthy of a husband so good, what it is you desire?' Having spoken a few words to Baucis, Philemon discovered their joint request to the Gods: 'We desire to be your priests, and to have the care of your temple; and, since we have passed our years in harmony, let the same hour take us off both together; and let me not ever see the tomb of my wife, nor let me be destined to be buried by her.' Fulfilment attended their wishes. So long as life was granted, they were the keepers of the temple; and when, enervated by years and old age, they were standing, by chance, before the sacred steps, and were relating the fortunes of the spot, Baucis beheld Philemon, and the aged Philemon saw Baucis, too, shooting into leaf. And now the tops of the trees growing above their two faces, so long as they could they exchanged words with each other, and said together, 'Farewell! my spouse;' and at the same moment the branches covered their concealed faces. The inhabitants of Tyana[90] still shew these adjoining trees, made of their two bodies. Old men, no romancers, (and there was no reason why they should wish to deceive me) told me this. I, indeed, saw garlands hanging on the branches, and placing there some fresh ones myself, I said, 'The good are the peculiar care of the Gods, and those who worshipped the Gods, are now worshipped themselves.'"

He had now ceased; and the thing itself and the relator of it had astonished them all; and especially Theseus, whom, desiring to hear of the wonderful actions of the Gods, the Calydonian river leaning on his elbow, addressed in words such as these: "There are, O most valiant hero, some things, whose form has been once changed, and then has continued under that change. There are some whose privilege it is to pass into many shapes, as thou, Proteus, inhabitant of the sea that embraces the earth. For people have seen thee one while a young man, and again a lion; at one time thou wast a furious boar, at another a serpent, which they dreaded to touch; and sometimes, horns rendered thee a bull. Ofttimes thou mightst be seen as a stone; often, too, as a tree. Sometimes imitating the appearance of flowing water, thou wast a river; sometimes fire, the very contrary of water."

[Footnote 82: Laughed at them.—Ver. 612. The Centaurs, from one of whom Pirithoüs was sprung, were famed for their contempt of, and enmity to, the Gods.]

[Footnote 83: By a low wall.—Ver. 620. As a memorial of the wonderful events here related by Lelex.]

[Footnote 84: Thatched with straw.—Ver. 630. It was the custom with the ancients, when reaping, to take off only the heads of the corn, and to leave the stubble to be reaped at another time. From this passage, we see that straw was used for the purpose of thatching.]

[Footnote 85: Lifts down.—Ver. 647. The lifting down the flitch of bacon might induce us to believe that the account of this story was written yesterday, and not nearly two thousand years since. So true is it, that there is nothing new under the sun.]

[Footnote 86: Feet and frame.—Ver. 659. 'Sponda.' This was the frame of the bedstead, and more especially the sides of it. In the case of a bed used for two persons, the two sides were distinguished by different names; the side at which they entered was open, and was called 'sponda:' the other side, which was protected by a board, was called 'pluteus.' The two sides were also called 'torus exterior,' or 'sponda exterior,' and 'torus interior,' or 'sponda interior.']

[Footnote 87: Double-tinted berries.—Ver. 664. Green on one side, and swarthy on the other.]

[Footnote 88: A short pause.—Ver. 671. This was the second course. The Roman 'cœna,' or chief meal, consisted of three stages. First, the 'promulsis,' 'antecœna,' or 'gustatio,' when they ate such things as served to stimulate the appetite. Then came the first course, which formed the substantial part of the meal; and next the second course, at which the 'bellaria,' consisting of pastry and fruits, such as are now used at dessert, were served.]

[Footnote 89: Immortals forbade it.—Ver. 688. This act of humanity reflects credit on the two Deities, and contrasts favourably with their usual cruel and revengeful disposition, in common with their fellow Divinities of the heathen Mythology.]

[Footnote 90: Of Tyana.—Ver. 719. This was a city of Cappadocia, in Asia Minor.]

EXPLANATION

The story of Baucis and Philemon, which is here so beautifully related by the Poet, is a moral tale, which shows the merit of hospitality, and how, in some cases at least, virtue speedily brings its own reward. If the story is based upon any actual facts, the history of its origin is entirely unknown. Huet, the theologian, indeed, supposes that it is founded on the history of the reception of the Angels by Abraham. This is a bold surmise, but entirely in accordance with his position, that the greatest part of the fictions of the heathen mythology were mere glosses or perversions of the histories of the Old Testament. If derived from Scripture, the story is just as likely to be founded on the hospitable reception of the Prophet Elijah by the woman of Zarephath; and the miraculous increase of the wine in the goblet, calls to mind 'the barrel of meal that wasted not, and the cruse of oil that did not fail.' The story of the wretched fate of the inhospitable neighbours of Baucis and Philemon is thought, by some modern writers, to be founded upon the Scriptural account of the destruction of the wicked cities of the plain.

Ancient writers have made many attempts to solve the wondrous story of Proteus. Some say that he was an elegant orator, who charmed his auditors by the force of his eloquence. Lucian says that he was an actor of pantomime, so supple that he could assume various postures. Herodotus, Diodorus Siculus, and Clement of Alexandria, assert that he was an ancient king of Egypt, successor to Pheron, and that he lived at the time, of the Trojan war. Herodotus, who represents him as a prince of great wisdom and justice, does not make any allusion to his powers of transformation, which was his great merit in the eyes of the poets. Diodorus Siculus says that his alleged changes may have had their rise in a custom which Proteus had of adorning his helmet, sometimes with the skin of a panther, sometimes with that of a lion, and sometimes with that of a serpent, or of some other animal. When Lycophron states that Neptune saved Proteus from the fury of his children, by making him go through caverns from Pallene to Egypt, he follows the tradition which says that he originally came from that town in Thessaly, and that he retired thence to Egypt. Virgil, and Servius, his Commentator, assert that Proteus returned to Thessaly after the death of his children, who were slain by Hercules; in which assertion, however, they are not supported by Homer or Herodotus.

FABLE VII [VIII.738-884]

Acheloüs continues his narrative with the story of Metra, the daughter of Erisicthon, who is attacked with insatiable hunger, for having cut down an oak, in one of the groves of Ceres. Metra begs of Neptune, who was formerly in love with her, the power of transforming herself into different shapes; that she may be enabled, if possible, to satisfy the voracious appetite of her father. By these means, Erisicthon, being obliged to expose her for sale, in order to purchase himself food, always recovers her again; until, by his repeated sale of her, the fraud is discovered. He at last becomes the avenger of his own impiety, by devouring his own limbs.

"Nor has the wife of Autolycus,[91] the daughter of Erisicthon, less privileges than he. Her father was one who despised the majesty of the Gods; and he offered them no honours on their altars. He is likewise said to have profaned with an axe a grove of Ceres, and to have violated her ancient woods with the iron. In these there was standing an oak with an ancient trunk, a wood in itself alone, fillets and tablets, as memorials,[92] and garlands, proofs of wishes that had been granted, surrounded the middle of it. Often, beneath this tree, did the Dryads lead up the festive dance; often, too, with hands joined in order, did they go round the compass of its trunk; and the girth of the oak made up three times five ells. The rest of the wood, too, lay as much under this oak as the grass lay beneath the whole of the wood. Yet not on that account even did the son of Triopas[93] withhold the axe from it; and he ordered his servants to cut down the sacred oak; and when he saw them hesitate, thus ordered, the wicked wretch, snatching from one of them an axe, uttered these words: 'Were it not only beloved by a Goddess, but even were it a Goddess itself, it should now touch the ground with its leafy top.' Thus he said; and while he was poising his weapon for a side stroke, the Deoïan oak[94] shuddered, and uttered a groan; and at once, its green leaves, and, with them, its acorns began to turn pale; and the long branches to be moistened with sweat. As soon as his impious hand had made an incision in its trunk, the blood flowed from the severed bark no otherwise than, as, at the time when the bull, a large victim, falls before the altars, the blood pours forth from his divided neck. All were amazed and one of the number attempted to hinder the wicked design, and to restrain the cruel axe. The Thessalian eyes him, and says, 'Take the reward of thy pious intentions,' and turns the axe from the tree upon the man, and hews off his head; and then hacks at the oak again; when such words as these are uttered from the middle of the oak: 'I, a Nymph,[95] most pleasing to Ceres, am beneath this wood; I, now dying, foretell to thee that the punishment of thy deeds, the solace of my death, is at hand.'

"He pursued his wicked design; and, at last, weakened by numberless blows, and pulled downward with ropes, the tree fell down, and with its weight levelled a great part of the wood. All her sisters, the Dryads, being shocked at the loss of the grove and their own, in their grief repaired to Ceres, in black array,[96] and requested the punishment of Erisicthon. She assented to their request, and the most beauteous Goddess, with the nodding of her head, shook the fields loaded with the heavy crops; and contrived for him a kind of punishment, lamentable, if he had not, for his crimes, been deserving of the sympathy of none, namely, to torment him with deadly Famine. And since that Goddess could not be approached by herself (for the Destinies do not allow Ceres and Famine to come together), in such words as these she addressed rustic Oreas, one of the mountain Deities: 'There is an icy region in the extreme part of Scythia, a dreary soil, a land, desolate, without corn and without trees; there dwell drowsy Cold, and Paleness, and Trembling, and famishing Hunger; order her to bury herself in the breast of this sacrilegious wretch. Let no abundance of provisions overcome her; and let her surpass my powers in the contest. And that the length of the road may not alarm thee, take my chariot, take the dragons, which thou mayst guide aloft with the reins;' and then she gave them to her.

"She, borne through the air on the chariot thus granted, arrived in Scythia; and, on the top of a steep mountain (they call it Caucasus), she unyoked the neck of the dragons, and beheld Famine, whom she was seeking, in a stony field, tearing up herbs, growing here and there, with her nails and with her teeth. Rough was her hair, her eyes hollow, paleness on her face, her lips white with scurf,[97] her jaws rough with rustiness; her skin hard, through which her bowels might be seen; her dry bones were projecting beneath her crooked loins; instead of a belly, there was only the place for a belly. You would think her breast was hanging, and was only supported from the chine[98] of the back. Leanness had, to appearance, increased her joints, and the caps of her knees were stiff, and excrescences projected from her overgrown ancles. Soon as Oreas beheld her at a distance (for she did not dare come near her), she delivered the commands of the Goddess; and, staying for so short a time, although she was at a distance from her, and although she had just come thither, still did she seem to feel hunger; and, turning the reins, she drove aloft the dragon's back to Hæmonia.

"Famine executes the orders of Ceres (although she is ever opposing her operations), and is borne by the winds through the air to the assigned abode, and immediately enters the bedchamber of the sacrilegious wretch, and embraces him, sunk in a deep sleep (for it is night-time), with her two wings. She breathes herself into the man, and blows upon his jaws, and his breast, and his face; and she scatters hunger through his empty veins. And having thus executed her commission, she forsakes the fruitful world, and returns to her famished abode, her wonted fields. Gentle sleep is still soothing[99] Erisicthon with its balmy wings. In a vision of his sleep he craves for food, and moves his jaws to no purpose, and tires his teeth grinding upon teeth, and wearies his throat deluded with imaginary food; and, instead of victuals, he devours in vain the yielding air. But when sleep is banished, his desire for eating is outrageous, and holds sway over his craving jaws, and his insatiate entrails. And no delay is there; he calls what the sea, what the earth, what the air produces, and complains of hunger with the tables set before him, and requires food in the midst of food. And what might be enough for whole cities, and what might be enough for a whole people, is not sufficient for one man. The more, too, he swallows down into his stomach, the more does he desire. And just as the ocean receives rivers from the whole earth, and yet is not satiated with water, and drinks up the rivers of distant countries, and as the devouring fire never refuses fuel, and burns up beams of wood without number, and the greater the quantity that is given to it, the more does it crave, and it is the more voracious through the very abundance of fuel; so do the jaws of the impious Erisicthon receive all victuals presented, and at the same time ask for more. In him all food is only a ground for more food, and there is always room vacant for eating still more.

"And now, through his appetite, and the voracity of his capacious stomach, he had diminished his paternal estate; but yet, even then, did his shocking hunger remain undiminished, and the craving of his insatiable appetite continued in full vigour. At last, after he has swallowed down his estate into his paunch,[100] his daughter alone is remaining, undeserving of him for a father; her, too, he sells, pressed by want. Born of a noble race, she cannot brook a master; and stretching out her hands, over the neighbouring sea, she says, 'Deliver me from a master, thou who dost possess the prize of my ravished virginity.' This prize Neptune had possessed himself of. He, not despising her prayer, although, the moment before, she has been seen by her master in pursuit of her, both alters her form, and gives her the appearance of a man, and a habit befitting such as catch fish. Looking at her, her master says, 'O thou manager of the rod, who dost cover the brazen hook, as it hangs, with tiny morsels, even so may the sea be smooth for thee, even so may the fish in the water be ever credulous for thee, and may they perceive no hook till caught; tell me where she is, who this moment was standing upon this shore (for standing on the shore I saw her), with her hair dishevelled, and in humble garb; for no further do her footsteps extend.' She perceives that the favour of the God has turned to good purpose, and, well pleased that she is inquired after of herself, she replies to him, as he inquires, in these words: 'Whoever thou art, excuse me, but I have not turned my eyes on any side from this water, and, busily employed, I have been attending to my pursuit. And that thou mayst the less disbelieve me, may the God of the sea so aid this employment of mine, no man has been for some time standing on this shore, myself only excepted, nor has any woman been standing here.' Her master believed her, and, turning his feet to go away, he paced the sands, and, thus deceived, withdrew. Her own shape was restored to her.

"But when her father found that his daughter had a body capable of being transformed, he often sold the grand-daughter of Triopas to other masters. But she used to escape, sometimes as a mare, sometimes as a bird, now as a cow, now as a stag; and so provided a dishonest maintenance for her hungry parent. Yet, after this violence of his distemper had consumed all his provision, and had added fresh fuel to his dreadful malady: he himself, with mangling bites, began to tear his own limbs, and the miserable wretch used to feed his own body by diminishing it. But why do I dwell on the instances of others? I, too, O youths,[101] have a power of often changing my body, though limited in the number of those changes. For, one while, I appear what I now am, another while I am wreathed as a snake; then as the leader of a herd, I receive strength in my horns. In my horns, I say, so long as I could. Now, one side of my forehead is deprived of its weapons, as thou seest thyself." Sighs followed his words.

[Footnote 91: Autolycus.—Ver. 738. He was the father of Anticlea, the mother of Ulysses, and was instructed by Mercury in the art of thieving. His wife was Metra, whose transformations are here described by the Poet.]

[Footnote 92: Tablets as memorials.—Ver. 744. That is, they had inscribed on them the grateful thanks of the parties who placed them there to Ceres, for having granted their wishes.]

[Footnote 93: Son of Triopas.—Ver. 751. Erisicthon was the son of Triopas.]

[Footnote 94: Deoïan oak.—Ver. 758. Belonging to Ceres. See Book vi. line 114.]

[Footnote 95: I, a Nymph.—Ver. 771. She was one of the Hamadryads, whose lives terminated with those of the trees which they respectively inhabited.]

[Footnote 96: In black array.—Ver. 778. The Romans wore mourning for the dead; which seems, in the time of the Republic, to have been black or dark blue for either sex. Under the Empire, the men continued to wear black, but the women wore white. On such occasions all ornaments were laid aside.]

[Footnote 97: With scurf.—Ver. 802. Clarke gives this translation of 'Labra incana situ:' 'Her lips very white with nasty stuff.']

[Footnote 98: From the chine.—Ver. 806. 'A spinæ tantummodo crate teneri,' is translated by Clarke, 'Was only supported by the wattling of her backbone.']

[Footnote 99: Is still soothing.—Ver. 823. Clarke renders the words 'Lenis adhuc somnus—Erisicthona pennis mulcebat;' 'Gentle sleep as yet clapped Erisicthon with her wings.']

[Footnote 100: Into his paunch.—Ver. 846. Clarke translates 'Tandem, demisso in viscera censu;' 'at last, after he had swallowed down all his estate into his g—ts.']

[Footnote 101: I too, O youths.—Ver. 880. Acheloüs is addressing Theseus, Pirithoüs, and Lelex. The words, 'Etiam mihi sæpe novandi Corporis, O Juvenes,' is rendered by Clarke, 'I too, gentlemen, have the power of changing my body.']

EXPLANATION

The story of Metra and Erisicthon has no other foundation, in all probability, than the diligent care which she took, as a dutiful daughter, to support her father, when he had ruined himself by his luxury and extravagance. She, probably, was a young woman, who, in the hour of need, could, in common parlance, 'turn her hand' to any useful employment. Some, however, suppose that, by her changes are meant the wages she received from those whom she served in the capacity of a slave, and which she gave to her father; and it must be remembered that, in ancient times, as money was scarce, the wages of domestics were often paid in kind. Other writers again suggest, less to the credit of the damsel, that her changes denote the price she received for her debaucheries. Ovid adds, that she married Autolycus, the robber, who stole the oxen of Eurytus. Callimachus also, in his Hymn to Ceres, gives the story of Erisicthon at length. He was the great grandfather of Ulysses, and was probably a man noted for his infidelity and impiety, as well as his riotous course of life. The story is probably of Eastern origin, and if a little expanded might vie with many of the interesting fictions which we read in the Arabian Night's Entertainments.

BOOK THE NINTH

FABLE I [IX.1-100]

Deïanira, the daughter of Œneus, having been wooed by several suitors, her father gives his consent that she shall marry him who proves to be the bravest of them. Her other suitors, having given way to Hercules and Acheloüs, they engage in single combat. Acheloüs, to gain the advantage over his rival, transforms himself into various shapes, and, at length, into that of a bull. These attempts are in vain, and Hercules overcomes him, and breaks off one of his horns. The Naiads, the daughters of Acheloüs, take it up, and fill it with the variety of fruits which Autumn affords; on which it obtains the name of the Horn of Plenty.

Theseus, the Neptunian hero,[1] inquires what is the cause of his sighing, and of his forehead being mutilated; when thus begins the Calydonian river, having his unadorned hair crowned with reeds:

"A mournful task thou art exacting; for who, when overcome, is desirous to relate his own battles? yet I will relate them in order; nor was it so disgraceful to be overcome, as it is glorious to have engaged; and a conqueror so mighty affords me a great consolation. If, perchance, Deïanira,[2] by her name, has at last reached thy ears, once she was a most beautiful maiden, and the envied hope of many a wooer; together with these, when the house of him, whom I desired as my father-in-law, was entered by me, I said, 'Receive me, O son of Parthaon,[3] for thy son-in-law.' Alcides, too, said the same; the others yielded to us two. He alleged that he was offering to the damsel both Jupiter as a father-in-law, and the glory of his labours; the orders, too, of his step-mother, successfully executed. On the other hand (I thought it disgraceful for a God to give way to a mortal, for then he was not a God), I said, 'Thou beholdest me, a king of the waters, flowing amid thy realms,[4] with my winding course; nor am I some stranger sent thee for a son-in-law, from foreign lands, but I shall be one of thy people, and a part of thy state. Only let it not be to my prejudice, that the royal Juno does not hate me, and that all punishment, by labours enjoined, is afar from me. For, since thou, Hercules, dost boast thyself born of Alcmena for thy mother; Jupiter is either thy pretended sire, or thy real one through a criminal deed: by the adultery of thy mother art thou claiming a father. Choose, then, whether thou wouldst rather have Jupiter for thy pretended father, or that thou art sprung from him through a disgraceful deed?'

"While I was saying such things as these, for some time he looked at me with a scowling eye, and did not very successfully check his inflamed wrath; and he returned me just as many words as these: 'My right hand is better than my tongue. If only I do but prevail in fighting, do thou get the better in talking;' and then he fiercely attacked me. I was ashamed, after having so lately spoken big words, to yield. I threw on one side my green garment from off my body, and opposed my arms to his, and I held my hands bent inwards,[5] from before my breast, on their guard, and I prepared my limbs for the combat. He sprinkled me with dust, taken up in the hollow of his hands, and, in his turn, grew yellow with the casting of yellow sand[6] upon himself. And at one moment he aimed at my neck, at another my legs, as they shifted about, or you would suppose he was aiming at them; and he assaulted me on every side. My bulk defended me, and I was attacked in vain; no otherwise than a mole, which the waves beat against with loud noise: it remains unshaken, and by its own weight is secure.

"We retire a little, and then again we rush together in conflict, and we stand firm, determined not to yield; foot, too, is joined to foot; and then I, bending forward full with my breast, press upon his fingers with my fingers, and his forehead with my forehead. In no different manner have I beheld the strong bulls engage, when the most beauteous mate[7] in all the pasture is sought as the reward of the combat; the herds look on and tremble, uncertain which the mastery of so great a domain awaits. Thrice without effect did Alcides attempt to hurl away from him my breast, as it bore hard against him; the fourth time, he shook off my hold, and loosened my arms clasped around him; and, striking me with his hand, (I am resolved to confess the truth) he turned me quite round, and clung, a mighty load, to my back. If any credit is to be given me, (and, indeed, no glory is sought by me through an untrue narration) I seemed to myself as though weighed down with a mountain placed upon me. Yet, with great difficulty, I disengaged my arms streaming with much perspiration, and, with great exertion, I unlocked his firm grasp from my body. He pressed on me as I panted for breath, and prevented me from recovering my strength, and then seized hold of my neck. Then, at last, was the earth pressed by my knee, and with my mouth I bit the sand. Inferior in strength, I had recourse to my arts,[8] and transformed into a long serpent, I escaped from the hero.

"After I had twisted my body into winding folds, and darted my forked tongue with dreadful hissings, the Tirynthian laughed, and deriding my arts, he said, 'It was the labour of my cradle to conquer serpents;[9]

and although, Acheloüs, thou shouldst excel other snakes, how large a part wilt thou, but one serpent, be of the Lernæan Echidna? By her very wounds was she multiplied, and not one head of her hundred in number[10] was cut off by me without danger to myself; but rather so that her neck became stronger, with two successors to the former head. Yet her I subdued, branching with serpents springing from each wound, and growing stronger by her disasters; and, so subdued, I slew her. What canst thou think will become of thee, who, changed into a fictitious serpent, art wielding arms that belong to another, and whom a form, obtained as a favour, is now disguising?' Thus he spoke; and he planted the grip of his fingers on the upper part of my neck. I was tortured, just as though my throat was squeezed with pincers; and I struggled hard to disengage my jaws from his fingers.

"Thus vanquished, too, there still remained for me my third form, that of a furious bull; with my limbs changed into those of a bull I renewed the fight. He threw his arms over my brawny neck, on the left side, and, dragging at me, followed me in my onward course; and seizing my horns, he fastened them in the hard ground, and felled me upon the deep sand. And that was not enough; while his relentless right hand was holding my stubborn horn, he broke it, and tore it away from my mutilated forehead. This, heaped with fruit and odoriferous flowers, the Naiads have consecrated, and the bounteous Goddess, Plenty, is enriched by my horn." Thus he said; but a Nymph, girt up after the manner of Diana, one of his handmaids, with her hair hanging loose on either side, came in, and brought the whole of the produce of Autumn in the most plentiful horn, and choice fruit for a second course.

Day comes on, and the rising sun striking the tops of the hills, the young men depart; nor do they stay till the stream has quiet restored to it, and a smooth course, and till the troubled waters subside. Acheloüs conceals his rustic features, and his mutilated horn, in the midst of the waves; yet the loss of this honour, taken from him, alone affects him; in other respects, he is unhurt. The injury, too, which has befallen his head, is now concealed with willow branches, or with reeds placed upon it.

[Footnote 1: The Neptunian hero.—Ver. 1. Theseus was the grandson of Neptune, through his father Ægeus.]

[Footnote 2: Deïanira.—Ver. 9. She was the daughter of Œneus, king of Ætolia, and became the wife of Hercules.]

[Footnote 3: Parthaon.—Ver. 12. He was the son of Agenor and Epicaste. Homer, however, makes Portheus, and not Parthaon, to have been the father of Œneus.]

[Footnote 4: Amid thy realms.—Ver. 18. The river Acheloüs flowed between Ætolia and Acarnania.]

[Footnote 5: Bent inwards.—Ver. 33. 'Varus,' which we here translate 'bent inwards,' according to some authorities, means 'bent outwards.']

[Footnote 6: Casting of yellow sand.—Ver. 35. It was the custom of wrestlers, after they had anointed the body with 'ceroma' or wrestler's oil, in order to render the body supple and pliant, to sprinkle the body with sand, or dust, to enable the antagonist to take a firm hold. It was, however, considered more praiseworthy to conquer in a contest which was ἀκονιτὶ 'without the use of sand.']

[Footnote 7: Most beauteous mate.—Ver. 47. Clarke translates 'nitidissima conjux,' 'the neatest cow.']

[Footnote 8: Recourse to my arts.—Ver. 62. 'Devertor ad artes,' is rendered by Clarke, 'I fly to my tricks.']

[Footnote 9: To conquer serpents.—Ver. 67. Hercules, while an infant in his cradle, was said to have strangled two serpents, which Juno sent for the purpose of destroying him.]

[Footnote 10: Hundred in number.—Ver. 71. The number of heads of the Hydra varies in the accounts given by different writers. Seven, nine, fifty, and a hundred are the numbers mentioned. This, however, is not surprising, as we are told that where one was cut off, two sprang up in their place, until Hercules, to prevent such consequences, adopted the precaution of searing the neck, where the head had been cut off, with a red hot iron.]

EXPLANATION

The river Acheloüs, which ran between Acarnania and Ætolia, often did considerable damage to those countries by its inundations, and, at the same time, by confounding or sweeping away the limits which separated those nations, it engaged them in continual warfare with each other. Hercules, who seems really to have been a person of great scientific skill, which he was ever ready to employ for the service of his fellow men, raised banks to it, and made its course so uniform and straight, that he was the means of establishing perpetual peace between these adjoining nations.

The early authors who recorded these events have narrated them under a thick and almost impenetrable veil of fiction. They say that Hercules engaged in combat with the God of that river, who immediately transformed himself into a serpent, by which was probably meant merely the serpentine windings of its course. Next they say, that the God changed himself into a bull, under which allegorical form they refer to the rapid and impetuous overflowing of its banks, ever rushing onwards, bearing down everything in its course, and leaving traces of its ravages throughout the country in its vicinity. This mode of description the more readily occurred to them in the case of Acheloüs, as from the roaring noise which they often make in their course, rivers in general were frequently represented under the figure of a bull, and, of course, as wearing horns, the great instruments of the havoc which they created.

It was said, then, that Hercules at length overcame this bull, and broke off one of his horns; by which was meant, according to Strabo, that he brought both the branches of the river into one channel. Again, this horn became the Horn of Plenty in that region; or, in other words, being withdrawn from its bed, the river left a large track of very fertile ground for agricultural purposes. As to the Cornucopia, or Horn of Plenty of the heathen Mythology, there is some variation in the accounts respecting it. Some writers say that by it was meant the horn of the goat Amalthea, which suckled Jupiter, and that the Nymphs gave it to Acheloüs, who again gave it in exchange for that of which Hercules afterwards deprived him. Deïanira, having given her hand to Hercules, as the recompense of the important services which he had rendered to her father, Œneus, it was fabled that she had been promised to Acheloüs, who was vanquished by his rival; and on this foundation was built the superstructure of the famous combat which the Poet here describes. After having remained for some time at the court of his father-in-law, Hercules was obliged to leave it, in consequence of having killed the son of Architritilus, who was the cupbearer of that prince.

FABLE II [IX.101-272]

Hercules, returning with Deïanira, as the prize of his victory, entrusts her to the Centaur Nessus, to carry her over the river Evenus. Nessus seizes the opportunity of Hercules being on the other side of the river, and attempts to carry her off; on which Hercules, perceiving his design, shoots him with an arrow, and thus prevents its execution. The Centaur, when expiring, in order to gratify his revenge, gives Deïanira his tunic dipped in his blood, assuring her that it contains an effectual charm against all infidelity on the part of her husband. Afterwards, on hearing that Hercules is in love with Iole, Deïanira sends him the tunic, that it may have the supposed effect. As soon as he puts it on, he is affected with excruciating torments, and is seized with such violent fits of madness, that he throws Lychas, the bearer of the garment, into the sea, where he is changed into a rock. Hercules, then, in obedience to a response of the oracle, which he consults, prepares a funeral pile, and laying himself upon it, his friend Philoctetes applies the torch to it, on which the hero, having first recounted his labours, expires in the flames. After his body is consumed, Jupiter translates him to the heavens, and he is placed in the number of the Gods.

But a passion for this same maiden proved fatal to thee, fierce Nessus,[11] pierced through the back with a swift arrow. For the son of Jupiter, as he was returning to his native city with his new-made wife, had now come to the rapid waters of the river Evenus.[12] The stream was swollen to a greater extent than usual with the winter rains, and was full of whirlpools, and impassable. Nessus came up to him, regardless of himself, but feeling anxiety for his wife, both strong of limb,[13] and well acquainted with the fords, and said, "Alcides, she shall be landed on yonder bank through my services, do thou employ thy strength in swimming;" and the Aonian hero entrusted to Nessus the Calydonian damsel full of alarm, and pale with apprehension, and equally dreading both the river and Nessus himself. Immediately, just as he was, loaded both with his quiver and the spoil of the lion, (for he had thrown his club and his crooked bow to the opposite side), he said, "Since I have undertaken it, the stream must be passed."

And he does not hesitate; nor does he seek out where the stream is the smoothest, and he spurns to be borne over by the compliance of the river. And now having reached the bank, and as he is taking up the bow which he had thrown over, he recognizes the voice of his wife; and as Nessus is preparing to rob him of what he has entrusted to his care, he cries out, "Whither, thou ravisher, does thy vain confidence in thy feet hurry thee? to thee am I speaking, Nessus, thou two-shaped monster. Listen; and do not carry off my property. If no regard for myself influences thee, still the wheel of thy father[14] might have restrained thee from forbidden embraces. Thou shall not escape, however, although thou dost confide[15] in thy powers of a horse; with a wound, and not with my feet, will I overtake thee." These last words he confirms by deeds, and pierces him through the back, as he is flying, with an arrow discharged at him. The barbed steel stands out from his breast; soon as it is wrenched out, the blood gushes forth from both wounds, mingled with the venom of the Lernæan poison. Nessus takes it out, and says to himself, "And yet I shall not die unrevenged;" and gives his garment, dyed in the warm blood, as a present to her whom he is carrying off, as though an incentive to love.

Long was the space of intervening time, and the feats of the mighty Hercules and the hatred of his step-mother had filled the earth. Returning victorious from Œchalia, he is preparing a sacrifice which he had vowed to Cenæan Jupiter,[16] when tattling Rumour (who takes pleasure in adding false things to the truth, and from a very little beginning, swells to a great bulk by her lies) runs before to thy ears, Deïanira, to the effect that the son of Amphitryon is seized with a passion for Iole. As she loves him, she believes it; and being alarmed with the report of this new amour, at first she indulges in tears and in her misery gives vent to her grief in weeping. Soon, however, she says, "But why do I weep? My rival will be delighted with these tears; and since she is coming I must make haste, and some contrivance must be resolved on while it is still possible, and while, as yet, another has not taken possession of my bed. Shall I complain, or shall I be silent? Shall I return to Calydon, or shall I stay here? Shall I depart from this abode? or, if nothing more, shall I oppose their entrance? What if, O Meleager, remembering that I am thy sister, I resolve on a desperate deed, and testify, by murdering my rival, how much, injury and a woman's grief can effect?"

Her mind wavers, amid various resolves. Before them all, she prefers to send the garment dyed in the blood of Nessus, to restore strength to his declining love. Not knowing herself what she is giving, she delivers the cause of her own sorrows to the unsuspecting Lichas,[17] and bids him, in gentle words, to deliver this most fatal gift to her husband. In his ignorance, the hero receives it, and places upon his shoulders the venom of the Lernæan Echidna. He is placing frankincense on the rising flames, and is offering the words of prayer, and pouring wine from the bowl upon the marble altars. The virulence of the bane waxes warm, and, melted by the flames, it runs, widely diffused over the limbs of Hercules. So long as he is able, he suppresses his groans with his wonted fortitude. After his endurance is overcome by his anguish, he pushes down the altars, and fills the woody Œta with his cries. There is no further delay; he attempts to tear off the deadly garment; but where it is torn off, it tears away the skin, and, shocking to relate, it either sticks to his limbs, being tried in vain to be pulled off, or it lays bare his mangled limbs, and his huge bones. The blood itself hisses, just as when a red hot plate of metal is dipped in cold water; and it boils with the burning poison. There is no limit to his misery; the devouring flames prey upon his entrails, and a livid perspiration flows from his whole body; his half-burnt sinews also crack; and his marrow being now dissolved by the subtle poison, lifting his hands towards the stars of heaven, he exclaims, "Daughter of Saturn, satiate thyself with my anguish; satiate thyself, and look down from on high, O cruel Goddess, at this my destruction, and glut thy relentless heart. Or, if I am to be pitied even by an enemy (for an enemy I am to thee), take away a life insupportable through these dreadful agonies, hateful, too, to myself, and only destined to trouble. Death will be a gain to me. It becomes a stepmother to grant such a favour.

"And was it for this that I subdued Busiris, who polluted the temples of the Gods with the blood of strangers? And did I for this, withdraw from the savage Antæus[18] the support given him by his mother? Did neither the triple shape of the Iberian shepherd[19], nor thy triple form, O Cerberus, alarm me? And did you, my hands, seize the horns of the mighty bull? Does Elis, too, possess the result of your labours, and the Stymphalian waters, and the Parthenian[20] grove as well? By your valour was it that the belt, inlaid with the gold of Thermodon[21], was gained, the apples too, guarded in vain by the wakeful dragon? And could neither the Centaurs resist me, nor yet the boar, the ravager of Arcadia? And was it not of no avail to the Hydra to grow through its own loss, and to recover double strength? And what besides? When I beheld the Thracian steeds fattened with human blood, and the mangers filled with mangled bodies, did I throw them down when thus beheld, and slay both the master and the horses themselves? And does the carcass of the Nemean lion lie crushed by these arms? With this neck did I support the heavens?[22] The unrelenting wife of Jupiter[23] was weary of commanding, but I was still unwearied with doing. But now a new calamity is come upon me, to which resistance can be made neither by valour, nor by weapons, nor by arms. A consuming flame is pervading the inmost recesses of my lungs, and is preying on all my limbs. But Eurystheus still survives. And are there," says he, "any who can believe that the Deities exist?"

And then, racked with pain, he ranges along the lofty Œta, no otherwise than if a tiger should chance to carry the hunting spears fixed in his body, and the perpetrator of the deed should be taking to flight. Often might you have beheld him uttering groans, often shrieking aloud, often striving to tear away the whole of his garments, and levelling trees, and venting his fury against mountains, or stretching out his arms towards the heaven of his father. Lo! he espies Lichas, trembling and lying concealed in a hollow rock, and, as his pain has summoned together all his fury, he says, "Didst thou, Lichas, bring this fatal present; and shalt thou be the cause of my death?" He trembles, and turning pale, is alarmed, and timorously utters some words of excuse. As he is speaking, and endeavouring to clasp his knees with his hands, Alcides seizes hold of him, and whirling him round three or four times, he hurls him into the Eubœan waves, with greater force than if sent from an engine of war. As he soars aloft in the aerial breeze he grows hard; and as they say that showers freeze with the cold winds, and that thence snow is formed, and that from the snow, revolving in its descent, the soft body is compressed, and is then made round in many a hailstone,[24] so have former ages declared, that, hurled through the air by the strong arms of Hercules, and bereft of blood through fear, and having no moisture left in him, he was transformed into hard stone. Even to this day, in the Eubœan sea, a small rock projects to a height, and retains the traces of the human form. This, the sailors are afraid to tread upon, as though it could feel it; and they call it Lichas.

But thou, the famous offspring of Jupiter, having cut down, trees which lofty Œta bore, and having raised them for a pile, dost order the son of Pœas[25] to take the bow and the capacious quiver, and the arrows which are again to visit[26] the Trojan realms; by whose assistance flames are put beneath the pile; and while the structure is being seized by the devouring fires, thou dost cover the summit of the heap of wood with the skin of the Nemean lion, and dost lie down with thy neck resting on thy club, with no other countenance than if thou art lying as a guest crowned with garlands, amid the full cups of wine.

And now, the flames, prevailing and spreading on every side, roared,[27] and reached the limbs thus undismayed, and him who despised them. The Gods were alarmed for this protector of the earth;[28] Saturnian Jupiter (for he perceived it) thus addressed them with joyful voice: "This fear of yours is my own delight, O ye Gods of heaven, and, with all my heart, I gladly congratulate myself that I am called the governor and the father of a grateful people, and that my progeny, too, is secure in your esteem. For, although this concern is given in return for his mighty exploits, still I myself am obliged by it. But, however, that your affectionate breasts may not be alarmed with vain fears, despise these flames of Œta. He who has conquered all things, shall conquer the fires which you behold; nor shall he be sensible of the potency of the flame, but in the part of him which he derived from his mother. That part of him, which he derived from me, is immortal, and exempt and secure from death, and to be subdued by no flames. This, too, when disengaged from earth, I will receive into the celestial regions, and I trust that this act of mine will be agreeable to all the Deities. Yet if any one, if any one, I say, perchance should grieve at Hercules being a Divinity, and should be unwilling that this honour should be conferred on him; still he shall know that he deserves it to be bestowed on him, and even against his will, shall approve of it."

To this the Gods assented; his royal spouse, too, seemed to bear the rest of his remarks with no discontented air, but only the last words with a countenance of discontent, and to take it amiss that she was so plainly pointed at. In the mean time, whatever was liable to be destroyed by flame, Mulciber consumed; and the figure of Hercules remained, not to be recognized; nor did he have anything derived from the form of his mother, and he only retained the traces of immortal Jupiter. And as when a serpent revived, by throwing off old age with his slough, is wont to be instinct with fresh life, and to glisten in his new-made scales; so, when the Tirynthian hero has put off his mortal limbs, he flourishes in his more æthereal part, and begins to appear more majestic, and to become venerable in his august dignity. Him the omnipotent Father, taking up among encircling clouds, bears aloft amid the glittering stars, in his chariot drawn by its four steeds.

[Footnote 11: Nessus.—Ver. 101. He was one of the Centaurs which were begotten by Ixion the cloud sent by Jupiter, under the form of Juno.]

[Footnote 12: Evenus.—Ver. 104. This was a river of Ætolia, which was also called by the name of 'Lycormas.']

[Footnote 13: Strong of limb.—Ver. 108. 'Membrisque valens,' is rendered by Clarke, 'being an able-limbed fellow.']

[Footnote 14: Wheel of thy father.—Ver. 124. He alludes to the punishment of Ixion, the father of Nessus, who was fastened to a revolving wheel in the Infernal Regions, as a punishment for his attempt on the chastity of Juno.]

[Footnote 15: Thou dost confide.—Ver. 125. 'Quamvis ope fidis equinâ,' is translated by Clarke, 'Although thou trustest to the help of thy horse part.']

[Footnote 16: Cenæan Jupiter.—Ver. 136. Jupiter was called Cenæan, from Cenæum, a promontory of Eubœa, where Hercules, after having taken the town of Œchalia, built an altar in honour of Jupiter. Hercules slew Eurytus, the king of Œchalia, and carried away his daughter Iole.]

[Footnote 17: Lichas.—Ver. 155. This was the attendant of Hercules, whom he sent to Deïanira for the garment which he used to wear while performing sacrifice.]

[Footnote 18: The savage Antæus.—Ver. 183. He alludes to the fresh strength which the giant Antæus gained each time he touched the earth.]

[Footnote 19: Iberian shepherd.—Ver. 184. Allusion is here made to Geryon, who had three bodies, and whom Hercules slew, and then carried away his herds. It has been suggested that the story of his triple form originated in the fact that he and his two brothers reigned amicably in conjunction over some portion of Spain, or the islands adjoining to it.]

[Footnote 20: Parthenian.—Ver. 188. A part of Arcadia was so called from Parthenium, a mountain which divided it from Argolis; there was also, according to Pliny the Elder, a town of the same name in Arcadia.]

[Footnote 21: Gold of Thermodon.—Ver. 189. The Thermodon was a river of Scythia, near which the Amazons were said to dwell. Eurystheus ordered Hercules to bring to him the belt of Hippolyta, the queen of the Amazons.]

[Footnote 22: Support the heavens.—Ver. 198. Atlas, king of Mauritania, was said to support the heavens on his shoulders, of which burden Hercules relieved him for a time, when he partook of his hospitality. It has been suggested that the meaning of this story is, that Hercules learned the study of astronomy from Atlas.]

[Footnote 23: Wife of Jupiter.—Ver. 199. Juno gave her commands to Hercules through Eurystheus, the son of Sthenelus, king of Mycenæ, who imposed upon him his various labours.]

[Footnote 24: Many a hailstone.—Ver. 222. Ovid here seems to think that snow is an intermediate state between rain and hail, and that hail is formed by the rapid motion of the snow as it falls.]

[Footnote 25: The son of Pœas.—Ver. 233. Philoctetes was the son of Pœas.]

[Footnote 26: Again to visit.—Ver. 232. It was decreed by the destinies that Troy should not be taken, unless the bow and arrows of Hercules were present; for which reason it was necessary to send for Philoctetes, who was the possessor of them. Troy had already seen them, when Hercules punished Laomedon, its king, for his perfidious conduct.]

[Footnote 27: Roared.—Ver. 239. 'Diffusa sonabat—flamma' is translated by Clarke, 'The flame, being diffused on all sides, rattled.']

[Footnote 28: Protector of the earth.—Ver. 241. Hercules merited this character, for having cleared the earth of monsters, robbers, and tyrants.]

EXPLANATION

Hercules, leaving the court of Calydon with his wife, proceeded on the road to the city of Trachyn, in Thessaly, to atone for the accidental death of Eunomus, and to be absolved from it by Ceyx, who was the king of that territory. Being obliged to cross the river Evenus, which had overflowed its banks, the adventure happened with the Centaur Nessus, which the Poet has here related. We learn from other writers, that after Nessus had expired, he was buried on Mount Taphiusa; and Strabo informs us, that his tomb (in which, probably, the ashes of other Centaurs were deposited) sent forth so offensive a smell, that the Locrians, who were the inhabitants of the adjacent country, were surnamed the 'Ozolæ,' that is, the 'ill-smelling,' or 'stinking,' Locrians. Although the river Evenus lay in the road between Calydon and Trachyn, still it did not run through the middle of the latter city, as some authors have supposed; for in such case Hercules would have been more likely to have passed it by the aid of a bridge or of a boat, than to have recourse to the assistance of the Centaur Nessus, and to have availed himself of his acquaintance with the fords of the stream.

Hercules, in lapse of time, becoming tired of Deïanira, by whom he had one son, named Hyllus, fell in love with Iole, the daughter of Eurytus; and that prince, refusing to give her to him, he made war upon Œchalia, and, having slain Eurytus, he bore off his daughter. Upon his return from that expedition, he sent Lychas for the vestments which he had occasion to use in a sacrifice which it was his intention to offer. Deïanira, jealous on account of his passion for Iole, sent him either a philtre or love potion, which unintentionally caused his death, or else a tunic smeared on the inside with a certain kind of pitch, found near Babylon, which, when thoroughly warmed, stuck fast to his skin; and this it is, most probably, which has been termed by poets and historians, the tunic of Nessus. It seems, however, pretty clear that Hercules fell into a languishing distemper, without any hopes of recovery, and, probably, in a fit of madness, he threw Lychas into the sea, which circumstance was made by the poets to account for the existence there of a rock known by that name.

Proceeding afterwards to Trachyn, he caused Deïanira to hang herself in despair; and, having consulted the oracle concerning his distemper, he was ordered to go with his friends to Mount Œta, and there to raise a funeral pile. He understood the fatal answer, and immediately prepared to execute its commands. When the pile was ready, Hercules ascended it, and laid himself down with an air of resignation, on which Philoctetes kindled the fire, which consumed him. Some, however, of the ancient authors say, with more probability, that Hercules died at Trachyn, and that his corpse was burned on Mount Œta. His apotheosis commenced at the ceremonial of his funeral, and, from the moment of his death, he was worshipped as a Demigod. Diodorus Siculus says that it was Iolus who first introduced this worship. It was also said that, as soon as Philoctetes had applied fire to the pile, it thundered, and the lightnings descending from heaven immediately consumed Hercules. A tomb was raised for him on Mount Œta, with an altar, upon which a bull, a wild boar, and a he-goat were yearly sacrificed in his honour, at the time of his festival. The Thebans, and, after them, the other people of Greece, soon followed the example of the Trachinians, and temples and altars were raised to him in various places, where he was honoured as a Demigod.

FABLE III [IX.273-323]

Juno, to be revenged on Alcmena for her amour with Jupiter, desires Ilithyïa, the Goddess who presides over births, not to assist her on the occasion of the birth of Hercules. Lucina complies with her request, and places herself on an altar at the gate of Alcmena's abode, where, by a magic spell, she increases her pains and impedes her delivery. Galanthis, one of her maids, seeing the Goddess at the door, imagines that she may possibly exercise some bad influence on her mistress's labour, and, to make her retire, declares that Alcmena is already delivered. Upon Ilithyïa withdrawing, Alcmena's pains are assuaged, and Hercules is born. The Goddess, to punish Galanthis for her officiousness, transforms her into a weazel, a creature which was supposed to bring forth its young through its mouth.

Atlas was sensible[29] of this burden. Nor, as yet, had Eurystheus, the son of Sthenelus, laid aside his wrath against Hercules; and, in his fury, he vented his hatred for the father against his offspring. But the Argive Alcmena, disquieted with prolonged anxieties for her son has Iole, to whom to disclose the complaints of her old age, to whom to relate the achievements of her son attested by all the world, or to whom to tell her own misfortunes. At the command of Hercules, Hyllus had received her both into his bed and his affections, and had filled her womb with a noble offspring. To her, thus Alcmena began her story:—

"May the Gods be propitious to thee at least; and may they shorten the tedious hours, at the hour when, having accomplished thy time, thou shalt be invoking Ilithyïa,[30] who presides over the trembling parturient women; her whom the influence of Juno rendered inexorable to myself. For, when now the natal hour of Hercules, destined for so many toils, was at hand, and the tenth sign of the Zodiac was laden with the great luminary, the heavy weight was extending my womb; and that which I bore was so great, that you might easily pronounce Jupiter to be the father of the concealed burden. And now I was no longer able to endure my labours: even now, too, as I am speaking, a cold shudder seizes my limbs, and a part of my pain is the remembrance of it. Tormented for seven nights, and during as many days, tired out with misery, and extending my arms towards heaven, with loud cries I used to invoke Lucina and the two Nixi.[31] She came, indeed, but corrupted beforehand, and she had the intention to give my life to the vengeful Juno. And when she heard my groans, she seated herself upon that altar before the door, and pressing her left knee with her right knee, her fingers being joined together in form of a comb,[32] she retarded my delivery; she uttered charms, too, in a low voice; and those charms impeded the birth now begun. I struggled hard, and, in my frenzy, I vainly uttered reproaches against the ungrateful Jupiter, and I desired to die, and complained in words that would have moved even the hard stones. The Cadmeian matrons attended me, and offered up vows, and encouraged me in my pains.

"There was present one of my hand-maids of the lower class of people, Galanthis by name, with yellow hair, and active in the execution of my orders; one beloved for her good services. She perceived that something unusual[33] was being done by the resentful Juno; and, while she was often going in and out of the door, she saw the Goddess, sitting upon the altar, and supporting her arms upon her knees, linked by the fingers; and then she said, 'Whoever thou art, congratulate my mistress; the Argive Alcmena is delivered, and, having brought forth, she has gained her wishes.' The Goddess who presides[34] over pregnancy leaped up, and, struck with surprise, loosened her joined hands. I, myself, on the loosening of those bonds, was delivered. The story is, that Galanthis laughed, upon deceiving the Divinity. The cruel Goddess dragged her along thus laughing and seized by her very hair, and she hindered her as she attempted to raise her body from the earth, and changed her arms into fore feet.

"Her former activity still remains, and her back has not lost its colour; but her shape is different from her former one. Because she had assisted me in labour by a lying mouth, she brings forth from the mouth,[35] and, just as before, she frequents my house."

[Footnote 29: Atlas was sensible.—Ver. 273. By reason of his supporting the heavens, to the inhabitants of which Hercules was now added.]

[Footnote 30: Ilithyïa.—Ver. 283. This Goddess is said by some to have been the daughter of Jupiter and Juno, while other writers consider her to have been the same either with Diana, or Juno Lucina.]

[Footnote 31: The two Nixi.—Ver. 294. Festus says, 'the three statues in the Capitol, before the shrine of Minerva, were called the Gods Nixii.' Nothing whatever is known of these Gods, who appear to have been obstetrical Divinities. It has been suggested, as there were three of them, that the reading should be, not 'Nixosque pares,' but 'Nixosque Lares,' 'and the Lares the Nixi.']

[Footnote 32: Form of a comb.—Ver. 299. This charm probably was suggestive of difficult or impeded parturition, the bones of the pelvis being firmly knit together in manner somewhat resembling the fingers when inserted one between the other, instead of yielding for the passage of the infant. Pliny the Elder informs us how parturition may be impeded by the use of charms.]

[Footnote 33: Something unusual.—Ver. 309. 'Nescio quid.' This very indefinite phrase is repeatedly used by Ovid; and in such cases, it expresses either actual doubt or uncertainty, as in the present instance; or it is used to denote something remarkable or indescribable, or to show that a thing is insignificant, mean, and contemptible.]

[Footnote 34: Goddess who presides.—Ver. 315. This was Ilithyïa, or Lucina, who was acting as the emissary of Juno.]

[Footnote 35: From the mouth.—Ver. 323. This notion is supposed to have been grounded on the fact of the weasel (like many other animals) carrying her young in her mouth from place to place.]

EXPLANATION

According to Diodorus Siculus and Apollodorus, Amphitryon was the son of Alceus, the son of Perseus, and his wife, Alcmena, was the daughter of Electryon, also the son of Perseus; and thus they were cousins. When their marriage was about to take place, an unforeseen accident prevented it. Electryon, who was king of Mycenæ, being obliged to revenge the death of his children, whom the sons of Taphius, king of the Teleboans, had killed in combat, returned victorious, and brought back with him his flocks, which he had recovered from Taphius. Amphitryon, who went to meet his uncle, to congratulate him upon the success of his expedition, throwing his club at a cow, which happened to stray from the herd, unfortunately killed him. This accidental homicide lost him the kingdom of Mycenæ, which was to have formed the dower of Alcmena. Sthenelus, the brother of Electryon, taking advantage of the public indignation, which was the result of the accident, drove Amphitryon out of the country of Argos, and made himself master of his brother's dominions, which he left, at his death, to his son Eurystheus, the inveterate persecutor of Hercules.

Amphitryon, obliged to retire to Thebes, was there absolved by Creon; but when, as he thought, he was about to receive the hand of Alcmena, who accompanied him to the court of that prince, she declared that, not being satisfied with the revenge which her father had taken on the Teleboans, she would consent to be the prize of him who would undertake to declare war against them. Amphitryon accepted these conditions, and, forming an alliance with Creon, Cephalus, and some other princes, made a descent upon the islands which the enemy possessed, and, making himself master of them, bestowed one of them on his ally, Cephalus.

It was during this war that Hercules came into the world; and whether Amphitryon had secretly consummated his marriage before his departure, or whether he had returned privately to Thebes, or to Tirynthus, where Hercules was said to have been born, it was published, that Jupiter, to deceive Alcmena, had taken the form of her husband, and was the father of the infant Hercules. If this is not the true explanation of the story, it may have been invented to conceal some intrigue in which Alcmena was detected; or, in process of time, to account for the extraordinary strength and valour of Hercules, it may have been said that Jupiter, and not Amphitryon, was the father of Hercules. Indeed, we find Seneca, in one of his Tragedies, putting these words into the mouth of Hercules:—'Whether all that has been said upon this subject be held as undoubted truth, or whether it proves to be but a fable, and that my father was, after all, in reality, but a mortal; my mother's fault is sufficiently effaced by my valour, and I have merit sufficient to have had Jupiter for my father.' The more readily, perhaps, to account for the transcendent strength and prowess of Hercules, the story was invented, that Jupiter made the night on which he was received by Alcmena under the form of Amphitryon, as long as three, or, according to Plautus, Hyginus, and Seneca, nine nights. Some writers say that Alcmena brought forth twins, one of which, Iphiclus, was the son of Amphitryon, while Hercules had Jupiter for his father.

With respect to the metamorphosis of Galanthis, it is but a little episode here introduced by Ovid, to give greater plausibility to the other part of the story. It most probably originated in the resemblance of the names of that slave to that of the weazel, which the Greeks called γαλῆ. Ælian, indeed, tells us that the Thebans paid honour to that animal, because it had helped Alcmena in her labour. The more ancient poets also added, that Juno retarded the birth of Hercules till the mother of Eurystheus was delivered, which was the cause of his being the subject of that king; though others state that this came to pass by the command of the oracle of Delphi. This king of Mycenæ having ordered him to rid Greece of the numerous robbers and wild beasts that infested it, it is most probable that, as we learn from Dionysius of Halicarnassus, he performed this service at the head of the troops of Eurystheus. If this is the case, the persecutions which the poets have ascribed to the jealousy of Juno, really originated either in the policy or the jealousy of the court of Mycenæ.

As Ovid has here cursorily taken notice of the labours of Hercules, we may observe, that it is very probable that his history is embellished with the pretended adventures of many persons who bore his name, and, perhaps, with those of others besides. Cicero, in his 'Treatise on the Nature of the Gods,' mentions six persons who bore the name of Hercules; and possibly, after a minute examination, a much greater number might be reckoned, many nations of antiquity having given the name to such great men of their own as had rendered themselves famous by their actions. Thus, we find one in Egypt in the time of Osiris, in Phœnicia, among the Gauls, in Spain, and in other countries. Confining ourselves to the Grecian Hercules, surnamed Alcides, we find that his exploits have generally been sung of by the poets, under the name of the Twelve Labours; but, on entering into the detail of them, we find them much more numerous. Killing some serpents in his youth, it was published, not only that he had done so, but that they had been sent by Juno for the purpose of destroying him. The forest of Nemea serving as a retreat for a great number of lions that ravaged the country, Hercules hunted them, and, killing the most furious of them, always wore his skin.

Several thieves, having made the neighbourhood of Lake Stymphalus, in Arcadia, their resort, he freed the country of them; the nails and wings which the poets gave them, in representing them as birds, being typical of their voracity and activity. The marshes of Lerna, near Argos, were infested by great numbers of serpents, which, as fast as they were destroyed, were replaced by new swarms; draining the marshes, and, probably, setting fire to the adjacent thickets or jungles, he destroyed these pestilent reptiles, on which it was fabled that he had destroyed the Hydra of Lerna, with its heads, which grew as fast as they were cut off. The forest of Erymanthus was full of wild boars, which laid waste all the neighbouring country: he destroyed them all, and brought one with him to the court of Eurystheus, of a size so monstrous, that the king was alarmed on seeing it, and was obliged to run and hide himself.

The stables of Augeas, king of Elis, were so filled with manure, by reason of the great quantity of oxen that he kept, that Hercules being called upon to cleanse them, employed his engineering skill in bringing the river Alpheus through them. Having pursued a hind for a whole year, which Eurystheus had commanded him to take, it was circulated, probably on account of her untiring swiftness, that she had feet of brass. The river Acheloüs having overflowed the adjacent country, he raised banks to it, as already mentioned. Theseus was a prisoner in Epirus, where he had been with Pirithous, to bring away the daughter of Aidoneus. Hercules delivered him; and that was the foundation of the Fable which said that he had gone down to Hades, or Hell. In the cavern of Tænarus there was a monstrous serpent; this he was ordered to kill, and, probably, this gave rise to the story of Cerberus being chained by him. Pelias having been killed by his daughters, his son Acastus pursued them to the court of Admetus, who, refusing to deliver up Alcestis, of whom he was enamoured, was taken prisoner in an engagement, and was delivered by that princess, who herself offered to be his ransom. Hercules being then in Thessaly, he took her away from Acastus, who was about to put her to death, and returned her to Admetus. This, probably, was the foundation of the fable which stated, that he had recovered her from the Infernal Regions, after having vanquished death, and bound him in chains.

The Amazons were a nation of great celebrity in the time of Hercules, and their frequent victories had rendered them very formidable to their neighbours. Eurystheus ordered him to go and bring away the girdle of Hippolyta, or, in other words, to make war upon them, and to pillage their treasures. Embarking on the Euxine Sea, Hercules arrived on the banks of the Thermodon, and, giving battle to the female warriors, defeated them; killing some, and putting the rest to flight. He took Antiope, or Hippolyta, prisoner, whom he gave to Theseus; but her sister, Menalippa, redeemed herself by giving up the famous girdle, or, in other words, by paying a large ransom. It is very probable, that in that expedition, he slew Diomedes, the barbarous king of Thrace, and brought away his mares, which were said to have been fed by him on human flesh. In returning by way of Thessaly, he embarked in the expedition of the Argonauts; but, leaving them soon afterwards, he went to Troy, and delivered Hesione from the monster which was to have devoured her; but not receiving from Laomedon, the king, the recompense which had been promised him, he killed that prince, sacked the city, and brought away Hesione, whom he gave to Telamon, who had accompanied him on the expedition.

This is probably the extent of the labours of Hercules in Greece, Thrace, and Phrygia. The poets have made him engage in many other laborious undertakings in distant countries, which most probably ought not to be attributed to the Grecian Hercules. Among other stories told of him, it is said, that having set out to fight with Geryon, the king of Spain, he was so much incommoded by the heat of the sun, that his wrath was excited against the luminary, and he fired his arrows at it, on which, the Sun, struck with admiration at his spirited conduct, made him a present of a golden goblet. After this, embarking and arriving in Spain, he defeated Geryon, a prince who was famed for having three heads, which probably either meant that he reigned over the three Balearic islands of Maiorca, Minorca, and Iviza, or else that Hercules defeated three princes who were strictly allied. Having thence passed the straits of Gibraltar to go over to Africa, he fought with the Giant Antæus, who sought to oppose his landing. That prince was said to be a son of the Earth, and was reported to recover fresh strength every time he was thrown on the ground; consequently, Hercules was obliged to hold him in his arms, till he had squeezed him to death. The solution of this fable is most probably that Antæus, always finding succour in a country where he was known as a powerful monarch, Hercules took measures to deprive him of aid, by engaging him in a sea fight, and thereby defeated him, without much trouble, as well as the Pygmies, who were probably some African tribes of stunted stature, who came to his assistance.

Hercules, returning from these two expeditions, passed through Gaul with the herds of Geryon, and went into Italy, where Cacus, a celebrated robber, who had made the caverns of Mount Aventine his haunts, having stolen some of his oxen, he, with the assistance, according to Dionysius of Halicarnassus, of Evander and Faunus, destroyed him, and shared his spoils with his allies. In his journey from Africa, Hercules delivered Atlas from the enmity of Busiris, the tyrant of Egypt, whom he killed; and gave such good advice to the Mauritanian king, that it was said that he supported the heavens for some time on his own shoulders, to relieve those of Atlas. The latter, by way of acknowledgment of his services, made him a present of several fine sheep, or rather, according to Diodorus Siculus, of some orange and lemon trees, which he carried with him into Greece. These were represented as the golden apples watched by a dragon in the garden of the Hesperides. As the ocean there terminated the scene of his conquests, he was said to have raised two pillars on those shores, to signify the fact of his having been there, and the impossibility of proceeding any further.

The deliverance of Prometheus, as already mentioned; the death of the two brothers, the Cercopes, famous robbers; the defeat of the Bull of Marathon; the death of Lygis, who disputed the passage of the Alps with him; that of the giant Alcyaneus, who hurled at him a stone so vast that it crushed twenty-four men to death; that of Eryx, king of Sicily, whom he killed with a blow of the cestus, for refusing to deliver to him the oxen which he had stolen; the combat with Cycnus, which was terminated by a peal of thunder, which separated the combatants; another combat against the Giants in Gaul, during which, as it was said, Jupiter rained down vast quantities of stones; all these are also attributed to Hercules, besides many more stories, which, if diligently collected, would swell to a large volume.

The foregoing remarks on the history of Hercules, give us an insight into the ideas which, based upon the explanations given by the authors of antiquity, the Abbè Banier, one of the most accomplished scholars of his age, entertained on this subject. We will conclude with some very able and instructive remarks on this mythus, which we extract from Mr. Keightley's Mythology of Ancient Greece and Italy. He says—

"Various theories have been formed respecting the mythus of Hercules. It is evidently one of very remote antiquity, long perhaps, anterior to the times of Homer. We confess that we cannot see any very valid reason for supposing no such real personage to have existed; for it will, perhaps, be found that mythology not unfrequently prefers to absolute fiction, the assuming of some real historic character, and making it the object of the marvels devised by lively and exuberant imagination, in order thereby to obtain more ready credence for the strange events which it creates. Such, then, may the real Hercules have been,—a Dorian, a Theban, or an Argive hero, whose feats of strength lived in the traditions of the people, and whom national vanity raised to the rank of a son of Zeus [Jupiter], and poetic fancy, as geographic knowledge extended, sent on journies throughout the known world, and accumulated in his person the fabled exploits of similar heroes of other regions.

"We may perceive, by the twelve tasks, that the astronomical theory was applied to the mythus of the hero, and that he was regarded as a personification of the Sun, which passes through the twelve signs of the Zodiac. This, probably, took place during the Alexandrian period. Some resemblance between his attributes and those of the Deity, with whom the Egyptian priests were pleased to identify him, may have given occasion to this notion; and he also bore some similitude to the God whom the Phœnicians chiefly worshipped, and who, it is probable, was the Sun. But we must steadily bear in mind, that Hercules was a hero in the popular legend long before any intercourse was opened between Greece and Egypt; and that, however (which is certainly not very likely) a God might be introduced from Phœnicia, the same could hardly be the case with a popular hero.—A very ingenious theory on the mythus of Hercules is given by Buttmann (Mythologus, vol. i., p. 246). Though acknowledging that Perseus, Theseus, and Hercules may have been real persons, he is disposed, from an attentive consideration of all the circumstances in the mythus of the last, to regard him as one of those poetical persons or personifications, who, as he says, have obtained such firm footing in the dark periods of antiquity, as to have acquired the complete air of historic personages.

"In his view of the life of Hercules, it is a mythus of extreme antiquity and great beauty, setting forth the ideal of human perfection, consecrated to the weal of mankind, or rather, in its original form, to that of his own nation. This perfection, according to the ideas of the heroic age, consists in the greatest bodily strength, united with the advantages of mind and soul recognised by that age. Such a hero is, he says, a man; but these noble qualities in him are of divine origin. He is, therefore, the son of the king of the Gods by a mortal mother. To render his perfection the more manifest, the Poet makes him to have a twin brother, the child of a mortal sire. As virtue is not to be learned, Hercules exhibits his strength and courage in infancy; he strangles the snakes, which fills his brother with terror. The character of the hero throughout life, as that of the avenger of injustice and punisher of evil, must exhibit itself in the boy as the wild instinct of nature; and the mythus makes him kill his tutor Linus with a blow of the lyre. When sent away by Amphitryon, he prepares himself, in the stillness and solitude of the shepherd's life, by feats of strength and courage, for his future task of purifying the earth of violence.

"—The number of tasks may not originally have been twelve, though most accounts agree in that number, but they were all of a nature agreeable to the ideas of an heroic age—the destruction of monsters, and bringing home to his own country the valuable productions of other regions. These are, however, regarded by Buttmann as being chiefly allegorical. The Hydra, for instance, he takes to have been meant to represent the evils of democratic anarchy, with its numerous heads, against which, though one may not be able to effect anything, yet the union of even two may suffice to become dominant over it.

"The toils of the hero conclude with the greatest and most rare of all in the heroic age—the conquest over death. This is represented by his descent into the under world, and dragging Cerberus to light is a proof of his victory. In the old mythus, he was made to engage with and wound Hades; and the Alcestis of Euripides exhibits him in conflict with Death. But virtue, to be a useful example, must occasionally succumb to human weakness in the power of the evil principle. Hence, Hercules falls into fits of madness, sent on him by Hera [Juno]; and hence—he becomes the willing slave of Omphale, the fair queen of Lydia, and changes his club and lion's skin for the distaff and the female robe.

"The mythus concludes most nobly with the assumption of the hero into Olympus. His protecting Deity abandons him to the power of his persevering enemy; his mortal part is consumed by fire, the fiercest of elements; his shade (εἴδωλον), like those of other men, descends to the realms of Hades, while the divine portion himself (αὐτὸς) mounts from the pyre in a thunder-cloud, and the object of Hera's persecution being now accomplished, espouses youth, the daughter of his reconciled foe.

"Muller (Dorians, vol. i. part ii. ch. 11, 12) is also disposed to view in Hercules a personification of the highest powers of man in the heroic age. He regards him as having been the national hero of the Dorian race, and appropriates to him all the exploits of the hero in Thessaly, Ætolia, and Epirus, which last place he supposes to have been the original scene of the Geryoneia, which was afterwards transformed to the western stream of the ocean. He thinks, however, that the Argives had an ancient hero of perhaps the same name, to whom the Peloponnesus adventures belong, and whom the Dorians combined with their own hero. The servitude to Eurystheus, and the enmity of Hera, he looks on as inventions of the Dorians to justify their own invasion of the Peloponnesus. This critic also proves that the Theban Hercules had nothing to do with the Gods and traditions of the Cadmeians; and he thinks that it was the Dorian Heracleides who introduced the knowledge of him into Thebes, or that he came from Delphi with the worship of Apollo, a Deity with whom, as the tutelar God of the Dorians, he supposes their national hero to have been closely connected."

FABLE IV [IX.324-425]

The Nymph Lotis, pursued by Priapus, in her flight, is changed into a tree. Dryope, going to sacrifice to the Naiads at the same spot, and ignorant of the circumstance, breaks a branch off the tree for her child, which she is carrying with her, and is subjected to a similar transformation. While Iole is relating these circumstances to Alcmena, she is surprised to see her brother Iolaüs restored to youth. The Poet here introduces the prediction of Themis concerning the children of Calirrhoë.

Thus she said; and, moved by the remembrance of her old servant, she heaved a deep sigh. Her daughter-in-law[36] addressed her, thus grieving. "Even her form being taken away from one that was an alien to thy blood, affects thee, O mother. What if I were to relate to thee the wondrous fate of my own sister? although tears and sorrow hinder me, and forbid me to speak. Dryope, the most remarkable for her beauty of the Œchalian maids, was the only daughter of her mother (for my father had me by another wife). Deprived of her virginity, and having suffered violence from the God that owns Delphi and Delos, Andræmon married her, and he was esteemed fortunate in his wife.

"There is a lake that gives the appearance of a sloping shore, by its shelving border; groves of myrtle crown the upper part. Hither did Dryope come, unsuspecting of her fate; and, that thou mayst be the more indignant at her lot, she was about to offer garlands to the Nymphs. In her bosom, too, she was bearing her son, who had not yet completed his first year, a pleasing burden; and she was nursing him, with the help of her warm milk. Not far from the lake was blooming a watery lotus that vied with the Tyrian tints, in hope of future berries. Dryope had plucked thence some flowers, which she might give as playthings to her child; and I, too, was just on the point of doing the same; for I was present. I saw bloody drops fall from the flower, and the boughs shake with a tremulous quivering; for, as the swains say, now, at length, too late in their information, the Nymph Lotis, flying from the lust of Priapus,[37] had transferred her changed form into this plant, her name being still preserved.

"Of this my sister was ignorant. When, in her alarm, she is endeavouring to retire and to depart, having adored the Nymphs, her feet are held fast by a root. She strives hard to tear them up, but she moves nothing except her upper parts. From below, a bark slowly grows up, and, by degrees, it envelopes the whole of her groin. When she sees this, endeavouring to tear her hair with her hands, she fills her hand with leaves, for leaves are covering all her head. But the boy Amphissos (for his grandfather Eurytus gave him this name) feels his mother's breast growing hard; nor does the milky stream follow upon his sucking. I was a spectator of thy cruel destiny, and I could give thee no help, my sister; and yet, as long as I could, I delayed the growing trunk and branches by embracing them; and, I confess it, I was desirous to be hidden beneath the same bark. Behold! her husband Andræmon and her most wretched father[38] appear, and inquire for Dryope: on their inquiring for Dryope, I show them the lotus. They give kisses to the wood still warm with life, and, extended on the ground, they cling to the roots of their own tree. And now, dear sister, thou hadst nothing except thy face, that was not tree. Tears drop upon the leaves made out of thy changed body; and, while she can, and while her mouth gives passage to her voice, she pours forth such complaints as these into the air:—

"'If any credit is to be given to the wretched, I swear by the Deities that I merited not this cruel usage. I suffer punishment without a crime. I lived in innocence; if I am speaking false, withered away, may I lose the leaves which I bear, and, cut down with axes, may I be burnt. Yet take this infant away from the branches of his mother, and give him to his nurse; and often, beneath my tree, make him drink milk, and beneath my tree let him play; and, when he shall be able to speak, make him salute his mother, and let him in sadness say, 'Beneath this trunk is my mother concealed.' Yet let him dread the ponds, and let him not pluck flowers from the trees; and let him think that all shrubs are the bodies of Goddesses. Farewell, dear husband; and thou, sister; and, thou my father; in whom, if there is any affection towards me, protect my branches from the wounds of the sharp pruning-knife, and from the bite of the cattle. And since it is not allowed me to bend down towards you, stretch your limbs up hither, and come near for my kisses, while they can still be reached, and lift up my little son. More I cannot say. For the soft bark is now creeping along my white neck, and I am being enveloped at the top of my head. Remove your hands from my eyes;[39] and, without your help, let the bark, closing over them, cover my dying eyes.' Her mouth ceased at once to speak, at once to exist; and long after her body was changed, were her newly formed branches still warm."

And now, while Iole was relating the wretched fate of her sister, and while Alcmena was drying away the tears of the daughter of Eurytus, with her fingers applied to her face, and still she herself was weeping, a novel event hushed all their sorrow; for Iolaüs[40] stood at the lofty threshold, almost a boy again, and covering his cheeks with a down almost imperceptible, having his visage changed to that of the first years of manhood. Hebe, the daughter of Juno had granted him this favour, overcome by the solicitations of her husband. When she was about to swear that she would hereafter grant such favours to no one, Themis did not allow her. "For now," said she, "Thebes is commencing civil warfare,[41] and Capaneus will not be able to be overcome, except by Jupiter, and the two brothers will engage in bloody combat, and the earth dividing, the prophet Amphiaraüs will see his destined shades, while he still lives;[42] and the son avenging one parent, by the death of the other parent, will be dutiful and wicked in the same action; and confounded by his misfortunes, deprived both of his reason and of his home, he will be persecuted both by the features of the Eumenides, and by the ghost of his mother; until his wife shall call upon him for the fatal gold, and the Phegeïan sword shall stab the side of their kinsman. Then, at last, shall Calirrhoë, the daughter of Acheloüs, suppliantly ask of mighty Jupiter these years of youth for her infant sons. Jupiter, concerned for them, will prescribe for them the peculiar gift of her who is both his step-daughter and his daughter-in-law,[43] and will make them men in their years of childhood."

When Themis, foreseeing the future, had said these words with prophetic voice, the Gods above murmured in varying discourse; and the complaint was,[44] why it might not be allowed others to grant the same gifts. Aurora, the daughter of Pallas, complained of the aged years of her husband; the gentle Ceres complained that Iäsion[45] was growing grey; Mulciber demanded for Ericthonius a life to live over again; a concern for the future influenced Venus, too, and she made an offer to renew the years of Anchises.

[Footnote 36: Her daughter-in-law.—Ver. 325. Iole was the wife of Hyllus, the son of Deïanira, by Hercules.]

[Footnote 37: Lust of Priapus.—Ver. 347. 'Fugiens obscœna Priapi,' is rendered by Clarke, 'Flying from the nasty attempts of Priapus upon her.']

[Footnote 38: Most wretched father.—Ver. 363. Eurytus was the father of Dryope.]

[Footnote 39: From my eyes.—Ver. 390. This alludes to the custom among the ancients of closing the eyes of the dying, which duty was performed by the nearest relations, who, closing the eyes and mouth, called upon the dying person by name, and exclaimed 'Vale,' 'farewell.']

[Footnote 40: Iolaüs.—Ver. 399. He was the son of Iphiclus, the brother of Hercules. See the Explanation in the next page.]

[Footnote 41: Civil warfare.—Ver. 404. This alludes to the Theban war, carried on between Eteocles and Polynices, the sons of Œdipus and Jocasta. Agreeing to reign in alternate years, Eteocles refused to give place to his brother when his year had terminated, on which Polynices fled to the court of Adrastus, king of Argos, and raised troops against his brother.]

[Footnote 42: While he still lives.—Ver. 407. This was Amphiaraüs, the son of Œcleus, and Hypermnestra, who was betrayed by his wife Eriphyle.]

[Footnote 43: Daughter-in-law.—Ver. 415. Hebe, the Goddess of Youth, was the daughter of Juno alone, without the participation of Jupiter; and from this circumstance she is styled the step-daughter of Jupiter. She was also his daughter-in-law on becoming the wife of Hercules.]

[Footnote 44: The complaint was.—Ver. 420. 'Murmur erat,' is rendered by Clarke, 'The grumbling was, why, &c.']

[Footnote 45: Iāsion.—Ver. 422. Iāsius, or Iāsion, was the son of Jupiter and Electra, and was the father of Plutus, the God of Riches, by the Goddess Cybele.]

EXPLANATION

The adventure of Dryope is one of those narratives which have no connexion with the main story which the Poet is relating, and, if really founded on fact, it would almost baffle any attempt to guess at its origin. It is, most probably, built entirely upon the name of the damsel who was said to have met with the untimely and unnatural fate so well depicted by the Poet.

The name of Dryope comes, very probably, from the Greek word Δρῦς, 'an oak,' which tree has a considerable resemblance to the lotus tree. If we seek for an historical solution, perhaps Dryope was punished for attempting to profane a tree consecrated to the Gods, a crime of which Erisicthon was guilty, and for which he was so signally punished. All the particulars that we know of Dryope are, that she was the daughter of Eurytus, and the sister of Iole; and that she was the wife of Andræmon.

Ovid says, that while Iole was relating this adventure to Alcmena, Iolaüs, who, according to some, was the son of Hercules, by Hebe, after his apotheosis, and, according to others, was the son of Iphiclus, the brother of Hercules, became young, at the intercession of that Goddess, who had appeased Juno. This was, probably, no other than a method of accounting for the great age to which and individual of the name of Iolaüs had lived.

Ovid then passes on to the surprising change in the children of Calirrhoë, the outline of which the story may be thus explained:—Amphiaraüs, foreseeing, (by the aid of the prophetic art, as we learn from Homer, Diodorus Siculus, Pliny and Statius), that the civil wars of Thebes, his native country, would prove fatal to him, retired from the court of Adrastus, King of Argos, whose sister he had married, to conceal himself in some place of safety. The Argives, to whom the oracle had declared, that Thebes could not be taken unless they had Amphiaraüs with their troops, searched for him in every direction; but their labour would have been in vain, if Eriphyle, his wife, gained by a necklace of great value, which her brother Adrastus gave her, had not discovered where he was. Discovered in his retreat, Amphiaraüs accompanied the Argives, and while, according to the rules of the soothsaying art, he was observing a flight of birds, in order to derive an augury from it, his horses fell down a precipice, and he lost his life. Statius and other writers, to describe this event in a poetical manner, say that the earth opened and swallowed up him and his chariot.

Amphiaraüs had engaged his son Alcmæon, in case he lost his life in the war, to kill Eriphyle; which injunction he performed as soon as he heard of the death of his father. Alcmæon, going to the court of Phegeus, to receive expiation for his crime, and to deliver himself from the persecution of the Furies, or, in other words, by the ceremonial of expiation, to tranquillize his troubled conscience, that prince received him with kindness, and gave him his daughter Alphesibæa in marriage. Alcmæon made her a present of his mother Eriphyle's necklace; but, having afterwards repudiated her to marry Calirrhoë, or Arsinoë, the daughter of Acheloüs, he went to demand the necklace from his brothers-in-law, who assassinated him. Amphiterus and Acarnanus, who were his sons by Calirrhoë, revenged the death of their father when they were very young; and this it is, possibly, which is meant by the Poet when he says that the Goddess Hebe augmented the number of their years, the purpose being, to put them speedily in a position to enable them to avenge the death of their father.

Thus we see, that Iolaüs was, like Æson, who also renewed his youth, a person who, in his old age, gave marks of unusual vigour; while in Amphiterus and Arcananus, to whom Hebe added years, are depicted two young men, who, by a deed of blood, exacted retribution for the death of their father, at a time when they were in general only looked upon as mere children.

FABLE V [IX.426-665]

Byblis falls in love with her brother Caunus, and her passion is inflamed to such a degree, that he is obliged to leave his native country, to avoid any encouragement of her incestuous flame. On this, she follows him; and, in her way through Caria, she is changed into a fountain.

Every God has[46] some one to favour; and their jarring discord is increasing by their various interests, until Jupiter opens his mouth, and says, "O, if you have any regard for me, to what rash steps are you proceeding? Does any one of you seem to himself so powerful as to overcome even the Fates? By the Fates has Iolaüs returned to those years which he has spent; by the Fates ought the sons of Calirrhoë to become young men, and not by ambition or by dint of arms. And do you, too, endure this as well with more contented mind, for even me do the Fates govern; could I but change them, declining years should not be making my son Æacus to bend beneath them; and Rhadamanthus should have the everlasting flower of age, together with my son, Minos, who is now looked down upon on account of the grievous weight of old age, and does not reign with the dignity with which once he did."

The words of Jupiter influenced the Divinities; and no one continued to complain when they saw Rhadamanthus and Æacus, and Minos, weary with years; Minos, who, when he was in the prime of life, had alarmed great nations with his very name. Then, however, he was enfeebled by age, and was alarmed by Miletus, the son of Deione,[47] exulting in the strength of youth, and in Phœbus as his sire; and though believing that he was aiming at his kingdom, still he did not dare to drive him away from his native home. Of thy own accord, Miletus, thou didst fly, and in the swift ship thou didst pass over the Ægean waters, and in the land of Asia didst build a city, bearing the name of its founder. Here Cyane, the daughter of the river Mæander, that so often returns to the same place, while she was following the windings of her father's bank, of a body excelling in beauty, being known by thee, brought forth a double offspring, Byblis, with Caunus, her brother.

Byblis is an example that damsels only ought to love what it is allowed them to love; Byblis, seized with a passion for her brother, the descendant of Apollo, loved him not as a sister loves a brother, nor in such manner as she ought. At first, indeed, she understands nothing of the flame, and she does not think[48] that she is doing wrong in so often giving him kisses, and in throwing her arms round the neck of her brother; and for a long time she herself is deceived, by this resemblance of natural affection. By degrees this affection degenerates, and decked out, she comes to see her brother, and is too anxious to appear beautiful; and if there is any woman there more beautiful, she envies her. But, as yet she is not fully discovered to herself, and under that flame conceives no wishes; but still, inwardly she is agitated. At one moment she calls him sweetheart,[49] at another, she hates the mention of his relationship; and now she prefers that he should call her Byblis, rather than sister. Still, while awake, she does not dare admit any criminal hopes into her mind; but when dissolved in soft sleep, she often sees the object which she is in love with. She seems to be even embracing her brother, and she blushes, though she is lying buried in sleep. Slumber departs; for a long time she is silent, and she recalls to memory the appearance of her dream, and thus she speaks with wavering mind:

"Ah, wretched me! What means this vision of the silent night? How far am I from wishing it real. Why have I seen this dream? He is, indeed, beautiful, even to envious eyes. He pleases me, too; and were he not my brother, I could love him, and he would be worthy of me. But it is my misfortune that I am his sister. So long as I strive, while awake, to commit no such attempt, let sleep often return with the like appearance. No witness is there in sleep; and yet there is the resemblance of the delight. O Venus and winged Cupid, together with thy voluptuous mother, how great the joys I experienced! how substantial the transport which affected me! How I lay dissolved in delight throughout my whole marrow! How pleasing to remember it; although short-lived was that pleasure, and the night sped onward rapidly, and was envious of my attempts at bliss. Oh, could I only be united to thee, by changing my name, how happily, Caunus, could I become the daughter-in-law of thy father! how happily, Caunus, couldst thou become the son-in-law of my father! O, that the Gods would grant that all things were in common with us, except our ancestors. Would that thou wast more nobly born than myself. For this reason then, most beauteous one, thou wilt make some stranger, whom I know not, a mother; but to me, who have unhappily got the same parents as thyself, thou wilt be nothing more than a brother. That tie alone we shall have, which bars all else. What, then, do my visions avail me? And what weight have dreams? And do dreams have any weight? The Gods fare better; for the Gods have their own sisters in marriage. Thus Saturn married Ops,[50] related to him by blood; Ocean Tethys, the ruler of Olympus Juno. The Gods above have their privileges. Why do I attempt to reduce human customs to the rule of divine ordinances, and those so different? Either this forbidden flame shall be expelled from my heart, or if I cannot effect that, I pray that I may first perish, and that when dead I may be laid out on my bed, and that my brother may give me kisses as I lie. And besides, this matter requires the inclination of us both; suppose it pleases me; to him it will seem to be a crime. But the sons of Æolus[51] did not shun the embraces of their sisters. But whence have I known of these? Why have I furnished myself with these precedents? Whither am I hurried onward? Far hence begone, ye lawless flames! and let not my brother be loved by me, but as it is lawful for a sister to love him. But yet, if he had been first seized with a passion for me, perhaps I might have indulged his desires. Am I then, myself, to court him, whom I would not have rejected, had he courted me? And canst thou speak out? And canst thou confess it? Love will compel me. I can. Or if shame shall restrain my lips, a private letter shall confess the latent flame."

This thought pleases her, this determines her wavering mind. She raises herself on her side, and leaning on her left elbow, she says, "He shall see it; let me confess my frantic passion. Ah, wretched me! How am I degrading myself! What flame is my mind now kindling!" And then, with trembling hand, she puts together the words well weighed. Her right hand holds the iron pen, the other, clean wax tablets.[52] She begins, and then she hesitates; she writes, and then corrects what is written; she marks, and then scratches out; she alters, and condemns, and approves; and one while she throws them down when taken up, and at another time, she takes them up again, when thrown aside. What she would have, she knows not. Whatever she seems on the point of doing, is not to her taste. In her features are assurance mingled with shame. The word 'sister' is written; it seems as well to efface the word 'sister,' and then to write such words as these upon the smoothed wax: "Thy lover wishes thee that health which she, herself, is not to enjoy, unless thou shalt grant it. I am ashamed! Oh, I am ashamed to disclose my name! and shouldst thou inquire what it is I wish; without my name[53] could I wish my cause to be pleaded, and that I might not be known as Byblis, until the hopes of enjoying my desires were realized. There might have been as a proof to thee of my wounded heart, my pale complexion, my falling away, my downcast looks, and my eyes often wet with tears, sighs, too, fetched without any seeming cause; frequent embraces too, and kisses, which, if perchance thou didst observe, could not be deemed to be those of a sister. Still I, myself, though I had a grievous wound in my soul, and although there was a raging fire within, have done everything, as the Gods are my witnesses, that at last I might be cured; and long, in my wretchedness, have I struggled to escape the ruthless weapon of Cupid; and I have endured more hardships than thou wouldst believe that a maiden could endure.

"Vanquished at length, I am forced to own my passion; and with timorous prayers, to entreat thy aid. Thou alone canst save, thou destroy, one who loves thee. Choose which thou wilt do. She is not thy enemy who begs this; but one who, though most nearly connected with thee, desires to be still more closely connected, and to be united to thee in a nearer tie. Let aged men be acquainted with ordinances, and make inquiry what is lawful, and what is wicked, and what is proper; and let them employ themselves in considering the laws. A passion that dares all consequences is suited to our years. As yet, we know not what is lawful, and we believe that all things are lawful, and so follow the example of the great Gods. Neither a severe father, nor regard for character, nor fear, shall restrain us, if only the cause for fearing is removed. Under a brother's name will we conceal our stolen joys so sweet. I have the liberty of conversing with thee in private; and even before others do we give embraces, and exchange kisses. How little is it that is wanting! do have pity on the love of her who confesses it, and who would not confess it, did not extreme passion compel her; and merit not to be inscribed on my tomb as the cause of my death."

The filled tablets fall short for her hand, as it vainly inscribes such words as these, and the last line is placed in the margin.[54] At once she seals up her own condemnation, with the impress of a signet, which she wets with her tears, for the moisture has deserted her tongue. Filled with shame, she then calls one of her male domestics, and gently addressing him in timorous tones, she said, "Carry these, most trusty one, to my," and, after a long pause, she added, "brother." While she was delivering them, the tablets, slipping from her hands, fell down. She was shocked by this omen, but still she sent them. The servant, having got a fit opportunity, goes to her brother and delivers the secret writing. The Mæandrian youth,[55] seized with sudden anger, throws away the tablets so received, when he has read a part; and, with difficulty withholding his hands from the face of the trembling servant, he says, "Fly hence, O thou accursed pander to forbidden lust, who shouldst have given me satisfaction by thy death, if it was not that thy destruction would bring disgrace on my character." Frightened, he hastens away, and reports to his mistress the threatening expressions of Caunus. Thou, Byblis, on hearing of his refusal, turnest pale, and thy breast, beset with an icy chill, is struck with alarm; yet when thy senses return, so, too, does thy frantic passion return, and thy tongue with difficulty utters such words as these, the air being struck by thy accents:

"And deservedly am I thus treated; for why, in my rashness, did I make the discovery of this wound? why have I so speedily committed words to a hasty letter, which ought rather to have been concealed? The feelings of his mind ought first to have been tried beforehand by me, with ambiguous expressions. Lest he should not follow me in my course, I ought, with some part of my sail[56] only, to have observed what kind of a breeze it was, and to have scudded over the sea in safety; whereas, now, I have filled my canvass with winds before untried. I am driven upon rocks in consequence; and sunk, I am buried beneath the whole ocean, and my sails have now no retreat. And besides, was I not forbidden, by unerring omens, to indulge my passion, at the time when the waxen tablets fell, as I ordered him to deliver them, and made my hopes sink to the ground? and ought not either the day to have been changed, or else my whole intentions; but rather, of the two,[57] the day? Some God himself warned me, and gave me unerring signs, if I had not been deranged; and yet I ought to have spoken out myself, and not to have committed myself to writing, and personally I ought to have discovered my passion; then he would have seen my tears, then he would have seen the features of her who loved him; I might have given utterance to more than what the letter contained. I might have thrown my arms around his reluctant neck, and have embraced his feet, and lying on the ground, I might have begged for life; and if I had been repelled, I might have seemed on the point of death. All this, I say, I might then have done; if each of these things could not singly have softened his obdurate feelings, yet all of them might.

"Perhaps, too, there may be some fault in the servant that was sent. He did not wait on him at a convenient moment; he did not choose, I suppose, a fitting time; nor did he request both the hour and his attention to be disengaged. 'Tis this that has undone me; for he was not born of a tigress, nor does he carry in his breast hard flints, or solid iron, or adamant; nor yet did he suck the milk of a lioness. He will yet be won. Again must he be attacked.[58] And no weariness will I admit of in the accomplishment of my design, so long as this breath of mine shall remain. For the best thing (if I could only recall what has been destined) would have been, not to have made the attempt; the next best thing is, to urge the accomplishment of what is begun; for he cannot (suppose I were to relinquish my design) ever be unmindful of this my attempt; and because I have desisted, I shall appear to have desired for but an instant, or even to have been trying him, and to have solicited him with the intention to betray; or, at least, I shall be thought not to have been overcome by this God, who with such intensity now burns, and has burnt my breast, but rather by lust. In fine, I cannot now be guiltless of a wicked deed; I have both written to him, and I have solicited him; my inclination has been defiled. Though I were to add nothing more, I cannot be pronounced innocent: as to what remains, 'twill add much to the gratifying of my wishes, but little to my criminality."

Thus she says; and (so great is the unsteadiness of her wavering mind) though she is loath to try him, she has a wish to try him, and she exceeds all bounds, and, to her misery, exposes herself to be often repulsed. At length, when there is now no end to this, he flies from his country and the commission of this crime, and founds a new city[59] in a foreign land. But then, they say that the daughter of Miletus, in her sadness, was bereft of all understanding. Then did she tear her garments away from her breast, and in her frenzy beat her arms. And now she is openly raving, and she proclaims the unlawful hopes of unnatural lust. Deprived of these hopes, she deserts her native land, and her hated home, and follows the steps of her flying brother. And as the Ismarian[60] Bacchanals, son of Semele, aroused by thy thyrsus, celebrate thy triennial festivals, as they return, no otherwise did the Bubasian matrons[61] see Byblis howling over the wide fields; leaving which, she wandered through the country of the Carians, and the warlike Leleges,[62] and Lycia.

And now she has left behind Cragos,[63] and Lymira,[64] and the waves of Xanthus, and the mountain in which the Chimæra had fire in its middle parts, the breast and the face of a lioness, and the tail of a serpent. The woods at length fail thee; when thou, Byblis, wearied with following him, dost fall down, and laying thy tresses upon the hard ground, art silent, and dost press the fallen leaves with thy face. Often, too, do the Lelegeïan Nymphs endeavour to raise her in their tender arms; often do they advise her to curb her passion, and they apply consolation to a mind insensible to their advice. Silent does Byblis lie, and she tears the green herbs with her nails, and waters the grass with the stream of her tears. They say that the Naiads placed beneath these tears a channel which could never become dry; and what greater gift had they to bestow? Immediately, as drops from the cut bark of the pitch tree, or as the viscid bitumen distils from the impregnated earth, or as water which has frozen with the cold, at the approach of Favonius, gently blowing, melts away in the sun, so is Byblis, the descendant of Phœbus, dissolving in her tears, changed into a fountain, which even now, in those vallies, bears the name of its mistress, and flows beneath a gloomy oak.

[Footnote 46: Every God has.—Ver. 425-6. 'Cui studeat, Deus omnis habet crescitque favore Turbida seditio.' Clarke thus renders these words, 'Every God has somebody to stickle for, and a turbulent sedition arises by their favours for their darlings.']

[Footnote 47: Son of Deione.—Ver. 442. According to some writers, Miletus was the son of Apollo and Deione, though others say that Thia was the name of his mother. He was the founder of the celebrated city of Miletus, in Caria, a country of Asia Minor.]

[Footnote 48: Does not think.—Ver. 457. Clarke translates this line, 'Nor does she think she does amiss that she so often tips him a kiss.' Antoninus Liberalis says, that Eidothea, the daughter of the king of Paria, and not Cyane, was the mother of Byblis and Caunus.]

[Footnote 49: Sweetheart.—Ver. 465. The word 'dominus' was often used as a term of endearment between lovers.]

[Footnote 50: Married Ops.—Ver. 497. Ops, the daughter of Cœlus or Uranus, who was also called Cybele, Rhea, and 'the great Mother,' was fabled to have been the wife of her brother Saturn; while Oceanus, the son of Cœlus and Vesta, married his sister Tethys.]

[Footnote 51: Sons of Æolus.—Ver. 506. Æolus had six sons, to whom he was said to have given their sisters for wives. In the case, however, of his daughter Canace, who was pregnant by her brother Macareus, Æolus was more severe, as he sent her a sword, with which to put herself to death.]

[Footnote 52: Clean wax tablets.—Ver. 521. Before the tablet was written upon, the wax was 'vacua,' empty; or, as we say of writing-paper, 'clean.' There was a blunt end to the upper part of the 'stylus,' or iron pen, with which the wax was smoothed down when any writing was erased.]

[Footnote 53: Without my name.—Ver. 531-2. 'Sine nomine vellem Posset agi mea causa meo,' is rendered by Clarke, 'I could wish my business might be transacted without my name.']

[Footnote 54: In the margin.—Ver. 564. Clarke translates, 'Summusque in margine versus adhæsit,' 'And the last line was clapped into the margin.']

[Footnote 55: Meandrian youth.—Ver. 573. Caunus was the grandson of the river Mæander.]

[Footnote 56: Part of my sail.—Ver. 589. She borrows this metaphor from sailors, who, before setting out, sometimes unfurl a little portion of the sail, to see how the wind blows.]

[Footnote 57: Rather of the two.—Ver. 598. Willing to believe anything in the wrong rather than herself; she is sure that the day was an unlucky one.]

[Footnote 58: Be attacked.—Ver. 615. 'Repeteudas erit,' Clarke translates, 'I must at him again.']

[Footnote 59: Founds a new city.—Ver. 633. This was Caunus, a city of Caria.]

[Footnote 60: Ismarian.—Ver. 641. Ismarus was a mountain of Thrace. The festival here alluded to was the 'trieterica,' or triennial feast of Bacchus.]

[Footnote 61: Bubasian matrons.—Ver. 643. We learn from Pliny the Elder that Bubasus was a region of Caria.]

[Footnote 62: Leleges.—Ver. 644. The Leleges were a warlike people of Caria, in Asia Minor, who were supposed to have sprung from Grecian emigrants, who first inhabited the adjacent island, and afterwards the continent. They were said to have their name from the Greek word λελεγμένοι 'gathered,' because they were collected from various places.]

[Footnote 63: Cragos.—Ver. 645. Cragos was a mountain of Lycia.]

[Footnote 64: Lymira.—Ver. 645. This was a city of Lycia, near Cragos.]

EXPLANATION

This shocking story has been also recounted by Antoninus Liberalis and both he and Ovid have embellished it with circumstances, which are the fruit of a lively imagination. They make Byblis travel over several countries in search of her brother, who flies from her extravagant passion, and they both agree in tracing her to Caria. There, according to Antoninus Liberalis, she was transformed into a Hamadryad, just as she was on the point of throwing herself from the summit of a mountain. Ovid, on the other hand, says that she was changed into a fountain, which afterwards bore her name.

It is, however, most probable, that if the story is founded on truth, the whole of the circumstances happened in Caria; since we learn, both from Apollodorus and Pausanias, that Miletus, her father, went from the island of Crete to lead a colony into Caria, when he conquered a city, to which he gave his own name. Pausanias says, that all the men of the city being killed during the siege, the conquerors married their wives and daughters. Cyanea, the daughter of Mæander, fell to the share of Miletus, and Caunus and Byblis were the offspring of that marriage. Byblis, having conceived a criminal passion for her brother, he was obliged to leave his father's court, that he might avoid her importunities; upon which she died of grief. As she often went to weep by a fountain, which was outside of the town, those who related the adventure, magnified it, by stating that she was changed into the fountain, which, after her death, bore her name. We are informed by Photius, on the authority of the historian Conon, that it was Caunus who fell in love with Byblis, and that she hanged herself upon a walnut tree. Ovid also, in his 'Art of Love,' follows the tradition that she hanged herself. 'Arsit et est laqueo fortiter ulta nefas.' Miletus lived in the time of the first Minos, and, according to some writers, married his daughter Acallis; but, having disagreed with his father-in-law, he was obliged to leave Crete, and retired to Caria.

The Persians had certain state ordinances, by which their monarchs were enjoined to marry their own sisters; and, as Asia Minor was overrun by them at the time when Crœsus was conquered by Cyrus, it is possible that the story of Byblis and Caunus may have originated in the disgust which the natives felt for their conquerors, and as a covert reproach to them for sanctioning alliances of so incestuous a nature. While Ovid enters into details in the story, which trench on the rules of modesty and decorum, the moral of the tale, aided by some of his precepts, is not uninstructive as a warning to youth to learn betimes how to regulate the passions.

Ligdus commands his wife Telethusa, who is pregnant, to destroy the infant, should it prove to be a girl; on which, the Goddess Isis appears to her in a dream, and, forbidding her to obey, promises her her protection. Telethusa is delivered of a daughter, who is called Iphis, and passes for a son. Iphis is afterwards married to Ianthe, on which, Isis, to reward her mother's piety, transforms her into a man.

The fame of this new prodigy would, perhaps, have filled the hundred cities of Crete, if Crete had not lately produced a nearer wonder of her own, in the change of Iphis.

For once on a time the Phæstian land[65] adjoining to the Gnossian kingdom produced one Ligdus, of obscure name, a man of the freeborn class of common people. Nor were his means any greater than his rank, but his life and his honour were untainted. He startled the ears of his wife in her pregnancy, with these words, when her lying-in was near at hand: "Two things there are which I wish for; that thou mayst be delivered with very little pain, and that thou mayst bring forth a male child. The other alternative is a cause of greater trouble, and providence has denied us means for bringing up a female. The thing I abominate; but if a female should, by chance, be brought forth at thy delivery, (I command it with reluctance, forgive me, natural affection) let it be put to death." Thus he said, and they bathed their faces with tears streaming down; both he who commanded, and she to whom the commands were given. But yet Telethusa incessantly urged her husband, with fruitless entreaties, not to confine his hopes within a compass so limited. But Ligdus's resolution was fixed.

And now was she hardly able to bear her womb big with the burden ripe for birth; when in the middle of the night, under the form of a vision, the daughter of Inachus, attended by a train of her votaries, either stood, or seemed to stand, before her bed. The horns of the moon were upon her forehead, with ears of corn with their bright golden colour, and the royal ornament of the diadem; with her was the barking Anubis,[66] and the holy Bubastis,[67] and the particoloured Apis;[68] he, too, who suppresses[69] his voice, and with his finger enjoins silence. There were the sistra too, and Osiris,[70] never enough sought for; and the foreign serpent,[71] filled with soporiferous poison. When thus the Goddess addressed her, as though roused from her sleep, and seeing all distinctly: "O Telethusa, one of my votaries, lay aside thy grievous cares, and evade the commands of thy husband; and do not hesitate, when Lucina shall have given thee ease by delivery, to bring up the child, whatever it shall be. I am a befriending Goddess,[72] and, when invoked, I give assistance; and thou shalt not complain that thou hast worshipped an ungrateful Divinity."

Thus she advises her, and then retires from her chamber. The Cretan matron arises joyful from her bed; and suppliantly raising her pure hands towards the stars of heaven, prays that her vision may be fulfilled. When her pains increased, and her burden forced itself into the light, and a girl was born to the father unaware of it, the mother ordered it to be brought up, pretending it was a boy; and the thing gained belief, nor was any one but the nurse acquainted with the fact. The father performed his vows, and gave the child the name of its grandfather. The grandfather had been called Iphis. The mother rejoiced in that name because it was common to both sexes, nor would she be deceiving[73] any one by it. Her deception lay unperceived under this fraud, the result of natural affection. The child's dress was that of a boy; the face such, that, whether you gave it to a girl or to a boy, either would be beautiful. In the meantime the third year had now succeeded the tenth, when her father, O Iphis, promised to thee, in marriage, the yellow-haired Iänthe, who was a virgin the most commended among all the women of Phæstus, for the endowments of her beauty; the daughter of the Dictæan Telestes. Equal was their age, their beauty equal; and they received their first instruction, the elements suited to their age, from the same preceptor.

Love, in consequence, touches the inexperienced breasts of them both, and inflicts on each an equal wound; but how different are their hopes! Iänthe awaits the time of their union, and of the ceremonial agreed upon, and believes that she, whom she thinks to be a man, will be her husband. Iphis is in love with her whom she despairs to be able to enjoy, and this very thing increases her flame; and, herself a maid, she burns with passion for a maid. And, with difficulty, suppressing her tears, she says, "What issue of my love awaits me, whom the anxieties unknown to any before, and so unnatural, of an unheard-of passion, have seized upon? if the Gods would spare me, (they ought to have destroyed me, and if they would not have destroyed me), at least they should have inflicted some natural evil, and one common to the human race. Passion for a cow does not inflame a cow, nor does that for mares inflame the mares. The ram inflames the ewes; its own female follows the buck. And so do birds couple; and among all animals, no female is seized with passion for a female. Would that I did not exist.

"Yet, lest Crete might not be the producer of all kinds of prodigies, the daughter of the Sun loved a bull; that is to say, a female loved a male. My passion, if I confess the truth, is more extravagant than that. Still she pursued the hopes of enjoyment; still, by a subtle contrivance, and under the form of a cow, did she couple with the bull, and her paramour was one that might be deceived. But though the ingenuity of the whole world were to centre here, though Dædalus himself were to fly back again with his waxen wings, what could he do? Could he, by his skilful arts, make me from a maiden into a youth? or could he transform thee, Iänthe? But why dost thou not fortify thy mind, and recover thyself, Iphis? And why not shake off this passion, void of all reason, and senseless as it is? Consider what it was thou wast born (unless thou art deceiving thyself as well), and pursue that which is allowable, and love that which, as a woman, thou oughtst to love. Hope it is that produces, Hope it is that nourishes love. This, the very case itself deprives thee of. No guard is keeping thee away from her dear embrace; no care of a watchful husband, no father's severity; does not she herself deny thy solicitations. And yet she cannot be enjoyed by thee; nor, were everything possible done, couldst thou be blessed; not, though Gods and men were to do their utmost. And now, too, no portion of my desires is baffled, and the compliant Deities have granted me whatever they were able, and what I desire, my father wishes, she herself wishes, and so does my destined father-in-law; but nature, more powerful than all these, wills it not; she alone is an obstacle to me. Lo, the longed-for time approaches, and the wedding-day is at hand, when Iänthe should be mine; and yet she will not fall to my lot. In the midst of water, I shall be athirst. Why, Juno, guardian of the marriage rites, and why, Hymenæus, do you come to this ceremonial, where there is not the person who should marry the wife, and where both of us females, we are coupled in wedlock?"

After saying these words, she closes her lips. And no less does the other maid burn, and she prays thee, Hymenæus, to come quickly. Telethusa, dreading the same thing that she desires, at one time puts off the time of the wedding, and then raises delays, by feigning illness. Often, by way of excuse, she pretends omens and visions. But now she has exhausted all the resources of fiction; and the time for the marriage so long delayed is now at hand, and only one day remains; whereon she takes off the fillets for the hair from her own head and from that of her daughter,[74] and embracing the altar with dishevelled locks, she says, "O Isis, thou who dost inhabit Parætonium,[75] and the Mareotic fields,[76] and Pharos,[77] and the Nile divided into its seven horns, give aid, I beseech thee, and ease me of my fears. Thee, Goddess, thee, I once beheld, and these thy symbols; and all of them I recognized; both thy attendants, and thy torches, and the sound of the sistra, and I noted thy commands with mindful care.

That this girl[78] now sees the light, that I, myself, am not punished, is the result of thy counsel, and thy admonition; pity us both, and aid us with thy assistance."

Tears followed her words. The Goddess seemed to move, (and she really did move) her altars; and the doors of her temple shook. Her horns, too,[79] shone, resembling those of the moon, and the tinkling sistrum sounded. The mother departs from the temple, not free from concern indeed, still pleased with this auspicious omen. Iphis follows her, her companion as she goes, with longer strides than she had been wont; her fairness does not continue on her face; both her strength is increased, and her features are more stern; and shorter is the length of her scattered locks. There is more vigour, also, than she had as a female. And now thou art a male, who so lately wast a female. Bring offerings to the temple, and rejoice with no hesitating confidence. They do bring their offerings to the temple. They add, too, an inscription; the inscription contains one short line: "Iphis, a male, offers the presents, which, as a female, he had vowed."

The following morn has disclosed the wide world with the rays of the Sun; when Venus, and Juno, and Hymenæus, repair to the social fires[80]; and Iphis, now a youth, gains his dear Iänthe.

[Footnote 65: Phæstian land.—Ver. 668. Phæstus was a city of Crete, built by Minos.]

[Footnote 66: Anubis.—Ver. 689. This was an Egyptian Deity, which had the body of a man, and the head of a dog. Some writers say that it was Mercury who was so represented, and that this form was given him in remembrance of the fact of Isis having used dogs in her search for Osiris, when he was slain by his brother Typhon. Other authors say, that Anubis was the son of Osiris, and that he distinguished himself with an helmet, bearing the figure of a dog, when he followed his father to battle.]

[Footnote 67: Bubastis.—Ver. 690. Though she is here an attendant of Isis, Diodorus Siculus represents her to have been the same divinity as Isis. Herodotus, however, says that Diana was worshipped by the Egyptians under that name. There was a city of Lower Egypt, called Bubastis, in which Isis was greatly venerated.]

[Footnote 68: Apis.—Ver. 690. This is supposed to have been another name for Osiris, whose body, having been burned on the funeral pile, the Egyptians believed that he re-appeared under the form of a bull; the name for which animal was 'apis.']

[Footnote 69: Who suppresses.—Ver. 691. This was the Egyptian divinity Harpocrates, the God of Secresy and Silence, who was represented with his finger laid on his lips.]

[Footnote 70: Osiris.—Ver. 692. When slain by his brother Typhon, Isis long sought him in vain, till, finding his scattered limbs by the aid of dogs, she entombed them. As the Egyptians had a yearly festival, at which they bewailed the loss of Osiris, and feigned that they were seeking him, Ovid calls that God, 'Nunquam satis quæsitus,' 'Never enough sought for.']

[Footnote 71: Foreign serpent.—Ver. 693. This is, most probably, the asp, a small serpent of Egypt, which is frequently found represented on the statues of Isis. Its bite was said to produce a lethargic sleep, ending in death. Cleopatra ended her life by the bite of one, which she ordered to be conveyed to her in a basket of fruit. Some commentators have supposed that the crocodile is here alluded to; but, as others have justly observed, the crocodile has no poisonous sting, but rather a capacity for devouring.]

[Footnote 72: A befriending Goddess.—Ver. 698. Diodorus Siculus says, that Isis was the discoverer of numerous remedies for disease, and that she greatly improved the healing art.]

[Footnote 73: Be deceiving.—Ver. 709. The name 'Iphis' being equally well for a male or a female.]

[Footnote 74: Of her daughter.—Ver. 770. We must suppose that Iphis wore the 'vitta,' which was an article of female dress, in private only, and in presence of her mother. Of course, in public, such an ornament would not have suited her, when appearing in the character of a man.]

[Footnote 75: Parætonium.—Ver. 772. Strabo says, that Parætonium was a city of Libya, with a capacious harbour.]

[Footnote 76: Mareotic fields.—Ver. 772. The Mareotic Lake was in the neighbourhood of the city of Alexandria.]

[Footnote 77: Pharos.—Ver. 772. This was an island opposite to Alexandria, famed for its light-house, which was erected to warn sailors from off the dangerous quicksands in the neighbourhood.]

[Footnote 78: This girl.—Ver. 778. Pointing at Iphis, who had attended her, Antoninus Liberalis says, that Telethusa prayed that Iphis might be transformed into a man, and cited a number of precedents for such a change.]

[Footnote 79: Her horns too.—Ver. 783. Isis was sometimes worshipped under the form of a cow, to the horns of which reference is here made.]

[Footnote 80: The social fires.—Ver. 795. On the occasion of marriages, offerings were made on the altars of Hymenæus and the other Deities, who were the guardians of conjugal rites.]

EXPLANATION

The story of Iphis being changed from a young woman into a man, of which Ovid lays the scene in the isle of Crete, is one of those facts upon which ancient history is entirely silent. Perhaps, the origin of the story was a disguise of a damsel in male dress, carried on, for family reasons, even to the very point of marriage; or it may have been based upon an account of some remarkable instance of androgynous formation.

Ovid may possibly have invented the story himself, merely as a vehicle for showing how the Deities recompense piety and strict obedience to their injunctions.

BOOK THE TENTH

FABLE I [X.1-85]

Eurydice, the wife of Orpheus, while sporting in the fields, with other Nymphs, is bitten by a serpent, which causes her death. After having mourned for her, Orpheus resolves to go down to the Infernal Regions in quest of her. Pluto and the Fates consent to her return, on condition that Orpheus shall not look on her till he is out of their dominions. His curiosity prevailing, he neglects this injunction, on which she is immediately snatched away from him, beyond the possibility of recovery. Upon this occasion, the Poet relates the story of a shepherd, who was turned into a rock by a look of Cerberus; and that of Olenus and Lethæa, who were transformed into stones.

Thence Hymenæus, clad in a saffron-coloured[1] robe, passed through the unmeasured tract of air, and directed his course to the regions of the Ciconians[2], and, in vain, was invoked by the voice of Orpheus. He presented himself indeed, but he brought with him neither auspicious words, nor joyful looks, nor yet a happy omen. The torch, too, which he held, was hissing with a smoke that brought tears to the eyes, and as it was, it found no flames amid its waving. The issue was more disastrous than the omens; for the newmade bride, while she was strolling along the grass, attended by a train of Naiads, was killed, having received the sting of a serpent on her ancle.

After the Rhodopeïan bard had sufficiently bewailed her in the upper realms of air, that he might try the shades below as well, he dared to descend to Styx by the Tænarian gate, and amid the phantom inhabitants and ghosts that had enjoyed the tomb, he went to Persephone, and him that held these unpleasing realms, the Ruler of the shades; and touching his strings in concert with his words, he thus said, "O ye Deities of the world that lies beneath the earth, to which we all come at last, each that is born to mortality; if I may be allowed, and you suffer me to speak the truth, laying aside[3] the artful expressions of a deceitful tongue; I have not descended hither from curiosity to see dark Tartarus, nor to bind the threefold throat of the Medusæan monster, bristling with serpents. But my wife was the cause of my coming; into whom a serpent, trodden upon by her, diffused its poison, and cut short her growing years. I was wishful to be able to endure this, and I will not deny that I have endeavoured to do so. Love has proved the stronger. That God is well known in the regions above. Whether he be so here, too, I am uncertain; but yet I imagine that even here he is; and if the story of the rape of former days is not untrue, 'twas love that united you two together. By these places filled with horrors, by this vast Chaos, and by the silence of these boundless realms, I entreat you, weave over again the quick-spun thread of the life of Eurydice.

"To you we all belong; and having staid but a little while above, sooner or later we all hasten to one abode. Hither are we all hastening. This is our last home; and you possess the most lasting dominion over the human race. She, too, when, in due season she shall have completed her allotted number of years, will be under your sway. The enjoyment of her I beg as a favour. But if the Fates deny me this privilege in behalf of my wife, I have determined that I will not return. Triumph in the death of us both."

As he said such things, and touched the strings to his words, the bloodless spirits wept. Tantalus did not catch at the retreating water, and the wheel of Ixion stood still, as though in amazement; the birds did not tear the liver of Tityus; and the granddaughters of Belus paused at their urns; thou, too, Sisyphus, didst seat thyself on thy stone. The story is, that then, for the first time, the cheeks of the Eumenides, overcome by his music, were wet with tears; nor could the royal consort, nor he who rules the infernal regions, endure to deny him his request; and they called for Eurydice. She was among the shades newly arrived, and she advanced with a slow pace, by reason of her wound.

The Rhodopeïan hero receives her, and, at the same time, this condition, that he turn not back his eyes until he has passed the Avernian vallies, or else that the grant will be revoked. The ascending path is mounted in deep silence, steep, dark, and enveloped in deepening gloom. And now they were not far from the verge of the upper earth. He, enamoured, fearing lest she should flag, and impatient to behold her, turned his eyes; and immediately she sank back again. She, hapless one! both stretching out her arms, and struggling to be grasped, and to grasp him, caught nothing but the fleeting air. And now, dying a second time, she did not at all complain of her husband; for why should she complain of being beloved? And now she pronounced the last farewell, which scarcely did he catch with his ears; and again was she hurried back to the same place.

No otherwise was Orpheus amazed at this twofold death of his wife, than he who, trembling, beheld the three necks[4] of the dog, the middle one supporting chains; whom fear did not forsake, before his former nature deserted him, as stone gathered over his body: and than Olenus,[5] who took on himself the crime of another, and was willing to appear guilty; and than thou, unhappy Lethæa, confiding in thy beauty; breasts, once most united, now rocks, which the watery Ida supports. The ferryman drove him away entreating, and, in vain, desiring again to cross the stream. Still, for seven days, in squalid guise[6] did he sit on the banks without the gifts of Ceres. Vexation, and sorrow of mind, and tears were his sustenance. Complaining that the Deities of Erebus[7] were cruel, he betook himself to lofty Rhodope, and Hæmus,[8] buffeted by the North winds. The third Titan had now ended the year bounded by the Fishes of the ocean;[9] and Orpheus had avoided all intercourse with woman, either because it had ended in misfortune to him, or because he had given a promise to that effect. Yet a passion possessed many a female to unite herself to the bard, and many a one grieved when repulsed. He also was the first adviser of the people of Thrace to transfer their affections to tender youths; and, on this side of manhood, to enjoy the short spring of life, and its early flowers.

[Footnote 1: Saffron-coloured.—Ver. 1. This was in order to be dressed in a colour similar to that of the 'flammeum,' which was a veil of a bright yellow colour, worn by the bride. This custom prevailed among the Romans, among whom the shoes worn by the bride were of the same colour with the veil.]

[Footnote 2: Ciconians.—Ver. 2. These were a people of Thrace, near the river Hebrus and the Bistonian Lake.]

[Footnote 3: Laying aside.—Ver. 19. 'Falsi positis ambagibus oris,' is rendered by Clarke, 'Laying aside all the long-winded fetches of a false tongue.']

[Footnote 4: The three necks.—Ver. 65. There was a story among the ancients, that when Cerberus was dragged by Hercules from the Infernal Regions, a certain man, through fear of Hercules, hid himself in a cave; and that on peeping out, and beholding Cerberus, he was changed into a stone by his fright. Suidas says, that in his time the stone was still to be seen, and that the story gave rise to a proverb.]

[Footnote 5: Olenus.—Ver. 69. Olenus, who was supposed to be the son of Vulcan, had a beautiful wife, whose name was Lethæa. When about to be punished for comparing her own beauty to that of the Goddesses, Olenus offered to submit to the penalty in her stead, on which they were both changed into stones.]

[Footnote 6: In squalid guise.—Ver. 74. 'Squallidus in ripa—sedit,' is rendered by Clarke, 'He sat in a sorry pickle on the bank.']

[Footnote 7: Erebus.—Ver. 76. Erebus was the son of Chaos and Darkness; but his name is often used to signify the Infernal Regions.]

[Footnote 8: Hæmus.—Ver. 77. This was a mountain of Thrace, which was much exposed to the North winds.]

[Footnote 9: Fishes of the ocean.—Ver. 78. 'Pisces,' 'the Fishes,' being the last sign of the Zodiac, when the sun has passed through it, the year is completed.]

EXPLANATION

Though Ovid has separated the adventures of Orpheus, whose death he does not relate till the beginning of the eleventh Book, we will here shortly enter upon an examination of some of the more important points of his history.

As, in his time, Poetry and Music were in a very low state of perfection, and as he excelled in both of those arts, it was said that he was the son of Apollo and the Muse Calliope; and it was added, that he charmed lions and tigers, and made even the trees sensible of the melodious tones of his lyre. These were mere hyperbolical expressions, which signified the wondrous charms of his eloquence and of his music combined, which he employed in cultivating the genius of a savage and uncouth people. Some conjecture that this personage originally came from Asia into Thrace, and suppose that he, together with Linus and Eumolpus, brought poetry and music into Greece, the use of which, till then, was unknown in that country; and that they introduced, at the same time, the worship of Ceres, Mars, and the orgies of Bacchus, which, from him who instituted them, received their name of 'Orphica.' Orpheus, too, is supposed to have united the office of high priest with that of king. Horace styles him the interpreter of the Gods; and he was said to have interposed with the Deities for the deliverance of the Argonauts from a dangerous tempest. It is thought that he passed some part of his life in Egypt, and became acquainted with many particulars of the ancient religion of the Egyptians, which he introduced into the theology of Greece. Some modern writers even go so far as to suggest that he learned from the Hebrews, who were then sojourning in Egypt, the knowledge of the true God.

His wife, Eurydice, dying very young, he was inconsolable for her loss. To alleviate his grief, he went to Thesprotia, in Epirus, the natives of which region were said to possess incantations, for the purpose of raising the ghosts of the departed. Here, according to some accounts, being deceived by a phantom, which was made to appear before him, he died of sorrow; but, according to other writers, he renounced the society of mankind for ever and retired to the mountains of Thrace. His journey to that distant country gave occasion to say, that he descended to the Infernal Regions. This is the more likely, as he is supposed to have there promulgated his notions of the infernal world, which, according to Diodorus Siculus, he had learned among the Egyptians.

Tzetzes, however, assures us that this part of his history is founded on the circumstance, that Orpheus cured his wife of the bite of a serpent, which had till then been considered to be mortal; and that the poets gave an hyperbolical version of the story, in saying that he had rescued her from Hell. He says, too, that he had learned in Egypt the art of magic, which was much cultivated there, and especially the method of charming serpents.

After the loss of his wife, he retired to mount Rhodope, to assuage the violence of his grief. There, according to Ovid and other poets, the Mænades, or Bacchanals, to be revenged for his contempt of them and their rites, tore him in pieces; which story is somewhat diversified by the writers who relate that Venus, exasperated against Calliope, the mother of Orpheus, for having adjudged to Proserpine the possession of Adonis, caused the women of Thrace to become enamoured of her son, and to tear him in pieces while disputing the possession of him. An ancient author, quoted by Hyginus, says that Orpheus was killed by the stroke of a thunderbolt, while he was accompanying the Argonauts; and Apollodorus says the same. Diodorus Siculus calls him one of the kings of Thrace; while other writers, among whom are Cicero and Aristotle, assert that there never was such a person as Orpheus. The learned Vossius says, that the Phœnician word 'ariph,' which signifies 'learned,' gave rise to the story of Orpheus. Le Clerc thinks that in consequence of the same Greek word signifying 'an enchanter,' and also meaning 'a singer,' he acquired the reputation of having been a most skilful magician.

We may, perhaps, safely conclude, that Orpheus really did introduce the worship of many Gods into Greece; and that, possibly, while he promulgated the necessity of expiating crimes, he introduced exorcism, and brought magic into fashion in Greece. Lucian affirms that he was also the first to teach the elements of astronomy. Several works were attributed to him, which are now no longer in existence; among which were a Poem on the Expedition of the Argonauts, one on the War of the Giants, another on the Rape of Proserpine, and a fourth upon the Labours of Hercules. The Poem on the Argonautic Expedition, which now exists, and is attributed to him, is supposed to have been really written by a poet named Onomacritus, who lived in the sixth century B.C., in the time of Pisistratus.

After his death, Orpheus was reckoned in the number of Heroes or Demigods; and we are informed by Philostratus that his head was preserved at Lesbos, where it gave oracular responses. Orpheus is not mentioned by Homer or Hesiod. The learned scholar Lobeck, in his Aglaophamus, has entered very deeply into an investigation of the real nature of the discoveries and institutions ascribed to him.

FABLE II [X.86-105]

Orpheus, retiring to Mount Rhodope, by the charms of his music, attracts to himself all kinds of creatures, rocks, and trees; among the latter is the pine tree, only known since the transformation of Attis.

There was a hill, and upon the hill a most level space of a plain, which the blades of grass made green: all shade was wanting in the spot. After the bard, sprung from the Gods, had seated himself in this place, and touched his tuneful strings, a shade came over the spot. The tree of Chaonia[10] was not absent, nor the grove of the Heliades,[11] nor the mast-tree with its lofty branches, nor the tender lime-trees, nor yet the beech, and the virgin laurel,[12] and the brittle hazels, and the oak, adapted for making spears, and the fir without knots, and the holm bending beneath its acorns, and the genial plane-tree,[13] and the parti-coloured maple,[14] and, together with them, the willows growing by the rivers, and the watery lotus, and the evergreen box, and the slender tamarisks, and the two-coloured myrtle, and the tine-tree,[15] with its azure berries.

You, too, the ivy-trees, with your creeping tendrils, came, and together, the branching vines, and the elms clothed with vines; the ashes, too, and the pitch-trees, and the arbute, laden with its blushing fruit, and the bending palm,[16] the reward of the conqueror; the pine, too, with its tufted foliage,[17] and bristling at the top, pleasing to the Mother of the Gods; since for this the Cybeleïan Attis put off the human form, and hardened into that trunk.

[Footnote 10: Tree of Chaonia.—Ver. 90. This was the oak, for the growth of which Chaonia, a province of Epirus, was famous.]

[Footnote 11: Grove of the Heliades.—Ver. 91. He alludes to the poplars, into which tree, as we have already seen, the Heliades, or daughters of the sun, were changed after the death of Phaëton.]

[Footnote 12: Virgin laurel.—Ver. 92. The laurel is so styled from the Virgin Daphne, who refused to listen to the solicitations of Apollo.]

[Footnote 13: Genial plane-tree.—Ver. 95. The plane tree was much valued by the ancients, as affording, by its extending branches, a pleasant shade to festive parties. Virgil says, in the Fourth Book of the Georgics, line 146, 'Atque ministrantem platanum potantibus umbram,' 'And the plane-tree that gives its shade for those that carouse.']

[Footnote 14: Parti-coloured maple.—Ver. 95. The grain of the maple being of a varying colour, it was much valued by the ancients, for the purpose of making articles of furniture.]

[Footnote 15: The tine tree.—Ver. 98. The 'tinus,' or 'tine tree,' according to Pliny the Elder, was a wild laurel, with green berries.]

[Footnote 16: The bending palm.—Ver. 102. The branches of the palm were remarkable for their flexibility, while no superincumbent weight could break them. On this account they were considered as emblematical of victory.]

[Footnote 17: Tufted foliage.—Ver. 103. The pine is called 'succincta,' because it sends forth its branches from the top, and not from the sides.]

EXPLANATION

The story of Attis, or Athis, here briefly referred to, is related by the ancient writers in many different ways; so much so, that it is not possible to reconcile the discrepancy that exists between them. From Diodorus Siculus we learn that Cybele, the daughter of Mæon, King of Phrygia, falling in love with a young shepherd named Attis, her father ordered him to be put to death. In despair, at the loss of her lover, Cybele left her father's abode, and, accompanied by Marsyas, crossed the mountains of Phrygia. Apollo, (or, as Vossius supposes, some priest of that God,) touched with the misfortunes of the damsel, took her to the country of the Hyperboreans in Scythia, where she died. Some time after, the plague ravaging Phrygia, and the oracle being consulted, an answer was returned, that, to ensure the ceasing of the contagion, they must look for the body of Attis, and give it funeral rites, and render to Cybele the same honour which they were wont to pay to the Gods: all which was done with such scrupulous care, that in time she became one of the most esteemed Divinities.

Arnobius, says that Attis was a shepherd, with whom Cybele fell in love in her old age. Unmoved by her rank, and repelled by her faded charms, he despised her advances. Midas, King of Pessinus, on seeing this, destined his own daughter, Agdistis, for the young Attis. Fearing the resentment of Cybele, he caused the gates of the city to be shut on the day on which the marriage was to be solemnized. Cybele being informed of this, hastened to Pessinus, and, destroying the gates, met with Attis, who had concealed himself behind a pine tree, and caused him to be emasculated; on which Agdistis committed self-destruction in a fit of sorrow.

Servius, Lactantius, and St. Augustine, give another version of the story, which it is not necessary here to enlarge upon, any farther than to say, that it depicts the love of a powerful queen for a young man who repulsed her advances. Ovid, also, gives a similar account in the fourth Book of the Fasti, line 220. Other authors, quoted by Arnobius, have given some additional circumstances, the origin of which it is almost impossible to guess at. They say that a female called Nana, by touching a pomegranate or an almond tree, which grew from the blood of Agdistis whom Bacchus had slain, conceived Attis, who afterwards became very dear to Cybele.

All that we can conclude from these accounts, and more especially from that given by Ovid in the Fasti, is, that the worship of Cybele being established in Phrygia, Attis was one of her priests; and that, as he led the example of mutilating himself, all her other priests, who were called Galli, submitted to a similar operation, to the great surprise of the uninitiated, who were not slow in inventing some wonderful story to account for an act so extraordinary.

FABLE III [X.106-142]

Cyparissus is about to kill himself for having slain, by accident, a favourite deer; but, before he is able to execute his design, Apollo transforms him into a Cypress.

Amid this throng was present the cypress, resembling the cone,[18] now a tree, but once a youth, beloved by that God who fits the lyre with the strings, and the bow with strings. For there was a large stag, sacred to the Nymphs who inhabit the Carthæan fields; and, with his horns extending afar, he himself afforded an ample shade to his own head. His horns were shining with gold, and a necklace studded with gems,[19] falling upon his shoulders, hung down from his smooth round neck; a silver ball,[20] fastened with little straps, played upon his forehead; and pendants of brass,[21] of equal size, shone on either ear around his hollow temples. He, too, void of fear, and laying aside his natural timorousness, used to frequent the houses, and to offer his neck to be patted by any hands, even though unknown to him.

But yet, above all others, he was pleasing to thee, Cyparissus, most beauteous of the nation of Cea.[22] Thou wast wont to lead the stag to new pastures, and to the streams of running waters; sometimes thou didst wreathe flowers of various colours about his horns, and at other times, seated on his back, like a horseman, first in this direction and then in that, thou didst guide his easy mouth with the purple bridle. 'Twas summer and the middle of the day, and the bending arms of the Crab, that loves the sea-shore, were glowing with the heat of the sun; the stag, fatigued, was reclining his body on the grassy earth, and was enjoying the coolness from the shade of a tree. By inadvertence the boy Cyparissus pierced him with a sharp javelin; and, when he saw him dying from the cruel wound, he resolved to attempt to die as well. What consolations did not Phœbus apply? and he advised him to grieve with moderation, and according to the occasion. Still did he lament, and as a last favour, he requested this of the Gods above, that he might mourn for ever. And now, his blood quite exhausted by incessant weeping, his limbs began to be changed into a green colour, and the hair, which but lately hung from his snow-white forehead, to become a rough bush, and, a stiffness being assumed, to point to the starry heavens with a tapering top. The God Phœbus lamented deeply, and in his sorrow he said, "Thou shalt be mourned by me, and shalt mourn for others, and shalt ever attend upon those who are sorrowing[23] for the dead."

[Footnote 18: Resembling the cone.—Ver. 106. In the Roman Circus for the chariot races, a low wall ran lengthways down the course, which, from its resemblance in position to the spinal bone, was called by the name of 'spina.' At each extremity of this 'spina,' there were placed upon a base, three large cones, or pyramids of wood, in shape very much like cypress trees, to which fact allusion is here made. They were called 'metæ,' 'goals.']

[Footnote 19: Studded with gems.—Ver. 113. Necklaces were much worn in ancient times by the Indians, Persians, and Egyptians. They were more especially used by the Greek and Roman females as bridal ornaments. The 'monile baccatum,' or 'bead necklace,' was the most common, being made of berries, glass, or other materials, strung together. They were so strung with thread, silk, or wire, and links of gold. Emeralds seem to have been much used for this purpose, and amber was also similarly employed. Thus Ovid says, in the second Book of the Metamorphoses, line 366, that the amber distilled from the trees, into which the sisters of Phaëton were changed, was sent to be worn by the Latin matrons. Horses and favourite animals, as in the present instance, were decked with 'monilia,' or necklaces.]

[Footnote 20: A silver ball.—Ver. 114. The 'bulla' was a ball of metal, so called from its resemblance in shape to a bubble of water. These were especially worn by the Roman children, suspended from the neck, and were mostly made of thin plates of gold, being of about the size of a walnut. The use of these ornaments was derived from the people of Etruria; and though originally worn only by the children of the Patricians, they were subsequently used by all of free birth. The children of the Libertini, or 'freedmen,' indeed wore 'bullæ,' but they were only made of leather. The 'bulla' was laid aside at the same time as the 'toga prætexta,' and was on that occasion consecrated to the Lares. The bulls of the Popes of Rome, received their names from this word; the ornament which was pendent from the rescript or decree being used to signify the document itself.]

[Footnote 21: Pendants of brass.—Ver. 116. The ear-ring was called among the Greeks ἐνώτιον, and by the Romans 'inauris.' The Greeks also called it ἐλλόβιον, from its being inserted in the lobe of the ear. Earrings were worn by both sexes among the Lydians, Persians, Libyans, Carthaginians, and other nations. Among the Greeks and Romans, the females alone were in the habit of wearing them. As with us, the ear-ring consisted of a ring and drop, the ring being generally of gold, though bronze was sometimes used by the common people. Pearls, especially those of elongated form, which were called 'elenchi,' were very much valued for pendants.]

[Footnote 22: Nation of Cea.—Ver. 120. Cea was one of the Cyclades, and Carthæa was one of its four cities.]

[Footnote 23: Who are sorrowing.—Ver. 142. The Poet in this manner accounts for the Roman custom of placing branches of Cypress before the doors of houses in which a dead body lay. Pliny the Elder says, that the Cypress was sacred to Pluto, and that for that reason it was used at funerals, and was placed upon the pile. Varro says, that it was used for the purpose of removing, by its own strong scent, the bad smell of the spot where the bodies were burnt, and also of the bodies themselves. It was also said to be so used, because, when once its bark is cut, it withers, and is consequently emblematical of the frail tenure of human life.]

Cyparissus, who, according to Ovid was born at Carthæa, a town in the isle of Cea, was probably a youth of considerable poetical talent and proficiency in the polite arts, which caused him to be deemed the favourite of Apollo. His transformation into a Cypress is founded on the resemblance between their names, that tree being called by the Greeks κυπάρισσος. The conclusion of the story is that Apollo, to console himself, enjoined that the Cypress tree should be the symbol of sorrow, or in other words that it should be used at funerals and be planted near graves and sepulchres; which fiction was most likely founded on the fact, that the tree was employed for those purposes; perhaps because its branches, almost destitute of leaves, have a somewhat melancholy aspect.

Some ancient writers also tell us that Cyparissus was a youth beloved by the God Sylvanus, for which reason that God is often represented with branches of Cypress in his hand.

FABLE IV [X.143-161]

Jupiter, charmed with the beauty of the youth Ganymede, transforms himself into an Eagle, for the purpose of carrying him off. He is taken up into Heaven, and is made the Cup-bearer of the Divinities.

Such a grove of trees had the bard attracted round him, and he sat in the midst of an assembly of wild beasts, and of a multitude of birds. When he had sufficiently tried the strings struck with his thumb, and perceived that the various tones, though they gave different sounds, still harmonize, in this song he raised his voice: "Begin, my parent Muse, my song from Jove, all things submit to the sway of Jove. By me, often before has the power of Jove been sung. In loftier strains have I sung of the Giants, and the victorious thunderbolts scattered over the Phlegræan plains.[24] Now is there occasion for a softer lyre; and let us sing of youths beloved by the Gods above, and of girls surprised by unlawful flames, who, by their wanton desires, have been deserving of punishment.

"The king of the Gods above was once inflamed with a passion for Ganymede, and something was found that Jupiter preferred to be, rather than what he was. Yet into no bird does he vouchsafe to be transformed, but that which can carry his bolts.[25] And no delay is there. Striking the air with his fictitious wings, he carries off the youth of Ilium; who even now mingles his cups for him, and, much against the will of Juno, serves nectar to Jove."

[Footnote 24: Phlegræan plains.—Ver. 151. Some authors place the Phlegræan plains near Cumæ, in Italy, and say that in a spot near there, much impregnated with sulphur, Jupiter, aided by Hercules and the other Deities, conquered the Giants with his lightnings. Others say that their locality was in that part of Macedonia which was afterwards called Pallene; others again, in Thessaly, or Thrace.]

[Footnote 25: Carry his bolts.—Ver. 158. The eagle was feigned to be the attendant bird of Jove, among other reasons, because it was supposed to fly higher than any other bird, to be able to fix its gaze on the sun without being dazzled, and never to receive injury from lightning. It was also said to have been the armour-bearer of Jupiter in his wars against the Titans, and to have carried his thunderbolts.]

The rape of Ganymede is probably based upon an actual occurrence, which may be thus explained. Tros, the king of Troy, having conquered several of his neighbours, as Eusebius, Cedrenus, and Suidas relate, sent his son Ganymede into Lydia, accompanied by several of the nobles of his court, to offer sacrifice in the temple dedicated to Jupiter; Tantalus, the king of that country, who was ignorant of the designs of the Trojan king, took his people for spies, and put Ganymede in prison. He having been arrested in a temple of Jupiter, by order of a prince, whose ensign was an eagle, it gave occasion for the report that he had been carried off by Jupiter in the shape of an eagle.

The reason why Jupiter is said to have made Ganymede his cup-bearer is difficult to conjecture, unless we suppose that he had served his father, in that employment at the Trojan court. The poets say that he was placed by the Gods among the Constellations, where he shines as Aquarius, or the Water-bearer.

The capture of Ganymede occasioned a protracted and bloody war between Tros and Tantalus; and after their death, Ilus, the son of Tros, continued it against Pelops, the son of Tantalus, and obliged him to quit his kingdom and retire to the court of Œnomaüs, king of Pisa, whose daughter he married, and by her had a son named Atreus, who was the father of Agamemnon and Menelaüs. Thus we see that probably Paris, the great grandson of Tros, carried off Helen, as a reprisal on Menelaüs, the great grandson of Tantalus, the persecutor of Ganymede. Agamemnon did not fail to turn this fact to his own advantage, by putting the Greeks in mind of the evils which his family had suffered from the kings of Troy.

FABLE V [X.162-219]

As Apollo is playing at quoits with the youth Hyacinthus, one of them, thrown by the Divinity, rebounds from the earth, and striking Hyacinthus on the head, kills him. From his blood springs up the flower which still bears his name.

"Phœbus would have placed thee too, descendant of Amycla,[26] in the heavens, if the stern Fates had given him time to place thee there. Still, so far as is possible, thou art immortal; and as oft as the spring drives away the winter, and the Ram succeeds the watery Fish, so often dost thou spring up and blossom upon the green turf. Thee, beyond all others, did my father love, and Delphi, situate in the middle[27] of the earth, was without its guardian Deity, while the God was frequenting the Eurotas, and the unfortified Sparta;[28] and neither his lyre nor his arrows were held in esteem by him.

"Unmindful of his own dignity, he did not refuse to carry the nets, or to hold the dogs, or to go, as his companion, over the ridges of the rugged mountains; and by lengthened intimacy he augmented his flame. And now Titan was almost in his mid course between the approaching and the past night, and was at an equal distance from them both; when they stripped their bodies of their garments, and shone with the juice of the oily olive, and engaged in the game of the broad quoit.[29] First, Phœbus tossed it, well poised, into the airy breeze, and clove the opposite clouds with its weight. After a long pause, the heavy mass fell on the hard ground, and showed skill united with strength. Immediately the Tænarian youth,[30] in his thoughtlessness, and urged on by eagerness for the sport, hastened to take up the circlet; but the hard ground sent it back into the air with a rebound against thy face, Hyacinthus.

"Equally as pale as the youth does the Divinity himself turn; and he bears up thy sinking limbs; and at one moment he cherishes thee, at another, he stanches thy sad wound; and now he stops the fleeting life by the application of herbs. His skill is of no avail. The wound is incurable. As if, in a well-watered garden, any one should break down violets, or poppies, and lilies, as they adhere to their yellow stalks; drooping, they would suddenly hang down their languid heads, and could not support themselves; and would look towards the ground with their tops. So sink his dying features; and, forsaken by its vigour, the neck is a burden to itself, and reclines upon the shoulder. 'Son of Œbalus,' says Phœbus, 'thou fallest, deprived of thy early youth; and I look on thy wound as my own condemnation. Thou art the object of my grief, and the cause of my crime. With thy death is my right hand to be charged; I am the author of thy destruction. Yet what is my fault? unless to engage in sport can be termed a fault; unless it can be called a fault, too, to have loved thee. And oh! that I could give my life for thee, or together with thee; but since I am restrained by the decrees of destiny, thou shalt ever be with me, and shalt dwell on my mindful lips. The lyre struck with my hand, my songs, too, shall celebrate thee; and, becoming a new flower, by the inscription on thee, thou shalt imitate[31] my lamentations. The time, too, shall come, at which a most valiant hero[32] shall add his name to this flower, and it shall be read upon the same leaves.'

"While such things are being uttered by the prophetic lips of Apollo, behold! the blood which, poured on the ground, has stained the grass, ceases to be blood, and a flower springs up, more bright than the Tyrian purple, and it assumes the appearance which lilies have, were there not in this a purple hue, and in them that of silver. This was not enough for Phœbus, for 'twas he that was the author of this honour. He himself inscribed his own lamentations on the leaves, and the flower has 'ai, ai,' inscribed thereon; and the mournful characters[33] there are traced. Nor is Sparta ashamed to have given birth to Hyacinthus; and his honours continue to the present time; the Hyacinthian festival[34] returns, too, each year, to be celebrated with the prescribed ceremonials, after the manner of former celebrations."

[Footnote 26: Descendant of Amycla.—Ver. 162. Hyacinthus is here called Amyclides, as though being the son of Amycla, whereas, in line 196 he is called 'Œbalides,' as though the son of Œbalus. Pausamas and Apollodorus (in one instance) say that he was the son of Amycla, the Lacedæmonian, who founded the city of Amyclæ; though, in another place, Apollodorus says that Piërus was his father. On the other hand, Hyginus, Lucian, and Servius say that he was the son of Œbalus. Some explain 'Amyclide,' as meaning 'born at Amyclæ;' and, indeed, Claudian says that he was born there. Others, again, would have Œbalide to signify 'born at Œbalia.' But, if he was the son of Amycla, this could not be the signification, as Œbalia was founded by Œbalus, who was the grandson of Amycla. The poet, most probably, meant to style him the descendant of Amycla, as being his great grandson, and the son of Œbalus. Again, in the 217th line of this Book, the Poet says that he was born at Sparta; but, in the fifth Book of the Fasti, line 223, he mentions Therapnæ, a town of Laconia, as having been his birthplace. Perizonius thinks that Ovid has here inadvertently confounded the different versions of the story of Hyacinthus.]

[Footnote 27: In the middle.—Ver. 168. Delphi, situated on a ridge of Parnassus, was styled the navel of the world, as it was supposed to be situate in the middle of the earth. The story was, that Jupiter, having let go two eagles, or pigeons, at the opposite extremities of the earth, with the view of ascertaining the central spot of it, they met in their flight at this place.]

[Footnote 28: Unfortified Sparta.—Ver. 169. Sparta was not fortified, because Lycurgus considered that it ought to trust for its defence to nothing but the valour and patriotism of its citizens.]

[Footnote 29: The broad quoit.—Ver. 177. The 'discus,' or quoit, of the ancients, was made of brass, iron, stone, or wood, and was about ten or twelve inches in diameter. Sometimes, a heavy mass of iron, of spherical form, was thrown instead of the 'discus.' It was perforated in the middle, and a rope or thong being passed through, was used in throwing it.]

[Footnote 30: The Tænarian youth.—Ver. 183. Hyacinthus is so called, not as having been born there, but because Tænarus was a famous headland or promontory of Laconia, his native country.]

[Footnote 31: Thou shalt imitate.—Ver. 206. The blood of Hyacinthus, changing into a flower, according to the ideas of the poets, the words Ai, Ai, expressive, in the Greek language, of lamentation, were said to be impressed on its leaves.]

[Footnote 32: Most valiant hero.—Ver. 207. He alludes to Ajax, the son of Telamon, from whose blood, when he slew himself, a similar flower was said to have arisen, with the letters Ai, Ai, on its leaves, expressive either of grief, or denoting the first two letters of his name, Αἴας. See Book xiii. line 397. The hyacinth was the emblem of death, among the ancient Greeks.]

[Footnote 33: Mournful characters.—Ver. 216. The letters are called 'funesta,' because the words αι, αι were the expressions of lamentation at funerals.]

[Footnote 34: Hyacinthian festival.—Ver. 219. The Hyacinthia was a festival celebrated every year at Amyclæ, in Laconia, by the people of that town and of Sparta. Some writers say that it was held solely in honour of Apollo; others, of Hyacinthus; but it is much more probable, that it was intended to be in honour of both Apollo and Hyacinthus. The festival lasted for three days, and began on the longest day of the Spartan month, Hecatombæus. On the first and last day, sacrifices were offered to the dead, and the fate of Hyacinthus was lamented. Garlands were forbidden to be worn on those days, bread was not allowed to be eaten, and no songs were recited in praise of Apollo. On the second day, rejoicing and amusements prevailed; the praises of Apollo were sung, and horse races were celebrated; after which, females, riding in chariots made of wicker-work, and splendidly adorned, formed a beautiful procession. On this day, sacrifices were offered, and the citizens kept open houses for their friends and relations. Athenæus mentions a favourite meal of the Laconians on this occasion, which was called κοπίς, and consisted of cakes, bread, meat, broth, raw herbs, figs, and other fruits, with the seeds of the lupine. Macrobius says, that chaplets of ivy were worn at the Hyacinthia; but, of course, that remark can only apply to the second day. Even when they had taken the field against an enemy, the people of Amyclæ were in the habit of returning home on the approach of the Hyacinthia, to celebrate that festival.]

EXPLANATION

Hyacinthus, as Pausanias relates, was a youth of Laconia. His father educated him with so much care, that he was looked upon as the favourite of Apollo, and of the Muses. As he was one day playing with his companions, he unfortunately received a blow on the head from a quoit, from the effects of which he died soon after. Some funeral verses were probably composed on the occasion; in which it was said, with the view of comforting his relations, that Boreas, jealous of the affection which Apollo had evinced for the youth, had turned aside the quoit with which they played; and thus, by degrees, in length of time the name of Apollo became inseparably connected with the story.

The Lacedæmonians each year celebrated a solemn festival near his tomb, where they offered sacrifices to him; and we are told by Athenæus, that they instituted games in his honour, which were called after his name. Pausanias makes mention of his tomb, upon which he says was engraved the figure of Apollo. His alleged change into the flower of the same name is probably solely owing to the similarity of their names. It is not very clear what flower it is that was known to the ancients under the name of Hyacinthus. Dioscorides believes it to be that called 'vaccinium' by the Romans, which is of a purple colour, and on which can be traced, though imperfectly, the letters αι (alas!) mentioned by Ovid. The lamentations of Apollo, on the death of Hyacinthus, formed the subject of bitter, and, indeed, deserved raillery, for several of the satirical writers among the ancients.

FABLE VI [X.220-242]

Venus, incensed at the Cerastæ for polluting the island of Cyprus, which is sacred to her, with the human sacrifices which they offer to their Gods, transforms them into bulls; and the Propœtides, as a punishment for their dissolute conduct, are transformed into rocks.

"But if, perchance, you were to ask of Amathus,[35] abounding in metals, whether she would wish to have produced the Propœtides; she would deny it, as well as those whose foreheads were of old rugged with two horns, from which they also derived the name of Cerastæ. Before the doors of these was standing an altar of Jupiter Hospes,[36] a scene of tragic horrors; if any stranger had seen it stained with blood, he would have supposed that sucking calves had been killed there, and Amathusian sheep;[37] strangers were slain there. Genial Venus, offended at the wicked sacrifices there offered, was preparing to abandon her own cities and the Ophiusian lands.[38] 'But how,' said she, 'have these delightful spots, how have my cities offended? What criminality is there in them? Let the inhuman race rather suffer punishment by exile or by death, or if there is any middle course between death and exile; and what can that be, but the punishment of changing their shape?'

"While she is hesitating into what she shall change them, she turns her eyes towards their horns, and is put in mind that those may be left to them; and then she transforms their huge limbs into those of fierce bulls.

"And yet the obscene Propœtides presumed to deny that Venus is a Goddess; for which they are reported the first of all women to have prostituted their bodies,[39] with their beauty, through the anger of the Goddess. And when their shame was gone, and the blood of their face was hardened, they were, by a slight transition, changed into hard rocks."

[Footnote 35: Amathus.—Ver. 220. Amathus was a city of Cyprus, sacred to Venus, and famous for the mines in its neighbourhood.]

[Footnote 36: Jupiter Hospes.—Ver. 224. Jupiter, in his character of Ζεῦς ξένιος, was the guardian and protector of travellers and wayfarers.]

[Footnote 37: Amathusian sheep.—Ver. 227. Amathusia was one of the names of the island of Cyprus.]

[Footnote 38: Ophiusian lands.—Ver. 229. Cyprus was anciently called Ophiusia, on account of the number of serpents that infested it; ὄφις being the Greek for a serpent.]

[Footnote 39: Their bodies.—Ver. 240. The women of Cyprus were notorious for the levity of their character. We learn from Herodotus that they had recourse to prostitution to raise their marriage portions.]

EXPLANATION

The Cerastæ, a people of the island of Cyprus, were, perhaps, said to have been changed into bulls, to show the barbarous nature and rustic manners of those islanders, who stained their altars with the blood of strangers, in sacrifice to the Gods.

An equivocation of names also, probably, aided in originating the story. The island of Cyprus is surrounded with promontories which rise out of the sea, and whose pointed rocks appear at a distance like horns, from which it had the name of Cerastis, the Greek word κέρας, signifying a 'horn.' Thus, the inhabitants having the name of Cerastæ, it was most easy to invent a fiction of their having been once turned into oxen, to account the more readily for their bearing that name.

The Propœtides, who inhabited the same island, were females of very dissolute character. Justin, and other writers, mention a singular and horrible custom in that island, of prostituting young girls in the very temple of Venus. It was most probably the utter disregard of these women for common decency, that occasioned the poets to say that they were transformed into rocks.

FABLE VII [X.243-297]

Pygmalion, shocked by the dissolute lives of the Propœtides, throws off all fondness for the female sex, and resolves on leading a life of perpetual celibacy. Falling in love with a statue which he has made, Venus animates it; on which he marries this new object of his affections, and has a son by her, who gives his name to the island.

"When Pygmalion saw these women spending their lives in criminal pursuits, shocked at the vices which Nature had so plentifully imparted to the female disposition, he lived a single life without a wife, and for a long time was without a partner of his bed. In the meantime, he ingeniously carved a statue of snow-white ivory with wondrous skill; and gave it a beauty with which no woman can be born; and then conceived a passion for his own workmanship. The appearance was that of a real virgin, whom you might suppose to be alive, and if modesty did not hinder her, to be desirous to move; so much did art lie concealed under his skill. Pygmalion admires it; and entertains, within his breast, a flame for this fictitious body.

"Often does he apply his hands to the work, to try whether it is a human body, or whether it is ivory; and yet he does not own it to be ivory. He gives it kisses, and fancies that they are returned, and speaks to it, and takes hold of it, and thinks that his fingers make an impression on the limbs which they touch, and is fearful lest a livid mark should come on her limbs when pressed. And one while he employs soft expressions, at another time he brings her presents that are agreeable to maidens, such as shells, and smooth pebbles, and little birds, and flowers of a thousand tints, and lilies, and painted balls, and tears of the Heliades, that have fallen from the trees. He decks her limbs, too, with clothing, and puts jewels on her fingers; he puts, too, a long necklace on her neck. Smooth pendants hang from her ears, and bows from her breast.[40] All things are becoming to her; and she does not seem less beautiful than when naked. He places her on coverings dyed with the Sidonian shell, and calls her the companion of his bed, and lays down her reclining neck upon soft feathers, as though it were sensible.

"A festival of Venus, much celebrated throughout all Cyprus, had now come; and heifers, with snow-white necks, having their spreading horns tipped with gold, fell, struck by the axe. Frankincense, too, was smoking, when, having made his offering, Pygmalion stood before the altar, and timorously said, 'If ye Gods can grant all things, let my wife be, I pray,' and he did not dare to say 'this ivory maid,' but 'like to this statue of ivory.' The golden Venus, as she herself was present at her own festival, understood what that prayer meant; and as an omen of the Divinity being favourable, thrice was the flame kindled up, and it sent up a tapering flame into the air. Soon as he returned, he repaired to the image of his maiden, and, lying along the couch, he gave her kisses. She seems to grow warm. Again he applies his mouth; with his hands, too, he feels her breast. The pressed ivory becomes soft, and losing its hardness, yields to the fingers, and gives way, just as Hymettian wax[41] grows soft in the sun, and being worked with the fingers is turned into many shapes, and becomes pliable by the very handling. While he is amazed, and is rejoicing, though with apprehension, and is fearing that he is deceived; the lover again and again touches the object of his desires with his hand. It is a real body; the veins throb, when touched with the thumb.

"Then, indeed, the Paphian hero conceives in his mind the most lavish expressions, with which to give thanks to Venus, and at length presses lips, no longer fictitious, with his own lips. The maiden, too, feels the kisses given her, and blushes; and raising her timorous eyes towards the light of day, she sees at once her lover and the heavens. The Goddess was present at the marriage which she thus effected. And now, the horns of the moon having been nine times gathered into a full orb, she brought forth Paphos; from whom the island derived its name."

[Footnote 40: Bows from her breast.—Ver. 265. The 'Redimiculum' was a sort of fillet, or head band, worn by females. Passing over the shoulders, it hung on each side, over the breast. In the statues of Venus, it was often imitated in gold. Clarke translates it by the word 'solitaire.']

[Footnote 41: Hymettian wax.—Ver. 284. Hymettus was a mountain of Attica, much famed for its honey.]

EXPLANATION

The Pygmalion here mentioned must not be mistaken for the person of the same name, who was the brother of Dido, and king of Tyre. The story is most probably an allegory, which was based on the fact that Pygmalion being a man of virtuous principles, and disgusted with the vicious conduct of the women of Cyprus, took a great deal of care in training the mind and conduct of a young female, whom he kept at a distance from the contact of the prevailing vices; and whom, after having recovered her from the obdurate and rocky state to which the other females were reduced, he made his wife, and had a son by her named Paphos; who was said to have been the founder of the city of Cyprus, known by his name.

FABLE VIII [X.298-518]

Myrrha, the daughter of Cinyras and Cenchris, having conceived an incestuous passion for her own father, and despairing of satisfying it, attempts to hang herself. Her nurse surprises her in the act, and prevents her death. Myrrha, after repeated entreaties and assurances of assistance, discloses to her the cause of her despair. The nurse, by means of a stratagem, procures her the object of her desires, which being discovered by her father, he pursues his daughter with the intention of killing her. Myrrha flies from her father's dominions and being delivered of Adonis, is transformed into a tree.

"Of him was that Cinyras sprung, who, if he had been without issue, might have been reckoned among the happy. Of horrible events shall I now sing. Daughters, be far hence; far hence be parents, too; or, if my verse shall charm your minds, let credit not be given to me in this part of my song, and do not believe that it happened; or, if you will believe, believe as well in the punishment of the deed.

"Yet, if Nature allows this crime to appear to have been committed, I congratulate the Ismarian matrons, and my own division of the globe. I congratulate this land, that it is afar from those regions which produced so great an abomination. Let the Panchæan land[42] be rich in amomum, and let it produce cinnamon, and its zedoary,[43] and frankincense distilling from its tree, and its other flowers, so long as it produces the myrrh-tree, as well. The new tree was not of so much worth as to be a recompense for the crime to which it owed its origin. Cupid himself denies, Myrrha, that it was his arrows that injured thee; and he defends his torches from that imputation; one of the three Sisters kindled this flame within thee, with a Stygian firebrand and with swelling vipers. It is a crime to hate a parent; but this love is a greater degree of wickedness than hatred. On every side worthy nobles are desiring thee in marriage, and throughout the whole East the youths come to the contest for thy bed. Choose out of all these one for thyself, Myrrha, so that, in all that number, there be not one person, namely, thy father.

"She, indeed, is sensible of her criminality, and struggles hard against her infamous passion, and says to herself, 'Whither am I being carried away by my feelings? What am I attempting? I beseech you, O ye Gods, and natural affection, and ye sacred ties of parents, forbid this guilt: defend me from a crime so great! if, indeed, this be a crime. But yet the ties of parent and child are said not to forbid this kind of union; and other animals couple with no distinction. It is not considered shameful for the heifer to mate with her sire; his own daughter becomes the mate of the horse; the he-goat, too, consorts with the flocks of which he is the father; and the bird conceives by him, from whose seed she herself was conceived. Happy they, to whom these things are allowed! The care of man has provided harsh laws, and what Nature permits, malignant ordinances forbid. And yet there are said to be nations[44] in which both the mother is united to the son, and the daughter to the father, and natural affection is increased by a twofold passion. Ah, wretched me! that it was not my chance to be born there, and that I am injured by my lot being cast in this place! but why do I ruminate on these things? Forbidden hopes, begone! He is deserving to be beloved, but as a father only. Were I not, therefore, the daughter of the great Cinyras, with Cinyras I might be united. Now, because he is so much mine, he is not mine, and his very nearness of relationship is my misfortune.

"'A stranger, I were more likely to succeed. I could wish to go far away hence, and to leave my native country, so I might but escape this crime. A fatal delusion detains me thus in love; that being present, I may look at Cinyras, and touch him, and talk with him, and give him kisses, if nothing more is allowed me. But canst thou hope for anything more, impious maid? and dost thou not perceive both how many laws, and how many names thou art confounding? Wilt thou be both the rival of thy mother, and the harlot of thy father? Wilt thou be called the sister of thy son, and the mother of thy brother? and wilt thou not dread the Sisters that have black snakes for their hair, whom guilty minds see threatening their eyes and their faces with their relentless torches? But do not thou conceive criminality in thy mind, so long as thou hast suffered none in body, and violate not the laws of all-powerful Nature by forbidden embraces. Suppose he were to be compliant, the action itself forbids thee; but he is virtuous, and regardful of what is right. And yet, O that there were a like infatuation in him!'

"Thus she says; but Cinyras, whom an honourable crowd of suitors is causing to be in doubt what he is to do, inquires of herself, as he repeats their names, of which husband she would wish to be the wife. At first she is silent; and, fixing her eyes upon her father's countenance, she is in confusion, and fills her eyes with the warm tears. Cinyras, supposing this to be the effect of virgin bashfulness, bids her not weep, and dries her cheeks, and gives her kisses. On these being given, Myrrha is too much delighted; and, being questioned what sort of a husband she would have, she says, 'One like thyself.' But he praises the answer not really[45] understood by him, and says, 'Ever be thus affectionate.' On mention being made of affection, the maiden, conscious of her guilt, fixed her eyes on the ground.

"It is now midnight, and sleep has dispelled the cares, and has eased the minds of mortals. But the virgin daughter of Cinyras, kept awake, is preyed upon by an unconquerable flame, and ruminates upon her wild desires. And one while she despairs, and at another she resolves to try; and is both ashamed, and yet is desirous, and is not certain what she is to do; and, just as a huge tree, wounded by the axe, when the last stroke now remains, is in doubt, as it were, on which side it is to fall, and is dreaded in each direction; so does her mind, shaken by varying passions, waver in uncertainty, this way and that, and receives an impulse in either direction; and no limit or repose is found for her love, but death: 'tis death that pleases her. She raises herself upright, and determines to insert her neck[46] in a halter; and tying her girdle to the top of the door-post, she says, 'Farewell, dear Cinyras, and understand the cause of my death;' and then fits the noose to her pale neck.

"They say that the sound of her words reached the attentive ears of her nurse,[47] as she was guarding the door of her foster-child. The old woman rises, and opens the door; and, seeing the instruments of the death she has contemplated, at the same moment she cries aloud, and smites herself, and rends her bosom, and snatching the girdle from her neck, tears it to pieces. And then, at last, she has time to weep, then to give her embraces, and to inquire into the occasion for the halter. The maid is silent, as though dumb, and, without moving, looks upon the earth; and thus detected, is sorry for her attempt at death in this slow manner. The old woman still urges her; and laying bare her grey hair, and her withered breasts, begs her, by her cradle and by her first nourishment, to entrust her with that which is causing her grief. She, turning from her as she asks, heaves a sigh. The nurse is determined to find it out, and not to promise her fidelity only. 'Tell me,' says she, 'and allow me to give thee assistance; my old age is not an inactive one. If it is a frantic passion, I have the means of curing it with charms and herbs; if any one has hurt thee by spells, by magic rites shalt thou be cured; or if it is the anger of the Gods, that anger can be appeased by sacrifice. What more than these can I think of? No doubt thy fortunes and thy family are prosperous, and in the way of continuing so; thy mother and thy father are still surviving.' Myrrha, on hearing her father's name, heaves a sigh from the bottom of her heart. Nor, even yet, does her nurse apprehend in her mind any unlawful passion; and still she has a presentiment that it is something connected with love. Persisting in her purpose, she entreats her, whatever it is, to disclose it to her, and takes her, as she weeps, in her aged lap; and so embracing her in her feeble arms, she says,

'Daughter, I understand it; thou art in love, and in this case (lay aside thy fears) my assiduity will be of service to thee; nor shall thy father ever be aware of it.'

"Furious, she sprang away from her bosom; and pressing the bed with her face, she said, 'Depart, I entreat thee, and spare my wretched shame.' Upon the other insisting, she said, 'Either depart, or cease to inquire why it is I grieve; that which thou art striving to know, is impious.' The old woman is struck with horror, and stretches forth her hands palsied both with years and with fear, and suppliantly falls before the feet of her foster-child. And one while she soothes her, sometimes she terrifies her with the consequences, if she is not made acquainted with it; and then she threatens her with the discovery of the halter, and of her attempted destruction, and promises her good offices, if the passion is confided to her. She lifts up her head, and fills the breast of her nurse with tears bursting forth; and often endeavouring to confess, as often does she check her voice; and she covers her blushing face with her garments, and says, 'O, mother, happy in thy husband!' Thus much she says; and then she sighs. A trembling shoots through the chilled limbs and the bones of her nurse, for she understands her; and her white hoariness stands bristling with stiff hair all over her head; and she adds many a word to drive away a passion so dreadful, if only she can. But the maiden is well aware that she is not advised to a false step; still she is resolved to die, if she does not enjoy him whom she loves. 'Live then,' says the nurse, 'thou shalt enjoy thy—' and, not daring to say 'parent,' she is silent; and then she confirms her promise with an oath.

"The pious matrons were now celebrating the annual festival of Ceres,[48] on which, having their bodies clothed with snow-white robes, they offer garlands made of ears of corn, as the first fruits of the harvest; and for nine nights they reckon embraces, and the contact of a husband, among the things forbidden. Cenchreïs, the king's wife, is absent in that company, and attends the mysterious rites. Therefore, while his bed is without his lawful wife, the nurse, wickedly industrious, having found Cinyras overcome with wine, discloses to him a real passion, but under a feigned name, and praises the beauty of the damsel. On his enquiring the age of the maiden, she says, 'She is of the same age as Myrrha.' After she is commanded to bring her, and as soon as she has returned home, she says, 'Rejoice, my fosterling, we have prevailed.' The unhappy maid does not feel joy throughout her entire body, and her boding breast is sad. And still she does rejoice: so great is the discord in her mind.

"'Twas the time when all things are silent, and Boötes had turned his wain with the pole obliquely directed among the Triones.[49] She approaches to perpetrate her enormity. The golden moon flies from the heavens; black clouds conceal the hiding stars; the night is deprived of its fires. Thou, Icarus, dost conceal thy rising countenance; and thou, Erigone, raised to the heavens through thy affectionate love for thy father. Three times was she recalled by the presage of her foot stumbling; thrice did the funereal owl give an omen by its dismal cry. Yet onward she goes, and the gloom and the dark night lessen her shame. In her left hand she holds that of her nurse, the other, by groping, explores the secret road. And now she is arrived at the door of the chamber; and now she opens the door; now she is led in; but her knees tremble beneath her sinking hams, her colour and her blood vanish; and her courage deserts her as she moves along. The nearer she is to the commission of her crime, the more she dreads it, and she repents of her attempt, and could wish to be able to return unknown. The old woman leads her on by the hand as she lingers, and when she has delivered her up on her approach to the lofty bed, she says, 'Take her, Cinyras, she is thy own,' and so unites their doomed bodies. The father receives his own bowels into the polluted bed, and allays her virgin fears, and encourages her as she trembles. Perhaps, too, he may have called her by a name suited to her age, and she may have called him 'father,' that the appropriate names might not be wanting in this deed of horror. Pregnant by her father, she departs from the chamber, and, in her impiety, bears his seed in her incestuous womb, and carries with her, criminality in her conception. The ensuing night repeats the guilty deed; nor on that night is there an end. At last, Cinyras, after so many embraces, longing to know who is his paramour, on lights being brought in, discovers both the crime and his own daughter.

"His words checked through grief, he draws his shining sword from the scabbard as it hangs. Myrrha flies, rescued from death by the gloom and the favour of a dark night; and wandering along the wide fields, she leaves the Arabians famed for their palms, and the Panchæan fields. And she wanders during nine horns of the returning moon; when, at length, being weary, she rests in the Sabæan country,[50] and with difficulty she supports the burden of her womb. Then, uncertain what to wish, and between the fear of death and weariness of life, she uttered such a prayer as this: 'O ye Deities, if any of you favour those who are penitent; I have deserved severe punishment, and I do not shrink from it. But that, neither existing, I may pollute the living, nor dead, those who are departed, expel me from both these realms; and transforming me, deny me both life and death.' Some Divinity ever regards the penitent; at least, the last of her prayers found its Gods to execute it. For the earth closes over her legs as she speaks, and a root shoots forth obliquely through her bursting nails, as a firm support to her tall trunk. Her bones, too, become hard wood, and her marrow continuing in the middle, her blood changes into sap, her arms into great branches, her fingers into smaller ones; her skin grows hard with bark. And now the growing tree has run over her heavy womb, and has covered her breast, and is ready to enclose her neck. She cannot endure delay, and sinks down to meet the approaching wood, and hides her features within the bark. Though she has lost her former senses together with her human shape, she still weeps on, and warm drops distil[51] from the tree. There is a value even in her tears, and the myrrh distilling from the bark, retains the name of its mistress, and will be unheard-of in no future age.

"But the infant conceived in guilt grows beneath the wood, and seeks out a passage, by which he may extricate himself, having left his mother. Her pregnant womb swells in the middle of the tree. The burden distends the mother, nor have her pangs words of their own whereby to express themselves; nor can Lucina be invoked by her voice while bringing forth. Yet she is like one struggling to be delivered; and the bending tree utters frequent groans, and is moistened with falling tears. Gentle Lucina stands by the moaning boughs, and applies her hands, and utters words that promote delivery. The tree gapes open, in chinks, and through the cleft bark it discharges the living burden. The child cries; the Naiads, laying him on the soft grass, anoint him with the tears of his mother.

"Even Envy herself would have commended his face; for just as the bodies of naked Cupids are painted in a picture, such was he. But that their dress may not make any difference, either give to him or take away from them, the polished quivers."

[Footnote 42: The Panchæan land.—Ver. 309. Panchæa was a region of Arabia Felix, abounding in the choicest wines and frankincense. Here, the Phœnix was said to find the materials for making its nest.]

[Footnote 43: Its zedoary.—Ver. 308. 'Costus,' or 'costum,' was an Indian shrub, which yielded a fragrant ointment, much esteemed by the ancients. Clarke translates it 'Coysts,' a word apparently of his own coining.]

[Footnote 44: Said to be nations.—Ver. 331. We do not read of any such nations, except the fabulous Troglodytes of Ethiopia, who were supposed to live promiscuously, like the brutes. Attica, king of the Huns, long after Ovid's time, married his own daughter, amid the rejoicings of his subjects.]

[Footnote 45: Not really.—Ver. 365. That is to say, not understood by him in the sense in which Myrrha meant it.]

[Footnote 46: To insert her neck.—Ver. 378. 'Laqueoque innectere fauces Destinat,' is translated by Clarke, 'And resolves to stitch up her neck in a halter.']

[Footnote 47: Of her nurse.—Ver. 382. Antoninus Liberalis gives this hag the name of Hippolyte.]

[Footnote 48: Festival of Ceres.—Ver. 431. Commentators, in general, suppose that he here alludes to the festival of the Thesmophoria, which was celebrated in honour of Demeter, or Ceres, in various parts of Greece; in general, by the married women, though the virgins joined in some of the ceremonies. Demosthenes, Diodorus Siculus, and Plutarch, say that it was first celebrated by Orpheus; while Herodotus states, that it was introduced from Egypt by the daughters of Danaüs; and that, after the Dorian conquest, it fell into disuse, being retained only by the people of Arcadia. It was intended to commemorate the introduction of laws and the regulations of civilized life, which were generally ascribed to Demeter. It is not known whether the festival lasted four or five days with the Athenians. Many days were spent by the matrons in preparing for its celebration. The solemnity was commenced by the women walking in procession from Athens to Eleusis. In this procession they carried on their heads representations of the laws which had been introduced by Ceres, and other symbols of civilized life. They then spent the night at Eleusis, in celebrating the mysteries of the Goddess. The second day was one of mourning, during which the women sat on the ground around the statues of Ceres, taking no food but cakes made of sesame and honey. On it no meetings of the people were held. Probably it was in the afternoon of this day that there was a procession at Athens, in which the women walked bare-footed behind a waggon, upon which were baskets, with sacred symbols. The third day was one of merriment and festivity among the women, in commemoration of Iämbe, who was said to have amused the Goddess during her grief at the loss of Proserpine. An atoning sacrifice, called ζήμια, was probably offered to the Goddess, at the end of this day. It is most probable that the ceremonial lasted but three days. The women wore white dresses during the period of its performance, and they adopted the same colour during the celebration of the Cerealia at Rome. Burmann thinks, that an Eastern festival, in honour of Ceres, is here referred to. If so, no accounts of it whatever have come down to us.]

[Footnote 49: Among the Triones.—Ver. 446. 'Triones'. This word, which is applied to the stars of the Ursa Major, or Charles's Wain, literally means 'oxen;' and is by some thought to come from 'tero,' 'to bruise,' because oxen were used for the purpose of threshing corn; but it is more likely to have its origin from 'terra,' 'the earth,' because oxen were used for ploughing. The Poet employs this periphrasis, to signify the middle of the night.]

[Footnote 50: Sabæan country.—Ver. 480. Sabæa, or Saba, was a region of Arabia Felix, now called 'Yemen.' It was famed for its myrrh, frankincense, and spices. In the Scriptures it is called Sheba, and it was the queen of this region, who came to listen to the wisdom of Solomon.]

[Footnote 51: Warm drops distil.—Ver. 500. He alludes to the manner in which frankincense is produced, it exuding from the bark of the tree in drops; this gum, Pliny the Elder and Lucretius call by the name of 'stacta,' or 'stacte.' The ancients flavoured their wines with myrrh.]

EXPLANATION

Le Clerc, forming his ideas on what Lucian, Phurnutus, and other authors have said on the subject, explains the story of Cinyras and Myrrha in the following manner. Cynnor, or Cinyras, the grandfather of Adonis, having one day drank to excess, fell asleep in a posture which violated the rules of decency. Mor, or Myrrha, his daughter-in-law, the wife of Ammon, together with her son Adonis, seeing him in that condition, acquainted her husband with her father's lapse. On his repeating this to Cinyras, the latter was so full of indignation, that he loaded Myrrha and Adonis with imprecations.

Loaded with the execrations of her father, Myrrha retired into Arabia, where she remained some time; and because Adonis passed some portion of his youth there, the poets feigned that Myrrha was delivered of him in that country. Her transformation into a tree was only invented on account of the equivocal character of her name, 'Mor,' which meant in the Arabic language 'Myrrh.' It is very probable that the story was founded on a tradition among the Phœnicians of the history of Noah, and of the malediction which Ham drew on himself by his undutiful conduct towards his father.

FABLE IX [X.519-707]

Adonis is educated by the Naiads. His beauty makes a strong impression on the Goddess Venus, and, in her passion, she traverses the same wilds in pursuit of the youth, which his mother did, when flying from the wrath of her father. After chasing the wild beasts, she invites Adonis to a poplar shade, where she warns him of his danger in hunting lions, wild boars, and such formidable animals. On this occasion, too, she relates the adventures of Hippomenes and Atalanta. The beauty of the latter was such, that her charms daily attracted crowds of suitors. Having consulted the oracle, whether she shall marry, she is answered that a husband will certainly prove her destruction. On this, to avoid marrying, she makes it a rule to offer to run with her suitors, promising that she herself will be the prize of the victor, but only on condition that immediate death shall be the fate of those who are vanquished by her. As she excels in running, her design succeeds, and several suitors die in the attempt to win her. Hippomenes, smitten with her charms, is not daunted at their ill success; but boldly enters the lists, after imploring the aid of Venus. Atalanta is struck with his beauty, and is much embarrassed, whether she shall yield to the charms of the youth, or to the dissuasions of the oracle. Hippomenes attracts her attention in the race, by throwing down some golden apples which Venus has given him, and then, reaching the goal before her, he carries off the reward of victory. Venus, to punish his subsequent ingratitude towards her, raises his desires to such a pitch, that he incurs the resentment of Cybele, by defiling her shrine with the embraces of his mistress; on which they are both transformed into lions, and thenceforth draw the chariot of the Goddess.

"Winged time glides on insensibly and deceives us; and there is nothing more fleeting than years. He, born of his own sister and of his grandfather, who, so lately enclosed in a tree, was so lately born, and but just now a most beauteous infant, is now a youth, now a man, and now more beauteous than he was before. And now he pleases even Venus,[52] and revenges the flames of his mother, kindled by her. For, while the boy that wears the quiver is giving kisses to his mother, he unconsciously grazes her breast with a protruding arrow. The Goddess, wounded, pushed away her son with her hand. The wound was inflicted more deeply than it seemed to be, and at first had deceived even herself. Charmed with the beauty of the youth, she does not now care for the Cytherian shores, nor does she revisit Paphos, surrounded with the deep sea, and Cnidos,[53] abounding in fish, or Amathus, rich in metals.

"She abandons even the skies; him she ever attends; and she who has been always accustomed to indulge in the shade, and to improve her beauty, by taking care of it, wanders over the tops of mountains, through the woods, and over bushy rocks, bare to the knee and with her robes tucked up after the manner of Diana, and she cheers on the dogs, and hunts animals that are harmless prey, either the fleet hares, or the stag with its lofty horns, or the hinds; she keeps afar from the fierce boars, and avoids the ravening wolves, and the bears armed with claws, and the lions glutted with the slaughter of the herds. Thee, too, Adonis, she counsels to fear them, if she can aught avail by advising thee. And she says, "Be brave against those animals that fly; boldness is not safe against those that are bold. Forbear, youth, to be rash at my hazard, and attack not the wild beasts to which nature has granted arms, lest thy thirst for glory should cost me dear. Neither thy age, nor thy beauty, nor other things which have made an impression on Venus, make any impression on lions and bristly boars, and the eyes and the tempers of wild beasts. The fierce boars carry lightning[54] in their curving tusks; there is rage and fury unlimited in the tawny lions; and the whole race is odious to me."

"Upon his asking, what is the reason, she says, 'I will tell thee, and thou wilt be surprised at the prodigious result of a fault long since committed. But this toil to which I am unaccustomed has now fatigued me, and see! a convenient poplar invites us, by its shade, and the turf furnishes a couch. Here I am desirous to repose myself, together with thee;' and forthwith she rests herself on the ground, and presses at once the grass and himself. And with her neck reclining on the bosom of the youth, smiling, she thus says, and she mingles kisses in the midst of her words:—

"Perhaps thou mayst have heard how a certain damsel excelled the swiftest men in the contest of speed. That report was no idle tale; for she did excel them. Nor couldst thou have said, whether she was more distinguished in the merit of her swiftness, or in the excellence of her beauty. Upon her consulting the oracle about a husband, the God said to her, 'Thou hast no need, Atalanta, of a husband; avoid obtaining a husband. And yet thou wilt not avoid it, and, while still living, thou wilt lose thyself.' Alarmed with the response of the God, she lives a single life in the shady woods, and determinedly repulses the pressing multitude of her suitors with these conditions. 'I am not,' says she, 'to be gained, unless first surpassed in speed. Engage with me in running. Both a wife and a wedding shall be given as the reward of the swift; death shall be the recompense of the slow. Let that be the condition of the contest.' She, indeed, was cruel in this proposal; but (so great is the power of beauty) a rash multitude of suitors agreed to these terms. Hippomenes had sat, as a spectator, of this unreasonable race, and said, 'Is a wife sought by any one, amid dangers so great?' And thus he condemned the excessive ardour of the youths. But when he beheld her face, and her body with her clothes laid aside, such as mine is, or such as thine would be, Adonis, if thou wast to become a woman, he was astonished, and raising his hands, he said, 'Pardon me, ye whom I was just now censuring; the reward which you contended for was not yet known to me.'

"In commending her, he kindles the flame, and wishes that none of the young men may run more swiftly than she, and, in his envy, is apprehensive of it. 'But why,' says he, 'is my chance in this contest left untried? The Divinity himself assists the daring.' While Hippomenes is pondering such things within himself, the virgin flies with winged pace. Although she appears to the Aonian youth to go no less swiftly than the Scythian arrow, he admires her still more in her beauty, and the very speed makes her beauteous. The breeze that meets her bears back her pinions on her swift feet, and her hair is thrown over her ivory shoulders and the leggings which are below her knees with their variegated border, and upon her virgin whiteness her body has contracted a blush; no otherwise than as when purple hangings[55] over a whitened hall tint it with a shade of a similar colour. While the stranger is observing these things, the last course is run,[56] and the victorious Atalanta is adorned with a festive crown. The vanquished utter sighs, and pay the penalty, according to the stipulation. Still, not awed by the end of these young men, he stands up in the midst; and fixing his eyes on the maiden, he says, 'Why dost thou seek an easy victory by conquering the inactive? Contend now with me. If fortune shall render me victorious, thou wilt not take it ill to be conquered by one so illustrious. For my father was Megareus, Onchestius his;[57] Neptune was his grandsire; I am the great grandson of the king of the waves. Nor is my merit inferior to my extraction. Or if I shall be conquered, in the conquest of Hippomenes thou wilt have a great and honourable name.'

"As he utters such words as these, the daughter of Schœneus regards him with a benign countenance, and is in doubt whether she shall wish to be overcome or to conquer; and thus she says: 'What Deity, a foe to the beauteous, wishes to undo this youth? and commands him, at the risk of a life so dear, to seek this alliance? In my own opinion, I am not of so great value. Nor yet am I moved by his beauty. Still, by this, too, I could be moved. But, 'tis because he is still a boy; 'tis not himself that affects me, but his age. And is it not, too, because he has courage and a mind undismayed by death? And is it not, besides, because he is reckoned fourth in descent from the monarch of the sea? And is it not, because he loves me, and thinks a marriage with me of so much worth as to perish for it, if cruel fortune should deny me to him? Stranger, while still thou mayst, begone, and abandon an alliance stained with blood. A match with me is cruelly hazardous. No woman will be unwilling to be married to thee; and thou mayst be desired even by a prudent maid. But why have I any concern for thee, when so many have already perished? Let him look to it; and let him die, since he is not warned by the fate of so many of my wooers, and is impelled onwards to weariness of life.

"'Shall he then die because he was desirous with me to live? And shall he suffer an undeserved death, the reward of his love? My victory will not be able to support the odium of the deed. But it is no fault of mine. I wish thou wouldst desist! or since thou art thus mad, would that thou wast more fleet than I! But what a feminine look[58] there is in his youthful face! Ah, wretched Hippomenes, I would that I had not been seen by thee! Thou wast worthy to have lived! And if I had been more fortunate; and if the vexatious Divinities had not denied me the blessings of marriage, thou wast one with whom I could have shared my bed.' Thus she said; and as one inexperienced, and smitten by Cupid for the first time, not knowing what she is doing, she is in love, and yet does not know that she is in love.

"And now, both the people and her father, demanded the usual race, when Hippomenes, the descendant of Neptune, invoked me with anxious voice; 'I entreat that Cytherea may favour my undertaking, and aid the passion that she has inspired in me.' The breeze, not envious, wafted to me this tender prayer; I was moved, I confess it; nor was any long delay made in giving aid. There is a field, the natives call it by name the Tamasenian field,[59] the choicest spot in the Cyprian land; this the elders of former days consecrated to me, and ordered to be added as an endowment for my temple. In the middle of this field a tree flourishes, with yellow foliage, and with branches tinkling with yellow gold. Hence, by chance as I was coming, I carried three golden apples, that I had plucked, in my hand; and being visible to none but him, I approached Hippomenes, and I showed him what was to be the use of them. The trumpets have now given the signal, when each of them darts precipitately from the starting place, and skims the surface of the sand with nimble feet. You might have thought them able to pace the sea with dry feet, and to run along the ears of white standing corn while erect. The shouts and the applause of the populace give courage to the youth, and the words of those who exclaim, 'Now, now, Hippomenes, is the moment to speed onward! make haste. Now use all thy strength! Away with delay! thou shalt be conqueror.' It is doubtful whether the Megarean hero, or the virgin daughter of Schœneus rejoiced the most at these sayings. O how often when she could have passed by him, did she slacken her speed, and then unwillingly left behind the features that long she had gazed upon.

"A parched panting is coming from his faint mouth, and the goal is still a great way off. Then, at length, the descendant of Neptune throws one of the three products of the tree. The virgin is amazed, and from a desire for the shining fruit, she turns from her course, and picks up the rolling gold. Hippomenes passes her. The theatres ring[60] with applause. She makes amends for her delay, and the time that she has lost, with a swift pace, and again she leaves the youth behind. And, retarded by the throwing of a second apple, again she overtakes the young man, and passes by him. The last part of the race now remained. 'And now,' said he, 'O Goddess, giver of this present, aid me;' and then with youthful might, he threw the shining gold, in an oblique direction, on one side of the plain, in order that she might return the more slowly. The maiden seemed to be in doubt, whether she should fetch it; I forced her to take it up, and added weight to the apple, when she had taken it up, and I impeded her, both by the heaviness of the burden, and the delay in reaching it. And that my narrative may not be more tedious than that race, the virgin was outrun, and the conqueror obtained the prize.

"And was I not, Adonis, deserving that he should return thanks to me, and the tribute of frankincense? but, in his ingratitude, he gave me neither thanks nor frankincense. I was thrown into a sudden passion; and provoked at being slighted, I provided by making an example, that I should not be despised in future times, and I aroused myself against them both. They were passing by a temple, concealed within a shady wood, which the famous Echion had formerly built for the Mother of the Gods, according to his vow; and the length of their journey moved them to take rest there. There, an unseasonable desire of caressing his wife seized Hippomenes, excited by my agency. Near the temple was a recess, with but little light, like a cave, covered with native pumice stone, one sacred from ancient religious observance; where the priest had conveyed many a wooden image of the ancient Gods. This he entered, and he defiled the sanctuary by a forbidden crime. The sacred images turned away their eyes, and the Mother of the Gods, crowned with turrets,[61] was in doubt whether she should plunge these guilty ones in the Stygian stream. That seemed too light a punishment. Wherefore yellow manes cover their necks so lately smooth; their fingers are bent into claws, of their shoulders are made fore-legs;[62] their whole weight passes into their breasts. The surface of the sand is swept by their tails.[63] Their look has anger in it; instead of words they utter growls; instead of chambers they haunt the woods; and dreadful to others, as lions, they champ the bits of Cybele with subdued jaws. Do thou, beloved by me, avoid these, and together with these, all kinds of wild beasts which turn not their backs in flight, but their breasts to the fight; lest thy courage should be fatal to us both."

[Footnote 52: Pleases even Venus.—Ver. 524. According to Apollodorus, Venus had caused Myrrha to imbibe her infamous passion, because she had treated the worship of that Goddess with contempt.]

[Footnote 53: Cnidos.—Ver. 531. This was a city of Caria, situate on a promontory. Strangers resorted thither, to behold a statue of Venus there, which was made by Praxiteles.]

[Footnote 54: Carry lightning.—Ver. 551. The lightning shock seems to be attributed to the wild boar, from the vehemence with which he strikes down every impediment in his way.]

[Footnote 55: Purple hangings.—Ver. 595. Curtains, or hangings, called 'aulæa,' were used by the ancients to ornament their halls, sitting rooms, and bed chambers. In private houses they were also sometimes hung as coverings over doors, and in the interior, as substitutes for them. In the palace of the Roman emperors, a slave, called 'velarius,' was posted at each of the principal doors, to raise the curtain when any one passed through. Window curtains were also used by the Romans, while they were employed in the temples, to veil the statue of the Divinity. Ovid here speaks of them as being of purple colour; while Lucretius mentions them as being of yellow, red, and rusty hue.]

[Footnote 56: Last course is run.—Ver. 597. Among the Romans, the race consisted of seven rounds of the Circus, or rather circuits of the 'spina,' or wall, in the midst of it, at each end of which was the 'meta,' or goal. Livy and Dio Cassius speak of seven conical balls, resembling eggs, which were called 'ova,' and were placed upon the 'spina.' Their use was to enable the spectators to count the number of rounds which had been run, for which reason they were seven in number; and as each round was run, one of the 'ova' was put up, or, according to Varro, taken down. The form of the egg was adopted in honour of Castor and Pollux, who were said to have been produced from eggs. The words 'novissima meta' here mean either 'the last part of the course,' or, possibly, 'the last time round the course.']

[Footnote 57: Onchestius his.—Ver. 605. But Hyginus says that Neptune was the father of Megareus, or Macareus, as the Scholiast of Sophocles calls him. Neptune being the father of Onchestius, Hippomenes was the fourth from Neptune, inclusively. Onchestius founded a city of that name in Bœotia, in honour of Neptune, who had a temple there; in the time of Pausanias the place was in ruins. That author tells us that Megareus aided Nisus against Minos, and was slain in that war.]

[Footnote 58: A feminine look.—Ver. 631. Clarke renders this line—'But what a lady-like countenance there is in his boyish face!']

[Footnote 59: Tamasenian field.—Ver. 644. Tamasis, or Tamaseus, is mentioned by Pliny as a city of Cyprus.]

[Footnote 60: The theatres ring.—Ver. 668. 'Spectacula' may mean either the seats, or benches, on which the spectators sat, or an amphitheatre. The former is most probably the meaning in the present instance.]

[Footnote 61: Crowned with turrets.—Ver. 696. Cybele, the Goddess of the Earth, was usually represented as crowned with turrets, and drawn in a chariot by lions.]

[Footnote 62: Are made fore-legs.—Ver. 700. 'Armus' is generally the shoulder of a brute; while 'humerus' is that of a man. 'Armus' is sometimes used to signify the human shoulder.]

[Footnote 63: By their tails.—Ver. 701. Pliny the Elder remarks that the temper of the lion is signified by his tail, in the same way as that of the horse by his ears. When in motion, it shows that he is angry; when quiet, that he is in a good temper.]

EXPLANATION

The Atalanta who is mentioned in this story was the daughter of Schœneus, and the granddaughter of Athamas, whose misfortunes obliged him to retire into Bœotia, where he built a little town, which was called after his name, as we learn from Pausanias and Eustathius. Ovid omits to say that it was one of the conditions of the agreement, that the lover was to have the start in the race. According to some writers, the golden apples were from the gardens of the Hesperides; while, according to others, they were plucked by Venus in the isle of Cyprus. The story seems to be founded merely on the fact, that Hippomenes contrived by means of bribes to find the way to the favour of his mistress.

Apollodorus, however, relates the story in a different manner; he says that the father of Atalanta desiring to have sons, but no daughters, exposed her, on her birth, in a desert, that she might perish. A she-bear found the infant, and nourished it, until it was discovered by some hunters. As the damsel grew up, she made hunting her favourite pursuit, and slew two Centaurs, who offered her violence, with her arrows. On her parents pressing her to marry, she consented to be the wife of that man only who could outrun her, on condition that those who were conquered by her in the race should be put to death. Several of her suitors having failed in the attempt, one of the name of Melanion, by using a similar stratagem to that attributed by Ovid to Hippomenes, conquered her in the race, and became her husband. Having profaned the temple of Jupiter, they were transformed, Melanion into a lion, and Atalanta into a lioness. According to Apollodorus, her father's name was Iasius, though in his first book he says she was the daughter of Schœneus. He also says that she was the same person that was present at the hunt of the Calydonian boar, though other writers represent them to have been different personages. Euripides makes Mænalus to have been the name of her father.

Atalanta had by Melanion, or, as some authors say, by Mars, a son named Parthenopæus, who was present at the Theban war. Ælian gives a long account of her history, which does not very much differ from the narrative of Apollodorus.

FABLE X [X.708-739]

Adonis being too ardent in the pursuit of a wild boar, the beast kills him, on which Venus changes his blood into a flower of crimson colour.

"She, indeed, thus warned him; and, harnessing her swans, winged her way through the air; but his courage stood in opposition to her advice. By chance, his dogs having followed its sure track, roused a boar, and the son of Cinyras pierced him, endeavouring to escape from the wood, with a wound from the side. Immediately the fierce boar, with his crooked snout, struck out the hunting-spear, stained with his blood, and then pursued him, trembling and seeking a safe retreat, and lodged his entire tusks in his groin, and stretched him expiring on the yellow sand.

"Cytherea, borne in her light chariot[64] through the middle of the air, had not yet arrived at Cyprus upon the wings of her swans. She recognized afar his groans, as he was dying, and turned her white birds in that direction. And when, from the lofty sky, she beheld him half dead, and bathing his body in his own blood, she rapidly descended, and rent both her garments and her hair, and she smote her breast with her distracted hands. And complaining of the Fates, she says, 'But, however, all things shall not be in your power; the memorials of my sorrow, Adonis, shall ever remain; and the representation of thy death, repeated yearly, shall exhibit an imitation of my mourning. But thy blood shall be changed into a flower. Was it formerly allowed thee, Persephone, to change the limbs[65] of a female into fragrant mint; and shall the hero, the son of Cinyras, if changed, be a cause of displeasure against me?' Having thus said, she sprinkles his blood with odoriferous nectar, which, touched by it, effervesces, just as the transparent bubbles are wont to rise in rainy weather. Nor was there a pause longer than a full hour, when a flower sprang up from the blood, of the same colour with it, such as the pomegranates are wont to bear, which conceal their seeds beneath their tough rind. Yet the enjoyment of it is but short-lived; for the same winds[66] which give it a name, beat it down, as it has but a slender hold, and is apt to fall by reason of its extreme slenderness."

[Footnote 64: In her light chariot.—Ver. 717. 'Vecta levi curru Cytherea,' Clarke quaintly renders, 'The Cytherean Goddess riding in her light chair.']

[Footnote 65: To change the limbs.—Ver. 729. Proserpine was said to have changed the Nymph, 'Mentha,' into a plant of that name, which we call 'mint.' Some writers say that she found her intriguing with Pluto while, according to other writers, she was the mistress of Pollux.]

[Footnote 66: The same winds.—Ver. 739. The flower which sprang from the blood of Adonis was the anemone, or wind-flower, of which Pliny the Elder says—'This flower never opens but when the wind is blowing, from which too, it receives its name, as ἄνεμος means the wind.'—(Book i. c. 23).]

EXPLANATION

Theocritus, Bion, Hyginus, and Antoninus Liberalis, beside several other authors, relate the history of the loves of Venus and Adonis. They inform us of many particulars which Ovid has here neglected to remark. They say that Mars, jealous of the passion which Venus had for Adonis, implored the aid of Diana, who, to gratify his revenge, sent the boar that destroyed the youth. According to some writers, it was Apollo himself that took the form of that animal; and they say that Adonis descending to the Infernal Regions, Proserpine fell in love with him, and refused to allow him to return, notwithstanding the orders of Jupiter. On this, the king of heaven fearing to displease both the Goddesses, referred the dispute to the Muse Calliope, who directed that Adonis should pass one half of his time with Venus on earth, and the other half in the Infernal Regions. They also tell us that it took up a year before the dispute could be determined, and that the Hours brought Adonis at last to the upper world, on which, Venus being dissatisfied with the decision of Calliope, instigated the women of Thrace to kill her son Orpheus.

The mythologists have considered this story to be based on grounds either historical or physical. Cicero, in his Discourse on the Nature of the Gods, says, that there were several persons who had the name of Venus, and that the fourth, surnamed Astarte, was a Syrian, who married Adonis, the son of Cinyras, king of Cyprus. Hunting in the forests of Mount Libanus, or Lebanon, he was wounded in the groin by a wild boar, which accident ultimately caused his death. Astarte caused the city of Byblos and all Syria to mourn for his loss; and, to keep his name and his sad fate in remembrance, established feasts in his honour, to be celebrated each year. Going still further, if we suppose the story to have originated in historical facts, it seems not improbable that Adonis did not die of his wound, and that, contrary to all expectation, he was cured; as the Syrians, after having mourned for several days during his festival, rejoiced as though he had been raised from the dead, at a second festival called 'The Return.' The worship both of Venus and Adonis probably originated in Syria, and was spread through Asia Minor into Greece; while the Carthaginians, a Phœnician colony introduced it into Sicily. The festival of Adonis is most amusingly described by Theocritus the Sicilian poet, in his 'Adoniazusæ.' Some authors have suggested that Adonis was the same with the Egyptian God Osiris, and that the affliction of Venus represented that of Isis at the death of her husband. According to Hesiod, Adonis was the son of Phœnix and Alphesibœa, while Panyasis says that he was son of Theias, the king of the Assyrians.

In support of the view which some commentators take of the story of Adonis having been founded on physical circumstance, we cannot do better than quote the able remarks of Mr. Keightley on the subject. He says (Mythology of Ancient Greece and Italy, p. 109)—"The tale of Adonis is apparently an Eastern mythus. His very name is Semitic (Hebrew 'Adon,' 'Lord'), and those of his parents also refer to that part of the world. He appears to be the same with the Thammuz, mentioned by the prophet Ezekiel, and to be a Phœnician personification of the sun who, during a part of the year is absent, or, as the legend expresses it, with the Goddess of the under world: during the remainder with Astarte, the regent of heaven. It is uncertain when the Adonia were first celebrated in Greece; but we find Plato alluding to the gardens of Adonis, as boxes of flowers used in them were called; and the ill fortune of the Athenian expedition to Sicily was in part ascribed to the circumstance of the fleet having sailed during that festival."

This notion of the mourning for Adonis being a testimony of grief for the absence of the Sun during the winter, is not, however, to be too readily acquiesced in. Lobeck (Aglaophamus, p. 691), for example, asks, with some appearance of reason, why those nations whose heaven was mildest, and their winter shortest, should so bitterly bewail the regular changes of the seasons, as to feign that the Gods themselves were carried off or slain; and he shrewdly observes, that, in that case, the mournful and the joyful parts of the festival should have been held at different times of the year, and not joined together, as they were. He further inquires, whether the ancient writers, who esteemed these Gods to be so little superior to men, may not have believed them to have been really and not metaphorically put to death? And, in truth, it is not easy to give a satisfactory answer to these questions.

BOOK THE ELEVENTH

FABLE I [XI.1-84]

While Orpheus is singing to his lyre on Mount Rhodope, the women of Thrace celebrate their orgies. During that ceremony they take advantage of the opportunity to punish Orpheus for his indifference towards their sex; and, in the fury inspired by their rites, they beat him to death. His head and lyre are carried by the stream of the river Hebrus into the sea, and are cast on shore on the isle of Lesbos. A serpent, about to attack the head when thrown on shore, is changed into a stone, and the Bacchanals who have killed him are transformed into trees.

While with songs such as these, the Thracian poet is leading the woods and the natures of savage beasts, and the following rocks, lo! the matrons of the Ciconians, having their raving breasts covered with the skins of wild beasts, from the summit of a hill, espy Orpheus adapting his voice to the sounded strings of his harp. One of these, tossing her hair along the light breeze, says, "See! see! here is our contemner!" and hurls her spear at the melodious mouth of the bard of Apollo: but, being wreathed at the end with leaves, it makes a mark without any wound. The weapon of another is a stone, which, when thrown, is overpowered in the very air by the harmony of his voice and his lyre, and lies before his feet, a suppliant, as it were, for an attempt so daring.

But still this rash warfare increases, and all moderation departs, and direful fury reigns triumphant. And yet all their weapons would have been conquered by his music; but the vast clamour, and the Berecynthian pipe[1] with the blown horns, and the tambourines, and the clapping of hands, and Bacchanalian yells, prevented the sound of the lyre from being heard. Then, at last, the stones became red with the blood of the bard, now no longer heard. But first the Mænades lay hands on innumerable birds, even yet charmed with his voice as he sang, and serpents, and a throng of wild beasts, the glory of this audience of Orpheus; and after that, they turn upon Orpheus with blood-stained right hands; and they flock together, as the birds, if at any time they see the bird of night strolling about by day; and as when the stag that is doomed to die[2] in the morning sand in the raised amphitheatre is a prey to the dogs; they both attack the bard, and hurl the thyrsi, covered with green leaves, not made for such purposes as these. Some throw clods, some branches torn from trees, others flint stones. And that weapons may not be wanting for their fury, by chance some oxen are turning up the earth with the depressed ploughshare; and not far from thence, some strong-armed peasants, providing the harvest with plenteous sweat, are digging the hard fields; they, seeing this frantic troop, run away, and leave the implements of their labour; and there lie, dispersed throughout the deserted fields, harrows and heavy rakes, and long spades.

After they, in their rage, have seized upon these, and have torn to pieces the oxen with their threatening horns, they return to the destruction of the bard; and they impiously murder him, extending his hands, and then for the first time uttering words in vain, and making no effect on them with his voice. And (Oh Jupiter!) through those lips listened to by rocks, and understood by the senses of wild beasts, his life breathed forth, departs into the breezes.[3] The mournful birds, the crowd of wild beasts, the hard stones, the woods that oft had followed thy song bewailed thee. Trees, too, shedding their foliage, mourned thee, losing their leaves. They say, too, that rivers swelled with their own tears; and the Naiads and Dryads had mourning garments of dark colour, and dishevelled hair. The limbs lie scattered[4] in various places. Thou, Hebrus, dost receive the head and the lyre; and (wondrous to relate!) while it rolls down the midst of the stream, the lyre complains in I know not what kind of mournful strain. His lifeless tongue, too, utters a mournful sound, to which the banks mournfully reply. And now, borne onward to the sea, they leave their native stream, and reach the shores of Methymnæan Lesbos.[5] Here an infuriated serpent attacks the head thrown up on the foreign sands, and the hair besprinkled with the oozing blood. At last Phœbus comes to its aid, and drives it away as it tries to inflict its sting, and hardens the open jaws of the serpent into stone, and makes solid its gaping mouth just as it is. His ghost descends under the earth, and he recognizes all the spots which he has formerly seen; and seeking Eurydice through the fields of the blessed, he finds her, and enfolds her in his eager arms. Here, one while, they walk together side by side,[6] and at another time he follows her as she goes before, and again at another time, walking in front, precedes her; and now, in safety, Orpheus looks back upon his own Eurydice.

Yet Lyæus did not suffer this wickedness to go unpunished; and grieving for the loss of the bard of his sacred rites, he immediately fastened down in the woods, by a twisting root, all the Edonian matrons who had committed this crime. For he drew out the toes of her feet, just as each one had pursued him, and thrust them by their sharp points into the solid earth. And, as when a bird has entangled its leg in a snare, which the cunning fowler has concealed, and perceives that it is held fast, it beats its wings, and, fluttering, tightens the noose with its struggles; so, as each one of these had stuck fast, fixed in the ground, in her alarm, she attempted flight in vain; but the pliant root held her fast, and confined her, springing forward[7] to escape. And while she is looking where her toes are, where, too, are her feet and her nails, she sees wood growing up upon her well-turned legs. Endeavouring, too, to smite her thigh, with grieving right hand, she strikes solid oak; her breast, too, becomes oak; her shoulders are oak. You would suppose that her extended arms are real boughs, and you would not be deceived in so supposing.

[Footnote 1: Berecynthian pipe.—Ver. 16. This pipe, made of box-wood, was much used in the rites of Cybele, or Berecynthia.]

[Footnote 2: Doomed to die.—Ver. 26. The Romans were wont to exhibit shows of hunting in the amphitheatre in the morning; and at mid-day the gladiatorial spectacles commenced. The 'arena' was the name given to the central open space, which derived its name from the sand with which it was covered, chiefly for the purpose of absorbing the blood of the wild beasts and of the combatants. Caligula, Nero, and Carus showed their extravagant disposition by using cinnabar and borax instead of sand. In the earlier amphitheatres there were ditches, called 'Euripi,' between the open space, or arena, and the seats, to defend the spectators from the animals. They were introduced by Julius Cæsar, but were filled up by Nero, to gain space for the spectators. Those who fought with the beasts (as it will be remembered St. Paul did at Ephesus) were either condemned criminals or captives, or persons who did so for pay, being trained for the purpose. Lucius Metellus was the first that we read of who introduced wild beasts in the theatre for the amusement of the public. He exhibited in the Circus one hundred and forty-two elephants, which he brought from Sicily, after his victory over the Carthaginians, and which are said to have been slain, more because the Romans did not know what to do with them, than for the amusement of the public. Lions and panthers were first exhibited by M. Fulvius, after the Ætolian war. In the Circensian games, exhibited by the Curule Ædiles, P. Cornelius Scipio Nasica, and P. Lentulus, B.C. 168, there were sixty-three African panthers and forty bears and elephants. These latter animals were sometimes introduced to fight with bulls. Sylla, when Prætor, exhibited one hundred lions, which were pierced with javelins. We also read of hippopotami and crocodiles being introduced for the same purpose, while cameleopards were also hunted in the games given by Julius Caesar in his third consulship. He also introduced bull fights, and Augustus first exhibited the rhinoceros, and a serpent, fifty cubits in length. When Titus constructed his great amphitheatre, five thousand wild beasts and four thousand tame animals were slain; while in the games celebrated by Trajan, after his victories over the Dacians, eleven thousand animals are said to have been killed. For further information on this subject, the reader is referred to the article 'Venatio,' in Smith's Dictionary of Greek and Roman Antiquities, which valuable work contains a large quantity of interesting matter on this barbarous practice of the Romans.]

[Footnote 3: Into the breezes.—Ver. 43. 'In ventos anima exhalata recessit' is rendered by Clarke—'his life breathed out, marches off into the wind.']

[Footnote 4: Limbs lie scattered.—Ver. 50. The limbs of Orpheus were collected by the Muses, and, according to Pausanias, were buried by them in Dium in Macedonia, while his head was carried to Lesbos.]

[Footnote 5: Methymnæan Lesbos.—Ver. 55. Methymna was a town in the isle of Lesbos, famed for its wines.]

[Footnote 6: Side by side.—Ver. 64. 'Conjunctis passibus' means 'at an equal pace, and side by side.']

[Footnote 7: Springing forward.—Ver. 78. 'Exsultantem' is rendered by Clarke, 'bouncing hard to get away.']

EXPLANATION

Some of the ancient mythologists say that the story of the serpent, changed into stone for insulting the head of Orpheus, was founded on the history of a certain inhabitant of the isle of Lesbos, who was punished for attacking the reputation of Orpheus. This critic excited contempt, as a malignant and ignorant person, who endeavoured, as it were, to sting the character of the deceased poet, and therefore, by way of exposing his spite and stupidity, he was said to have been changed from a serpent into a stone. According to Philostratus, the poet's head was preserved in the temple of Apollo at Lesbos; and he tells us that Diomedes, and Neoptolemus, the son of Achilles, brought Philoctetes to Troy, after having explained to him the oracular response which the head of Orpheus had given to him from the bottom of a cave at Lesbos.

The harp of Orpheus was preserved in the same temple; and so many wonders were reported of it, that Neanthus, the son of the tyrant Pytharus, purchased it of the priests of Apollo, believing that its sound would be sufficient to put rocks and trees in motion; but, according to Lucian, he succeeded so ill, that on his trying the harp, the dogs of the neighbouring villages fell upon him and tore him to pieces.

The transformation of the women of Thrace into trees, for the murder of Orpheus, is probably an allegory intended to show that these furious and ill-conditioned females did not escape punishment for their misdeeds; and that they were driven by society to pass the rest of their lives in woods and caverns.

FABLE II [XI.85-145]

Bacchus, having punished the Thracian women for the murder of Orpheus, leaves Thrace. His tutor, Silenus, having become intoxicated, loses his companions, and is brought by some Phrygian peasants to Midas. He sends him to Bacchus, on which the God, in acknowledgment of his kindness, promises him whatever favour he may desire. Midas asks to be able to turn everything that he touches into gold. This power is granted; but, soon convinced of his folly, Midas begs the God to deprive him of it, on which he is ordered to bathe in the river Pactolus. He obeys the God, and communicates the power which he possesses to the stream; from which time that river has golden sands.

And this is not enough for Bacchus. He resolves to forsake the country itself, and, with a superior train, he repairs to the vineyards of his own Tymolus, and Pactolus; although it was not golden at that time, nor to be coveted for its precious sands. The usual throng, both Satyrs and Bacchanals, surround him, but Silenus is away. The Phrygian rustics took him, as he was staggering with age and wine, and, bound with garlands, they led him to their king, Midas, to whom, together with the Cecropian Eumolpus,[8] the Thracian Orpheus had intrusted the mysterious orgies of Bacchus. Soon as he recognized this associate and companion of these rites, he hospitably kept a festival on the coming of this guest, for twice five days, and as many nights joined in succession.

"And now the eleventh Lucifer had closed the lofty host of the stars, when the king came rejoicing to the Lydian lands, and restored Silenus to the youth, his foster-child. To him the God, being glad at the recovery of his foster-father, gave the choice of desiring a favour, pleasing, indeed, but useless, as it turned out. He, destined to make a foolish use of the favour, says, 'Cause that whatever I shall touch with my body shall be turned into yellow gold.' Liber assents to his wish, and grants him the hurtful favour, and is grieved that he has not asked for something better. The Berecynthian hero[9] departs joyful, and rejoices in his own misfortune, and tries the truth of his promise by touching everything. And, hardly believing himself, he pulls down a twig from a holm-oak, growing on a bough not lofty; the twig becomes gold. He takes up a stone from the ground; the stone, too, turns pale with gold. He touches a clod, also; by his potent touch the clod becomes a mass of gold. He plucks some dry ears of corn, that wheat is golden. He holds an apple taken from a tree, you would suppose that the Hesperides had given it. If he places his fingers upon the lofty door-posts, then the posts are seen to glisten. When, too, he has washed his hands in the liquid stream, the water flowing from his hands might have deceived Danaë. He scarcely can contain his own hopes in his mind, imagining everything to be of gold. As he is thus rejoicing, his servants set before him a table supplied with dainties, and not deficient in parched corn. But then, whether he touches the gifts of Ceres with his right hand, the gifts of Ceres, as gold, become hard; or if he attempts to bite the dainties with hungry teeth, those dainties, upon the application of his teeth, shine as yellow plates of gold. Bacchus, the grantor of this favour, he mingles with pure water; you could see liquid gold flowing through his jaws.

"Astonished at the novelty of his misfortune, being both rich and wretched, he wishes to escape from his wealth, and now he hates what but so lately he has wished for; no plenty relieves his hunger, dry thirst parches his throat, and he is deservedly tormented by the now hated gold; and raising his hands towards heaven, and his shining arms, he says, "Grant me pardon, father Lenæus; I have done wrong, but have pity on me, I pray, and deliver me from this specious calamity!" Bacchus, the gentle Divinity among the Gods, restored him, as he confessed that he had done wrong, to his former state, and annulled his given promise, and the favour that was granted: "And that thou mayst not remain overlaid with thy gold, so unhappily desired, go," said he, "to the river adjoining to great Sardis,[10] and trace thy way, meeting the waters as they fall from the height of the mountain, until thou comest to the rise of the stream. And plunge thy head beneath the bubbling spring, where it bursts forth most abundantly, and at once purge thy body, at once thy crime." The king placed himself beneath the waters prescribed; the golden virtue tinged the river, and departed from the human body into the stream. And even now, the fields, receiving the ore of this ancient vein of gold, are hard, growing of pallid colour, from their clods imbibing the gold.

[Footnote 8: Eumolpus.—Ver. 93. There were three celebrated persons of antiquity named Eumolpus. The first was a Thracian, the son of Neptune and Chione, who lived in the time of Erectheus, king of Athens, against whom he led the people of Eleusis, and who established the Eleusinian mysteries. Some of his posterity settling at Athens, the Eumolpus here named was born there. He was the son of Musæus and the disciple of Orpheus. The third Eumolpus is supposed to have lived between the times of the two already named.]

[Footnote 9: Berecynthian hero.—Ver. 106. Midas is so called from mount Berecynthus in Phrygia.]

[Footnote 10: Sardis.—Ver. 137. The city of Sardis was the capital of Lydia, where Crœsus had his palace. The river Pactolus flowed through it.]

EXPLANATION

The ancients divided the Divinities into several classes, and in the last class, which Ovid calls the populace, or commonalty of the Gods, were the Satyrs and Sileni. The latter, according to Pausanias, were no other than Satyrs of advanced age. There seems, however, to have been one among them, to whom the name of Silenus was especially given, and to him the present story relates. According to Pindar and Pausanias he was born at Malea, in Laconia; while Theopompus, quoted by Ælian, represents him as being the son of a Nymph. He was inferior to the higher Divinities, but superior to man, in not being subject to mortality. He was represented as bald, flat-nosed, and red-faced, a perfect specimen of a drunken old man. He is often introduced either sitting on an ass, or reeling along on foot, with a thyrsus to support him.

He was said to have tended the education of the infant Bacchus, and indeed, according to the author whose works are quoted as those of Orpheus, he was an especial favourite of the Gods; while some writers represent him not as a drunken old man, but as a learned philosopher and a skilful commander. Lucian combines the two characters, and describes him as an aged man with large straight ears and a huge belly, wearing yellow clothes, and generally mounted on an ass, or supported by a staff, but, nevertheless, as being a skilful general. Hyginus says, that the Phrygian peasants found Midas near a fountain, into which, according to Xenophon, some one had put wine, which had made him drunk. In his interview with Midas, according to Theopompus, as quoted by Ælian, they had a conversation concerning that unknown region of the earth, to which Plato refers under the name of the New Atlantis, and which, after long employing the speculations of the ancient philosophers, was realized to the moderns in the discovery of America. The passage is sufficiently curious to deserve to be quoted. He says, "Asia, Europe, and Libya, are but three islands, surrounded by the ocean; but beyond that ocean there is a vast continent, whose bounds are entirely unknown to us. The men and the animals of that country are much larger, and live much longer than those of this part of the world. Their towns are fine and magnificent; their customs are different from ours; and they are governed by different laws. They have two cities, one of which is called 'the Warlike,' and the other 'the Devout.' The inhabitants of the first city are much given to warfare, and make continual attacks upon their neighbours, whom they bring under their subjection. Those who inhabit the other city are peaceable, and blessed with plenty; the earth without toil or tillage furnishing them with abundance of the necessaries of life. Except their sick, they all live in the midst of riches and continual festivity and pleasure; but they are so just and righteous that the Gods themselves delight to go frequently and pass their time among them.

"The warlike people of the first city having extended their conquests in their own vast continent, made an irruption into ours, with a million of men, as far as the country of the Hyperboreans; but when they saw their mode of living, they deemed them to be unworthy of their notice, and returned home. These warriors rarely die of sickness; they delight in warfare, and generally lose their lives in battle. There is also in this new world another numerous people called Meropes; and in their country is a place called 'Anostus,' that is to say, 'not to be repassed,' because no one ever comes back from thence. It is a dreadful abyss, having no other than a reddish sort of light. There are two rivers in that place; one called the River of Sorrow, and the other the River of Mirth. Trees as large as planes grow about these rivers. Those who eat of the fruit of the trees growing near the River of Sorrow, pass their lives in affliction, weeping continually, even to their last breath; but such as eat of the fruit of the other trees, forget the past, and revert through the different stages of their life, and then die."

Ælian regards the passage as a mere fable, and the latter part is clearly allegorical. The mention of the two cities, 'the Warlike' and 'the Devout,' can hardly fail to remind us of Japan, with its spiritual and temporal capitals.

Some writers say, that Silenus was the king of Caria, and was the contemporary and friend of Midas, to whom his counsel proved of considerable service, in governing his dominions. He was probably called the foster-father or tutor, of Bacchus, because he introduced his worship into Phrygia and the neighbouring countries.

FABLE III [XI.146-193]

Pan is so elated with the praises of some Nymphs who hear the music of his pipe, that he presumes to challenge Apollo to play with him. The mountain God, Tmolus, who is chosen umpire of the contest, decides in favour of Apollo, and the whole company approve of his judgment except Midas, who, for his stupidity in preferring Pan, receives a pair of asses' ears. He carefully conceals them till they are discovered by his barber, who publishes his deformity in a very singular manner.

He, abhorring riches, inhabited the woods and the fields, and followed Pan, who always dwells in caves of the mountains; but his obtuse understanding[11] still remained, and the impulse of his foolish mind was fated again, as before, to be an injury to its owner. For the lofty Tmolus, looking far and wide over the sea, stands erect, steep with its lofty ascent; and extending in its descent on either side, is bounded on the one side by Sardis, on the other by the little Hypæpæ.

While Pan is there boasting of his strains to the charming Nymphs, and is warbling a little tune upon the reeds joined with wax, daring to despise the playing of Apollo in comparison with his own, he comes to the unequal contest under the arbitration of Tmolus.[12] The aged umpire seats himself upon his own mountain, and frees his ears of the incumbering trees. His azure-coloured hair is only covered with oak, and acorns hang around his hollow temples. And looking at the God of the flocks, he says, "there is no delay in me, your umpire." He sounds his rustic reeds, and delights Midas with his uncouth music; for he, by chance, is present as he plays. After this the sacred Tmolus turns his face towards the countenance of Apollo; his words follow the direction of his face. He, having his yellow head wreathed with Parnassian laurel, sweeps the ground with his robe, soaked in Tyrian purple,[13] and supports with his left hand his lyre, adorned with gems and Indian ivory; the other hand holds the plectrum. The very posture is that of an artist. He then touches the strings with a skilful thumb; charmed by the sweetness of which, Tmolus bids Pan to hold his reeds in submission to the lyre; and the judgment and decision of the sacred mountain pleases them all. Yet it is blamed, and is called unjust by the voice of Midas alone. But the Delian God does not allow his stupid ears to retain their human shape: but draws them out to a great length, and he fills them with grey hairs, and makes them unsteady at the lower part, and gives them the power of moving. The rest of his body is that of a man; in one part alone is he condemned to punishment; and he assumes the ears of the slowly moving ass.

He, indeed, concealed them, and endeavoured to veil his temples, laden with this foul disgrace, with a purple turban. But a servant, who was wont to cut his hair, when long, with the steel scissars, saw it; who, when he did not dare disclose the disgraceful thing he had seen, though desirous to publish it, and yet could not keep it secret, retired, and dug up the ground, and disclosed, in a low voice, what kind of ears he had beheld on his master, and whispered it to the earth cast up. And then he buried this discovery of his voice with the earth thrown in again, and, having covered up the ditch, departed in silence.

There, a grove, thick set with quivering reeds, began to rise; and as soon as it came to maturity, after a complete year, it betrayed its planter. For, moved by the gentle South wind, it repeated the words there buried, and disclosed the ears of his master.

[Footnote 11: Obtuse understanding.—Ver. 148. 'Pingue sed ingenium mansit,' is rendered by Clarke, 'but he continued a blockhead still.']

[Footnote 12: Tmolus.—Ver. 156. This was the tutelary divinity of the mountain of Tmolus, or Tymolus.]

[Footnote 13: Soaked in Tyrian purple.—Ver. 166. Being saturated with Tyrian purple, the garment would be 'dibaphus,' or 'twice dipt;' being first dyed in the grain, and again when woven. Of course, these were the most valuable kind of cloths.]

EXPLANATION

Midas, according to Pausanias, was the son of Gordius and Cybele, and reigned in the Greater Phrygia. Strabo says that he and his father kept their court near the river Sangar, in cities which, in the time of that author had become mean villages. As Midas was very rich, and at the same time very frugal, it was reported that whatever he touched was at once turned into gold; and Bacchus was probably introduced into his story, because Midas had favoured the introduction of his worship, and was consequently supposed to have owed his success to the good offices of that Divinity. He was probably the first who extracted gold from the sands of the river Pactolus, and in that circumstance the story may have originated. Strabo says that Midas found the treasures which he possessed in the mines of Mount Bermius. It was said that in his infancy some ants were seen to creep into his cradle, and to put grains of wheat in his mouth, which was supposed to portend that he would be rich and frugal.

As he was very stupid and ignorant, the fable of his preference of the music of Pan to that of Apollo was invented, to which was added, perhaps, as a mark of his stupidity, that the God gave him a pair of asses' ears. The scholiast of Aristophanes, to explain the story, says either it was intended to shew that Midas, like the ass, was very quick of hearing, or in other words, had numerous spies in all parts of his dominions; or, it was invented, because his usual place of residence was called Onouta, ὄνου ὦτα, 'the ears of an ass.' Strabo says that he took a draught of warm bullock's blood, from the effects of which he died; and, according to Plutarch, he did so to deliver himself from the frightful dreams with which he was tormented.

Tmolus, the king of Lydia, according to Clitophon, was the son of Mars and the Nymph Theogene, or, according to Eustathius, of Sipylus and Eptonia. Having violated Arriphe, a Nymph of Diana, he was, as a punishment, tossed by a bull, and falling on some sharp pointed stakes, he lost his life, and was buried on the mountain that afterwards bore his name.

FABLE IV [XI.194-220]

Apollo and Neptune build the walls of Troy for king Laomedon, who refuses to give the Gods the reward which he has promised: on which Neptune punishes his perjury by an inundation of his country. Laomedon is then obliged to expose his daughter to a sea monster, in order to appease the God. Hercules delivers her; and Laomedon defrauds him likewise of the horses which he has promised him. In revenge, Hercules plunders the city of Troy, and carries off Hesione, whom he gives in marriage to his companion Telamon.

The son of Latona, having thus revenged himself, departs from Tmolus, and, borne through the liquid air, rests on the plains of Laomedon, on this side of the narrow sea of Helle, the daughter of Nephele. On the right hand of Sigæum and on the left of the lofty Rhœtæum,[14] there is an ancient altar dedicated to the Panomphæan[15] Thunderer. Thence, he sees Laomedon now first building the walls of rising Troy, and that this great undertaking is growing up with difficult labour, and requires no small resources. And then, with the trident-bearing father of the raging deep, he assumes a mortal form, and for the Phrygian king they build the walls,[16] a sum of gold being agreed on for the defences.

The work is now finished; the king refuses the reward, and, as a completion of his perfidy, adds perjury to his false words. "Thou shalt not escape unpunished," says the king of the sea; and he drives all his waters towards the shores of covetous Troy. He turns the land, too, into the form of the sea, and carries off the wealth of the husbandmen, and overwhelms the fields with waves. Nor is this punishment sufficient: the daughter of the king, is also demanded for a sea monster. Chained to the rugged rocks, Alcides delivers her, and demands the promised reward, the horses agreed upon; and the recompense of so great a service being denied him, he captures the twice-perjured walls of conquered Troy. Nor does Telamon, a sharer in the warfare, come off without honour; and he obtains Hesione, who is given to him.

But Peleus was distinguished by a Goddess for his wife; nor was he more proud of the name of his grandfather than that of his father-in-law.[17] Since, not to his lot alone did it fall to be the grandson of Jove; to him alone, was a Goddess given for a wife.

[Footnote 14: Rhœtæum.—Ver. 197. Sigæum and Rhœtæum were two promontories, near Troy, between which was an altar dedicated to Jupiter Panomphæus.]

[Footnote 15: Panomphæan.—Ver. 198. Jupiter had the title 'Panomphæus,' from πᾶν, 'all,' and ὀμφή, 'the voice,' either because he was worshipped by the voices of all, or because he was the author of all prophecy.]

[Footnote 16: Build the walls.—Ver. 204. It has been suggested that the story of Laomedon obtaining the aid of Neptune in building the walls of Troy, only meant that he built it of bricks made of clay mixed with water, and dried in the sun.]

[Footnote 17: His father-in-law.—Ver. 219. Nereus, the father of Thetis; was a Divinity of the sea, and was gifted with the power of prophecy.]

EXPLANATION

Laomedon, being King of Troy, and the city being open and defenceless, he undertook to enclose it with walls, and succeeded so well, that the work was attributed to Apollo. The strong banks which he was obliged to raise to keep out the sea and to prevent inundations, were regarded as the work of Neptune. In time, these banks being broken down by tempests, it was reported that the God of the sea had thus revenged himself on Laomedon, for refusing him the reward which had been agreed upon between them. This story received the more ready credit from the circumstance mentioned by Herodotus and Eustathius, that this king used the treasure belonging to the temple of Neptune, in raising these embankments, and building the walls of his city; having promised the priests to restore it when he should be in a condition to do so; which promise he never performed. Homer says that Neptune and Apollo tended the flocks while all the subjects of Laomedon were engaged in building the walls.

When these embankments were laid under water, and a plague began to rage within the city, the Trojans were told by an oracle that to appease the God of the sea, they must sacrifice a virgin of the royal blood. The lot fell upon Hesione, and she was exposed to the fury of a sea-monster. Hercules offered to deliver her for a reward of six horses, and having succeeded, was refused his recompense by Laomedon; whom he slew, and then plundered his city. He then gave the kingdom to Podarces, the son of Laomedon, and Hesione to his companion Telamon, who had assisted him. This monster was probably an allegorical representation of the inundations of the sea; and Hesione having been made the price of him that could succeed in devising a remedy, she was said to have been exposed to the fury of a monster. The six horses promised by Laomedon were perhaps so many ships, which Hercules demanded for his recompense; and this is the more likely, as the ancients said that these horses were so light and swift, that they ran upon the waves, which story seems to point at the qualities of a galley or ship under sail.

Lycophron gives a more wonderful version of the story. He says that the monster, to which Hesione was exposed, devoured Hercules, and that he was three days in its belly, and came out, having lost all his hair. This is, probably, a way of telling us that Hercules and his assistants were obliged to work in the water, which incommoded them very much. Palæphatus gives another explanation: he says that Hesione was about to be delivered up to a pirate, and that Hercules, on boarding his ship, was wounded, although afterwards victorious.

FABLES V AND VI [XI.221-409]

Proteus foretells that Thetis shall have a son, who shall be more powerful than his father, and shall exceed him in valour. Jupiter, who is in love with Thetis, is alarmed at this prediction, and yields her to Peleus. The Goddess flies from his advances by assuming various shapes, till, by the advice of Proteus, he holds her fast, and then having married her, she bears Achilles. Peleus goes afterwards to Ceyx, king of Trachyn, to expiate the death of his brother Phocus, whom he has killed. Ceyx is in a profound melancholy, and tells him how his brother Dædalion, in the transports of his grief for his daughter Chione, who had been slain for vying with Diana, has been transformed into a hawk. During this relation, Peleus is informed that a wolf which Psamathe has sent to revenge the death of Phocus, is destroying his herds. He endeavours to avert the wrath of the Goddess, but she is deaf to his entreaties, till, by the intercession of Thetis, she is appeased, and she turns the wolf into stone.

For the aged Proteus had said to Thetis, "Goddess of the waves, conceive; thou shalt be the mother of a youth, who by his gallant actions shall surpass the deeds of his father, and shall be called greater than he." Therefore, lest the world might contain something greater than Jove, although he had felt no gentle flame in his breast, Jupiter avoided the embraces of Thetis,[18] the Goddess of the sea, and commanded his grandson, the son of Æacus,[19] to succeed to his own pretensions, and rush into the embraces of the ocean maid. There is a bay of Hæmonia, curved into a bending arch; its arms project out; there, were the water but deeper, there would be a harbour, but the sea is just covering the surface of the sand. It has a firm shore, which retains not the impression of the foot, nor delays the step of the traveller, nor is covered with sea-weeds. There is a grove of myrtle at hand, planted with particoloured berries. In the middle there is a cave, whether formed by nature or art, it is doubtful; still, by art rather.

To this, Thetis, thou wast wont often to come naked, seated on thy harnessed dolphin. There Peleus seized upon thee, as thou wast lying fast bound in sleep; and because, being tried by entreaties, thou didst resist, he resolved upon violence, clasping thy neck with both his arms. And, unless thou hadst had recourse to thy wonted arts, by frequently changing thy shape, he would have succeeded in his attempt. But, at one moment, thou wast a bird (still, as a bird he held thee fast); at another time a large tree: to that tree did Peleus cling. Thy third form was that of a spotted tiger; frightened by that, the son of Æacus loosened his arms from thy body.

Then pouring wine upon its waters,[20] he worshipped the Gods of the sea, both with the entrails of sheep and with the smoke of frankincense; until the Carpathian[21] prophet said, from the middle of the waves, "Son of Æacus, thou shalt gain the alliance desired by thee. Do thou only, when she shall be resting fast asleep in the cool cave, bind her unawares with cords and tenacious bonds. And let her not deceive thee, by imitating a hundred forms; but hold her fast, whatever she shall be, until she shall reassume the form which she had before." Proteus said this, and hid his face in the sea, and received his own waves at his closing words. Titan was now descending, and, with the pole of his chariot bent downward, was taking possession of the Hesperian main; when the beautiful Nereid, leaving the deep, entered her wonted place of repose. Hardly had Peleus well seized the virgin's limbs, when she changed her shape, until she perceived her limbs to be held fast, and her arms to be extended different ways. Then, at last, she sighed, and said, "Not without the aid of a Divinity, dost thou overcome me;" and then she appeared as Thetis again. The hero embraced her thus revealed, and enjoyed his wish, and by her was the father of great Achilles.

And happy was Peleus in his son, happy, too, in his wife, and one to whose lot all blessings had fallen, if you except the crime of his killing Phocus. The Trachinian land[22] received him guilty of his brother's blood, and banished from his native home. Here Ceyx, sprung from Lucifer for his father, and having the comeliness of his sire in his face, held the sway without violence and without bloodshed, who, being sad at that time and unlike his former self, lamented the loss of his brother. After the son of Æacus, wearied, both with troubles and the length of the journey, has arrived there, and has entered the city with a few attending him, and has left the flocks of sheep and the herds which he has brought with him, not far from the walls, in a shady valley; when an opportunity is first afforded him of approaching the prince, extending the symbols of peace[23] with his suppliant hand, he tells him who he is, and from whom descended. He only conceals his crime, and, dissembling as to the true reason of his banishment, he entreats him to aid him by a reception either in his city or in his territory. On the other hand, the Trachinian prince addresses him with gentle lips, in words such as these: "Peleus, our bounties are open even to the lowest ranks, nor do I hold an inhospitable sway. To this my inclination, thou bringest in addition as powerful inducements, an illustrious name, and Jupiter as thy grandsire. And do not lose thy time in entreaty; all that thou askest thou shalt have. Look upon all these things, whatever thou seest, as in part thy own: would that thou couldst behold them in better condition!" and then he weeps. Pelcus and his companions enquire what it is that occasions grief so great. To them he thus speaks:—

"Perhaps you may think that this bird, which lives upon prey, and affrights all the birds, always had wings. It was a man; and as great is the vigour of its courage, as he who was Dædalion by name was active, and bold in war, and ready for violence; he was sprung from him, for his father, who summons forth[24] Aurora, and withdraws the last from the heavens. Peace was cherished by me; the care of maintaining peace and my marriage contract was mine; cruel warfare pleased my brother; that prowess of his subdued both kings and nations, which, changed, now chases the Thisbean doves.[25] Chione was his daughter, who, highly endowed with beauty, was pleasing to a thousand suitors, when marriageable at the age of twice seven years. By chance Phœbus, and the son of Maia, returning, the one from his own Delphi, the other from the heights of Cyllene, beheld her at the same moment, and at the same moment were inspired with passion. Apollo defers his hope of enjoyment until the hours of night; the other brooks no delay, and with his wand, that causes sleep, touches the maiden's face. At the potent touch she lies entranced, and suffers violence from the God. Night has now bespangled the heavens with stars; Phœbus personates an old woman, and takes those delights before enjoyed in imagination. When her mature womb had completed the destined time, Autolycus was born, a crafty offspring of the stock of the God with winged feet, ingenious at every kind of theft, and who used, not degenerating from his father's skill,[26] to make white out of black, and black out of white. From Phœbus was born (for she brought forth twins) Philammon, famous for his tuneful song, and for his lyre.

"But what avails it for her to have brought forth two children, and to have been pleasing to two Gods, and to have sprung from a valiant father, and the Thunderer as her ancestor?[27] Is even glory thus prejudicial to many? To her, at least, it was a prejudice; who dared to prefer herself to Diana, and decried the charms of the Goddess. But violent wrath was excited in her, and she said, 'We will please her by our deeds.'[28] And there was no delay: she bent her bow, and let fly an arrow from the string, and pierced with the reed the tongue that deserved it. The tongue was silent; nor did her voice, and the words which she attempted to utter, now follow; and life, with her blood, left her, as she endeavoured to speak. Oh hapless affection! What pain did I then endure in my heart, as her uncle, and what consolations did I give to my affectionate brother? These the father received no otherwise than rocks do the murmurs of the ocean, and he bitterly lamented his daughter thus snatched from him. But when he beheld her burning, four times had he an impulse to rush into the midst of the pile; thence repulsed, four times did he commit his swift limbs to flight, and, like an ox, bearing upon his galled neck the stings of hornets, he rushed where there was no path. Already did he seem to me to run faster than a human being, and you would have supposed that his feet had assumed wings. Therefore he outran all; and, made swift by the desire for death, he gained the heights of Parnassus.

"Apollo pitying him, when Dædalion would have thrown himself from the top of the rock, made him into a bird, and supported him, hovering in the air upon these sudden wings; and he gave him a curved beak, and crooked claws on his talons, his former courage, and strength greater in proportion than his body; and, now become a hawk, sufficiently benignant to none, he rages equally against all birds; and grieving himself, becomes the cause of grief to others."

While the son of Lucifer is relating these wonders about his brother, hastening with panting speed, Phocæan Antenor, the keeper of his herds, runs up to him. "Alas, Peleus! Peleus!" says he, "I am the messenger to thee of a great calamity;" and then Peleus bids him declare whatever news it is that he has brought; and the Trachinian hero himself is in suspense, and trembles through apprehension. The other tells his story: "I had driven the weary bullocks to the winding shore, when the Sun at his height, in the midst of his course, could look back on as much of it as he could see to be now remaining; and a part of the oxen had bent their knees on the yellow sands, and, as they lay, viewed the expanse of the wide waters; some, with slow steps, were wandering here and there; others were swimming, and appearing with their lofty necks above the waves. A temple is hard by the sea, adorned neither with marble nor with gold, but made of solid beams, and shaded with an ancient grove; the Nereids and Nereus possess it. A sailor, while he was drying his nets upon the shore, told us that these were the Gods of the temple. Adjacent to this is a marsh, planted thickly with numerous willows, which the water of the stagnating waves of the sea has made into a swamp. From that spot, a huge monster, a wolf, roaring with a loud bellowing, alarms the neighbouring places, and comes forth from the thicket of the marsh, both having his thundering jaws covered with foam and with clotted blood, and his eyes suffused with red flame. Though he was raging both with fury and with hunger, still was he more excited by fury; for he did not care to satisfy his hunger by the slaughter of the oxen, and to satiate his dreadful appetite, but he mangled the whole herd, and, like a true foe, pulled each to the ground. Some, too, of ourselves, while we were defending them, wounded with his fatal bite, were killed. The shore and the nearest waves were red with blood, and the fens were filled with the lowings of the herd. But delay is dangerous, and the case does not allow us to hesitate: while anything is still left, let us all unite, and let us take up arms, arms, I say, and in a body let us bear weapons."

Thus speaks the countryman. And the loss does not affect Peleus; but, remembering his crime, he considers that the bereaved Nereid has sent these misfortunes of his, as an offering to the departed Phocus. The Œtæan king[29] commands his men to put on their armour, and to take up stout weapons; together with whom, he himself is preparing to go. But Halcyone, his wife, alarmed at the tumult, runs out, and not yet having arranged all her hair, even that which is arranged she throws in disorder; and clinging to the neck of her husband, she entreats him, both with words and tears, to send assistance without himself, and so to save two lives in one. The son of Æacus says to her, "O queen, lay aside thy commendable and affectionate fears; the kindness of thy proposal is too great for me. It does not please me, that arms should be employed against this new monster. The Divinity of the sea must be adored." There is a lofty tower; a fire is upon the extreme summit,[30] a place grateful to wearied ships. They go up there, and with sighs they behold the bulls lying scattered upon the sea shore, and the cruel ravager with blood-stained mouth, having his long hair stained with gore. Peleus, thence extending his hands towards the open sea, entreats the azure Psamathe to lay aside her wrath, and to give him her aid. But she is not moved by the words of the son of Æacus, thus entreating. Thetis, interceding on behalf of her husband, obtains that favour for him.

But still the wolf persists, not recalled from the furious slaughter, and keenly urged by the sweetness of the blood; until she changes him into marble, as he is fastening on the neck of a mangled heifer. His body preserves every thing except its colour. The colour of the stone shows that he is not now a wolf, and ought not now to be feared. Still, the Fates do not permit the banished Peleus to settle in this land: the wandering exile goes to the Magnetes,[31] and there receives from the Hæmonian Acastus[32] an expiation of the murder.

[Footnote 18: Embraces of Thetis.—Ver. 226. Fulgentius suggests, that the meaning of this is, that Jupiter, or fire, will not unite with Thetis, who represents water.]

[Footnote 19: Son of Æacus.—Ver. 227. Peleus was the son of Æacus, who was the son of Jupiter, by Ægina, the daughter of Æsopus.]

[Footnote 20: Upon its waters.—Ver. 247. While libations were made to the other Divinities, either on their altars, or on the ground, the marine Deities were so honoured by pouring wine on the waves of the sea.]

[Footnote 21: Carpathian.—Ver. 249. The Carpathian sea was so called from the Isle of Carpathus, which lay between the island of Rhodes and the Egyptian coast.]

[Footnote 22: Trachinian land.—Ver. 269. Apollodorus says, that Peleus, when exiled, repaired to Phthia, and not to the city of Trachyn.]

[Footnote 23: Symbols of peace.—Ver. 276. The 'velamenta' were branches of olive, surrounded with bandages of wool, which were held in the hands of those who begged for mercy or pardon. The wool *covering the hand was emblematical of peace, the hand being thereby rendered powerless to effect mischief.]*

[Footnote 24: Who summons forth.—Ver. 296. This is a periphrasis for Lucifer, or the Morning Star, which precedes, and appears to summon the dawn.]

[Footnote 25: Thisbean doves.—Ver. 300. Thisbe was a town of Bœotia, so called from Thisbe, the daughter of Æsopus. It was famous for the number of doves which it produced.]

[Footnote 26: Father's skill.—Ver. 314. Being the son of Mercury, who was noted for his thieving propensities.]

[Footnote 27: Her ancestor.—Ver. 319. Jupiter was the great-grandfather of Chione, being the father of Lucifer, and the grandfather of Dædalion.]

[Footnote 28: By our deeds.—Ver. 323. This is said sarcastically, as much as to say, 'If I do not please her by my looks, at least I will by my actions.']

[Footnote 29: The Œtæan king.—Ver. 383. Namely, Ceyx, the king of Trachyn, which city Hercules had founded, at the foot of Mount Œta.]

[Footnote 30: The extreme summit.—Ver. 393. The upper stories of the ancient light-houses had windows looking towards the sea; and torches, or fires (probably in cressets, or fire-pans, at the end of poles), were kept burning on them by night, to guide vessels. 'Pharos,' or 'Pharus,' the name given to light-houses, is derived from the celebrated one built on the island of Pharos, at the entrance of the port of Alexandria. It was erected by Sostratus, of Cnidos, at the expense of one of the Ptolemies, and cost 800 talents. It was of huge dimensions, square, and constructed of white stone. It contained many stories, and diminished in width from below upwards. There were 'phari,' or 'light-houses,' at Ostia, Ravenna, Capreæ, and Brundisium.]

[Footnote 31: The Magnetes.—Ver. 408. The Magnetes were the people of Magnesia, a district of Thessaly. They were famed for their skill in horsemanship.]

[Footnote 32: Hæmonian Acastus.—Ver. 409. Acastus was the son of Pelias. His wife Hippolyta, being enamoured of Peleus, and he not encouraging her advances, she accused him of having made an attempt on her virtue. On this, Acastus determined upon his death; and having taken him to Mount Pelion, on the pretext of hunting, he took away his arms, and left him there, to be torn to pieces by the wild beasts. Mercury, or, according to some, Chiron, came to his assistance, and gave him a sword made by Vulcan, with which he slew Acastus and his wife.]

EXPLANATION

Thetis being a woman of extraordinary beauty, it is not improbable, that in the Epithalamia that were composed on her marriage, it was asserted, that the Gods had contended for her hand, and had been forced to give way, in obedience to the superior power of destiny. Hyginus says that Prometheus was the only person that was acquainted with the oracle; and that he imparted it to Jupiter, on condition that he would deliver him from the eagle that tormented him: whereupon the God sent Hercules to Mount Caucasus, to perform his promise. It was on the occasion of this marriage that the Goddess Discord presented the golden apple, the dispute for which occasioned the Trojan war. The part of the story which relates how she assumed various forms, to avoid the advances of Peleus, is perhaps an ingenious method of stating, that having several suitors, she was originally disinclined to Peleus, and used every pretext to avoid him, until, by the advice of a wise friend, he found means to remove all the difficulties which opposed his alliance with her.

Some writers state that Thetis was the daughter of Chiron; but Euripides, in a fragment of his Iphigenia, tells us that Achilles, who was the son of this marriage, took a pride in carrying the figure of a Nereid on his shield. The three sons of Æacus were Peleus, Telamon, and Phocus; while they were playing at quoits, the latter accidentally received a blow from Peleus, which killed him. Ovid, however, seems here to imply that Peleus killed his brother purposely.

The story of Chione most probably took its rise from the difference between the inclinations of the two children that she bore. Autolycus, being cunning, and addicted to theft, he was styled the son of Mercury; while Philammon being a lover of music, Apollo was said to be his father. According to Pausanias, Autolycus was the son of Dædalion, and not of Chione. The story of the wolf, the minister of the vengeance of Psamathe, for the death of Phocus, is probably built on historical grounds. Æacus had two wives, Ægina and Psamathe, the sister of Thetis; by the first he had Peleus and Telamon; by the second, Phocus. Lycomedes, the king of Scyros, the brother of Psamathe, resolved to revenge the death of his nephew, whom Peleus had killed: and declared war against Ceyx, for receiving him into his dominions. The troops of Lycomedes ravaged the country, and carried away the flocks of Peleus: on which prayers and entreaties were resorted to, with the view of pacifying him; which object having been effected, he withdrew his troops. On this, it was rumoured that he was changed into a rock, after having ravaged the country like a wild beast, which comparison was perhaps suggested by the fact of his name being partly compounded of the word λυκὸς, 'a wolf.'

FABLE VII [XI.410-748]

Ceyx, going to Claros, to consult the oracle about his brother's fate, is shipwrecked on the voyage. Juno sends Iris to the God of Sleep, who, at her request, dispatches Morpheus to Halcyone, in a dream, to inform her of the death of her husband. She awakes in the morning, full of solicitude, and goes to the shore where she finds the body of Ceyx thrown up by the waves. She is about to cast herself into the sea in despair, when the Gods transform them both into king-fishers.

In the mean time, Ceyx being disturbed in mind, both on account of the strange fate of his brother, and the wonders that had succeeded his brother, prepares to go to the Clarian God, that he may consult the sacred oracle, the consolation of mortals: for the profane Phorbas,[33] with his Phlegyans, renders the oracle of Delphi inaccessible. Yet he first makes thee acquainted with his design, most faithful Halcyone, whose bones receive a chill, and a paleness, much resembling boxwood, comes over her face, and her cheeks are wet with tears gushing forth. Three times attempting to speak, three times she moistens her face with tears, and, sobs interrupting her affectionate complaints, she says:—

"What fault of mine, my dearest, has changed thy mind? Where is that care of me, which once used to exist? Canst thou now be absent without anxiety, thy Halcyone being left behind? Now, is a long journey pleasing to thee? Now, am I dearer to thee when at a distance? But I suppose thy journey is by land, and I shall only grieve, and shall not fear as well, and my anxiety will be free from apprehension. The seas and the aspect of the stormy ocean affright me. And lately I beheld broken planks on the sea shore; and often have I read the names upon tombs,[34] without bodies there buried. And let not any deceitful assurance influence thy mind, that the grandson of Hippotas[35] is thy father-in-law; who confines the strong winds in prison, and assuages the seas when he pleases. When, once let loose, the winds have taken possession of the deep, nothing is forbidden to them; every land and every sea is disregarded by them. Even the clouds of heaven do they insult, and by their bold onsets strike forth the brilliant fires.[36] The more I know them, (for I do know them, and, when little, have often seen them in my father's abode,) the more I think they are to be dreaded. But if thy resolution, my dear husband, cannot be altered by my entreaties, and if thou art but too determined to go; take me, too, as well. At least, we shall be tossed together; nor shall I fear anything, but what I shall be then suffering; and together we shall endure whatever shall happen; together we shall be carried over the wide seas."

By such words and the tears of the daughter of Æolus, is her husband, son of the Morning Star, much affected; for the flame of love exists no less in him. But he neither wishes to abandon his proposed voyage, nor to admit Halcyone to a share in the danger; and he says, in answer, many things to console her timorous breast. And yet she does not, on that account, approve of his reasons. To them he adds this alleviation, with which alone he influences his affectionate wife: "All delay will, indeed, be tedious to me; but I swear to thee by the fire of my sire, (if only the fates allow me to return,) that I will come back before the moon has twice completed her orb." When, by these promises, a hope has been given her of his speedy return, he forthwith orders a ship, drawn out of the dock, to be launched in the sea, and to be supplied with its proper equipments. On seeing this, Halcyone again shuddered, as though presaging the future, and shed her flowing tears, and gave him embraces; and at last, in extreme misery, she said, with a sad voice, "Farewell!" and then she sank with all her body to the ground.

But the youths, while Ceyx is still seeking pretexts for delay, in double rows,[37] draw the oars towards their hardy breasts, and cleave the main with equal strokes. She raises her weeping eyes, and sees her husband standing on the crooked stern, and by waving his hand making the first signs to her; and she returns the signals. When the land has receded further, and her eyes are unable to distinguish his countenance: still, while she can, she follows the retreating ship with her sight. When this too, borne onward, cannot be distinguished from the distance; still she looks at the sails waving from the top of the mast. When she no longer sees the sails; she anxiously seeks her deserted bed, and lays herself on the couch. The bed, and the spot, renew the tears of Halcyone, and remind her what part of herself is wanting.

They have now gone out of harbour, and the breeze shakes the rigging; the sailor urges the pendent oars towards their sides;[38] and fixes the sailyards[39] on the top of the mast, and spreads the canvass full from the mast, and catches the coming breezes. Either the smaller part, or, at least, not more than half her course, had now been cut by the ship, and both lands were at a great distance, when, towards night, the sea began to grow white with swelling waves, and the boisterous East wind to blow with greater violence. Presently the master cries, "At once, lower the top sails, and furl the whole of the sail to the yards!" He orders, but the adverse storm impedes the execution; and the roaring of the sea does not allow any voice to be heard.

Yet, of their own accord, some hasten to draw in the oars, some to secure the sides, some to withdraw the sails from the winds. This one pumps up the waves, and pours back the sea into the sea; another takes off the yards. While these things are being done without any order, the raging storm is increasing, and the fierce winds wage war on every side, and stir up the furious main. The master of the ship is himself alarmed, and himself confesses that he does not know what is their present condition, nor what to order or forbid; so great is the amount of their misfortunes, and more powerful than all his skill. For the men are making a noise with their shouts, the cordage with its rattling, the heavy waves with the dashing of other waves, the skies with the thunder. The sea is upturned with billows, and appears to reach the heavens, and to sprinkle the surrounding clouds with its foam. And one while, when it turns up the yellow sands from the bottom, it is of the same colour with them; at another time it is blacker than the Stygian waves. Sometimes it is level, and is white with resounding foam. The Trachinian ship too, is influenced by these vicissitudes; and now aloft, as though from the summit of a mountain, it seems to look down upon the vallies and the depths of Acheron; at another moment, when the engulphing sea has surrounded it, sunk below, it seems to be looking at heaven above from the infernal waters. Struck on its side by the waves, it often sends forth a low crashing sound, and beaten against, it sounds with no less noise, than on an occasion when the iron battering ram, or the balista, is shaking the shattered towers. And as fierce lions are wont, gaining strength in their career, to rush with their breasts upon the weapons, and arms extended against them; so the water, when upon the rising of the winds it had rushed onwards, advanced against the rigging of the ship, and was much higher than it.

And now the bolts shrink, and despoiled of their covering of wax,[40] the seams open wide, and afford a passage to the fatal waves. Behold! vast showers fall from the dissolving clouds, and you would believe that the whole of the heavens is descending into the deep, and that the swelling sea is ascending to the tracts of heaven. The sails are wet with the rain, and the waves of the ocean are mingled with the waters of the skies. The firmament is without its fires; and the gloomy night is oppressed both with its own darkness and that of the storm. Yet the lightnings disperse these, and give light as they flash; the waters are on fire with the flames of the thunder-bolts. And now, too, the waves make an inroad into the hollow texture of the ship; and as a soldier, superior to all the rest of the number, after he has often sprung forward against the fortifications of a defended city, at length gains his desires; and, inflamed with the desire of glory, though but one among a thousand more, he still mounts the wall, so, when the violent waves have beaten against the lofty sides, the fury of the tenth wave,[41] rising more impetuously than the rest, rushes onward; and it ceases not to attack the wearied ship, before it descends within the walls, as it were, of the captured bark. Part, then, of the sea is still attempting to get into the ship, part is within it. All are now in alarm, with no less intensity than a city is wont to be alarmed, while some are undermining the walls without, and others within have possession of the walls. All art fails them, and their courage sinks; and as many shapes of death seem to rush and to break in upon them, as the waves that approach. One does not refrain from tears; another is stupefied; another calls those happy[42] whom funeral rites await; another, in his prayers, addresses the Gods, and lifting up his hands in vain to that heaven which he sees not, implores their aid. His brothers and his parent recur to the mind of another; to another, his home, with his pledges of affection, and so what has been left behind by each.

The remembrance of Halcyone affects Ceyx; on the lips of Ceyx there is nothing but Halcyone; and though her alone he regrets, still he rejoices that she is absent. Gladly, too, would he look back to the shore of his native land, and turn his last glance towards his home; but he knows not where it is. The sea is raging in a hurricane[43] so vast, and all the sky is concealed beneath the shade brought on by the clouds of pitchy darkness, and the face of the night is redoubled in gloom. The mast is broken by the violence of the drenching tempest; the helm, too, is broken; and the undaunted wave, standing over its spoil, looks down like a conqueror, upon the waves as they encircle below. Nor, when precipitated, does it rush down less violently, than if any God were to hurl Athos or Pindus, torn up from its foundations, into the open sea; and with its weight and its violence together, it sinks the ship to the bottom. With her, a great part of the crew overwhelmed in the deep water, and not rising again to the air, meet their fate. Some seize hold of portions and broken pieces of the ship. Ceyx himself seizes a fragment of the wreck, with that hand with which he was wont to wield the sceptre, and in vain, alas! he invokes his father, and his father-in-law. But chiefly on his lips, as he swims, is his wife Halcyone. Her he thinks of, and her name he repeats: he prays the waves to impel his body before her eyes; and that when dead he may be entombed by the hands of his friends. While he still swims, he calls upon Halcyone far away, as often as the billows allow[44] him to open his mouth, and in the very waves he murmurs her name. When, lo! a darkening arch[45] of waters breaks over the middle of the waves, and buries his head sinking beneath the bursting billow. Lucifer was obscured that night, and such that you could not have recognized him; and since he was not allowed to depart from the heavens,[46] he concealed his face beneath thick clouds.

In the meantime, the daughter of Æolus, ignorant of so great misfortunes, reckons the nights; and now she hastens to prepare the garments[47] for him to put on, and now, those which, when he comes, she herself may wear, and vainly promises herself his return. She, indeed, piously offers frankincense to all the Gods above; but, before all, she pays her adorations at the temple of Juno, and comes to the altars on behalf of her husband, who is not in existence. And she prays that her husband may be safe, and that he may return, and may prefer no woman before her. But this last alone can be her lot, out of so many of her wishes. But the Goddess endures not any longer to be supplicated on behalf of one who is dead; and, that she may repel her polluted hands[48] from the altars,—she says, "Iris, most faithful messenger of my words, hasten quickly to the soporiferous court of Sleep, and command him, under the form of Ceyx who is dead, to send a vision to Halcyone, to relate her real misfortune." Thus she says. Iris assumes garment of a thousand colours, and, marking the heavens with her curving arch, she repairs to the abode of the king, Sleep, as bidden, concealed beneath a rock.

There is near the Cimmerians[49] a cave with a long recess, a hollowed mountain, the home and the habitation of slothful Sleep, into which the Sun, whether rising, or in his mid course, or setting, can never come. Fogs mingled with darkness are exhaled from the ground, and it is a twilight with a dubious light. No wakeful bird, with the notes of his crested features, there calls forth the morn; nor do the watchful dogs, or the geese more sagacious[50] than the dogs, break the silence with their voices. No wild beasts, no cattle, no boughs waving with the breeze, no loud outbursts of the human voice, there make any sound; mute Rest has there her abode. But from the bottom of the rock runs a stream, the waters of Lethe,[51] through which the rivulet, trickling with a murmuring noise amid the sounding pebbles, invites sleep. Before the doors of the cavern, poppies bloom in abundance, and innumerable herbs, from the juice of which the humid night gathers sleep, and spreads it over the darkened Earth. There is no door in the whole dwelling, to make a noise by the turning of the hinges; no porter at the entrance. But in the middle is a couch, raised high upon black ebony, stuffed with feathers, of a dark colour, concealed by a dark coverlet; on which the God himself lies, his limbs dissolved in sloth. Around him lie, in every direction, imitating divers shapes, unsubstantial dreams as many as the harvest bears ears of corn, the wood green leaves, the shore the sands thrown up. Into this, soon as the maiden had entered, and had put aside with her hands the visions that were in her way, the sacred house shone with the splendour of her garment, and the God, with difficulty lifting up his eyes sunk in languid sloth, again and again relapsing, and striking the upper part of his breast with his nodding chin, at last aroused himself from his dozing; and, raised on his elbow, he inquired why she had come; for he knew who she was.

But she replied, "Sleep, thou repose of all things; Sleep, thou gentlest of the Deities; thou peace of the mind, from which care flies, who dost soothe the hearts of men, wearied with the toils of the day, and refittest them for labour, command a vision, that resembles in similitude the real shape, to go to Halcyone, in Herculean Trachyn, in the form of the king, and to assume the form of one that has suffered shipwreck. Juno commands this." After Iris had executed her commission, she departed; for she could no longer endure the effects of the vapour; and, as soon as she perceived sleep creeping over her limbs, she took to flight,[52] and departed along the bow by which she had come just before.

But Father Sleep, out of the multitude of his thousand sons, raises Morpheus,[53] a skilful artist, and an imitator of any human shape. No one more dexterously than he mimics the gait, and the countenance, and the mode of speaking; he adds the dress, too, and the words most commonly used by any one. But he imitates men only; for another one becomes a wild beast, becomes a bird, or becomes a serpent, with its lengthened body: this one, the Gods above call Icelos; the tribe of mortals, Phobetor. There is likewise a third, master of a different art, called Phantasos: he cleverly changes himself into earth, and stone, and water, and a tree, and all those things which are destitute of life. These are wont, by night, to show their features to kings and to generals, while others wander amid the people and the commonalty. These, Sleep, the aged God, passes by, and selects Morpheus alone from all his brothers, to execute the commands of the daughter of Thaumas; and again he both drops his head, sunk in languid drowsiness, and shrinks back within the lofty couch.

Morpheus flies through the dark with wings that make no noise, and in a short space of intervening time arrives at the Hæmonian city; and, laying aside his wings from off his body, he assumes the form of Ceyx; and in that form, wan, and like one without blood, without garments, he stands before the bed of his wretched wife. The beard of the hero appears to be dripping, and the water to be falling thickly from his soaking hair. Then leaning on the bed, with tears running down his face, he says these words: "My most wretched wife, dost thou recognise thy Ceyx, or are my looks so changed with death? Observe me; thou wilt surely know me: and, instead of thy husband, thou wilt find the ghost of thy husband. Thy prayers, Halcyone, have availed me nothing; I have perished. Do not promise thyself, thus deceived, my return. The cloudy South wind caught my ship in the Ægean Sea,[54] and dashed it to pieces, tossed by the mighty blasts; and the waves choked my utterance, in vain calling upon thy name. It is no untruthful messenger that tells thee this: thou dost not hear these things through vague rumours. I, myself, shipwrecked, in person, am telling thee my fate. Come, arise then, shed tears, and put on mourning; and do not send me unlamented to the phantom realms of Tartarus."

To these words Morpheus adds a voice, which she may believe to be that of her husband. He seems, too, to be shedding real tears, and his hands have the gesture of Ceyx. As she weeps, Halcyone groans aloud, and moves her arms in her sleep, and catching at his body, grasps the air; and she cries aloud, "Stay, whither dost thou hurry? We will go together." Disturbed by her own voice, and by the appearance of her husband, she shakes off sleep; and first she looks about there, to see if he, who has been so lately seen, is there; for the servants, roused by her voice, have brought in lights. After she has found him nowhere, she smites her face with her hands, and tears her garments from off her breast, and beats her breast itself. Nor cares she to loosen her hair; she tears it, and says to her nurse, as she inquires what is the occasion of her sorrow: "Halcyone is no more! no more! with her own Ceyx is she dead. Away with words of comfort. He has perished by shipwreck. I have seen him, and I knew him; and as he departed, desirous to detain him, I extended my hands towards him. The ghost fled: but, yet it was the undoubted and the real ghost of my husband. It had not, indeed, if thou askest me that, his wonted features; nor was he looking cheerful with his former countenance. Hapless, I beheld him, pale, and naked, and with his hair still dripping. Lo! ill-fated man, he stood on this very spot;" and she seeks the prints of his footsteps, if any are left. "This it was, this is what I dreaded in my ill-boding mind, and I entreated that thou wouldst not, deserting me, follow the winds. But, I could have wished, since thou didst depart to perish, that, at least, thou hadst taken me as well. To have gone with thee, yes, with thee, would have been an advantage to me; for then neither should I have spent any part of my life otherwise than together with thee, nor would my death have been divided from thee. Now, absent from thee, I perish; now, absent, I am tossed on the waves; and the sea has thee without me.

"My heart were more cruel than the sea itself, were I to strive to protract my life any further; and, were I to struggle to survive so great a misfortune. But I will not struggle, nor, hapless one, will I abandon thee; and, at least, I will now come to be thy companion. And, in the tomb, if the urn does not, yet the inscription[55] shall unite us: if I touch not thy bones with my bones, still will I unite thy name with my name." Grief forbids her saying more, and wailings come between each word, and groans are heaved from her sorrow-stricken breast.

It is now morning: she goes forth from her abode to the sea-shore, and, wretched, repairs to that place from which she had seen him go, and says, "While he lingered, and while he was loosening the cables, at his departure, he gave me kisses upon this sea-shore;" and while she calls to recollection the incidents which she had observed with her eyes, and looks out upon the sea, she observes on the flowing wave, I know not what object, like a body, within a distant space: and at first she is doubtful what it is. After the water has brought it a little nearer, and, although it is still distant, it is plain that it is a corpse. Ignorant who it may be, because it is ship-wrecked, she is moved at the omen, and, though unknown, would fain give it a tear. "Alas! thou wretched one!" she says, "whoever thou art; and if thou hast any wife!" Driven by the waves, the body approaches nearer. The more she looks at it, the less and the less is she mistress of her senses. And now she sees it brought close to the land, that now she can well distinguish it: it is her husband. "'Tis he!" she exclaims, and, on the instant, she tears her face, her hair, and her garments; and, extending her trembling hands towards Ceyx, she says, "And is it thus, Oh dearest husband! is it thus, Oh ill-fated one! that thou dost return to me?"

A mole, made by the hand of man, adjoins the waves, which breaks the first fury of the ocean, and weakens the first shock of its waters. Upon that she leaped, and 'tis wondrous that she could. She flew, and beating the light air with her wings newly formed, she, a wretched bird, skimmed the surface of the water. And, while she flew, her croaking mouth, with its slender bill, uttered a sound like that of one in sadness, and full of complaining. But when she touched the body, dumb, and without blood, embracing the beloved limbs with her new-made wings, in vain she gave him cold kisses with her hardened bill. The people were in doubt whether Ceyx was sensible of this, or whether, by the motion of the wave, he seemed to raise his countenance; but really he was sensible of it; and, at length, through the pity of the Gods above, both were changed into birds. Meeting with the same fate, even then their love remained. Nor, when now birds, is the conjugal tie dissolved: they couple, and they become parents; and for seven calm days,[56] in the winter-time, does Halcyone brood upon her nest floating on the sea.[57] Then the passage of the deep is safe; Æolus keeps the winds in, and restrains them from sallying forth, and secures a smooth sea for his descendants.

[Footnote 33: The profane Phorbas.—Ver. 414. The temple at Delphi was much nearer and more convenient for Ceyx to resort to; but at that period it was in the hands of the Phlegyans, a people of Thessaly, of predatory and lawless habits, who had plundered the Delphic shrine. They were destroyed by thunderbolts and pestilence, or, according to some authors, by Neptune, who swept them away in a flood. Phorbas, here mentioned, was one of the Lapithæ, a savage robber, who forced strangers to box with him, and then slew them. Having the presumption to challenge the Gods, he was slain by Apollo.]

[Footnote 34: Names upon tombs.—Ver. 429. Cenotaphs, or honorary tombs, were erected in honour of those, who having been drowned, their bodies could not be found. One great reason for erecting these memorials was the notion, that the souls of those who had received no funeral honours, wandered in agony on the banks of the Styx for the space of one hundred years.]

[Footnote 35: Hippotas.—Ver. 431. Æolus was the grandson of Hippotas, through his daughter Sergesta, who bore Æolus to Jupiter. Ovid says that he was the father of Halcyone; but, according to Lucian, she was the daughter of Æolus the Hellenian, the grandson of Deucalion.]

[Footnote 36: Brilliant fires.—Ver. 436. Ovid probably here had in view the description given by Lucretius, commencing Book i. line 272.]

[Footnote 37: In double rows.—Ver. 462. By this it is implied that the ship of Ceyx was a 'biremis,' or one with two ranks of rowers; one rank being placed above the other. Pliny the Elder attributes the invention of the 'biremis' to the Erythræans. Those with three ranks of rowers were introduced by the Corinthians; while Dionysius, the first king of Sicily, was the inventor of the Quadriremis, or ship with four ranks of rowers. Quinqueremes, or those with five ranks, are said to have been the invention of the Salaminians. The first use of those with six ranks has been ascribed to the Syracusans. Ships were sometimes built with twelve, twenty, and even forty ranks of rowers, but they appear to have been intended rather for curiosity than for use. As, of course, the labour of each ascending rank increased, through the necessity of the higher ranks using longer oars, the pay of the lowest rank was the lowest, their work being the easiest. Where there were twenty ranks or more, the upper oars required more than one man to manage them. Ptolemy Philopater had a vessel built as a curiosity, which had no less than four thousand rowers.]

[Footnote 38: Towards their sides.—Ver. 475. 'Obvertere lateri remos' most probably means 'To feather the oars,' which it is especially necessary to do in a gale, to avoid the retarding power of the wind against the surface of the blade of the oar.]

[Footnote 39: Fixes the sail-yards.—Ver. 476. 'Cornua' means, literally, 'The ends or points of the sail-yards,' or 'Antennæ:' but here the word is used to signify the sail-yards themselves.]

[Footnote 40: Covering of wax.—Ver. 514. The 'Cera' with which the seams of the ships were stopped, was most probably a composition of wax and pitch, or other bituminous and resinous substances.]

[Footnote 41: The tenth wave.—Ver. 530. This is said in allusion to the belief that every tenth wave exceeded the others in violence.]

[Footnote 42: Calls those happy.—Ver. 540. Those who died on shore would obtain funeral rites; while those who perished by shipwreck might become food for the fishes, a fate which was regarded by the ancients with peculiar horror. Another reason for thus regarding death by shipwreck, was the general belief among the ancients, that the soul was an emanation from æther, or fire, and that it was contrary to the laws of nature for it to be extinguished by water. Ovid says in his Tristia, or Lament (Book I. El. 2, l. 51-57), 'I fear not death: 'tis the dreadful kind of death; Take away the shipwreck: then death will be a gain to me. 'Tis something for one, either dying a natural death, or by the sword, to lay his breathless corpse in the firm ground, and to impart his wishes to his kindred, and to hope for a sepulchre, and not to be food for the fishes of the sea.']

[Footnote 43: A hurricane.—Ver. 548-9. 'Tanta vertigine pontus Fervet' is transcribed by Clarke, 'The sea is confounded with so great a vertigo.']

[Footnote 44: The billows allow.—Ver. 566. 'Quoties sinit hiscere fluctus' is rendered by Clarke, 'As oft as the waves suffer him to gape.']

[Footnote 45: A darkening arch.—Ver. 568. Possibly 'niger arcus' means a sweeping wave, black with the sand which it has swept from the depths of the ocean; or else with the reflection of the dark clouds.]

[Footnote 46: From the heavens.—Ver. 571. The word Olympus is frequently used by the poets to signify 'the heavens;' as the mountain of that name in Thessaly, from its extreme height, was supposed to be the abode of the Gods.]

[Footnote 47: Prepare the garments.—Ver. 575. Horace tells us that their clients wove garments for the Roman patricians; and the females of noble family did the same for their husbands, children, and brothers. Ovid, in the Fasti, describes Lucretia as making a 'lacerna,' or cloak, for her husband Collatinus. She says to her hand-maidens, 'With all speed there must be sent to your master a cloak made with our hands.' (Book ii. l. 746.) Suetonius tells us that Augustus would wear no clothes but those made by his wife, sister, or daughter.]

[Footnote 48: Polluted hands.—Ver. 584. All persons who had been engaged in the burial of the dead were considered to be polluted, and were not allowed to enter the temples of the Gods till they had been purified. Among the Greeks, persons who had been supposed to have died in foreign countries, and whose funeral rites had been performed in an honorary manner by their own relatives, if it turned out that they were not dead, and they returned to their own country, were considered impure, and were only purified by being dressed in swaddling clothes, and treated like new-born infants. We shall, then, be hardly surprised at Juno considering Halcyone to be polluted by the death of her husband Ceyx, although at a distance, and as yet unknown to her.]

[Footnote 49: The Cimmerians.—Ver. 592. Ovid appropriately places the abode of the drowsy God in the cold, damp, and foggy regions of the Cimmerians, who are supposed, by some authors, to have been a people of Sarmatia, or Scythia, near the Palus Mæotis, or sea of Azof. Other writers suppose that a fabulous race of people, said to live near Baiæ in Italy, and to inhabit dark caves throughout the day, while they sallied forth to plunder at night, are here referred to. This description of the abode of Sleep, and of his appearance and attendants, is supposed to have been borrowed by Ovid from one of the Greek poets.]

[Footnote 50: Geese more sagacious.—Ver. 599. This is said in compliment to the geese, for the service they rendered, in giving the alarm, and saving the Capitol, when in danger of being taken by the Gauls.]

[Footnote 51: Waters of Lethe.—Ver. 603. After the dead had tasted the waters of Lethe, one of the rivers of Hell, it was supposed that they lost all recollection of the events of their former life.]

[Footnote 52: Took to flight.—Ver. 632. Clarke translates this line, 'Away she scours, and returns through the bow through which she had come.']

[Footnote 53: Morpheus.—Ver. 635. Morpheus was so called from the Greek μορφὴ, 'shape,' or 'figure,' because he assumed various shapes. Icelos has his name from the Greek ἴκελος, 'like,' for a similar reason. Phobetor is from the Greek φοβὸς, 'fear,' because it was his office to terrify mortals. Lucian appears to mean the same Deity, under the name of Taraxion. Phantasos is from the Greek φάντασις, 'fancy.']

[Footnote 54: In the Ægean Sea.—Ver. 663. The Ægean Sea lay between the city of Trachyn and the coast of Ionia, whither Ceyx had gone.]

[Footnote 55: The inscription.—Ver. 706. The epitaphs on the tombs of the ancients usually contained the name of the person, his age, and (with the Greeks) some account of the principal events of his life. Halcyone, in her affectionate grief, promises her husband, at least, an honorary funeral, and a share in her own epitaph.]

[Footnote 56: Seven calm days.—Ver. 745. Simonides mentions eleven as being the number of the days; Philochorus, nine; but Demagoras says seven, the number here adopted by Ovid.]

[Footnote 57: Floating on the sea.—Ver. 746. The male of the kingfisher was said by the ancients to be so constant to his mate, that on her death he refused to couple with any other, for which reason the poets considered that bird as the emblem of conjugal affection. The sea was supposed to be always calm when the female was sitting; from which time of serenity, our proverb, which speaks of 'Halcyon days,' takes its rise.]

EXPLANATION

According to the testimony of several of the ancient writers, Ceyx was the king of Trachyn, and was a prince of great knowledge and experience; and many had recourse to him to atone for the murders which they had committed, whether through imprudence or otherwise. Pausanias says that Eurystheus having summoned Ceyx to deliver up to him the children of Hercules, that prince, who was not able to maintain a war against so powerful a king, sent the youths to Theseus, who took them into his protection.

To recover from the melancholy consequent upon the death of his brother Dædalion and his niece Chione, he went to Claros to consult the oracle of Apollo, and was shipwrecked on his return; on which, his wife, Halcyone, was so afflicted, that she died of grief, or else threw herself into the sea, as Hyginus informs us. It was said that they were changed into the birds which we call kingfishers, a story which, probably, has no other foundation than the name of Halcyone, which signifies that bird; which by the ancients was considered to be the symbol of conjugal affection.

Apollodorus, however, does not give us so favourable an idea of the virtue of these persons as Ovid has done. According to him, it was their pride which proved the cause of their destruction. Jupiter enraged at Ceyx, because he had assumed his name as Halcyone had done that of Juno, changed them both into birds, he becoming a cormorant, and she a kingfisher. This story is remarkable for the beautiful and affecting manner in which it is told.

FABLE VIII [XI.749-795]

The Nymph Hesperia flying from Æsacus, who is enamoured of her, is bitten by a serpent, and instantly dies from the effects of the wound. He is so afflicted at her death, that he throws himself into the sea, and is transformed into a didapper.

Some old man[58] observes them as they fly over the widely extended seas, and commends their love, preserved to the end of their existence. One, close by, or the same, if chance so orders it, says, "This one, too, which you see, as it cuts through the sea, and having its legs drawn up," pointing at a didapper, with its wide throat, "was the son of a king. And, if you want to come down to him in one lengthened series, his ancestors are Ilus, and Assaracus, and Ganymede,[59] snatched away by Jupiter, and the aged Laomedon, and Priam, to whom were allotted the last days of Troy. He himself was the brother of Hector, and had he not experienced a strange fate in his early youth, perhaps he would have had a name not inferior to that of Hector; although the daughter of Dymas bore this last. Alexirhoë, the daughter of the two-horned Granicus,[60] is said secretly to have brought forth Æsacus, under shady Ida.

"He loathed the cities, and distant from the splendid court, frequented the lonely mountains, and the unambitious fields; nor went but rarely among the throngs of Ilium. Yet, not having a breast either churlish, or impregnable to love, he espies Hesperie, the daughter of Cebrenus,[61] on the banks of her sire, who has been often sought by him throughout all the woods, drying her locks, thrown over her shoulders, in the sun. The Nymph, thus seen, takes to flight, just as the frightened hind from the tawny wolf; and as the water-duck, surprised at a distance, having left her wonted stream, from the hawk. Her the Trojan hero pursues, and, swift with love, closely follows her, made swift by fear. Behold! a snake, lurking in the grass, with its barbed sting, wounds her foot as she flies, and leaves its venom in her body. With her flight is her life cut short. Frantic, he embraces her breathless, and cries aloud,—"I grieve, I grieve that ever I pursued thee. But I did not apprehend this; nor was it of so much value to me to conquer. We two have proved the destruction of wretched thee. The wound was given by the serpent; by me was the occasion given. I should be more guilty than he, did I not give the consolation for thy fate by my own death." Thus he said; and from a rock which the hoarse waves had undermined, he hurled himself into the sea. Tethys, pitying him as he fell, received him softly, and covered him with feathers as he swam through the sea; and the power of obtaining the death he sought was not granted to him. The lover is vexed that, against his will, he is obliged to live on, and that opposition is made to his spirit, desirous to depart from its wretched abode. And, as he has assumed newformed wings on his shoulders, he flies aloft, and again he throws his body in the waves: his feathers break the fall. Æsacus is enraged; and headlong he plunges into the deep,[62] and incessantly tries the way of destruction. Love caused his leanness; the spaces between the joints of his legs are long; his neck remains long, and his head is far away from his body. He loves the sea, and has his name because he plunges[63] in it.

[Footnote 58: Some old man.—Ver. 749-50. 'Hos aliquis senior—spectat;' these words are translated by Clarke, 'Some old blade spies them.']

[Footnote 59: Ganymede.—Ver. 756. Ovid need not have inserted Assaracus and Ganymede, as they were only the brothers of Ilus, and the three were the sons of Tros. Ilus was the father of Laomedon, whose son was Priam, the father of Æsacus.]

[Footnote 60: Granicus.—Ver. 763. The Granicus was a river of Mysia, near which Alexander the Great defeated Darius with immense slaughter.]

[Footnote 61: Cebrenus.—Ver. 769. The Cebrenus was a little stream of Phrygia, not far from Troy.]

[Footnote 62: *Plunges into the deep.—Ver. 791-2. 'Inque profundum Pronus abit,' Clarke renders, 'Goes plumb down into the deep.' Certainly this is nearer to its French origin, 'a plomb,' than the present form, 'plump down;' but, like many other instances in his translation, it decidedly does not help us, as he professes to do, to 'the attainment of the elegancy of this great Poet.'*]

[Footnote 63: *Because he plunges.—Ver. 795. He accounts for the Latin name of the diver, or didapper, 'mergus,' by saying that it was so called, 'a mergendo,' from its diving, which doubtless was the origin of the name, though not taking its rise in the fiction here related by the Poet.*]

EXPLANATION

Ovid and Apollodorus agree that Æsacus was the son of Priam, and that he was changed into a didapper, or diver, but they differ in the other circumstances of his life. Instead of being the son of Alexirhoë, Apollodorus says that he was the son of Priam and Arisbe the daughter of Merope, his first wife; that his father made him marry Sterope, who dying very young, he was so afflicted at her death, that he threw himself into the sea. He also says that Priam having repudiated Arisbe to marry Hecuba, the daughter of Cisseus, Æsacus seeing his mother-in-law pregnant of her second son, foretold his father that her progeny would be the cause of a bloody war, which would end in the destruction of the kingdom of Troy; and that upon this prediction, the infant, when born, was exposed on Mount Ida.

Tzetzes adds, that Æsacus told his father that it was absolutely necessary to put to death both the mother and the infant which was born on that same day; on which Priam being informed that Cilla, the wife of Thymætes, being delivered on that day of a son, he ordered them both to be killed; thinking thereby to escape the realization of the prediction. Servius, on the authority of Euphorion, relates the story in much the same manner; but a poet quoted by Cicero in his first book on Divination, says that it was the oracle of Zelia, a little town at the foot of Mount Ida, which gave that answer as an interpretation of the dream of Hecuba. Pausanias says it was the sibyl Herophila who interpreted the dream, while other ancient writers state that it was Cassandra. Apollodorus says that Æsacus learned from his grandfather Merops the art of foretelling things to come.

BOOK THE TWELFTH

FABLES I AND II [XII.1-145]

The Greeks assemble their troops at Aulis, to proceed against the city of Troy, and revenge the rape of Helen; but the fleet is detained in port by contrary winds. Calchas, the priest, after a prediction concerning the success of the expedition, declares that the weather will never be favourable till Agamemnon shall have sacrificed his daughter Iphigenia. She is immediately led to the altar for that purpose; but Diana, appeased by this act of obedience, carries away the maiden, and substitutes a hind in her place, on which a fair wind arises. Upon the Greeks landing at Troy, a battle is fought, in which Protesilaüs is killed by Hector, and Achilles kills Cygnus, a Trojan, on which his father Neptune transforms him into a swan.

His father Priam mourned him, not knowing that Æsacus, having assumed wings, was still living; Hector, too, with his brothers, made unavailing offerings[1] at a tomb, that bore his name on it. The presence of Paris was wanting, at this mournful office: who, soon after, brought into his country a lengthened war, together with a ravished wife;[2] and a thousand ships[3] uniting together, followed him, and, together with them, the whole body[4] of the Pelasgian nation. Nor would vengeance have been delayed, had not the raging winds made the seas impassable, and the Bœotian land detained in fishy Aulis the ships ready to depart. Here, when they had prepared a sacrifice to Jupiter, after the manner of their country, as the ancient altar was heated with kindled fires, the Greeks beheld an azure-coloured serpent creep into a plane tree, which was standing near the sacrifice they had begun. There was on the top of the tree a nest of twice four birds, which the serpent seized[5] together, and the dam as she fluttered around the scene of her loss, and he buried them in his greedy maw. All stood amazed. But Calchas, the son of Thestor, a soothsayer, foreseeing the truth, says, "Rejoice, Pelasgians, we shall conquer. Troy will fall, but the continuance of our toil will be long;" and he allots the nine birds to the years of the war. The serpent, just as he is, coiling around the green branches in the tree, becomes a stone, and, under the form of a serpent, retains that stone form.

Nereus continued boisterous in the Ionian waves, and did not impel the sails onwards; and there are some who think that Neptune favoured Troy, because he made the walls of the city. But not so the son of Thestor. For neither was he ignorant, nor did he conceal, that the wrath of the virgin Goddess must be appeased by the blood of a virgin. After the public good had prevailed over affection, and the king over the father, and Iphigenia, ready to offer her chaste blood, stood before the altar, while the priests were weeping; the Goddess was appeased, and cast a mist before their eyes, and, amid the service and the hurry of the rites, and the voices of the suppliants, is said to have changed Iphigenia, the Mycenian maiden, for a substituted hind. Wherefore, when the Goddess was appeased by a death which was more fitting, and at the same moment the wrath of Phœbe, and of the sea was past, the thousand ships received the winds astern, and having suffered much, they gained the Phrygian shore.

There is a spot in the middle of the world, between the land and the sea, and the regions of heaven, the confines of the threefold universe, whence is beheld whatever anywhere exists, although it may be in far distant regions, and every sound pierces the hollow ears. Of this place Fame is possessed, and chooses for herself a habitation on the top[6] of a tower, and has added innumerable avenues, and a thousand openings to her house, and has closed the entrances with no gates. Night and day are they open. It is all of sounding brass; it is all resounding, and it reechoes the voice, and repeats what it hears. Within there is no rest, and silence in no part. Nor yet is there a clamour, but the murmur of a low voice, such as is wont to arise from the waves of the sea, if one listens at a distance, or like the sound which the end of the thundering makes when Jupiter has clashed the black clouds together. A crowd occupies the hall; the fickle vulgar come and go; and a thousand rumours, false mixed with true, wander up and down, and circulate confused words. Of these, some fill the empty ears with conversation; some are carrying elsewhere what is told them; the measure of the fiction is ever on the increase, and each fresh narrator adds something to what he has heard. There, is Credulity, there, rash Mistake, and empty Joy, and alarmed Fears, and sudden Sedition, and Whispers of doubtful origin. She sees what things are done in heaven and on the sea, and on the earth; and she pries into the whole universe.

She has made it known that Grecian ships are on their way, with valiant troops: nor does the enemy appear in arms unlooked for. The Trojans oppose their landing, and defend the shore, and thou, Protesilaüs,[7] art, by the decrees of fate, the first to fall by the spear of Hector;[8] and the battles now commenced, and the courageous spirits of the Trojans, and Hector, till then unknown, cost the Greeks dear. Nor do the Phrygians experience at small expense of blood what the Grecian right hand can do.

And now the Sigæan shores are red with blood: now Cygnus, the son of Neptune, has slain a thousand men. Now is Achilles pressing on in his chariot, and levelling the Trojan ranks, with the blow of his Peleian spear; and seeking through the lines either Cygnus or Hector, he engages with Cygnus: Hector is reserved for the tenth year. Then animating the horses, having their white necks pressed with the yoke, he directed his chariot against the enemy, and brandishing his quivering spear with his arm, he said, "O youth, whoever thou art, take this consolation in thy death, that thou art slain by the Hæmonian Achilles."

Thus far the grandson of Æacus. His heavy lance followed his words. But, although there was no missing in the unerring lance, yet it availed nothing, by the sharpness of its point, thus discharged; and as it only bruised his breast with a blunt stroke, the other said, "Thou son of a Goddess, (for by report have we known of thee beforehand) why art thou surprised that wounds are warded off from me? (for Achilles was surprised); not this helmet that thou seest tawny with the horse's mane, nor the hollowed shield, the burden of my left arm, are assistant to me; from them ornament alone is sought; for this cause, too, Mars is wont to take up arms. All the assistance of defensive armour shall be removed, and yet I shall come off unhurt. It is something to be born, not of a Nereid,[9] but of one who rules both Nereus and his daughter, and the whole ocean."

Thus he spoke; and he hurled against the descendant of Æacus his dart, destined to stick in the rim of his shield; it broke through both the brass and the next nine folds of bull's hide; but stopping in the tenth circle of the hide, the hero wrenched it out, and again hurled the quivering weapon with a strong hand; again his body was without a wound, and unharmed, nor was a third spear able even to graze Cygnus, unprotected, and exposing himself. Achilles raged no otherwise than as a bull,[10] in the open Circus,[11] when with his dreadful horns he butts against the purple-coloured garments, used as the means of provoking him, and perceives that his wounds are evaded. Still, he examines whether the point has chanced to fall from off the spear. It is still adhering to the shaft. "My hand then is weak," says he, "and it has spent all the strength it had before, upon one man. For decidedly it was strong enough, both when at first I overthrew the walls of Lyrnessus, or when I filled both Tenedos and Eëtionian[12] Thebes with their own blood. Or when Caÿcus[13] flowed empurpled with the slaughter of its people: and Telephus[14] was twice sensible of the virtue of my spear. Here, too, where so many have been slain, heaps of whom I both have made along this shore, and I now behold, my right hand has proved mighty, and is mighty."

Thus he spoke; and as if he distrusted what he had done before, he hurled his spear against Menœtes, one of the Lycian multitude,[15] who was standing opposite, and he tore asunder both his coat of mail, and his breast beneath it. He beating the solid earth with his dying head, he drew the same weapon from out of the reeking wound, and said, "This is the hand, this the lance, with which I conquered but now. The same will I use against him; in his case, I pray that the event may prove the same." Thus he said, and he hurled it at Cygnus, nor did the ashen lance miss him; and, not escaped by him, it resounded on his left shoulder: thence it was repelled, as though by a wall, or a solid rock. Yet Achilles saw Cygnus marked with blood, where he had been struck, and he rejoiced, but in vain. There was no wound; that was the blood of Menœtes.

Then indeed, raging, he leaps headlong from his lofty chariot, and hand to hand, with his gleaming sword striking at his fearless foe, he perceives that the shield and the helmet are pierced with his sword, and that his weapon, too, is blunted upon his hard body. He endures it no longer; and drawing back his shield, he three or four times strikes the face of the hero, and his hollow temples, with the hilt of the sword; and following, he presses onward as the other gives ground, and confounds him, and drives him on, and gives him no respite in his confusion. Horror seizes on him, and darkness swims before his eyes; and as he moves backwards his retreating steps, a stone in the middle of the field stands in his way. Impelled over this, with his breast upwards, Achilles throws Cygnus with great violence, and dashes him[16] to the earth. Then, pressing down his breast with his shield and his hard knees, he draws tight the straps of his helmet; which, fastened beneath his pressed chin, squeeze close his throat, and take away his respiration and the passage of his breath.

He is preparing to strip his vanquished foe; he sees nothing but his armour, left behind. The God of the Ocean changed his body into a white bird, of which he so lately bore the name.

[Footnote 1: Unavailing offerings.—Ver. 3. 'Inferias inanes' is a poetical expression, signifying the offering sacrifices of honey, milk, wine, blood, flowers, frankincense, and other things, at a tomb, which was empty or honorary. The Greeks called these kind of sacrifices by the name of χοαί.]

[Footnote 2: A ravished wife.—Ver. 5. This was Helen, the wife of Menelaüs, whose abduction by Paris was the cause of the Trojan war.]

[Footnote 3: A thousand ships.—Ver. 7. That is, a thousand in round numbers. For Homer makes them, 1186; Dictys Cretensis, 1225; and Dares, 1140.]

[Footnote 4: The whole body.—Ver. 7. The adjective 'commune' is here used substantively, and signifies 'the whole body.']

[Footnote 5: Serpent seized.—Ver. 16-17. Clarke translates this line, 'Which the snake whipt up, as also the dam flying about her loss, and buried them in his greedy paunch.']

[Footnote 6: On the top.—Ver. 43. 'Summaque domum sibi legit in arce,' is translated by Clarke, 'And chooses there a house for herself, on the very tip-top of it.']

[Footnote 7: Protesilaüs.—Ver. 68. He was the husband of Laodamia, the daughter of Acastus. His father was Iphiclus, who was noted for his extreme swiftness.]

[Footnote 8: Spear of Hector.—Ver. 67. Some writers say that he fell by the hand of Æneas.]

[Footnote 9: Of a Nereid.—Ver. 93. Cygnus says this sarcastically, in allusion to Achilles being born of Thetis, a daughter of Nereus.]

[Footnote 10: As a bull.—Ver. 103-4. Clarke translates these lines in this comical strain: 'Achilles was as mad as a bull in the open Circus, when he pushes at the red coat, stuffed, used on purpose to provoke him.']

[Footnote 11: The open Circus.—Ver. 104. We learn from Seneca, that it was the custom in the 'venationes' of the Circus to irritate the bull against his antagonist, by thrusting in his path figures stuffed with straw or hay, and covered with red cloth. Similar means are used to provoke the bull in the Spanish bull-fights of the present day.]

[Footnote 12: Eëtionian.—Ver. 110. Eëtion, the father of Andromache, the wife of Hector, was the king of Thebes in Cilicia, which place was ravaged by the Greeks for having sent assistance to the Trojans.]

[Footnote 13: Caÿcus.—Ver. 111. The Caÿcus was a river of Mysia, in Asia Minor, which country had incurred the resentment of the Greeks, for having assisted the Trojans.]

[Footnote 14: Telephus.—Ver. 112. Telephus, the son of Hercules and the Nymph Auge, was wounded in combat by Achilles. By the direction of the oracle, he applied to Achilles for his cure, which was effected by means of the rust of the weapon with which the wound was made.]

[Footnote 15: Lycian multitude.—Ver. 116. The Lycians, whose territory was in Asia Minor, between Caria and Pamphylia, were allies of the Trojans.]

[Footnote 16: And dashes him.—Ver. 139. Clarke renders this line, 'He overset him, and thwacked him against the ground.']

EXPLANATION

It is not improbable that the prediction of Calchas, at Aulis, that the war against Troy would endure nine years, had no other foundation than his desire to check an enterprise which must be attended with much bloodshed, and difficulties of the most formidable nature. It is not unlikely, too, that this interpretation of the story of the serpent devouring the birds may have been planned by some of the Grecian generals, who did not dare openly to refuse their assistance to Agamemnon. The story of Iphigenia was, perhaps, founded on a similar policy. The ancient poets and historians are by no means agreed as to the fate of Iphigenia, as some say that she really was sacrificed, while others state that she was transformed into a she-bear, others into an old woman, and Nicander affirms that she was changed into a heifer.

There is no story more celebrated among the ancients than that of the intended immolation of Iphigenia. Euripides wrote two tragedies on the subject. Homer, however, makes no allusion to the story of Iphigenia; but he mentions Iphianassa, the daughter of Agamemnon, who was sent for, to be a hostage on his reconciliation with Achilles; she is probably the same person that is meant by the later poets, under the name of Iphigenia.

It has been suggested by some modern commentators, that the story of Iphigenia was founded on the sacrifice of his own daughter, by Jeptha, the judge of Israel, which circumstance happened much about the same time. The story of the substitution of the hind for the damsel, when about to be slain, was possibly founded on the substituted offering for Isaac when about to be offered by his father; for it is not probable that the people of Greece were entirely ignorant of the existence of the books of Moses, and that wonderful narrative would be not unlikely to make an impression on minds ever ready to be attracted by the marvellous. Some writers have taken pains to show that Agamemnon did not sacrifice, or contemplate sacrificing, his own daughter, by asserting that the Iphigenia here mentioned was the daughter of Helen, who was educated by Clytemnestra, the wife of Agamemnon, and the sister of Helen. Pausanias also adopts this view, and gives for his authorities Euphorion of Chalcis, Alexander, Stesichorus, and the people of Argos, who preserved a tradition to the same effect.

Lucretius, Virgil, and Diodorus Siculus are in the number of those who assert that Iphigenia actually was immolated. According to Dictys the Cretan, and several of the ancient scholiasts, Ulysses having left the

Grecian camp without the knowledge of Agamemnon, went to Argos, and returned with Iphigenia, under the pretext that her father intended to marry her to Achilles. Some writers state that Achilles was in love with Iphigenia; and that he was greatly enraged at Ulysses for bringing her to the camp, and opposed her sacrifice to the utmost of his power.

Ovid then proceeds to recount the adventures of the Greeks, after their arrival at Troy. An oracle had warned the Greeks, that he who should be the first to land on the Trojan shores, would inevitably be slain. Protesilaüs seeing that this prediction damped the courage of his companions, led the way, and sacrificed his life for the safety of his friends, being slain by Hector immediately on his landing. Cygnus, signalizing himself by his bravery, attracted the attention of Achilles, who singled him out as a worthy antagonist. It was said that this hero was the son of Neptune; perhaps because he was powerful by sea, and the prince of some island in the Archipelago. He was said to be invulnerable, most probably because his shield was arrow-proof. The story of his transformation into a swan, has evidently no other foundation than the resemblance between his name and that of that bird.

FABLES III AND IV [XII.146-535]

A truce ensuing, the Grecian chiefs having assembled at a feast, express their surprise at the fact of Cygnus being invulnerable. Nestor, by way of showing a still more surprising instance, relates how the Nymph Cænis, the daughter of Elatus, having yielded to the caresses of Neptune, was transformed by him into a man, and made invulnerable. Cæneus being present at the wedding feast of Pirithoüs, the son of Ixion, where Eurytus was a guest, the latter, being elevated with wine, made an attempt upon Hippodamia, the bride; on which a quarrel arose between the Centaurs and the Lapithæ. After many on both sides had been slain, Cæneus still remained unhurt; on which, the Centaurs having heaped up trunks of trees upon him, he was pressed to death; Neptune then changed his body into a bird.

This toil[17] and this combat brought on a cessation for many days; and both sides rested, laying aside their arms. And while a watchful guard was keeping the Phrygian walls, and a watchful guard was keeping the Argive trenches, a festive day had arrived, on which Achilles, the conqueror of Cygnus, appeased Pallas with the blood of a heifer, adorned with fillets. As soon as he had placed its entrails[18] upon the glowing altars, and the smell, acceptable to the Deities, mounted up to the skies, the sacred rites had their share, the other part was served up at the table. The chiefs reclined on couches, and sated their bodies with roasted flesh,[19] and banished both their cares and their thirst with wine. No harps, no melody of voices,[20] no long pipe of boxwood pierced with many a hole, delights them; but in discourse they pass the night, and valour is the subject-matter of their conversation. They relate the combats of the enemy and their own; and often do they delight to recount, in turn, both the dangers that they have encountered and that they have surmounted. For of what else should Achilles speak? or of what, in preference, should they speak before the great Achilles? But especially the recent victory over the conquered Cygnus was the subject of discourse. It seemed wonderful to them all, that the body of the youth was penetrable by no weapon, and was susceptible of no wounds, and that it blunted the steel itself. This same thing, the grandson of Æacus, this, the Greeks wondered at.

When thus Nestor says to them: "Cygnus has been the only despiser of weapons in your time, and penetrable by no blows. But I myself formerly saw the Perrhæbean[21] Cæneus bear a thousand blows with his body unhurt; Cæneus the Perrhæbean, I say, who, famous for his achievements, inhabited Othrys. And that this, too, might be the more wondrous in him, he was born a woman." They are surprised, whoever are present, at the singular nature of this prodigy, and they beg him to tell the story. Among them, Achilles says, "Pray tell us, (for we all have the same desire to hear it,) O eloquent old man,[22] the wisdom of our age; who was this Cæneus, and why changed to the opposite sex? in what war, and in the engagements of what contest was he known to thee? by whom was he conquered, if he was conquered by any one?"

Then the aged man replied: "Although tardy old age is a disadvantage to me, and many things which I saw in my early years escape me now, yet I remember most of them; and there is nothing, amid so many transactions of war and peace, that is more firmly fixed in my mind than that circumstance. And if extended age could make any one a witness of many deeds, I have lived two hundred[23] years, and now my third century is being passed by me. Cænis, the daughter of Elatus, was remarkable for her charms; the most beauteous virgin among the Thessalian maids, and one sighed for in vain by the wishes of many wooers through the neighbouring cities, and through thy cities, Achilles, for she was thy countrywoman. Perhaps, too, Peleus would have attempted that alliance; but at that time the marriage of thy mother had either befallen him, or had been promised him. Cænis did not enter into any nuptial ties; and as she was walking along the lonely shore, she suffered violence from the God of the ocean. 'Twas thus that report stated; and when Neptune had experienced the pleasures of this new amour, he said, 'Be thy wishes secure from all repulse; choose whatever thou mayst desire.' The same report has related this too; Cænis replied, 'This mishap makes my desire extreme, that I may not be in a condition to suffer any such thing in future. Grant that I be no longer a woman, and thou wilt have granted me all.' She spoke these last words with a hoarser tone, and the voice might seem to be that of a man, as indeed it was.

"For now the God of the deep ocean had consented to her wish; and had granted moreover that he should not be able to be pierced by any wounds, or to fall by any steel. Exulting in his privilege, the Atracian[24] departed; and now spent his time in manly exercises, and roamed over the Peneïan plains. Pirithoüs, the son of the bold Ixion, had married Hippodame,[25] and had bidden the cloud-born monsters to sit down at the tables ranged in order, in a cave shaded with trees. The Hæmonian nobles were there; I, too, was there, and the festive palace resounded with the confused rout. Lo! they sing the marriage song, and the halls smoke with the fires;[26] the maiden, too, is there, remarkable for her beauty, surrounded by a crowd of matrons and newly married women. We all pronounce Pirithoüs fortunate in her for a wife; an omen which we had well nigh falsified. For thy breast, Eurytus, most savage of the savage Centaurs, is inflamed as much with wine as with seeing the maiden; and drunkenness, redoubled by lust, holds sway over thee. On the sudden the tables being overset, disturb the feast, and the bride is violently dragged away by her seized hair. Eurytus snatches up Hippodame, and the others such as each one fancies, or is able to seize; and there is all the appearance of a captured city. The house rings with the cries of women. Quickly we all rise; and first, Theseus says, 'What madness, Eurytus, is impelling thee, who, while I still live, dost provoke Pirithoüs, and, in thy ignorance, in one dost injure two?' And that the valiant hero may not say these things in vain, he pushes them off as they are pressing on, and takes her whom they have seized away from them as they grow furious.

"He says nothing in answer, nor, indeed, can he defend such actions by words; but he attacks the face of her protector with insolent hands, and strikes his generous breast. By chance, there is near at hand an ancient bowl, rough with projecting figures, which, huge as it is, the son of Ægeus, himself huger still, takes up and hurls full in his face. He, vomiting both from his wounds and his mouth clots of blood,[27] and brains and wine together, lying on his back, kicks on the soaking sand. The double-limbed[28] Centaurs are inflamed at the death of their brother; and all vying, with one voice exclaim, 'To arms! to arms!' Wine gives them courage, and, in the first onset, cups hurled are flying about, and shattered casks[29] and hollow cauldrons; things before adapted for a banquet, now for war and slaughter. First, the son of Ophion, Amycus, did not hesitate to spoil the interior of the house of its ornaments; and first, from the shrine he tore up a chandelier,[30] thick set with blazing lamps; and lifting it on high, like him who attempts to break the white neck of the bull with sacrificial axe, he dashed it against the forehead of Celadon the Lapithean, and left his skull mashed into his face, no longer to be recognized. His eyes started out, and the bones of his face being dashed to pieces, his nose was driven back, and was fixed in the middle of his palate. Him, Belates the Pellæan, having torn away the foot of a maple table, laid flat on the ground, with his chin sunk upon his breast, and vomiting forth his teeth mixed with blood; and sent him, by a twofold wound, to the shades of Tartarus.

"As Gryneus stood next, looking at the smoking altar with a grim look, he said, 'And why do we not make use of this?' and then he raised an immense altar, together with its fire; and hurled it into the midst of the throng of the Lapithæ, and struck down two of them, Broteus and Orius. The mother of Orius was Mycale, who was known by her incantations to have often drawn down the horns of the struggling moon. On this Exadius says, 'Thou shalt not go unpunished, if only the opportunity of getting a weapon is given me;' and, as his weapon, he wields the antlers of a votive stag,[31] which were upon a lofty pine-tree. With the double branches of these, Gryneus is pierced through the eyes, and has those eyes scooped out. A part of them adheres to the antlers, a part runs down his beard, and hangs down clotted with gore. Lo! Rhœtus snatches up an immense flaming brand, from the middle of the altar, and on the right side breaks through the temples of Charaxus, covered with yellow hair. His locks, seized by the violent flames, burn like dry corn, and the blood seared in the wound emits a terrific noise in its hissing, such as the iron glowing in the flames is often wont to emit, which, when the smith has drawn it out with the crooked pincers, he plunges into the trough; whereon it whizzes, and, sinking in the bubbling water, hisses. Wounded, he shakes the devouring fire from his locks, and takes upon his shoulders the threshold, torn up out of the ground, a whole waggon-load, which its very weight hinders him from throwing full against the foe. The stony mass, too, bears down Cometes, a friend, who is standing at a short distance; nor does Rhœtus then restrain his joy, and he says, 'In such manner do I pray that the rest of the throng of thy party may be brave;' and then he increases the wound, redoubled with the half-burnt stake, and three or four times he breaks the sutures of his head with heavy blows, and its bones sink within the oozing brains.

"Victorious, he passes on to Evagrus, and Corythus, and Dryas; of which number, when Corythus, having his cheeks covered[32] with their first down, has fallen, Evagrus says, 'What glory has been acquired by thee, in killing a boy?' Rhœtus permits him to say no more, and fiercely thrusts the glowing flames into the open mouth of the hero, as he is speaking, and through the mouth into the breast. Thee, too, cruel Dryas, he pursues, whirling the fire around his head, but the same issue does not await thee as well. Thou piercest him with a stake burnt at the end, while triumphing in the success of an uninterrupted slaughter, in the spot where the neck is united to the shoulder. Rhœtus groans aloud, and with difficulty wrenches the stake out of the hard bone, and, drenched in his own blood, he flies. Orneus flies, too, and Lycabas, and Medon, wounded in his right shoulder-blade, and Thaumas with Pisenor; Mermerus, too, who lately excelled all in speed of foot, but now goes more slowly from the wound he has received; Pholus, too, and Melaneus, and Abas a hunter of boars, and Astylos the augur, who has in vain dissuaded his own party from this warfare. He also says to Nessus,[33] as he dreads the wounds, 'Fly not! for thou shalt be reserved for the bow of Hercules.' But Eurynomus and Lycidas, and Areos, and Imbreus did not escape death, all of whom the right hand of Dryas pierced right through. Thou, too, Crenæus, didst receive a wound in front,[34] although thou didst turn thy back in flight; for looking back, thou didst receive the fatal steel between thy two eyes, where the nose is joined to the lower part of the forehead. In the midst of so much noise, Aphidas was lying fast asleep from the wine which he had drunk incessantly, and was not aroused, and in his languid hand was grasping the mixed bowl, stretched at full length upon the shaggy skin of a bear of Ossa. Soon as Phorbas beheld him from afar, wielding no arms, he inserted his fingers in the strap of his lance,[35] and said, 'Drink thy wine mingled with the water of Styx;' and, delaying no longer, he hurled his javelin against the youth, and the ash pointed with steel was driven into his neck, as, by chance, he lay there on his back. His death happened without his being sensible of it; and the blood flowed from his full throat, both upon the couch and into the bowl itself.

"I saw Petræus endeavouring to tear up an acorn-bearing oak from the earth; and, as he was grasping it in his embrace, and was shaking it on this side and that, and was moving about the loosened tree, the lance of Pirithoüs hurled at the ribs of Petræus, transfixed his struggling breast together with the tough oak. They said, too, that Lycus fell by the valour of Pirithoüs, and that Chromis fell by the hand of Pirithoüs. But each of them gave less glory to the conqueror, than Dictys and Helops gave. Helops was transfixed by the javelin, which passed right through his temples, and, hurled from the right side, penetrated to his left ear. Dictys, slipping from the steep point of a rock, while, in his fear, he is flying from the pursuing son of Ixion, falls down headlong, and, by the weight of his body, breaks a huge ash tree, and spits his own entrails upon it, thus broken. Aphareus advances as his avenger, and endeavours to hurl a stone torn away from the mountain. As he is endeavouring to do so, the son of Ægeus attacks him with an oaken club, and breaks the huge bones of his arm, and has neither leisure, nor, indeed, does he care to put his useless body to death; and he leaps upon the back of the tall Bianor, not used to bear[36] any other than himself; and he fixes his knees in his ribs, and holding his long hair, seized with his left hand, shatters his face, and his threatening features, and his very hard temples, with the knotty oak. With his oak, too, he levels Nedymnus, and Lycotas the darter, and Hippasus having his breast covered with his flowing beard, and Ripheus, who towered above the topmost woods, and Tereus, who used to carry home the bears, caught in the Hæmonian mountains, alive and raging.

"Demoleon could not any longer endure Theseus enjoying this success in the combat, and he tried with vast efforts to tear up from the thick-set wood an aged pine; because he could not effect this, he hurled it, broken short, against his foe. But Theseus withdrew afar from the approaching missile, through the warning of Pallas; so at least he himself wished it to be thought. Yet the tree did not fall without effect: for it struck off from the throat of the tall Crantor, both his breast and his left shoulder. He, Achilles, had been the armour-bearer of thy father: him Amyntor, king of the Dolopians,[37] when conquered in war, had given to the son of Æacus, as a pledge and confirmation of peace. When Peleus saw him at a distance, mangled with a foul wound, he said, 'Accept however, Crantor, most beloved of youths, this sacrifice;' and, with a strong arm, and energy of intention, he hurled his ashen lance against Demoleon, which broke through the enclosures of his ribs, and quivered, sticking amid the bones. He draws out with his hand the shaft without the point; even that follows, with much difficulty; the point is retained within his lungs. The very pain gives vigour to his resolution; though wounded, he rears against the enemy, and tramples upon the hero with his horse's feet. The other receives the re-echoing strokes upon his helmet and his shield, and defends his shoulders, and holds his arms extended before him, and through the shoulder-blades he pierces two breasts[38] at one stroke. But first, from afar, he had consigned to death Phlegræus, and Hyles; in closer combat, Hiphinoüs and Clanis. To these is added Dorylas, who had his temples covered with a wolf's skin, and the real horns of oxen reddened with much blood, that performed the duty of a cruel weapon.

"To him I said, for courage gave me strength, 'Behold, how much thy horns are inferior to my steel;' and then I threw my javelin. When he could not avoid this, he held up his right hand before his forehead, about to receive the blow; and to his forehead his hand was pinned. A shout arose; but Peleus struck him delaying, and overpowered by the painful wound, (for he was standing next to him) with his sword beneath the middle of his belly. He leaped forth, and fiercely dragged his own bowels on the ground, and trod on them thus dragged, and burst them thus trodden; and he entangled his legs, as well in them, and fell down, with his belly emptied of its inner parts. Nor did thy beauty, Cyllarus,[39] save thee while fighting, if only we allow beauty to that monstrous nature of thine. His beard was beginning to grow; the colour of his beard was that of gold; and golden-coloured hair was hanging from his shoulders to the middle of his shoulder-blades. In his face there was a pleasing briskness; his neck, and his shoulders, and his hands, and his breast were resembling the applauded statues of the artists, and so in those parts in which he was a man; nor was the shape of the horse beneath that shape, faulty and inferior to that of the man. Give him but the neck and the head of a horse, and he would be worthy of Castor. So fit is his back to be sat upon, so stands his breast erect with muscle; he is all over blacker than black pitch; yet his tail is white; the colour, too, of his legs is white. Many a female of his own kind longed for him; but Hylonome alone gained him, than whom no female more handsome lived in the lofty woods, among the half beasts. She alone attaches Cyllarus, both by her blandishments, and by loving, and by confessing that she loves him. Her care, too, of her person is as great as can be in those limbs: so that her hair is smoothed with a comb; so that she now decks herself with rosemary, now with violets or roses, and sometimes she wears white lilies; and twice a day she washes her face with streams that fall from the height of the Pagasæan wood; and twice she dips her body in the stream: and she throws over her shoulder or her left side no skins but what are becoming, and are those of choice beasts.

"Their love was equal: together they wandered upon the mountains; together they entered the caves; and then, too, together had they entered the Lapithæan house; together were they waging the fierce warfare. The author of the deed is unknown: but a javelin came from the left side, and pierced thee, Cyllarus, below the spot where the breast is joined to the neck. The heart, being pierced with a small wound, grew cold, together with the whole body, after the weapon was drawn out. Immediately, Hylonome receives his dying limbs, and cherishes the wound, by laying her hand on it, and places her mouth on his, and strives to stop the fleeting life. When she sees him dead, having uttered what the clamour hinders from reaching my ears, she falls upon the weapon that has pierced him, and as she dies, embraces her husband. He, too, now stands before my eyes, Phæocomes, namely, who had bound six lions' skins together with connecting knots; covered all over, both horse and man. He, having discharged the trunk of a tree, which two yokes of oxen joined together could hardly have moved, battered the son of Phonolenus on the top of his head. The very broad round form of his skull was broken; and through his mouth, and through his hollow nostrils, and his eyes, and his ears, his softened brains poured down; just as curdled milk is wont through the oaken twigs, or as any liquor flows under the weight of a well-pierced sieve, and is squeezed out thick through the numerous holes. But I, while he was preparing to strip him of his arms as he lay, (this thy sire knows,) plunged my sword into the lower part of his belly, as he was spoiling him. Chthonius, too, and Teleboas, lay pierced by my sword. The former was bearing a two-forked bough as his weapon, the latter a javelin; with his javelin he gave me a wound. You see the marks; look! the old scar is still visible.

"Then ought I[40] to have been sent to the taking of Troy; then I might, if not have overcome, still have stayed the arms of the mighty Hector. But at that time Hector was not existing, or but a boy; and now my age is failing. Why tell thee of Periphas, the conqueror of the two-formed Pyretus? Why of Ampyx, who fixed his cornel-wood spear, without a point, full in the face of the four-footed Oëclus? Macareus, struck down the Pelethronian[41] Erigdupus,[42] by driving a crowbar into his breast. I remember, too, that a hunting spear, hurled by the hand of Nessus, was buried in the groin of Cymelus. And do not believe that Mopsus,[43] the son of Ampycus, only foretold things to come; a two-formed monster was slain by Mopsus, darting at him, and Odites in vain attempted to speak, his tongue being nailed to his chin, and his chin to his throat. Cæneus had put five to death, Stiphelus, and Bromus, and Antimachus, and Helimus, and Pyracmos, wielding the axe. I do not remember their respective wounds, but I marked their numbers, and their names. Latreus, most huge both in his limbs and his body, sallied forth, armed with the spoils of Emathian[44] Halesus, whom he had consigned to death. His age was between that of a youth, and an old man; his vigour that of a youth; grey hairs variegated his temples. Conspicuous by his buckler, and his helmet, and his Macedonian pike;[45] and turning his face towards both sides, he brandished his arms, and rode in one same round, and vaunting, poured forth thus many words into the yielding air:—

"'And shall I put up with thee, too, Cænis? for to me thou shalt ever be a woman, to me always Cænis. Does not thy natal origin lower thy spirit? And does it not occur to thy mind for what foul deed thou didst get thy reward, and at what price the false resemblance to a man? Consider both what thou wast born, as well as what thou hast submitted to: go, and take up a distaff together with thy baskets, and twist the threads[46] with thy thumb; leave warfare to men.' As he is vaunting in such terms, Cæneus pierces his side, stretched in running, with a lance hurled at him, just where the man is joined to the horse. He raves with pain, and strikes at the exposed face of the Phylleian [47] youth with his pike. It bounds back no otherwise than hail from the roof of a house; or than if any one were to beat a hollow drum with a little pebble. Hand to hand he encounters him, and strives to plunge his sword into his tough side; but the parts are impervious to his sword. 'Yet,' says he, 'thou shalt not escape me; with the middle of the sword shalt thou be slain, since the point is blunt;' and then he slants the sword against his side, and grasps his stomach with his long right arm. The blow produces an echo, as on a body of marble when struck; and the shivered blade flies different ways, upon striking his neck.

"After Cæneus had enough exposed his unhurt limbs to him in his amazement, 'Come now,' said he, 'let us try thy body with my steel;' and up to the hilt he plunged his fatal sword into his shoulder-blade, and extended his hand unseen into his entrails, and worked it about, and in the wound made a fresh wound. Lo! the double-limbed monsters, enraged, rush on in an impetuous manner, and all of them hurl and thrust their weapons at him alone. Their weapons fall blunted. Unstabbed and bloodless the Elateïan Cæneus remains from each blow. This strange thing makes them astonished. 'Oh great disgrace!' cries Monychus; 'a whole people, we are overcome by one, and that hardly a man; although, indeed, he is a man; and we by our dastardly actions, are what he once was. What signify our huge limbs? What our twofold strength? What that our twofold nature has united in us the stoutest animals in existence? I neither believe that we are born of a Goddess for our mother, nor of Ixion, who was so great a person, that he conceived hopes of even the supreme Juno. By a half male foe are we baffled. Heap upon him stones and beams, and entire mountains, and dash out his long-lived breath, by throwing whole woods upon him. Let a whole wood press on his jaws; and weight shall be in the place of wounds.'

"Thus he said; and by chance having got a tree, thrown down by the power of the boisterous South wind, he threw it against the powerful foe: and he was an example to the rest; and in a short time, Othrys, thou wast bare of trees, and Pelion had no shades. Overwhelmed by this huge heap, Cæneus swelters beneath the weight of the trees, and bears on his brawny shoulders the piled-up oaks. But after the load has increased upon his face and his head, and his breath has no air to draw; at one moment he faints, at another he endeavours, in vain, to raise himself into the open air, and to throw off the wood cast upon him: and sometimes he moves it. Just as lo! we see, if lofty Ida is convulsed with earthquakes. The event is doubtful. Some gave out that his body was hurled to roomy Tartarus by the weight of the wood. The son of Ampycus denied this, and saw go forth into the liquid air, from amid the pile, a bird with tawny wings; which then was beheld by me for the first time, then, too, for the last. When Mopsus saw it with gentle flight surveying his camp, and making a noise around it with a vast clamour, following him both with his eyes and his feelings, he said, 'Hail! thou glory of the Lapithæan race, once the greatest of men, but now the only bird of thy kind, Cæneus.' This thing was credited from its assertor. Grief added resentment, and we bore it with disgust, that one was overpowered by foes so many. Nor did we cease to exercise our weapons, in shedding their blood, before a part of them was put to death, and flight and the night dispersed the rest."

[Footnote 17: This toil.—Ver. 146. Clarke translates 'Hic labor,' 'This laborious bout.']

[Footnote 18: Its entrails.—Ver. 152. The 'prosecta,' or 'prosiciæ,' or 'ablegamina,' were portions of the animal which were the first cut off, for the purpose of becoming as a sacrifice to the Deities. The 'prosecta,' in general, consisted of a portion of the entrails.]

[Footnote 19: Roasted flesh.—Ver. 155. We are informed by Servius, that boiled meat was not eaten in the heroic ages.]

[Footnote 20: Melody of voices.—Ver. 157. Plutarch remarks, that that entertainment is the most pleasant where no musician is introduced; conversation, in his opinion, being preferable.]

[Footnote 21: Perrhæbean.—Ver. 172. The Perrhæbeans were a people of Thessaly, who, having been conquered by the Lapithæ, betook themselves to the mountain fortresses of Pindus.]

[Footnote 22: Eloquent old man.—Ver. 176-181. Clarke renders these lines, 'Come, tell us, O eloquent old gentleman, the wisdom of our age, who was that Cæneus, and why he was turned into the other sex? in which war, or what engagement, he was known to you? by whom he was conquered, if he was conquered by any one?' Upon that, the old blade replied.']

[Footnote 23: Two hundred.—Ver. 188. Ovid does not here follow the more probable version, that the age of Nestor was three generations of thirty years each.]

[Footnote 24: The Atracian.—Ver. 209. 'Atracides' is an epithet, meaning 'Thessalian,' as Atrax, or Atracia, was a town of Thessaly, situated near the banks of the river Peneus.]

[Footnote 25: Hippodame.—Ver. 210. She is called Ischomache by Propertius, and Deidamia by Plutarch.]

[Footnote 26: With the fires.—Ver. 215. These fires would be those of the nuptial torches, and of the altars for sacrifice to Hymenæus and the other tutelary divinities of marriage.]

[Footnote 27: Clots of blood.—Ver. 238. Clarke renders 'Sanguinis globos,' 'goblets of blood.']

[Footnote 28: Double-limbed.—Ver. 240. Clarke translates, 'Ardescunt bimembres,' 'The double-limbed fellows are in a flame.']

[Footnote 29: Shattered cask.—Ver. 243. 'Cadi' were not only earthenware vessels, in which wine was kept, but also the vessels used for drawing water.]

[Footnote 30: A chandelier.—Ver. 247. 'Funale' ordinarily means, 'a link,' or 'torch,' made of fibrous substances twisted together, and smeared with pitch or wax. In this instance the word seems to mean a chandelier with several branches.]

[Footnote 31: A votive stag.—Ver. 267. It appears that the horns of a stag were frequently offered as a votive gift to the Deities, especially to Diana, the patroness of the chase. Thus in the seventh Eclogue of Virgil, Mycon vows to present to Diana, 'Vivacis cornua cervi,' 'The horns of a long-lived stag.']

[Footnote 32: Cheeks covered.—Ver. 291. 'Prima tectus lanugine malas,' is not very elegantly rendered by Clarke, 'Having his chaps covered with down, then first putting out.']

[Footnote 33: Nessus.—Ver. 309. We have already seen how Nessus the Centaur met his death from the arrow of Hercules, when about to offer violence to Deïanira.]

[Footnote 34: A wound in front.—Ver. 312. It has been suggested that, perhaps Ovid here had in his mind the story of one Pomponius, of whom Quintilian relates, that, having received a wound in his face, he was showing it to Cæsar, on which he was advised by the latter never to look behind him when he was running away.]

[Footnote 35: Strap of his lance.—Ver. 321. The 'amentum' was the thong, or strap of leather, with which the lance, or javelin, was fastened, in order to draw it back when thrown.]

[Footnote 36: Not used to bear.—Ver. 346. He alludes to the twofold nature, or 'horse-part' of the Centaur, as Clarke calls it.]

[Footnote 37: The Dolopians.—Ver. 364. They were a people of Phthiotis and Thessaly.]

[Footnote 38: Pierces two breasts.—Ver. 377. He says this by poetical license, in allusion to the two-fold form of the Centaurs.]

[Footnote 39: Cyllarus.—Ver. 393. This was also the name of the horse which Castor tamed, to which Ovid alludes in the 401st line.]

[Footnote 40: Then ought I.—Ver. 445. Nestor here shows a little of the propensity for boasting, which distinguishes him in the Iliad.]

[Footnote 41: Pelethronian.—Ver. 452. Pelethronia was a region of Thessaly, which contained a town and a mountain of that name.]

[Footnote 42: Erigdupus.—Ver. 453. The signification of this name is 'The noise of strife.']

[Footnote 43: Mopsus.—Ver. 456. He was a prophet, and one of the Lapithæ. There are two other persons mentioned in ancient history of the same name.]

[Footnote 44: Emathian.—Ver. 462. Properly, Emathia was a name of Macedonia; but it is here applied to Thessaly, which adjoined to that country.]

[Footnote 45: *Macedonian pike.—Ver. 466.* The 'sarissa' is supposed to have been a kind of pike with which the soldiers of the Macedonia phalanx were armed. Its ordinary length was twenty-one feet; but those used by the phalanx were twenty-four feet long.]

[Footnote 46: *Twist the threads.—Ver. 475.* The woof was called 'subtegmen,' 'subtemen,' or 'trama,' while the warp was called 'stamen,' from 'stare,' 'to stand,' on account of its erect position in the loom.]

[Footnote 47: *Phylleian.—Ver. 479.* Phyllus was a city of Phthiotis, in Thessaly.]

EXPLANATION

We learn from Diodorus Siculus, and other ancient authors, that the people of Thessaly, and those especially who lived near Mount Pelion, were the first who trained horses for riding, and used them as a substitute for chariots. Pliny the Elder says that they excelled all the other people of Greece in horsemanship, and that they carried it to such perfection, that the name of ἱππεὺς, 'a horseman,' and that of 'Thessalian,' became synonymous. Again, the Thessalians, from their dexterity in killing the wild bulls that infested the neighbouring mountains, sometimes with darts or spears, and at other times in close engagement, acquired the name of Hippocentaurs, that is, 'horsemen that hunted bulls,' or simply κένταυροι, 'Centaurs.'

It is not improbable that, because the Thessalians began to practise riding in the reign of Ixion, the poets made the Centaurs his sons; and they were said to have a cloud for their mother, which Jupiter put in the place of Juno, to baulk the attempt of Ixion on her virtue, because, according to Palæphatus, many of them lived in a city called Nephele, which, in Greek, signifies a cloud. As another method of accounting for their alleged descent from a cloud, it has been suggested that the Centaurs were a rapacious race of men, who ravaged the neighbouring country: that those who wrote the first accounts of them, in the ancient dialect of Greece, gave them the name of Nephelim, (the epithet of the giants of Scripture,) many Phœnician words having been imported in the early language of that country; and that in later times, finding them called by this name, the Greek word Nephelè, signifying 'a cloud,' persons readily adopted the fable that they were born of one.

The Centaurs being the descendants of Centaurus, the son of Ixion, and Pirithoüs being also the son of Ixion, by Dia, the former, declared war against Pirithoüs, asserting, that, as the descendants of Ixion, they had a right to share in the succession to his dominions. This quarrel, however, was made up, and they continued on friendly terms, until the attempt of Eurytus, or Eurytion, on Hippodamia, the bride of Pirithoüs, which was followed by the consequences here described by Ovid. The Centaurs are twice mentioned in the Iliad as φῆρες, or 'wild beasts,' and once under the name of 'Centaurs.' Pindar is the first writer that mentions them as being of a twofold form, partly man, and partly horse. In the twenty-first Book of the Odyssey, line 295, Eurytion is said to have had his ears and nose cut off by way of punishment, and that, from that period, 'discord arose between the Centaurs and men.'

Buttman, (Mythologus, ii. p. 22, as quoted by Mr. Keightley), says that the names of Centaurs and Lapithæ are two purely poetic names, used to designate two opposite races of men,—the former, the rude horse-riding tribes, which tradition records to have been spread over the north of Greece: the latter, the more civilized race, which founded towns, and gradually drove their wild neighbours back into the mountains. He thinks that the explanation of the word 'Centaurs,' as 'Air-piercers,' (from κεντεῖν τὴν αὔραν) not an improbable one, for the idea is suggested by the figure of a Cossack leaning forward with his protruded lance as he gallops along. But he regards the idea of κένταυρος, having been in its origin simply κέντωρ, as much more probable, [it meaning simply 'the spurrer-on.'] Lapithæ may, he thinks, have signified 'Stone persuaders,' from λᾶας πείθειν, a poetic appellation for the builders of towns. He supposes Hippodamia to have been a Centauress, married to the prince of the Lapithæ, and thus accounts for the Centaurs having been at the wedding. Mr. Keightley, in his 'Mythology of Ancient Greece and Italy,' remarks that 'it is certainly not a little strange that a rude mountain race like the Centaurs should be viewed as horsemen; and the legend which ascribes the perfecting of the art of horsemanship to the Lapithæ, is unquestionably the more probable one. The name Centaur, which so much resembles the Greek verb κεντέω, 'to spur,' we fancy gave origin to the fiction. This derivation of it is, however, rather dubious.'

After the battle here described, the Centaurs retreated to the mountains of Arcadia. The Lapithæ pursuing them, drove them to the Promontory of Malea in Laconia, where, according to Apollodorus, Neptune took them into his protection. Servius and Antimachus, as quoted by Comes Natalis, say that some of them fled to the Isle of the Sirens (or rather to that side of Italy which those Nymphs had made their abode); and that there they were destroyed by the voluptuous and debauched lives they led.

The fable of Cæneus, which Ovid has introduced, is perhaps simply founded on the prodigious strength and the goodness of the armour of a person of that name. The story of Halyonome killing herself on the body of Cyllarus, may possibly have been handed down by tradition. It is not unlikely that, if the Centaurs were horsemen, their women were not unacquainted with horsemanship; indeed, representations of female Centaurs are given, on ancient monuments, as drawing the chariot of Bacchus.

FABLES V AND VI [XII.536-628]

Periclymenus, the brother of Nestor, who has received from Neptune the power of transforming himself, is changed into an eagle, in a combat with Hercules; and in his flight is shot by him with an arrow. Neptune prays Apollo to avenge the death of Cygnus: because the Destinies will not permit him to do so himself. Apollo enters the Trojan camp in disguise, and directs the arrow which Paris aims at Achilles; who is mortally wounded in the heel, the only vulnerable part of his body.

As the Pylian related this fight between the Lapithæ and the Centaurs, but half human, Tlepolemus[48] could not endure his sorrow for Alcides being passed by with silent lips, and said, "It is strange, old man, that thou shouldst have a forgetfulness of the exploits of Hercules; at least, my father himself used often to relate to me, that these cloud-begotten monsters were conquered by him." The Pylian, sad at this, said, "Why dost thou force me to call to mind my misfortunes, and to rip up my sorrows, concealed beneath years, and to confess my hatred of, and disgust at, thy father? He, indeed, ye Gods! performed things beyond all belief, and filled the world with his services; which I could rather wish could be denied; but we are in the habit of praising neither Deiphobus nor Polydamas,[49] nor Hector himself: for who would commend an enemy? That father of thine once overthrew the walls of Messene, and demolished guiltless cities, Elis and Pylos, and carried the sword and flames into my abode. And, that I may say nothing of others whom he slew, we were twice six sons of Neleus, goodly youths; the twice six fell by the might of Hercules, myself alone excepted. And that the others were vanquished might have been endured; but the death of Periclymenus is wonderful; to whom Neptune, the founder of the Neleian family, had granted to be able to assume whatever shapes he might choose, and again, when assumed, to lay them aside. He, after he had in vain been turned into all other shapes, was turned into the form of the bird that is wont to carry the lightnings in his crooked talons, the most acceptable to the king of the Gods. Using the strength of that bird, his wings, and his crooked bill, together with his hooked talons, he tore the face of the hero. The Tirynthian hero aims at him his bow, too unerring, and hits him, as he moves his limbs aloft amid the clouds, and hovering in the air, just where the wing is joined to the side.

"Nor is the wound a great one, but his sinews, cut by the wound, fail him, and deny him motion and strength for flying. He fell down to the earth, his weakened pinions not catching the air; and where the smooth arrow had stuck in his wing, it was pressed still further by the weight of his pierced body, and it was driven, through the upper side, into the left part of the neck. Do I seem to be owing encomiums to the exploits of thy father Hercules, most graceful leader of the Rhodian fleet?[50] Yet I will no further avenge my brothers, than by being silent on his brave deeds: with thyself I have a firm friendship." After the son[51] of Neleus had said these things with his honied tongue, the gifts of Bacchus being resumed after the discourse of the aged man, they arose from their couches: the rest of the night was given to sleep.

But the God who commands the waters of the sea with his trident, laments, with the affection of a father, the body of his son, changed into the bird of the son of Sthenelus; and abhorring the ruthless Achilles, pursues his resentful wrath in more than an ordinary manner. And now, the war having been protracted for almost twice five years, with such words as these he addresses the unshorn Smintheus:[52] "O thou, most acceptable to me, by far, of the sons of my brother, who, together with me, didst build the walls of Troy in vain; and dost thou not grieve when thou lookest upon these towers so soon to fall? or dost thou not lament that so many thousands are slain in defending these walls? and (not to recount them all) does not the ghost of Hector, dragged around his Pergamus, recur to thee? Though still the fierce Achilles, more blood-stained than war itself, lives on, the destroyer of our toil, let him but put himself in my power, I will make him feel what I can do with my triple spear. But since it is not allowed us to encounter the enemy in close fight, destroy him, when off his guard, with a secret shaft."

He nodded his assent; and the Delian God, indulging together both his own resentment and that of his uncle, veiled in a cloud, comes to the Trojan army, and in the midst of the slaughter of the men, he sees Paris, at intervals, scattering his darts among the ignoble Greeks; and, discovering himself to be a Divinity, he says, "Why dost thou waste thy arrows upon the blood of the vulgar? If thou hast any concern for thy friends, turn upon the grandson of Æacus, and avenge thy slaughtered brothers." Thus he said; and pointing at the son of Peleus, mowing down the bodies of the Trojans with the sword, he turned his bow towards him, and directed his unerring arrow with a fatal right hand. This was the only thing at which, after the death of Hector, the aged Priam could rejoice. And art thou then, Achilles, the conqueror of men so great, conquered by the cowardly ravisher of a Grecian wife? But if it had been fated for thee to fall by the hand of a woman, thou wouldst rather have fallen by the Thermodontean[53] battle-axe.

Now that dread of the Phrygians, the glory and defence of the Pelasgian name, the grandson of Æacus, a head invincible in war, had been burnt: the same Divinity had armed him,[54] and had burned him. He is now but ashes; and there remains of Achilles, so renowned, I know not what; that which will not well fill a little urn. But his glory lives, which can fill the whole world: this allowance is befitting that hero, and in this the son of Peleus is equal to himself, and knows not the empty Tartarus. Even his very shield gives occasion for war, that you may know to whom it belongs; and arms are wielded for arms. The son of

Tydeus does not dare to claim them, nor Ajax, the son of Oïleus,[55] nor the younger son of Atreus, nor he who is his superior both in war and age, nor any others; the hope of so much glory exists only in him begotten by Telamon and the son of Laërtes. The descendant of Tantalus[56] removes from himself the burden and the odium of a decision, and orders the Argive leaders to sit in the midst of the camp, and transfers the judgment of the dispute to them all.

[Footnote 48: Tlepolemus.—Ver. 537. He was a son of Hercules, by Astioche.]

[Footnote 49: Polydamas.—Ver. 547. He was a noble Trojan, of great bravery, who had married a daughter of Priam.]

[Footnote 50: Rhodian fleet.—Ver. 575. Tlepolemus, when a youth, slew his uncle, Lycimnius, the son of Mars. Flying from his country with some followers, he retired to the Island of Rhodes, where he gained the sovereignty. He went to the Trojan war with nine ships, to aid the Greeks, where he fell by the hand of Sarpedon.]

[Footnote 51: After the son.—Ver. 578-9. 'A sermone senis repetito munere Bacchi Surrexere toris.' These words are thus quaintly rendered in Clarke's translation: 'From listening to the old gentleman's discourse, they return again to their bottle; and taking the other glass, they departed.']

[Footnote 52: Smintheus.—Ver. 585. Apollo was so called, in many of the cities of Asia, and was worshipped under this name, in the Isle of Tenedos. He is said by Eustathius, to have been so called from Smynthus, a town near Troy. But, according to other accounts, he received the epithet from the Cretan word σμίνϑος, a mouse; being supposed to protect man against the depredations of that kind of vermin.]

[Footnote 53: Thermodontean.—Ver. 611. He alludes to Penthesilea, the Queen of the Amazons, who, aiding the Trojans against the Greeks, was slain by Achilles. The battle-axe was the usual weapon of the Amazons]

[Footnote 54: Had armed him.—Ver. 614. Vulcan, the God of Fire, made his armour at the request of his mother, Thetis; and now his body was burned by fire.]

[Footnote 55: Son of Oïleus.—Ver. 622. This was Ajax, the King of the Locrians.]

[Footnote 56: Descendant of Tantalus.—Ver. 626. Agamemnon was the son of Atreus, grandson of Pelops, and great-grandson of Tantalus. He wisely refused to take upon himself alone the onus of deciding the contention between Ajax and Ulysses.]

EXPLANATION

Periclymenus was the son of Neleus and Chloris, as we are told by Homer, Apollodorus, and other authors. According to these authors, Neleus, king of Orchomenus, was the son of Neptune, who assumed the form of the river Enipeus, the more easily to deceive Tyro, the daughter of Salmoneus. Neleus married Chloris, the daughter of Amphion, king of Thebes, who bore him eleven sons and one daughter, of which number, Homer names but three. Periclymenus, the youngest of the family, was a warlike prince, and, according to Apollodorus, accompanied Jason in the expedition of the Argonauts.

Hercules, after having instituted the Olympic games, marched into Messenia, and declared war with Neleus. The ancient writers differ as to the cause of this expedition; but they agree in stating, that Hercules made himself master of Pylos, a town which Neleus had built, as a refuge from the capricious humours of his brother Pelias; and that Neleus and all his children were killed, except Nestor, who had been brought up among the Geranians, and who afterwards reigned in Pylos. The story which here relates how Periclymenus transformed himself into an eagle, and was then killed by Hercules, may possibly mean, that having long resisted the attacks of his formidable enemy, he was at length put to flight, and slain by an arrow. It is said that Neptune had given him the power to metamorphose himself into different figures, very probably because his grandfather, who was a maritime prince, had taught him the art of war and various stratagems, which he industriously made use of, to avert the ruin of his family.

In relation to the story of the death of Achilles, Dictys the Cretan tells us, that Achilles having seen Polyxena, the daughter of Priam, along with Cassandra, as she was sacrificing to Apollo, fell in love with her, and demanded her in marriage and that Hector would not consent to it, except on condition of his betraying the Greeks. This demand, so injurious to his honour, provoked Achilles so much, that he forthwith slew Hector, and dragged his body round the walls of the city. He further says that when Priam went to demand the body of Hector, he took Polyxena with him, in order to soften Achilles. His design succeeded, and Priam then agreed to give her to him in marriage. On the day appointed for the solemnity in the temple of Apollo, Paris, concealing himself behind the altar, while Deiphobus pretended to embrace Achilles, wounded him in the heel, and killed him on the spot, either because the arrow was poisoned, or because he was wounded on the great tendon, which has since been called 'tendon Achillis,' a spot where a wound might very easily be mortal.

This story of the death of Achilles does not seem to have been known to Homer; for he appears, in the twenty-fourth book of the Odyssey, to insinuate that that hero died in battle, fighting for the Grecian cause.

After his death Achilles was honoured as a Demigod, and Strabo says that he had a temple near the promontory of Sigæum. Pausanias and Pliny the Elder make mention of an island in the Euxine Sea, where the memory of Achilles was expressly honoured, from which circumstances it had the name of Achillea.

BOOK THE THIRTEENTH

FABLES I AND II [XIII.1-438]

After the death of Achilles, Ajax and Ulysses contend for his armour; the Greek chiefs having adjudged it to the last, Ajax kills himself in despair, and his blood is changed into a flower. When Ulysses has brought Philoctetes, who is possessed of the arrows of Hercules, to the siege, and the destinies of Troy are thereby accomplished, the city is taken and sacked, and Hecuba becomes the slave of Ulysses.

The chiefs were seated; and a ring of the common people standing around, Ajax, the lord of the seven-fold shield, arose before them. And as he was impatient in his wrath, with stern features he looked back upon the Sigæan shores, and the fleet upon the shore, and, stretching out his hands, he said, "We are pleading,[1] O Jupiter, our cause before the ships, and Ulysses vies with me! But he did not hesitate to yield to the flames of Hector, which I withstood, and which I drove from this fleet. It is safer, therefore, for him to contend with artful words than with his right hand. But neither does my talent lie in speaking, nor his[2] in acting; and as great ability as I have in fierce warfare, so much has he in talking. Nor do I think, O Pelasgians, that my deeds need be related to you; for you have been eye-witnesses of them. Let Ulysses recount his, which he has performed without any witness, and of which night alone[3] is conscious. I own that the prize that is sought is great; but the rival of Ajax lessens its value. It is no proud thing, great though it may be, to possess any thing which Ulysses has hoped for. Already has he obtained the reward of this contest, in which, when he shall have been worsted, he will be said to have contended with me. And I, if my prowess were to be questioned, should prevail by the nobleness of my birth, being the son of Telamon, who took the city[4] of Troy under the valiant Hercules, and entered the Colchian shores in the Pagasæan ship. Æacus was his father, who there gives laws to the silent shades, where the heavy stone urges downward Sisyphus,[5] the son of Æolus.

"The supreme Jupiter owns Æacus, and confesses that he is his offspring. Thus Ajax is the third[6] from Jupiter. And yet, O Greeks, let not this line of descent avail me in this cause, if it be not common to me with the great Achilles. He was my cousin;[7] I ask for what belonged to my cousin? Why does one descended from the blood of Sisyphus, and very like him in thefts and fraud, intrude the name of a strange family among the descendants of Æacus? Are the arms to be denied me, because I took up arms before him, and through the means of no informer?[8] and shall one seem preferable who was the last to take them up, and who, by feigning madness, declined war, until the son of Nauplius,[9] more cunning than he, but more unhappy for himself, discovered the contrivance[10] of his cowardly mind, and dragged him forth to the arms which he had avoided. Now let him take the best arms who would have taken none. Let me be dishonoured, and stripped of the gifts that belonged to my cousin, who presented myself in the front of danger. And I could wish that that madness had been either real or believed so to be, and that he had never attended us as a companion to the Phrygian towers, this counsellor of evil! Then, son of Pœas,[11] Lemnos would not have had thee exposed there through our guilt; who now, as they say, concealed in sylvan caves, art moving the very rocks with thy groans, and art wishing for the son of Laërtes what he has deserved; which, may the Gods, the Gods, I say, grant thee not to pray in vain.

"And now, he that was sworn upon the same arms with ourselves, one of our leaders, alas! by whom, as his successor, the arrows of Hercules are used, broken by disease and famine, is being clothed[12] and fed by birds; and in shooting fowls, he is employing the shafts destined for the destruction of Troy. Still, he lives, because he did not accompany Ulysses. And the unhappy Palamedes would have preferred that he had been left behind; then he would have been living, or, at least, he would have had a death without any criminality. Him, Ulysses remembering too well the unlucky discovery of his madness, pretended to be betraying the Grecian interests, and proved his feigned charge, and shewed the Greeks the gold, which he had previously hidden in the ground. By exile then, or by death,[13] has he withdrawn from the Greeks their best strength. Thus Ulysses fights, thus is he to be dreaded. Though he were to excel even the faithful Nestor in eloquence, yet he would never cause me to believe that the forsaking of Nestor[14] was not a crime; who, when he implored the aid of Ulysses, retarded by the wound of his steed, and wearied with the years of old age, was deserted by his companion. The son of Tydeus knows full well that these charges are not invented by me, who calling on him often by name, rebuked him, and upbraided[15] his trembling friend with his flight. The Gods above behold the affairs of men with just eyes. Lo! he wants help, himself, who gave it not; and as he left another, so was he doomed to be left: such law had he made for himself.

"He called aloud to his companions. I came, and I saw him trembling, and pale with fear, and shuddering at the impending death. I opposed the mass of my shield to the enemy, and covered him[16] as he lay; and I preserved (and that is the least part of my praise) his dastardly life. If thou dost persist in vying, let us return to that place; restore the enemy, and thy wound, and thy wonted fear; and hide behind my shield, and under that contend with me. But, after I delivered him, he to whom his wounds before gave no strength for standing, fled, retarded by no wound whatever. Hector approaches, and brings the Gods along with him to battle, and where he rushes on, not only art thou alarmed, Ulysses, but even the valiant are; so great terror does he bring. Him, as he exulted in the successes of his bloodstained slaughter, in close conflict, I laid flat with a huge stone. Him demanding one with whom he might engage, did I alone withstand; and you, Greeks, prayed it might fall to my lot;[17] and your prayers prevailed. If you inquire into the issue of this fight, I was not beaten by him.

"Lo! the Trojans bring fire and sword, and Jove, as well, against the Grecian fleet. Where is now the eloquent Ulysses? I, forsooth, protected a thousand ships, the hopes of your return, with my breast. Grant me the arms, in return for so many ships. But, if I may be allowed to speak the truth, a greater honour is sought for them than is for me, and our glory is united; and Ajax is sought for the arms, and not the arms by Ajax. Let the Ithacan Ulysses compare with these things Rhesus,[18] and the unwarlike Dolon,[19] and Helenus,[20] the son of Priam, made captive with the ravished Pallas. By daylight nothing was done; nothing when Diomedes was afar. If once you give these arms for services so mean, divide them, and that of Diomedes would be the greater share of them. But, why these for the Ithacan? who, by stealth and unarmed, ever does his work, and deceives the unwary enemy by stratagem? The very brilliancy of his helmet, as it sparkles with bright gold, will betray his plans, and discover him as he lies hid. But neither will the Dulichian[21] head, beneath the helm of Achilles, sustain a weight so great; and the spear[22] from Pelion must be heavy and burdensome for unwarlike arms. Nor will the shield, embossed with the form of the great globe, beseem a dastard left hand, and one formed for theft. Why then, caitiff, dost thou ask for a gift that will but weaken thee? should the mistake of the Grecian people bestow it on thee, there would be a cause for thee to be stripped, not for thee to be dreaded by the enemy. Thy flight, too, (in which, alone, most dastardly wretch! thou dost excel all others,) will be retarded, when dragging a load so great. Besides, that shield of thine, which has so rarely experienced the conflict, is unhurt; for mine, which is gaping in a thousand wounds from bearing the darts, a new successor must be obtained. In fine, what need is there for words? Let us be tried in action. Let the arms of that brave hero be thrown in the midst of the enemy: order them to be fetched thence, and adorn him that brings them back, with them so brought off."

The son of Telamon had now ended, and a murmur among the multitude ensued upon his closing words, until the Laërtian hero stood up, and fixing his eyes, for a short time, on the ground, raised them towards the chiefs, and opened his mouth in the accents that were looked for; nor was gracefulness wanting to his eloquent words.

"If my prayers had been of any avail together with yours, Pelasgians, the successor to a prize so great would not now be in question, and thou wouldst now be enjoying thine arms, and we thee, O Achilles. But since the unjust Fates have denied him to me and to yourselves, (and here he wiped his eyes with his hands as though shedding tears,) who could better succeed the great Achilles than he through whom[23] the great Achilles joined the Greeks? Only let it not avail him that he seems to be as stupid as he really is; and let not my talents, which ever served you, O Greeks, be a prejudice to me: and let this eloquence of mine, if there is any, which now pleads for its possessor, and has often done so for yourselves, stand clear of envy, and let each man not disown his own advantages. For as to descent and ancestors, and the things which we have not made ourselves, I scarce call these our own. But, indeed, since Ajax boasts that he is the great grandson of Jove, Jupiter, too, is the founder of my family, and by just as many degrees am I distant from him. For Laërtes is my father, Arcesius his, Jupiter his; nor was any one of these ever condemned[24] and banished. Through the mother,[25] too, Cyllenian Mercury, another noble stock, is added to myself. On the side of either parent there was a God. But neither because I am more nobly born on my mother's side, nor because my father is innocent of his brother's blood, do I claim the arms now in question. By personal merit weigh the cause. So that it be no merit in Ajax that Telamon and Peleus were brothers; and so that not consanguinity, but the honour of merit, be regarded in the disposal of these spoils. Or if nearness of relationship and the next heir is sought, Peleus is his sire, and Pyrrhus is his son. What room, then, is there for Ajax? Let them be taken to Phthia[26] or to Scyros. Nor is Teucer[27] any less a cousin of Achilles than he; and yet does he sue for, does he expect to bear away the arms?

"Since then the contest is simply one of deeds; I, in truth, have done more than what it is easy for me to comprise in words. Yet I shall proceed in the order of events. Thetis, the Nereid mother, prescient of coming death, conceals her son by his dress. The disguise of the assumed dress deceived all, among whom was Ajax. Amid woman's trinkets I mixed arms such as would affect the mind of a man. And not yet had the hero thrown aside the dress of a maiden, when, as he was brandishing a shield and a spear, I said, 'O son of a Goddess, Pergamus reserves itself to fall through thee. Why, then, dost thou delay to overthrow the mighty Troy?' And then I laid my hands on him, and to brave deeds I sent forth the brave. His deeds then are my own. 'Twas I that subdued Telephus, as he fought with his lance; 'twas I that recovered him, vanquished, and begging for his life. That Thebes has fallen, is my doing. Believe me, that I took Lesbos, that I took Tenedos, Chrysa[28] and Cylla, cities of Apollo, and Scyros too. Consider too, that the Lyrnessian[29] walls were levelled with the ground, shaken by my right hand. And, not to mention other things, 'twas I, in fact, that found one who might slay the fierce Hector; through me the renowned Hector lies prostrate. By those arms through which Achilles was found out, I demand these arms. To him when living I gave them; after his death I ask them back again.

"After the grief of one[30] had reached all the Greeks, and a thousand ships had filled the Eubœan Aulis, the breezes long expected were either not existing or adverse to the fleet; and the ruthless oracles commanded Agamemnon to slay his innocent daughter for the cruel Diana. This the father refuses, and is enraged against the Gods themselves, and, a king, he is still a father. By my words I swayed the gentle disposition of the parent to the public advantage. Now, indeed, I make this confession, and let the son of Atreus forgive me as I confess it; before a partial judge I upheld a difficult cause. Yet the good of the people and his brother, and the supreme power of the sceptre granted to him, influence him to balance praise against blood. I was sent, too, to the mother, who was not to be persuaded, but to be deceived with craft; to whom, if the son of Telamon had gone, until even now would our sails have been without wind. A bold envoy, too, I was sent to the towers of Ilium, and the senate-house of lofty Troy was seen and entered by me; and still was it filled with their heroes. Undaunted, I pleaded the cause which all Greece had entrusted to me; and I accused Paris, and I demanded back the plunder, and Helen as well; and I moved Priam and Antenor[31], related to Priam. But Paris and his brothers, and those who, under him, had been ravishers, scarce withheld their wicked hands; and this thou knowest, Menelaüs, and that was the first day of my danger in company with thee. It were a tedious matter to relate the things which, by my counsel and my valour, I have successfully executed in the duration of this tedious warfare.

"After the first encounter, the enemy for a long time kept themselves within the walls of the city, and there was no opportunity for open fight. At length, in the tenth year we fought. And what wast thou doing in the mean time, thou, who knowest of nothing but battles? what was the use of thee? But if thou inquirest into my actions: I lay ambuscades for the enemy; I surround the trenches[32] with redoubts; I cheer our allies that they may bear with patient minds the tediousness of a protracted war; I show, too, how we are to be supported, and how to be armed; I am sent[33] whither necessity requires. Lo! by the advice of Jove, the king, deceived by a form in his sleep, commands him to dismiss all care of the war thus begun. He is enabled, through the author of it, to defend his own cause. Ajax should not have allowed this, and should have demanded that Troy be razed. And he should have fought, the only thing he could do. Why, does he not stop them when about to depart? Why does he not take up arms, and why not suggest some course for the fickle multitude to pursue? This was not too much for him, who never says any thing but what is grand. Well, and didst thou take to flight? I was witness of it, and ashamed I was to see, when thou wast turning thy back, and wast preparing the sails of disgrace. Without delay, I exclaimed, 'What are you doing? What madness made you, O my friends, quit Troy, well nigh taken? And what, in this tenth year, are you carrying home but disgrace?'

"With these and other words, for which grief itself had made me eloquent, I brought back the resisting Greeks from the flying fleet. The son of Atreus calls together his allies, struck with terror; nor, even yet, does the son of Telamon dare to utter a word; yet Thersites[34] dares to launch out against the kings with impudent remarks, although not unpunished by myself. I am aroused, and I incite the trembling citizens against the foe, and by my voice I reclaim their lost courage. From that time, whatever that man, whom I drew away as he was turning his back, may seem to have done bravely, is all my own. In fine, who of the Greeks is either praising thee, or resorts to thee; but with me the son of Tydeus shares his exploits; he praises me, and is ever confident while Ulysses is his companion. It is something, out of so many thousands of the Greeks, to be singled out alone by Diomedes. Nor was it lot that ordered me to go forth; and yet, despising the dangers of the night and of the enemy, I slew Dolon, one of the Phrygian race, who dared the same things that we dared; though not before I had compelled him[35] to disclose everything, and had learned what perfidious Troy designed. Everything had I now discovered, and I had nothing further to find out, and I might now have returned, with my praises going before me. Not content with that, I sought the tent of Rhesus, and in his own camp slew himself and his attendants. And thus, as a conqueror, and having gained my own desires, I returned in the captured chariot, resembling a joyous triumph. Deny me the arms of him whose horses the enemy had demanded as the price for one night's service; and let Ajax be esteemed your greater benefactor.

"Why should I make reference to the troops of Lycian Sarpedon,[36] mowed down by my sword? With much bloodshed I slew Cœranos, the son of Iphitus, and Alastor, and Chromius, and Alcander, and Halius, and Noëmon, and Prytanis, and I put to death Thoön, with Chersidamas, and Charops, and Ennomos, impelled by his relentless fate; five of less renown fell by my hand beneath the city walls. I, too, fellow-citizens, have wounds, honourable in their place.[37] Believe not his crafty words; here! behold them." And then, with his hand, he pulls aside his garment, and, "this is the breast," says he, "that has been ever employed in your service."

"But the son of Telamon has spent none of his blood on his friends for so many years, and he has a body without a single wound.[38] But what signifies that, if he says that he bore arms for the Pelasgian fleet against both the Trojans and Jupiter himself? I confess it, he did bear them; nor is it any part of mine with malice to detract from the good deeds of others; but let him not alone lay claim to what belongs to all, and let him give to yourselves, as well, some of the honour. The descendant of Actor, safe under the appearance of Achilles, repelled the Trojans, with their defender, from the ships on the point of being burnt. He, too, unmindful of the king, and of the chiefs, and of myself, fancies that he alone dared to engage[39] with Hector in combat, being the ninth in that duty, and preferred by favour of the lot. But yet, most brave chief, what was the issue of thy combat? Hector came off, injured by no wound. Ah, wretched me! with how much grief am I compelled to recollect that time at which Achilles, the bulwark of the Greeks, was slain: nor tears, nor grief, nor fear, hindered me from carrying his body aloft from the ground; on these shoulders, I say, on these shoulders I bore the body of Achilles, and his arms together with him, which now, too, I am endeavouring to bear off. I have strength to suffice for such a weight, and, assuredly, I have a soul that will be sensible of your honours.

"Was then, forsooth! his azure mother so anxious in her son's behalf that the heavenly gifts, a work of so great ingenuity, a rough soldier, and one without any genius, should put on? For he will not understand the engravings on the shield; the ocean, and the earth, and the stars with the lofty heavens and the Pleïades, and the Hyades, and the Bear that avoids the sea, and the different cities, and the blazing sword of Orion; arms he insists on receiving, which he does not understand. What! and does he charge that I, avoiding the duties of this laborious war, came but late to the toil begun? and does he not perceive that in this he is defaming the brave Achilles? If he calls dissembling a crime, we have both of us dissembled. If delay stands for a fault, I was earlier than he. A fond wife detained me, a fond mother Achilles. The first part of our time was given to them, the rest to yourselves. I am not alarmed, if now I am unable to defend myself against this accusation, in common with so great a man. Yet he was found out by the dexterity of Ulysses, but not Ulysses by that of Ajax.

"And that we may not be surprised at his pouring out on me the reproaches of his silly tongue, against you, too, does he make objections worthy of shame. Is it base for me, with a false crime to have charged Palamedes, and honourable for you to have condemned him? But neither could Palamedes, the son of Nauplius, defend a crime so great, and so manifest; nor did you only hear the charges against him, but you witnessed them, and in the bribe itself the charge was established. Nor have I deserved to be accused, because Lemnos, the isle of Vulcan, still receives Philoctetes, the son of Pœas. Greeks, defend your own acts! for you consented to it. Nor yet shall I deny that I advised him to withdraw himself from the toils of the warfare and the voyage, and to try by rest to assuage his cruel pains. He consented, and still he lives. This advice was not only well-meant, but it was fortunate as well, when 'twas enough to be well-meant. Since our prophets demand him for the purpose of destroying Troy, entrust not that to me. The son of Telamon will be better to go, and by his eloquence will soften the hero, maddened by diseases and anger, or by some wile will skilfully bring him thence. Sooner will Simoïs flow backward, and Ida stand without foliage, and Achaia promise aid to Troy, than, my breast being inactive in your interest, the skill of stupid Ajax shall avail the Greeks.

"Though thou be, relentless Philoctetes, enraged against thy friends and the king, and myself, though thou curse and devote my head, everlastingly, and though thou wish to have me in thy anguish thrown in thy way perchance, and to shed my blood; and though if I meet thee, so thou wilt have the opportunity of meeting me, still will I attempt thee, and will endeavour to bring thee back with me. And, if Fortune favours me, I will as surely be the possessor of thy arrows, as I was the possessor of the Dardanian prophet[40] whom I took prisoner; and so I revealed the answers of the Deities and the fates of Troy; and as I carried off the hidden statue[41] of the Phrygian Minerva from the midst of the enemy. And does Ajax, then, compare himself with me? The Fates, in fact, would not allow Troy to be captured without that statue. Where is the valiant Ajax? where are the boastful words of that mighty man? Why art thou trembling here? Why dares Ulysses to go through the guards, and to entrust himself to the night, and, through fell swords, to enter not only the walls of Troy, but even its highest towers, and to tear the Goddess from her shrine, and, thus torn, to bear her off amid the enemy?

"Had I not done these things, in vain would the son of Telamon been bearing the seven hides of the bulls on his left arm. On that night was the victory over Troy gained by me; then did I conquer Pergamus, when I rendered it capable of being conquered. Forbear by thy looks,[42] and thy muttering, to show me the son of Tydeus; a part of the glory in these things is his own. Neither wast thou alone, when for the allied fleet thou didst grasp thy shield: a multitude was attending thee, while but one fell to me: who, did he not know that a fighting man is of less value than a wise one, and that the reward is not the due of the invincible right hand, would himself, too, have been suing for these arms; the more discreet Ajax would have been suing, and the fierce Eurypilus,[43] and the son of the famous Andremon;[44] no less, too would Idomeneus,[45] and Meriones[46] sprung from the same land, and the brother of the greater son of Atreus have sought them. But these, brave in action, (nor are they second to thee in war,) have all yielded to my wisdom. Thy right hand is of value in war, but thy temper is one that stands in need of my direction. Thou hast strength without intelligence; I have a care for the future. Thou art able to fight; with me, the son of Atreus chooses the proper time for fighting. Thou only art of service with thy body; I with my mind: and as much as he who guides the bark, is superior to the capacity of the rower, as much as the general is greater than the soldier, so much do I excel thee; and in my body there is an intellect that is superior to hands: in that lies all my vigour.

"But you, ye chieftains, give the reward to your watchful servant; and for the cares of so many years which I have passed in anxiety, grant this honour as a compensation for my services. Our toil is now at its close; I have removed the opposing Fates, and by rendering it capable of being taken, in effect I have taken the lofty Pergamus. Now, by our common hopes, and the walls of the Trojans doomed to fall, and by those Gods whom lately I took from the enemy, by anything that remains, through wisdom to be done; if, too, anything remains of bold enterprize, and to be recovered from a dangerous spot; if you think that anything is still wanting for the downfall of Troy; then remember me; or if you give not me the arms, concede them to this;" and then he discovers the fatal statue of Minerva.

The body of the chiefs is moved, and then, in fact appears what eloquence can do; and the fluent man receives the arms of a brave one. He, who so often has alone withstood both Hector, and the sword, and flames, and Jove himself, cannot now withstand his wrath alone, and grief conquers the man that is invincible. He seizes his sword, and he says:—"This, at least, is my own; or will Ulysses claim this, too, for himself. This must I use against myself; and the blade, which has often been wet with the blood of the Phrygians, will now be wet with the slaughter of its owner: that no one but Ajax himself, may be enabled to conquer Ajax."

Thus he said; and he plunged the fatal sword into his breast, then for the first time suffering a wound, where it lay exposed to the steel. Nor were his hands able to draw out the weapon there fixed: the blood itself forced it out. And the earth, made red by the blood, produced a purple flower from the green turf, the same which had formerly been produced from the Œbalian wound. Letters common to that youth and to the hero, were inscribed in the middle of the leaves; the latter belonging to the name,[47] the former to the lamentation.

The conqueror, Ulysses, set sail for the country of Hypsipyle,[48] and of the illustrious Thoas, and the regions infamous for the slaughter there of the husbands of old; that he might bring back the arrows, the weapons of the Tirynthian hero. After he had carried them back to the Greeks, their owner attending too, the concluding hand was put, at length, to this protracted war. Troy and Priam fell together; the wretched wife of Priam lost after every thing else her human form, and alarmed a foreign air[49] with her barkings. Where the long Hellespont is reduced into a narrow compass, Ilion was in flames; nor had the flames yet ceased; and the altar of Jove had drank up the scanty blood of the aged Priam. The priestess of Apollo[50] dragged by the hair, extends her unavailing hands towards the heavens. The victorious Greeks drag along the Dardanian matrons, embracing, while they may, the statues of their country's Gods, and clinging to the burning temples, an envied spoil. Astyanax[51] is hurled from those towers from which he was often wont, when shown by his mother, to behold his father, fighting for himself, and defending the kingdom of his ancestors.

And now Boreas bids them depart, and with a favourable breeze, the sails, as they wave, resound, and the sailors bid them take advantage of the winds. "Troy, farewell!" the Trojan women cry;—"We are torn away!" and they give kisses to the soil, and leave the smoking roofs of their country. The last that goes on board the fleet, a dreadful sight, is Hecuba, found amid the sepulchres of her children. Dulichian hands have dragged her away, while clinging to their tombs and giving kisses to their bones; yet the ashes of one has she taken out, and, so taken out, has carried with her in her bosom the ashes of Hector. On the tomb of Hector she leaves the grey hair of her head, an humble offering, her hair and her tears. There is opposite to Phrygia, where Troy stood, a land inhabited by the men of Bistonia. There, was the rich palace of Polymnestor, to whom thy father, Polydorus, entrusted thee, to be brought up privately, and removed thee afar from the Phrygian arms. A wise resolution; had he not added, as well, great riches, the reward of crime, the incentive of an avaricious disposition. When the fortunes of the Phrygians were ruined, the wicked king of the Phrygians took a sword, and plunged it in the throat of his fosterchild; and, as though the crime could be removed with the body, he hurled him lifeless from a rock into the waters below.

[Footnote 1: We are pleading.—Ver. 5. The skill of the Poet is perceptible in the abrupt commencement of the speech of the impetuous Ajax.]

[Footnote 2: Nor his.—Ver. 11. Ajax often uses the pronoun 'iste' as a term of reproach.]

[Footnote 3: Night alone.—Ver. 15. By this he means that the alleged exploits of Ulysses were altogether fictitious; or that they were done in the dark to conceal his fear.]

[Footnote 4: Took the city.—Ver. 23. Telamon, was the companion of Hercules when he sacked Troy, as a punishment for the perfidy of Laomedon.]

[Footnote 5: Sisyphus.—Ver. 26. This is intended as a reproachful hint against Ulysses, whose mother, Anticlea, was said to have been seduced by Sisyphus before her marriage to Laërtes.]

[Footnote 6: Ajax is the third.—Ver. 28. That is the third, exclusive of Jupiter; for Ajax was the grandson of Æacus, and the great grandson of Jupiter.]

[Footnote 7: My cousin.—Ver. 31. 'Frater' here means, not 'brother,' but 'cousin,' as Peleus and Telamon, the fathers of Achilles and Ajax, were brothers.]

[Footnote 8: No informer.—Ver. 34. He alludes to the means which Ulysses adopted to avoid going to the Trojan war. Pretending to be seized with madness, he ploughed the sea-shore, and sowed it with salt. To ascertain the truth, Palamedes placed his infant son, Telemachus, before the plough; on which Ulysses turned on one side, to avoid hurting the child, which was considered a proof that his madness was not real.]

[Footnote 9: Son of Nauplius.—Ver. 39. Palamedes was the son of Nauplius, the king of Eubœa, and a son of Neptune.]

[Footnote 10: The contrivance.—Ver. 38. Ulysses forged a letter from Priam, in which the king thanked Palamedes for his intended assistance to the Trojan cause, and begged to present him a sum of money. By bribing the servants of Palamedes, he caused a large quantity of gold to be buried in the ground, under his tent. He then caused the letter to be intercepted, and to be carried to Agamemnon. On the appearance of Palamedes to answer the charge, Ulysses appeared seemingly as his friend, and suggested, that if no gold should be found in his possession, he must be innocent. The gold, however, being found, Palamedes was stoned to death.]

[Footnote 11: Son of Pœas.—Ver. 45. Philoctetes was the possessor of the arrows of Hercules, without the presence of which Troy could not be taken. Accompanying the Greeks to the Trojan war, he was wounded in the foot by one of the arrows; and the smell arising from the wound was so offensive, that, by the advice of Ulysses, he was left behind, in the island of Lemnos, one of the Cyclades.]

[Footnote 12: Is being clothed.—Ver. 53. The Poet Attius, as quoted by Cicero, says that Philoctetes, while in Lemnos, made himself clothing out of the feathers of birds.]

[Footnote 13: Or by death.—Ver. 61. Exile in the case of Philoctetes; death, in that of Palamedes.]

[Footnote 14: Forsaking of Nestor.—Ver. 64. Nestor having been wounded by Paris, and being overtaken by Hector, was on the point of perishing, when Diomedes came to his rescue, Ulysses having taken to flight. See the Iliad, Book iii.]

[Footnote 15: And upbraided.—Ver. 69. He alludes to the words in the Iliad, which Homer puts in the mouth of Diomedes.]

[Footnote 16: And covered him.—Ver. 75. Ajax, at the request of Menelaüs, protected Ulysses with his shield, when he was wounded.]

[Footnote 17: Fall to my lot.—Ver. 85. He alludes to the occasion when some of the bravest of the Greeks drew lots which should accept the challenge of Hector: the Greeks wishing, according to Homer, that the lot might fall to Ajax Telamon, Ajax Oïleus, or Agamemnon.]

[Footnote 18: Rhesus.—Ver. 98. He was slain by Ulysses and Diomedes on the night on which he arrived, Iliad, Book x.]

[Footnote 19: Dolon.—Ver. 98. Being sent out by Hector to spy, he was intercepted by Ulysses and Diomedes, and slain at Troy. Iliad, Book x.]

[Footnote 20: Helenus.—Ver. 99. Being skilled in prophesy, after he was taken prisoner by Diomedes and Ulysses, his life was saved; and marrying Andromache, after the death of Pyrrhus, he succeeded to the throne of part of the kingdom of Chaonia.]

[Footnote 21: Dulichian.—Ver. 107. Dulichium was an island of the Ionian Sea, near Ithaca, and part of the realms of Ulysses.]

[Footnote 22: The spear.—Ver. 109. The spear of Achilles had been cut from the wood on Mount Pelion, and given by the Centaur Chiron to his father Peleus.]

[Footnote 23: He through whom.—Ver. 134. Through whom Achilles had been discovered, concealed among the daughters of Lycomedes, king of Seyros.]

[Footnote 24: Ever condemned.—Ver. 145. He alludes to the joint crime of Peleus the uncle, and Telamon, the father of Ajax, who were banished for the murder of their brother Phocus.]

[Footnote 25: Through the mother.—Ver. 146. Anticlea, the mother of Ulysses, was the daughter of Autolycus, of whom Mercury was the father by Chione, the daughter of Dædalion.]

[Footnote 26: Phthia.—Ver. 156. Phthia was the city of Thessaly, where Peleus, the father of Achilles, was residing; while Pyrrhus, his son, was living with his mother Deidamia, in the isle of Scyros, one of the Cyclades.]

[Footnote 27: Teucer.—Ver. 157. Teucer was the cousin of Achilles, being the son of Telamon, and the half-brother of Ajax; Hesione being the mother of Teucer, while Ajax was the son of Eubœa.]

[Footnote 28: Chrysa.—Ver. 174. Chrysa and Cylla were cities in the vicinity of Troy. This Scyros was, probably, not the island of that name, but some place near Troy.]

[Footnote 29: Lyrnessian.—Ver. 176. This was a city of the Troad, on the taking of which by Achilles, Hippodamia, or Briseïs, the daughter of Bryses, was made captive by Achilles.]

[Footnote 30: Grief of one.—Ver. 181. He alludes to the misfortune of Menelaüs in losing his wife, if, indeed, it could be deemed a misfortune.]

[Footnote 31: Antenor.—Ver. 201. Antenor, who was related to Priam, always advocated peace with the Greeks; for which reason, according to Livy, the Greeks did not treat him as an enemy.]

[Footnote 32: Surround the trenches.—Ver. 212. He probably alludes to the trenches thrown up before the ships of the Greeks, and defended by embankments, which were afterwards destroyed by Neptune.]

[Footnote 33: I am sent.—Ver. 215. As on the occasion when he was sent to restore Chryseis to her father Chryses, the priest of Apollo, that the pestilence might be stayed, which had been sent by the offended God.]

[Footnote 34: Thersites.—Ver. 233. He was the most deformed, cowardly, and impudent of the Greeks, who, always abusing his betters, was beaten by Ulysses, and was at last killed by Achilles with a blow of his fist.]

[Footnote 35: Compelled him.—Ver. 245. When he was taken prisoner by them, Ulysses and Diomedes compelled Dolon to disclose what was going on in the Trojan camp, and learned from him the recent arrival of Rhesus, the son of either Mars or Strymon, and the king of Thrace.]

[Footnote 36: Sarpedon.—Ver. 255. He was the son of Jupiter and Europa, and was king of Lycia. Aiding the Trojans, he was slain by Patroclus.]

[Footnote 37: In their place.—Ver. 263. That is, inflicted on the breast, and not on the back.]

[Footnote 38: A single wound.—Ver. 267. He alludes to his being invulnerable, from having been wrapped in the lion's skin of Hercules.]

[Footnote 39: Dared to engage.—Ver. 275. Hector and Ajax Telamon meeting in single combat, neither was the conqueror; but on parting they exchanged gifts, which were fatal to them both. Hector was dragged round the walls of Troy by the belt which he received from Ajax; while the latter committed suicide with the sword which was given to him by Hector.]

[Footnote 40: Dardanian prophet.—Ver. 335. Helenus, the son of Priam.]

[Footnote 41: The hidden statue.—Ver. 337. This was the Palladium, or statue of Minerva, which was destined to be the guardian of the safety of Troy, so long as it was in the possession of the Trojans.]

[Footnote 42: By thy looks.—Ver. 350. We are to suppose, that here Ajax is nodding at, or pointing towards Diomedes, as having helped Ulysses on all the occasions which he names, he having been his constant companion in his exploits.]

[Footnote 43: Eurypilus.—Ver. 357. He was the son of Evæmon, and came with forty ships to aid the Greeks. He was from Ormenius, a city of Thessaly.]

[Footnote 44: Andremon.—Ver. 357. Thoas, the son of Andremon, was the leader of the Ætolians; he came with forty ships to the Trojan war.]

[Footnote 45: Idomeneus.—Ver. 358. He was the son of Deucalion, king of Crete. After the siege of Troy, he settled at Salentinum, a promontory of Calabria, in Italy.]

[Footnote 46: Meriones.—Ver. 359. He was the nephew and charioteer of Idomeneus.]

[Footnote 47: To the name.—Ver. 398. See note to Book x., line 207.]

[Footnote 48: Country of Hypsipyle.—Ver. 399. The island of Lemnos is here called the country of Hypsipyle, who saved the life of her father Thoas, when the other women of the island slew the males.]

[Footnote 49: A foreign air.—Ver. 406. Namely, Thrace, which was far away from her native country.]

[Footnote 50: Priestess of Apollo.—Ver. 410. Cassandra was the priestess of Apollo. Being ravished by Ajax Oïleus, she became the captive of Agamemnon, and was slain by Clytemnestra.]

[Footnote 51: Astyanax.—Ver. 415. He was the only child of Hector and Andromache. Ulysses threw him from the top of a high tower, that none of the royal blood might survive.]

EXPLANATION

It may with justice be said, that in the speeches of Ajax Telamon, and Ulysses, here given, the Poet has presented us with a masterpiece of genius; both in the lively colours in which he has described the two rivals, and the ingenious manner in which he has throughout sustained the contrast between their respective characters.

The ancient writers are not agreed upon the question, who was the mother of Ajax Telamon; Dares says that it was Hesione; while Apollodorus, Plutarch, Tzetzes and others, allege that it was Peribœa, the daughter of Alcathoüs, the son of Pelops. Pindar and Apollodorus say, that Hercules, on going to visit his friend Telamon, prayed to Jupiter that Telamon might have a son, whose skin should be as impenetrable as that of the Nemæan lion, which he then wore. As he prayed, he espied an eagle; upon which, he informed his friend that a favourable event awaited his prayer, and desired him to call his son after the name of an eagle, which in the Greek is αἰετὸς. The Scholiast on Sophocles, Suidas and Tzetzes, say further, that when Hercules returned to see Telamon, after the birth of Ajax, he covered him with the lion's skin, and that by this means Ajax became invulnerable except in that spot of his body, which was beneath the hole which the arrow of Hercules had made in the skin of the beast.

Dictys, Suidas, and Cedrenus affirm, that the dispute of Ulysses and Ajax Telamon was about the Palladium, to which each of them laid claim. They add, that the Grecian nobles, having adjudged it to Ulysses, Ajax threatened to slay them, and was found dead in his tent the next morning; but it is more generally stated to the effect here related by Ovid, that he killed himself, because he could not obtain the armour of Achilles. Filled with grief and anger combined, he became distracted; and after falling on some flocks, which in his madness he took for enemies, he at last stabbed himself with the sword which he had received from Hector. This account has been followed by Euripides, in his tragedy on the subject of the death of Ajax; and Homer seems to allude to this story, when he makes Ulysses say, that on his descent to the Infernal Regions, the shades of all the Grecian heroes immediately met him, except that of Ajax, whose resentment at their former dispute about the armour of Achilles was still so warm, that he would not come near him. The Scholiast on Homer, and Eustathius, say that Agamemnon being much embarrassed how to behave in a dispute which might have proved fatal to the Grecian cause, ordered the Trojan prisoners to come before the council to give their opinion, as to which of them had done the most mischief; and that they answered in favour of Ulysses. The Scholiast on Aristophanes also adds, that Agamemnon, not satisfied with this enquiry, sent out spies to know what was the opinion of the Trojans on the relative merits of Ulysses and Ajax; and that upon their report, he decided in favour of Ulysses.

According to Pliny and Pausanias, Ajax was buried near the promontory of Sigæum, where a tomb was erected for him; though other writers, on the authority of Dictys, place his tomb on the promontory of Rhœtæum. Horace speaks of him as being denied the honour of a funeral; but he evidently alludes to a passage in the tragedy of Sophocles, where the poet introduces Agamemnon as obstinately refusing to allow him burial, till he is softened by the entreaties of Teucer.

It is probable that Homer knew nothing of the story here mentioned relative to the concealment of Achilles, disguised in female apparel, by Thetis, in the court of Lycomedes, her brother; for speaking of the manner in which Achilles engaged in the war, he says that Nestor and Ulysses went to visit Peleus and Menœtius, and easily prevailed with them that Achilles and Patroclus should accompany them to the war. It was, however, at the court of Lycomedes that Achilles fell in love with and married Deidamia, by whom he had Pyrrhus, or Neoptolemus, who was present at the taking of Troy, at a very early age.

The story of Polydorus is related in the third Book of the Æneid, and is also told by Hyginus, with some variations. He says that Polydorus was sent by Priam to Polymnestor, king of Thrace, while he was yet in his cradle; and that Ilione, the daughter of Priam, distrusting the cruelty and avarice of Polymnestor, who was her husband, educated the child as her own son, and made their own son Deiphylus pass for Polydorus, the two infants being of the same age. He also says that the Greeks, after the taking of Troy, offered Electra to Polymnestor in marriage, on condition that he should divorce Ilione, and slay Polydorus, and that Polymnestor, having acceded to their proposal, unconsciously killed his own son Deiphylus. Polydorus going to consult the oracle concerning his future fortune, was told, that his father was dead, and his native city reduced to ashes; on which he imagined that the oracle had deceived him; but returning to Thrace, his sister informed him of the secret, on which he deprived Polymnestor of his sight.

FABLES III AND IV [XIII.439-622]

In returning from Troy, the Greeks are stopped in Thrace by the shade of Achilles, who requests that Polyxena shall be sacrificed to his manes. While Hecuba is fetching water with which to bathe the body of her daughter, she espies the corpse of her son Polydorus. In her exasperations she repairs to the court of Polymnestor; and having torn out his eyes, is transformed into a bitch. Memnon, who has been slain by Achilles, is honoured with a magnificent funeral, and, at the prayer of Aurora, his ashes are transformed by Jupiter into birds, since called Memnonides.

On the Thracian shore the son of Atreus had moored his fleet, until the sea was calm, and until the wind was more propitious. Here, on a sudden, Achilles, as great as he was wont to be when alive, rises from the ground, bursting far and wide, and, like to one threatening, revives the countenance of that time when he fiercely attacked Agamemnon with his lawless sword. "And are you departing, unmindful of me, ye Greeks?" he says; "and is all grateful remembrance of my valour buried together with me? Do not so. And that my sepulchre may not be without honour, let Polyxena slain appease the ghost of Achilles." Thus he said; and his companions obeying the implacable shade, the noble and unfortunate maid, and more than an ordinary woman, torn from the bosom of her mother, which she now cherished almost alone, was led to the tomb, and became a sacrifice at his ruthless pile.

She, mindful of herself, after she was brought to the cruel altar, and had perceived that the savage rites were preparing for her; and when she saw Neoptolemus standing by, and wielding his sword, and fixing his eyes upon her countenance, said—"Quickly make use of this noble blood: in me there is no resistance: and do thou bury thy weapons either in my throat or in my breast!" and, at the same time she laid bare her throat and her breast; "should I, Polyxena, forsooth,[52] either endure to be the slave of any person, or will any sacred Deity be appeased by such a sacrifice. I only wish that my death could be concealed from my mother. My mother is the impediment; and she lessens my joys at death. Yet it is not my death, but her own life, that should be lamented by her. Only, stand ye off, lest I should go to the Stygian shades not a free woman: if in this I demand what is just; and withhold the hands of males from the contact of a virgin. My blood will be the more acceptable to him, whoever it is that you are preparing to appease by my slaughter. Yet, if the last prayers of my lips move any of you,—'tis the daughter of king Priam, and not a captive that entreats—return my body unconsumed to my mother, and let her not purchase for me with gold, but with tears, the sad privilege of a sepulchre. When in former times she could, then used she to purchase with gold."

Thus she said; but the people did not restrain those tears which she restrained. Even the priest himself, weeping and reluctant, divided her presented breast with the piercing steel. She, sinking to the earth on her failing knees, maintained an undaunted countenance to the last moment of her life. Even then was it her care, when she fell, to cover the features that ought to be concealed, and to preserve the honour of her chaste modesty. The Trojan matrons received her, and reckoned the children of Priam whom they had had to deplore; and how much blood one house had expended. And they lament thee, Oh virgin! and thee, Oh thou! so lately called a royal wife and a royal mother, once the resemblance of flourishing Asia, but now a worthless prey amid the plunder of Troy; which the conquering Ulysses would have declined as his, but that thou hadst brought Hector forth. And scarce did Hector find an owner for his mother. She, embracing the body bereft of a soul so brave, gave to that as well, those tears which so oft she had given for her country, her children, and her husband; and her tears she poured in his wounds. And she impressed kisses with her lips, and beat her breast now accustomed to it; and trailing her grey hairs in the clotted blood, many things indeed did she say, but these as well, as she tore her breast:

"My daughter, the last affliction (for what now remains?) to thy mother: my daughter, thou liest prostrate, and I behold thy wound as my own wounds. Lo! lest I should have lost any one of my children without bloodshed, thou, too, dost receive thy wound. Still, because thou wast a woman, I supposed thee safe from the sword; and yet, a woman, thou hast fallen by the sword. The same Achilles, the ruin of Troy, and the bereaver of myself, the same has destroyed thus many of thy brothers, and thyself. But, after he had fallen by the arrows of Paris and of Phœbus, 'Now, at least,' I said, 'Achilles is no longer to be dreaded;' and yet even now, was he to be dreaded by me. The very ashes of him, as he lies buried, rage against this family; and even in the tomb have we found him an enemy. For the descendant of Æacus have I been thus prolific. Great Ilion lies prostrate, and the public calamity is completed by a dreadful catastrophe; if indeed, it is completed. Pergamus alone remains for me: and my sorrow is still in its career. So lately the greatest woman in the world, powerful in so many sons-in-law, and children[53], and daughters-in-law, and in my husband, now I am dragged into exile, destitute, and torn away from the tombs of my kindred, as a present to Penelope. She, pointing me out to the matrons of Ithaca, as I tease my allotted task, will say, 'This is that famous mother of Hector; this is the wife of Priam.' And, now thou, who after the loss of so many children, alone didst alleviate the sorrows of thy mother, hast made the atonement at the tomb of the enemy. Atoning sacrifices for an enemy have I brought forth. For what purpose, lasting like iron, am I reserved? and why do I linger here? To what end dost thou, pernicious age, detain me? Why, ye cruel Deities, unless to the end that I may see fresh deaths, do ye reprieve an aged woman of years so prolonged? Who could have supposed, that after the fall of Troy, Priam could have been pronounced happy? Blessed in his death, he has not beheld thee, my daughter, thus cut off; and at the same moment, he lost his life and his kingdom.

"But, I suppose, thou, a maiden of royal birth, wilt be honoured with funeral rites, and thy body will be deposited in the tombs of thy ancestors. This is not the fortune of thy house; tears and a handful of foreign sand will be thy lot, the only gifts of a mother. We have lost all; a child most dear to his mother, now alone remains as a reason for me to endure to live yet for a short time, once the youngest of all my male issue, Polydorus, entrusted on these coasts to the Ismarian king. Why, in the mean time, am I delaying to bathe her cruel wounds with the stream, her features, too, besmeared with dreadful blood?"

Thus she spoke; and with aged step she proceeded towards the shore, tearing her grey locks. "Give me an urn, ye Trojan women," the unhappy mother had just said, in order that she might take up the flowing waters, when she beheld[54] the body of Polydorus thrown up on the shore, and the great wounds made by the Thracian weapons. The Trojan women cried out aloud; with grief she was struck dumb; and very grief consumed both her voice and the tears that arose within; and much resembling a hard rock she became benumbed. And at one moment she fixed her eyes on the ground before her; and sometimes she raised her haggard features towards the skies; and now she viewed the features, now the wounds of her son, as he lay; the wounds especially; and she armed and prepared herself for vengeance by rage. Soon as she was inflamed by it, as though she still remained a queen, she determined to be revenged, and was wholly employed in devising a fitting form of punishment. And as the lioness rages when bereft of her sucking whelp, and having found the tracks of his feet, follows the enemy that she sees not; so Hecuba, after she had mingled rage with mourning, not forgetful of her spirit, but forgetful of her years, went to Polymnestor, the contriver of this dreadful murder, and demanded an interview; for that it was her wish to show him a concealed treasure left for him to give to her son.

The Odrysian king believes her, and, inured to the love of gain, comes to a secret spot. Then with soothing lips, he craftily says, "Away with delays, Hecuba, and give the present to thy son; all that thou givest, and what thou hast already given, I swear by the Gods above, shall be his." Sternly she eyes him as he speaks, and falsely swears; and she boils with heaving rage; and so flies on him, seized by a throng of the captive matrons, and thrusts her fingers into his perfidious eyes; and of their sight she despoils his cheeks, and plunges her hands into the sockets, ('tis rage that makes her strong); and, defiled with his guilty blood, she tears not his eyes, for they are not left, but the places for his eyes.

Provoked by the death of their king, the Thracian people begin to attack the Trojan matron with the hurling of darts and of stones. But she attacks the stones thrown at her with a hoarse noise, and with bites; and attempting to speak, her mouth just ready for the words, she barks aloud. The place still exists, and derives its name[55] from the circumstance; and long remembering her ancient misfortunes, even then did she howl dismally through the Sithonian plains. Her sad fortune moved both her own Trojans, and her Pelasgian foes, and all the Gods as well; so much so, that even the wife and sister of Jove herself denied that Hecuba had deserved that fate.

Although she has favoured those same arms, there is not leisure for Aurora to be moved by the calamities and the fall of Troy. A nearer care and grief at home for her lost Memnon is afflicting her. Him his rosy-coloured mother saw perish by the spear of Achilles on the Phrygian plains. This she saw; and that colour with which the hours of the morning grow ruddy, turned pale, and the æther lay hid in clouds. But the parent could not endure to behold his limbs laid on the closing flames. But with loose hair, just as she was, she disdained not to fall down at the knees of great Jove, and to add these words to her tears: "Inferior to all the Goddesses which the golden æther does sustain, (for throughout all the world are my temples the fewest), still, a Goddess, I am come; not that thou shouldst grant me temples and days of sacrifice, and altars to be heated with fires. But if thou considerest how much I, a female, perform for thee, at the time when, with the early dawn, I keep the confines of the night, thou wouldst think that some reward ought to be given to me. But that is not my care, nor is such now the condition of Aurora such that she should demand the honours deserved by her. Bereft of my Memnon am I come; of him who, in vain, wielded valiant arms for his uncle, and who in his early years ('twas thus ye willed it,) was slain by the brave Achilles. Give him, I pray, supreme ruler of the Gods, some honour, as a solace for his death, and ease the wounds of a mother."

Jove nods his assent; when suddenly the lofty pile of Memnon sinks with its towering fires, and volumes of black smoke darken the light of day. Just as when the rivers exhale the rising fogs, and the sun is not admitted below them. The black embers fly, and rolling into one body, they thicken, and take a form, and assume heat and life from the flames. Their own lightness gives them wings; and first, like birds, and then real birds, they flutter with their wings. At once innumerable sisters are fluttering, whose natal origin is the same. And thrice do they go around the pile, and thrice does their clamour rise in concert into the air. In the fourth flight they separate their company. Then two fierce tribes wage war from opposite sides, and with their beaks and crooked claws expend their rage, and weary their wings and opposing breasts; and down their kindred bodies fall, a sacrifice to the entombed ashes, and they remember that from a great man they have received their birth. Their progenitor gives a name to these birds so suddenly formed, called Memnonides after him; when the Sun has run through the twelve signs of the Zodiac, they fight, doomed to perish in battle, in honour of their parent.[56]

To others, therefore, it seemed a sad thing, that the daughter of Dymas was now barking; but Aurora was intent on her own sorrows; and even now she sheds the tears of affection, and sprinkles them in dew over all the world.

[Footnote 52: Forsooth.—460. Clarke translates 'scilicet,' 'I warrant ye.']

[Footnote 53: And children.—Ver. 509. Hyginus names fifty-four children of Priam, of whom seventeen were by Hecuba.]

[Footnote 54: She beheld.—Ver. 536. Euripides represents, in his tragedy of Hecuba, that a female servant, sent by Hecuba to bring water from the sea shore for the purpose of washing the body of Polyxena, was the first to see the corpse of Polydorus.]

[Footnote 55: Derives its name.—Ver. 569. Strabo places it near Sestos, in the Thracian Chersonesus, and calls it κυνὸς σῆμα, 'The bitches' tomb.']

[Footnote 56: Of their parent.—Ver. 619. He perhaps alludes to the fights of the Gladiators, on the occasion of the funerals of the Roman patricians. 'Parentali perituræ Marte,' is rendered by Clarke, 'to fall in the fight of parentation.']

EXPLANATION

The particulars which Ovid here gives of the misfortunes that befell the family of Priam, with the exception of a few circumstances, agree perfectly with the narratives of the ancient historians.

According to Dictys, Philostratus, and Hyginus, after Achilles was slain by the treachery of Paris, on the eve of his marriage with Polyxena, she became inconsolable at his death, and returning to the Grecian camp, she was kindly received by Agamemnon; but being unable to get the better of her despair, she stole out of the camp at night, and stabbed herself at the tomb of Achilles. Philostratus adds, that the ghost of Achilles appeared to Apollonius Tyanæus, the hero of his story, and gave him permission to ask him any questions he pleased, assuring him, that he would give him full information on the subject of them. Among other things, Apollonius desired to know if it was the truth that the Greeks had sacrificed Polyxena on his tomb; to which the ghost replied, that her grief made her take the resolution not to survive her intended husband, and that she had killed herself.

Other writers, agreeing with Ovid as to the manner of her death, tell us that it was Pyrrhus who sacrificed Polyxena to his father's shade, to revenge his death, of which, though innocently, she had been the cause. Pausanias, who says that this was the general opinion, avers, on what ground it is difficult to conceive, that Homer designedly omitted this fact, because it was so dishonourable to the Greeks; and in his description of the paintings at Delphi, by Polygnotus, of the destruction of Troy, he says that Polyxena was there represented as being led out to the tomb of Achilles, where she was sacrificed by the Greeks. He also says, that he had seen her story painted in the same manner at Pergamus, Athens, and other places. Many of the poets, and Virgil in the number, affirm that Polyxena was sacrificed in Phrygia, near Troy, on the tomb of Achilles, he having desired it at his death; while Euripides says that it was in the Thracian Chersonesus, on a cenotaph, which was erected there in honour of Achilles: and that his ghost appearing, Calchas was consulted, who answered, that it was necessary to sacrifice Polyxena, which was accordingly done by Pyrrhus.

The ancient writers are divided as to the descent of Hecuba. Homer, who has been followed by his Scholiast, and by Ovid and Suidas, says that she was the daughter of Dymas, King of Phrygia. Euripides says that she was the daughter of Cisscus, and with him Virgil and Servius agree. Apollodorus, again, makes her to be descended from Sangar and Merope. In the distribution of spoil after the siege of Troy, Hecuba fell to the share of Ulysses, and became his slave; but died soon after, in Thrace. Plautus and Servius allege that the Greeks themselves circulated the story of her transformation into a bitch, because she was perpetually railing at them, to provoke them to put her to death, rather than condemn her to pass her life as a slave. According to Strabo and Pomponius Mela, in their time, the place of her burial was still to be seen in Thrace. Euripides, in his Hecuba, has not followed this tradition, but represents her as complaining that the Greeks had chained her to the door of Agamemnon like a dog. Perhaps she became the slave of Agamemnon after Ulysses had left the army, on his return to Ithaca; and it is possible that the story of her transformation may have been solely founded on this tradition. She bore to Priam ten sons and seven daughters, and survived them all except Helenus; most of her sons having fallen by the hand of Achilles.

Many ancient writers, with whom Ovid here agrees, affirm that Memnon was the son of Tithonus, the brother of Priam, and Aurora, or Eos, the Goddess of the morn. They also say that he came to assist the Trojans with ten thousand Persians, and as many Æthiopians. Diodorus Siculus asserts that Memnon was said to have been the son of Aurora, because he left Phrygia, and went to settle in the East. It is not clear in what country he fixed his residence. Some say that it was at Susa, in Persia; others that it was in Egypt, or in Æthiopia, which perhaps amounts to the same, as Æthiopia was not in general distinguished from the Higher or Upper Egypt. Marsham is of opinion that Memnon was the same with Amenophis, one of the kings of Egypt: while Le Clerc considers him to have been the same person as Ham, the son of Noah; and Vossius identifies him with Boalcis, a God of the Syrians. It seems probable that he was an Egyptian, who had perhaps formed an alliance with the reigning family of Troy.

FABLES V AND VI [XIII.623-718]

After the taking of Troy, Æneas escapes with his father and his son, and goes to Delos. Anius, the priest of Apollo, recounts to him how his daughters have been transformed into doves, and at parting they exchange presents. The Poet here introduces the story of the daughters of Orion, who, having sacrificed their lives for the safety of Thebes, when ravaged by a plague, two young men arise out of their ashes.

But yet the Fates do not allow the hope of Troy to be ruined even with its walls. The Cytherean hero bears on his shoulders the sacred relics and his father, another sacred relic, a venerable burden. In his affection, out of wealth so great, he selects that prize, and his own Ascanius, and with his flying fleet is borne through the seas from Antandros,[57] and leaves the accursed thresholds of the Thracians, and the earth streaming with the blood of Polydorus; and, with good winds and favouring tide, he enters the city of Apollo, his companions attending him.

Anius, by whom, as king, men were, and by whom, as priest, Phœbus was duly provided for, received him both into his temple and his house, and showed him the city and the dedicated temples, and the two trunks of trees once grasped[58] by Latona in her labour. Frankincense being given to the flames, and wine poured forth on the frankincense, and the entrails of slain oxen[59] being duly burnt, they repair to the royal palace, and reclining on lofty couches, with flowing wine, they take the gifts of Ceres. Then the pious Anchises says, "O chosen priest of Phœbus, am I deceived? or didst thou not have a son, also, when first I beheld these walls, and twice two daughters, so far as I remember?" To him Anius replies, shaking his temples wreathed with snow-white fillets, and says, "Thou art not mistaken, greatest hero; thou didst see me the parent of five children, whom now (so great a vicissitude of fortune affects mankind) thou seest almost bereft of all. For what assistance is my absent son to me, whom Andros, a land so called after his name, possesses, holding that place and kingdom on behalf of his father?

"The Delian God granted him the art of augury; to my female progeny Liber gave other gifts, exceeding both wishes and belief. For, at the touch of my daughters, all things were transformed into corn, and the stream of wine, and the berry of Minerva; and in these were there rich advantages. When the son of Atreus, the destroyer of Troy, learned this (that thou mayst not suppose that we, too, did not in some degree feel your storms) using the force of arms, he dragged them reluctantly from the bosom of their father, and commanded them to feed, with their heavenly gifts, the Argive fleet. Whither each of them could, they made their escape. Eubœa was sought by two; and by as many of my daughters, was Andros, their brother's island, sought. The forces came, and threatened war if they were not given up. Natural affection, subdued by fear, surrendered to punishment those kindred breasts; and, that thou mayst be able to forgive a timid brother, there was no Æneas, no Hector to defend Andros, through whom you Trojans held out to the tenth year. And now chains were being provided for their captive arms. Lifting up towards heaven their arms still free, they said, 'Father Bacchus, give us thy aid!' and the author of their gift did give them aid; if destroying them, in a wondrous manner, be called giving aid. By what means they lost their shape, neither could I learn, nor can I now tell. The sum of their calamity is known to me: they assumed wings, and were changed into birds of thy consort,[60] the snow-white doves."

With such and other discourse, after they have passed the time of feasting, the table being removed, they seek sleep. And they rise with the day, and repair to the oracle of Phœbus, who bids them seek the ancient mother and the kindred shores. The king attends, and presents them with gifts when about to depart; a sceptre to Anchises, a scarf and a quiver to his grandson, and a goblet to Æneas, which formerly Therses, his Ismenian guest, had sent him from the Aonian shores; this Therses had sent to him, but the Mylean Alcon had made it, and had carved it with this long device:

There was a city, and you might point out its seven gates: these were in place of[61] a name, and showed what city it was. Before the city was a funeral, and tombs, and fires, and funeral piles; and matrons, with hair dishevelled and naked breasts, expressed their grief; the Nymphs, too, seem to be weeping, and to mourn their springs dried up. Without foliage the bared tree runs straight up; the goats are gnawing the dried stones. Lo! he represents the daughters of Orion in the middle of Thebes; the one, as presenting her breast, more than woman's, with her bared throat; the other, thrusting a sword in her valorous wounds, as dying for her people, and as being borne, with an honoured funeral, through the city, and as being burnt in a conspicuous part of it; and then from the virgin embers, lest the race should fail, twin youths arising, whom Fame calls 'Coronæ,'[62] and for their mothers' ashes leading the funeral procession.

Thus far for the figures that shine on the ancient brass; the summit of the goblet is rough with gilded acanthus. Nor do the Trojans return gifts of less value than those given; and to the priest they give an incense-box, to keep the frankincense; they give a bowl, too, and a crown, brilliant with gold and gems. Then recollecting that the Trojans, as Teucrians, derived their origin from the blood of Teucer, they make for Crete, and cannot long endure the air of that place;[63] and, having left behind the hundred cities, they desire to reach the Ausonian harbours. A storm rages, and tosses the men to and fro; and winged Aëllo frightens them, when received in the unsafe harbours of the Strophades.[64] And now, borne along, they have passed the Dulichian harbours, and Ithaca, and Same,[65] and the Neritian abodes, the kingdom of the deceitful Ulysses; and they behold Ambracia,[66] contended for in a dispute of the Deities, which now is renowned for the Actian Apollo,[67] and the stone in the shape of the transformed judge, and the land of Dodona, vocal with its oaks; and the Chaonian bays, where the sons of the Molossian king escaped the unavailing flames, with wings attached to them.

[Footnote 57: Antandros.—Ver. 628. This was a city of Phrygia, at the foot of Mount Ida, where the fleet of Æneas was built.]

[Footnote 58: Trees once grasped.—Ver. 635. These were a palm and an olive tree, which were pointed out by the people of Delos, as having been held by Latona, when in the pangs of labour.]

[Footnote 59: Of slain oxen.—Ver. 637. This, however, was contrary to the usual practice; for if we credit Macrobius, no victim was slain on the altars of Apollo, in the island of Delos.]

[Footnote 60: Of thy consort.—Ver. 673. It must be remembered, that he is addressing Anchises, who was said to have enjoyed the favour of Venus; to which Goddess the dove was consecrated.]

[Footnote 61: In place of.—Ver. 686. For the seven gates, would at once lead to the conclusion that it represented the city of Thebes, in Bœotia. Myla, before referred to, was a town of Sicily.]

[Footnote 62: Calls 'Coronæ'.—Ver. 698. The word 'Coronas' is here employed as the plural of a female name 'Corona;' in Greek Κώρωνις.]

[Footnote 63: Of that place.—Ver. 707. Æneas and his followers founded in Crete the city of Pergamea; but the pestilence which raged there, and a continued drought, combined with the density of the atmosphere, obliged them to leave the island.]

[Footnote 64: The Strophades.—Ver. 709. These were two islands in the Ionian Sea, on the western side of Peloponnesus. They received their name from the Greek work στροφὴ, 'a return,' because Calais and Zethes pursued the Harpies, which persecuted Phineus so far, and then returned home by the command of Jupiter.]

[Footnote 65: Same.—Ver. 711. This island was also called Cephalenia. It was in the Ionian Sea, and formed part of the kingdom of Ulysses.]

[Footnote 66: Ambracia.—Ver. 714. This was a famous city of Epirus, which gave its name to the gulf of Ambracia.]

[Footnote 67: Actian Apollo.—Ver. 715. Augustus built a temple to Apollo, at Actium, in Epirus, near which he had defeated the fleet of Antony and Cleopatra. He also instituted games, to be celebrated there every fifth year in honour of his victory.]

EXPLANATION

Virgil describes Anius as the king of Delos, and the priest of Apollo at the same time. 'Rex Anius, rex idem hominum Phœbique sacerdos.' Æneid, Book III. He was descended from Cadmus, through his mother Rhea, the daughter of Staphilus. Having engaged in some intrigue, as Diodorus Siculus conjectures, her father exposed her on the sea in an open boat, which drove to Delos, and she was there delivered of Anius, who afterwards became the king of the island. By his wife Dorippe he had three daughters, who were extremely frugal, and by means of the offerings and presents that were brought to the temple of Apollo, amassed a large store of provisions. During the siege of Troy, the Greeks sent Palamedes to Delos, to demand food for the army; and, as a security for his compliance with these demands, they exacted the daughters of Anius as hostages. The damsels soon afterwards finding means to escape, it was said that Bacchus, who was their kinsman through Cadmus, had transformed them into doves. Probably the story of their transforming every thing they touched, into wine, corn, and oil, was founded solely on their thriftiness and parsimony. Bochart, however, explains the story from the circumstance of their names being, as he conjectures, Oëno, Spermo, and Elaï, which, in the old Phœnician dialect, signified wine, corn, and oil; and he thinks that the story was confirmed in general belief by the fact that large quantities of corn, wine, and oil were supplied from Delos to the Grecian army when before Troy.

In the reign of Orion, Thebes being devastated by a plague, the oracles were consulted, and the Thebans were told that the contagion would cease as soon as the daughters of the king should be sacrificed to the wrath of heaven. The two maidens immediately presented themselves at the altar; and on their immolation, the Gods were appeased, and the plague ceased. This example of patriotism and fortitude filled the more youthful Thebans with so much emulation, that they shook off their former inactivity, and soon became conspicuous for their bravery: which sudden change gave occasion to the saying, that the ashes of these maidens had been transformed into men.

The Poet follows Æneas on his voyage, to gain an opportunity of referring to several other current stories. Among other places, he passes the city of Ambracia, about which the Gods had contended, and sees the rock into which the umpire of their dispute, who had decided in favour of Hercules, was changed. Ambracia was on the coast of Epirus, and gave its name to an adjacent inlet of the sea, called the Ambracian Gulf. Antoninus Liberalis tells us, on the authority of Nicander, that Apollo, Diana, and Hercules disputed about this city, and left the decision to Cragaleus, who gave it in favour of Hercules; on which, Apollo transformed him into a rock. Very possibly the meaning of this may be, that when the people of Ambracia were considering to which of these Deities they should dedicate their city, Cragaleus preferred Hercules to the other two, or, in other words, the feats of war to the cultivation of the arts and sciences. Apollo was said to have turned him into a stone, either because he met with his death near the promontory where a temple of Apollo stood, or to show the stupidity of his decision. Antoninus Liberalis is the only writer besides Ovid that makes mention of the adventure of the sons of the Molossian king; he tells us that Munychus, king of the Molossi, had three sons, Alcander, Megaletor, and Philæus, and a daughter named Hyperippe. Some robbers setting fire to their father's house, they were transformed by Jupiter into birds. This, in all probability, is a poetical way of saying that the youths escaped from the flames, contrary to universal expectation.

The opinions of writers have been very conflicting as to the origin of the oracle of Dodona. Silius Italicus says that two pigeons flew from Thebes in Egypt, one of which went to Libya, and occasioned the founding of the oracle of Jupiter Ammon; while the other settled upon an oak in Chaonia, and signified thereby to the inhabitants, that it was the will of heaven that there should be an oracle in that place. Herodotus says that two priestesses of Egyptian Thebes being carried off by some Phœnician merchants, one of them was sold to the Greeks, after which she settled in the forest of Dodona, where a little chapel was founded by her in honour of Jupiter, in which she gave responses. He adds, that they called her 'the dove,' because being a foreigner they did not understand her language. At length, having learned the language of the Pelasgians, it was said that the dove had spoken. On that foundation grew the tradition that the oaks themselves uttered oracular responses.

Notwithstanding this plausible account of Herodotus, it is not impossible that some equivocal expressions in the Hebrew and Arabian languages may have given rise to the story. 'Himan,' in the one language, signified 'a priest;' and 'Heman,' in the other, was the name for 'a pigeon.' Possibly those who found the former word in the history of ancient Greece, written in the dialect of the original Phœnician settlers, did not understand it, and by their mistake, caused it to be asserted that a dove had founded the oracle of Dodona. Bochart tells us that the same word, in the Phœnician tongue, signifies either 'pigeons,' or 'women;' but the Abbè Sallier has gone still further, and has shown that, in the language of the ancient inhabitants of Epirus, the same word had the two significations mentioned by Bochart.

This oracle afterwards grew famous for its responses, and the priests used considerable ingenuity in the delivery of their answers. They cautiously kept all who came to consult them at a distance from the dark recess where the shrine was situated; and took care to deliver their responses in a manner so ambiguous, as to make people believe whatever they pleased. In this circumstance originates the variation in the descriptions of the oracle which the ancients have left us. According to some, it was the oaks that spoke; according to others, the beeches; while a third account was that pigeons gave the answers; and, lastly, it was said that the ringing of certain cauldrons there suspended, divulged the will of heaven. Stephanus Byzantinus has left a curious account of this contrivance of the cauldrons; he says that in that part of the forest of Dodona, where the oracle stood, there were two pillars erected, at a small distance from each other. On one there was placed a brazen vessel, about the size of an ordinary cauldron: and on the other a little boy, which was most probably a piece of mechanism, who held a brazen whip with several thongs which hung loose, and were easily moved. When the wind blew, the lashes struck against the vessel, and occasioned a noise while the wind continued. It was from them, he says, that the forest took the name of Dodona; 'dodo,' in the ancient language, signifying 'a cauldron.'

Strabo says that the responses were originally given by three priestesses: and he gives the reason why two priests were afterwards added to them. The Bœotians having been treacherously attacked by the people of Thrace during a truce which they had made, went to consult the oracle of Dodona; and the priestess answering them that if they would act impiously their design would succeed to their wish, the envoys suspected that this response had been suggested by the enemy, and burned her in revenge; after which they vindicated their cruelty by saying that if the priestess designed to deceive them, she well deserved her punishment; and that if she spoke with truthfulness, they had only followed the advice of the oracle. This argument not satisfying the people of the district, the Bœotian envoys were seized; but as they pleaded that it was unjust that two women already prejudiced against them should be their judges, two priests were added to decide the matter. These, in return for their being the occasion of putting them in an office so honourable and lucrative, acquitted the Bœotians; whose fellow countrymen were always in the habit from that time of addressing the priests when they consulted the oracle. These priests were called by the name of 'Selli.'

FABLE VII [XIII.719-897]

Polyphemus, one of the Cyclops, jealous of Acis, who is in love with Galatea, kills the youth with a rock which he hurls at him; on which, his blood is changed into a river which bears his name.

They make for the neighbouring land of the Phæacians,[68] planted with beauteous fruit. After this, Epirus and Buthrotos,[69] ruled over by the Phrygian prophet, and a fictitious Troy, are reached. Thence, acquainted with the future, all which, Helenus, the son of Priam, in his faithful instructions has forewarned them of, they enter Sicania. With three points this projects into the sea. Of these, Pachynos is turned towards the showery South: Lilybæum is exposed to the soft Zephyrs: but Peloros looks towards the Bear, free from the sea, and towards Boreas. By this part the Trojans enter; and with oars and favouring tide, at nightfall the fleet makes the Zanclæan sands. Scylla infests the right hand side, the restless Charybdis the left. This swallows and vomits forth again ships taken down; the other, having the face of a maiden, has her swarthy stomach surrounded with fierce dogs; and (if the poets have not left the whole a fiction) once on a time, too, she was a maiden. Many suitors courted her; who being repulsed, she, most beloved by the Nymphs of the ocean, went to the ocean Nymphs, and used to relate the eluded loves of the youths.

While Galatea[70] was giving her hair be to combed, heaving sighs, she addressed her in such words as these: "And yet, O maiden, no ungentle race of men does woo thee; and as thou dost, thou art able to deny them with impunity. But I, whose sire is Nereus, whom the azure Doris bore, who am guarded, too, by a crowd of sisters, was not able, but through the waves, to escape the passion of the Cyclop;" and as she spoke, the tears choked her utterance. When, with her fingers like marble, the maiden had wiped these away, and had comforted the Goddess, "Tell me, dearest," said she, "and conceal not from me (for I am true to thee) the cause of thy grief." In these words did the Nereid reply to the daughter of Cratæis:[71] "Acis was the son of Faunus and of the Nymph Symæthis, a great delight, indeed, to his father and his mother, yet a still greater to me. For the charming youth had attached me to himself alone, and eight birth-days having a second time been passed, he had now marked his tender cheeks with the dubious down. Him I pursued; incessantly did the Cyclop me pursue. Nor can I, shouldst thou enquire, declare whether the hatred of the Cylops, or the love of Acis, was the stronger in me. They were equal. O genial Venus! how great is the power of thy sway. For that savage, and one to be dreaded by the very woods, and beheld with impunity by no stranger, the contemner of great Olympus with the Gods themselves, now feels what love is; and, captivated with passion for me, he burns, forgetting his cattle and his caves.

"And now, Polyphemus, thou hast a care for thy looks, and now for the art of pleasing; now thou combest out thy stiffened hair with rakes, and now it pleases thee to cut thy shaggy beard with the sickle, and to look at thy fierce features in the water, and so to compose them. Thy love for carnage, and thy fierceness, and thy insatiate thirst for blood, now cease; and the ships both come and go in safety. Telemus, in the mean time arriving at the Sicilian Ætna, Telemus, the son of Eurymus, whom no omen had ever deceived, accosts the dreadful Polyphemus, and says, 'The single eye that thou dost carry in the midst of thy forehead, Ulysses shall take away from thee.' He laughed, and said, 'O most silly of the prophets, thou art mistaken, for another has already taken it away.' Thus does he slight him, in vain warning him of the truth; and he either burdens the shore, stalking along with huge strides, or, wearied, he returns to his shaded cave.

"A hill, in form of a wedge, runs out with a long projection into the sea: and the waves of the ocean flow round either side. Hither the fierce Cyclop ascended, and sat down in the middle. His woolly flocks followed, there being no one to guide them. After the pine tree,[72] which afforded him the service of a staff, but more fitted for sail-yards, was laid before his feet, and his pipe was taken up, formed of a hundred reeds; all the mountains were sensible of the piping of the shepherd: the waves, too, were sensible. I, lying hid within a rock, and reclining on the bosom of my own Acis, from afar caught such words as these with my ears, and marked them so heard in my mind: 'O Galatea, fairer than[73] the leaf of the snow-white privet,[74] more blooming than the meadows, more slender than the tall alder, brighter than glass, more wanton than the tender kid, smoother than the shells worn by continual floods, more pleasing than the winter's sun, or than the summer's shade, more beauteous than the apples, more sightly than the lofty plane tree, clearer than ice, sweeter than the ripened grape, softer than both the down of the swan, and than curdled milk, and, didst thou not fly me, more beauteous than a watered garden. And yet thou, the same Galatea, art wilder than the untamed bullocks, harder than the aged oak, more unstable than the waters, tougher than both the twigs of osier and than the white vines, more immoveable than these rocks, more violent than the torrent, prouder than the bepraised peacock, fiercer than the fire, rougher than the thistles, more cruel than the pregnant she-bear, more deaf than the ocean waves, more savage than the trodden water-snake: and, what I could especially wish to deprive thee of, fleeter not only than the deer when pursued by the loud barkings, but even than the winds and the fleeting air.

"'But didst thou but know me well, thou wouldst repine at having fled, and thou thyself wouldst blame thy own hesitation, and wouldst strive to retain me. I have a part of the mountain for my cave, pendent with the native rock; in which the sun is not felt in the middle of the heat, nor is the winter felt: there are apples that load the boughs; there are grapes on the lengthening vines, resembling gold; and there are purple ones as well; both the one and the other do I reserve for thee. With thine own hands thou shalt thyself gather the soft strawberries growing beneath the woodland shade; thou thyself shalt pluck the cornels of autumn, and plums not only darkened with their black juice, but even of the choicest kinds, and resembling new wax. Nor, I being thy husband, will there be wanting to thee chesnuts, nor the fruit of the arbute tree:[75] every tree shall be at thy service. All this cattle is my own: many, too, are wandering in the valleys: many the wood conceals: many more are penned in my caves. Nor, shouldst thou ask me perchance, could I tell thee, how many there are; 'tis for the poor man to count his cattle. For the praises of these trust not me at all; in person thou thyself mayst see how they can hardly support with their legs their distended udders. Lambs, too, a smaller breed, are in the warm folds: there are kids, too, of equal age to them in other folds. Snow-white milk I always have: a part of it is kept for drinking, another part the liquified rennet hardens. Nor will common delights, and ordinary enjoyments alone fall to thy lot, such as does, and hares, and she-goats, or a pair of doves, or a nest taken from the tree top. I have found on the mountain summit the twin cubs of a shaggy she-bear, which can play with thee, so like each other that thou couldst scarce distinguish them. These I found, and I said, 'These for my mistress will I keep.'

"'Do now but raise thy beauteous head from out of the azure sea; now, Galatea, come, and do not scorn my presents. Surely I know myself, and myself but lately I beheld in the reflection of the limpid water; and my figure[76] pleased me as I saw it. See how huge I am. Not Jove, in heaven, is greater than this body; for thou art wont to tell how one Jupiter reigns, who he is I know not. Plenty of hair hangs over my grisly features, and, like a grove, overshadows my shoulders; nor think it uncomely that my body is rough, thick set with stiff bristles. A tree without leaves is unseemly; a horse is unseemly, unless a mane covers his tawny neck. Feathers cover the birds; their wool is an ornament to the sheep; a beard and rough hair upon their body is becoming to men. I have but one eye in the middle of my forehead, but it is like a large buckler. Well! and does not the Sun from the heavens behold all these things? and yet the Sun has but one eye. And, besides, in your seas does my father reign. Him do I offer thee for a father-in-law; only do take pity on a suppliant, and hear his prayer, for to thee alone do I give way. And I, who despise Jove, and the heavens, and the piercing lightnings, dread thee, daughter of Nereus; than the lightnings is thy wrath more dreadful to me. But I should be more patient under these slights, if thou didst avoid all men. For why, rejecting the Cyclop, dost thou love Acis? And why prefer Acis to my embraces? Yet, let him please himself, and let him please thee, too, Galatea, though I wish he could not; if only the opportunity is given, he shall find that I have strength proportioned to a body so vast. I will pull out his palpitating entrails; and I will scatter his torn limbs about the fields, and throughout thy waves, and thus let him be united to thee. For I burn: and my passion, thus slighted, rages with the greater fury; and I seem to be carrying in my breast Ætna, transferred there with all its flames; and yet, Galatea, thou art unmoved.'

"Having in vain uttered such complaints (for all this I saw), he rises; and like an enraged bull, when the heifer is taken away from him, he could not stand still, and he wandered in the wood, and the well known forests. When the savage monster espied me, and Acis unsuspecting and apprehensive of no such thing; and he exclaimed:—'I see you, and I shall cause this to be the last union for your affection.' And that voice was as loud as an enraged Cyclop ought, for his size, to have. Ætna trembled at the noise; but I, struck with horror, plunged into the adjoining sea. The hero, son of Symæthis, turned his back and fled, and cried,—'Help me, Galatea, I entreat thee; help me, ye parents of hers; and admit me, now on the point of destruction, within your realms.' The Cyclop pursued, and hurled a fragment, torn from the mountain; and though the extreme angle only of the rock reached him, yet it entirely crushed Acis. But I did the only thing that was allowed by the Fates to be done, that Acis might assume the properties of his grandsire. The purple blood flowed from beneath the rock, and in a little time the redness began to vanish; and at first it became the colour of a stream muddied by a shower; and, in time, it became clear. Then the rock, that had been thrown, opened, and through the chinks, a reed vigorous and stately arose, and the hollow mouth of the rock resounded with the waters gushing forth. And, wondrous event! a youth suddenly emerged, as far as the midriff, having his new-made horns encircled with twining reeds. And he, but that he was of larger stature, and azure in all his features, was Acis still. But, even then, still it was Acis, changed into a river; and the stream has since retained that ancient name."

[Footnote 68: The Phæacians.—Ver. 719. The Phæacians were the people of the Island of Corcyra (now Corfu), who were so called from Phæax, the son of Neptune. This island was famous for the gardens of Alcinoüs, which are mentioned in the Odyssey. The Corcyrans were the originators of the disastrous Peloponnesian war.]

[Footnote 69: Buthrotos.—Ver. 721. This was a city of Epirus, not far from Corcyra. It received its name from its founder.]

[Footnote 70: Galatea.—Ver. 738. She was a sea Nymph, the daughter of Nereus and Doris.]

[Footnote 71: Daughter of Cratæis.—Ver. 749. Cratæis was a river of Calabria, in Italy. Symæthis was a stream of Sicily, opposite to Calabria.]

[Footnote 72: The pine tree.—Ver. 782. By way of corroborating this assertion, Boccaccio tells us, that the body of Polyphemus was found in Sicily, his left hand grasping a walking-stick longer than the mast of a ship.]

[Footnote 73: Fairer than.—Ver. 789. This song of Polyphemus is, in some measure, imitated from that of the Cyclop, in the Eleventh Idyll of Theocritus.]

[Footnote 74: Snow-white privet.—Ver. 789. Hesiod says, that Galatea had her name from her extreme fairness; γάλα being the Greek word for milk. To this the Poet here alludes.]

[Footnote 75: Arbute tree.—Ver. 820. The fruit of the arbutus, or strawberry tree, were so extremely sour, that they were called, as Pliny the Elder tells us, 'unedones;' because people could not eat more than one. The tree itself was valued for the beauty and pleasing shade of its foliage.]

[Footnote 76: My figure.—Ver. 841. Virgil and Theocritus also represent Polyphemus as boasting of his good looks.]

EXPLANATION

Homer, who, in the ninth Book of the Odyssey, has entered fully into the subject of Polyphemus and the other Cyclops, does not recount this adventure, which Ovid has borrowed from Theocritus, the Sicilian poet. Some writers have suggested that Acis was a Sicilian youth, who, having met with a repulse from Galatea, threw himself into the river, which was afterwards called by his name. It is, however, more probable that this river was so called from the rapidity of its course. Indeed, the scholiast on Theocritus and Eustathius distinctly say that the stream was called Acis, because the swiftness of its course resembled that of an arrow, which was called ἀκὶς, in the Greek language.

Homer, in describing the Cyclops, informs us that they were a lawless race, who, neglecting husbandry, lived on the spontaneous produce of a rich soil, and dwelling in mountain caves, devoted themselves entirely to the pleasures of a pastoral life. He says that they were men of monstrous stature, and had but one eye, in the middle of their forehead. Thucydides supposes them to have been the original inhabitants of Sicily. As their origin was unknown, it was said that they were the offspring of Neptune, or, in other words, that they had come by sea, to settle in Sicily. According to Justin, they retained possession of the island till the time of Cocalus; but in that point he disagrees with Homer, who represents them as being in the island after the time of Cocalus, who was a contemporary of Minos, and lived long before the Trojan war.

They inhabited the western parts of Sicily, near the promontories of Lilybæum and Drepanum; and from that circumstance, according to Bochart, they received their name. He supposes that the Cyclopes were so called from the Phœnician compound word Chek-lub, contracted for Chek-le-lub, which, according to him, was the name of the Gulf of Lilybæum. Because, in the Greek language κυκλὸς signified 'a circle,' and ὢπς, 'an eye,' it was given out that the name of Cyclops was given to them, because they had but one round eye in the middle of the forehead. It is possible that they may have acquired their character of being cannibals on true grounds, or, perhaps, only because they were noted for their extreme cruelty. Living near the volcanic mountain of Ætna, they were called the workmen of Vulcan; and Virgil describes them as forging the thunderbolts of Jupiter. Some writers represent them as having armed the three

Deities, who divided the empire of the world: Jupiter with thunder; Pluto with his helmet; and Neptune with his trident. Statius represents them as the builders of the walls of Argos and Virgil as the founders of the gates of the Elysian fields. Aristotle supposes that they were the first builders of towers.

Diodorus Siculus and Tzetzes say that Polyphemus was king of a part of Sicily, when Ulysses landed there; who, falling in love with Elpe, the daughter of the king, carried her off. The Læstrygons, the neighbours of Polyphemus, pursued him, and obliged him to give up the damsel, who was brought back to her father. Ulysses, in relating the story to the Phæacians, artfully concealed circumstances so little to his credit, and with impunity invented the absurdities which he related concerning a country to which his audience were utter strangers.

FABLE VIII [XIII.898-968]

Glaucus having observed some fishes which he has laid upon the grass revive and leap again into the water, is desirous to try the influence of the grass on himself. Putting some of it into his mouth, he immediately becomes mad, and leaping into the sea, is transformed into a sea God.

Galatea ceases[77] speaking, and the company breaking up, they depart; and the Nereids swim in the becalmed waves. Scylla returns, (for, in truth, she does not trust herself in the midst of the ocean) and either wanders about without garments on the thirsty sand, or, when she is tired, having lighted upon some lonely recess of the sea, cools her limbs in the enclosed waves. When, lo! cleaving the deep, Glaucus comes, a new-made inhabitant of the deep sea, his limbs having been lately transformed at Anthedon,[78] near Eubœa; and he lingers from passion for the maiden now seen, and utters whatever words he thinks may detain her as she flies. Yet still she flies, and, swift through fear, she arrives at the top of a mountain, situate near the shore.

In front of the sea, there is a huge ridge, terminating in one summit, bending for a long distance over the waves, and without trees. Here she stands, and secured by the place, ignorant whether he is a monster or a God, she both admires his colour, and his flowing hair that covers his shoulders and his back, and how a wreathed fish closes the extremity of his groin. This he perceives; and leaning upon a rock that stands hard by, he says, "Maiden, I am no monster, no savage beast; I am a God of the waters: nor have Proteus, and Triton, and Palæmon, the son of Athamas, a more uncontrolled reign over the deep. Yet formerly I was a mortal; but, still, devoted to the deep sea, even then was I employed in it. For, at one time, I used to drag the nets that swept up the fish; at another time, seated on a rock, I managed the line with the rod. The shore was adjacent to a verdant meadow, one part of which was surrounded with water, the other with grass, which, neither the horned heifers had hurt with their browsing, nor had you, ye harmless sheep, nor you, ye shaggy goats, ever cropped it. No industrious bee took thence the collected blossoms, no festive garlands were gathered thence for the head; and no mower's hands had ever cut it. I was the first to be seated on that turf, while I was drying the dripping nets. And that I might count in their order the fish that I had taken; I laid out those upon it which either chance had driven to my nets, or their own credulity to my barbed hooks.

"The thing is like a fiction (but of what use is it to me to coin fictions?); on touching the grass my prey began to move, and to shift their sides, and to skip about on the land, as though in the sea. And while I both paused and wondered, the whole batch flew off to the waves, and left behind their new master and the shore. I was amazed, and, in doubt for a long time, I considered what could be the cause;

whether some Divinity had done this, or whether the juice of some herb. 'And yet,' said I, 'what herb has these properties?' and with my hand I plucked the grass, and I chewed it, so plucked, with my teeth. Hardly had my throat well swallowed the unknown juices, when I suddenly felt my entrails inwardly throb, and my mind taken possession of by the passions of another nature. Nor could I stay in that place; and I exclaimed, 'Farewell, land, never more to be revisited;' and plunged my body beneath the deep. The Gods of the sea vouchsafed me, on being received by them, kindred honours, and they entreated Oceanus and Tethys to take away from me whatever mortality I bore. By them was I purified; and a charm being repeated over me nine times, that washes away all guilt, I was commanded to put my breast beneath a hundred streams.

"There was no delay; rivers issuing from different springs, and whole seas, were poured over my head. Thus far I can relate to thee what happened worthy to be related, and thus far do I remember; but my understanding was not conscious of the rest. When it returned to me, I found myself different throughout all my body from what I was before, and not the same in mind. Then, for the first time, did I behold this beard, green with its deep colour, and my flowing hair, which I sweep along the spacious seas, and my huge shoulders, and my azurecoloured arms, and the extremities of my legs tapering in the form of a finny fish. But still, what does this form avail me, what to have pleased the ocean Deities, and what to be a God, if thou art not moved by these things?"

As he was saying such things as these, and about to say still more, Scylla left the God. He was enraged, and, provoked at the repulse, he repaired to the marvellous court of Circe, the daughter of Titan.

[Footnote 77: Ceases.—Ver. 898. 'Desierat Galatea loqui,' is translated by Clarke, 'Galatea gave over talking.']

[Footnote 78: Anthedon.—Ver. 905. Anthedon was a maritime city of Bœotia, only separated from the Island of Eubœa, by the narrow strait of the Euripus.]

EXPLANATION

The ancient writers mention three persons of the name of Glaucus: one was the son of Minos, the second of Hippolochus, and the third is the one here mentioned. Strabo calls him the son of Polybus, while other writers make him to have been the son of Phorbas, and others of Neptune. Being drowned, perhaps by accident, to do honour to his memory, it was promulgated that he had become a sea God, and the city of Anthedon, of which he was a native, worshipped him as such.

Athenæus says that he carried off Ariadne from the isle of Naxos, where Theseus had left her; on which Bacchus punished him by binding him to a vine. According to Diodorus Siculus, he appeared to the Argonauts, when overtaken by a storm. From Apollonius Rhodius we learn that he foretold to them that Hercules, and Castor and Pollux, would be received into the number of the Gods. It was also said, that in the battle which took place between Jason and the Tyrrhenians, he was the only person that escaped unwounded. Euripides, who is followed by Pausanias, says that he was the interpreter of Nereus, and was skilled in prophecy; and Nicander even says that it was from him that Apollo learned the art of prediction. Strabo and Philostratus say that he was metamorphosed into a Triton, which is a-kin to the description of his appearance here given by Ovid.

The place where he leaped into the sea was long remembered; and in the days of Pausanias 'Glaucus' Leap' was still pointed out by the people of Anthedon. It is not improbable that he drowned himself for some reason which tradition failed to hand down to posterity.

BOOK THE FOURTEENTH

FABLE I [XIV.1-74]

Circe becomes enamoured of Glaucus, who complains to her of his repulse by Scylla. She endeavours, without success, to make him desert Scylla for herself. In revenge, she poisons the fountain where the Nymph is wont to bathe, and communicates to her a hideous form; which is so insupportable to Scylla, that she throws herself into the sea, and is transformed into a rock.

And now Glaucus, the Eubœan plougher of the swelling waves, had left behind Ætna, placed upon the jaws of the Giant, and the fields of the Cyclops, that had never experienced the harrow or the use of the plough, and that were never indebted to the yoked oxen; he had left Zancle, too, behind, and the opposite walls of Rhegium,[1] and the sea, abundant cause of shipwreck, which, confined by the two shores, bounds the Ausonian and the Sicilian lands. Thence, swimming with his huge hands through the Etrurian seas, Glaucus arrived at the grass-clad hills, and the halls of Circe, the daughter of the Sun, filled with various wild beasts. Soon as he beheld her, after salutations were given and received, he said, "Do thou, a Goddess, have compassion on me a God; for thou alone (should I only seem deserving of it,) art able to relieve this passion of mine. Daughter of Titan, by none is it better known how great is the power of herbs, than by me, who have been transformed by their agency; and, that the cause of my passion may not be unknown to thee, Scylla has been beheld by me on the Italian shores, opposite the Messenian walls. I am ashamed to recount my promises, my entreaties, my caresses, and my rejected suit. But, do thou, if there is any power in incantations, utter the incantation with thy holy lips; or, if any herb is more efficacious, make use of the proved virtues of powerful herbs. But I do not request thee to cure me, and to heal these wounds; and there is no necessity for an end to them; but let her share in the flame." But Circe, (for no one has a temper more susceptible of such a passion, whether it is that the cause of it originates in herself, or whether it is that Venus, offended[2] by her father's discovery, causes this,) utters such words as these:—

"Thou wilt more successfully court her who is willing, and who entertains similar desires, and who is captivated with an equal passion. Thou art worthy of it, and assuredly thou oughtst to be courted spontaneously; and, if thou givest any hopes, believe me, thou shalt be courted[3] spontaneously. That thou mayst entertain no doubts, or lest confidence in thy own beauty may not exist, behold! I who am both a Goddess, and the daughter of the radiant Sun, and am so potent with my charms, and so potent with my herbs, wish to be thine. Despise her who despises thee; her, who is attached to thee, repay by like attachment, and, by one act, take vengeance on two individuals."

Glaucus answered her, making such attempts as these,—"Sooner shall foliage grow in the ocean, and sooner shall sea-weed spring up on the tops of the mountains, than my affections shall change, while Scylla is alive." The Goddess is indignant; and since she is not able to injure him, and as she loves him she does not wish to do so, she is enraged against her, who has been preferred to herself; and, offended with these crosses in love, she immediately bruises herbs, infamous for their horrid juices, and, when bruised, she mingles with them the incantations of Hecate. She puts on azure vestments too, and through the troop of fawning wild beasts she issues from the midst of her hall; and making for Rhegium, opposite to the rocks of Zancle, she enters the waves boiling with the tides; on these, as though on the firm shore, she impresses her footsteps, and with dry feet she skims along the surface of the waves.

There was a little bay, curving in the shape of a bent bow, a favourite retreat of Scylla, whither she used to retire from the influence both of the sea and of the weather, when the sun was at its height in his mid career, and made the smallest shadow from the head downwards. This the Goddess infects beforehand, and pollutes it with monster-breeding drugs; on it she sprinkles the juices distilled from the noxious root, and thrice nine times, with her magic lips, she mutters over the mysterious charm, enwrapt in the dubious language of strange words.[4] Scylla comes; and she has now gone in up to the middle of her stomach, when she beholds her loins grow hideous with barking monsters; and, at first believing that they are no part of her own body, she flies from them and drives them off, and is in dread of the annoying mouths of the dogs; but those that she flies from, she carries along with herself; and as she examines the substance of her thighs, her legs, and her feet, she meets with Cerberean jaws in place of those parts. The fury of the dogs still continues, and the backs of savage monsters lying beneath her groin, cut short, and her prominent stomach, still adhere to them.

Glaucus, still in love, bewailed her, and fled from an alliance with Circe, who had thus too hostilely employed the potency of herbs. Scylla remained on that spot; and, at the first moment that an opportunity was given, in her hatred of Circe, she deprived Ulysses of his companions. Soon after, the same Scylla would have overwhelmed the Trojan ships, had she not been first transformed into a rock, which even now is prominent with its crags; this rock the sailor, too, avoids.

[Footnote 1: Rhegium.—Ver. 5. Rhegium was a city of Calabria, opposite to the coast of Sicily.]

[Footnote 2: Venus offended.—Ver. 27. The Sun, or Apollo, the father of Circe, as the Poet has already related in his fourth Book, betrayed the intrigues of Mars with Venus.]

[Footnote 3: Shalt be courted.—Ver. 31. She means that he shall be courted, but by herself.]

[Footnote 4: Of strange words.—Ver. 57. 'Obscurum verborum ambage novorum' is rendered by Clarke, 'Darkened with a long rabble of new words.']

EXPLANATION

According to Hesiod, Circe was the daughter of the Sun and of the Nymph Perse, and the sister of Pasiphaë, the wife of Minos. Homer makes her the sister of Æetes, the king of Colchis, while other authors represent her as the daughter of that monarch, and the sister of Medea. Being acquainted with the properties of simples, and having used her art in mixing poisonous draughts, she was generally looked upon as a sorceress. Apollonius Rhodius says that she poisoned her husband, the king of the Sarmatians, and that her father Apollo rescued her from the rage of her subjects, by transporting her in his chariot into Italy. Virgil and Ovid say that she inhabited one of the promontories of Italy, which afterwards bore her name, and which at the present day is known by the name of Monte Circello.

It is not improbable that the person who went by the name of Circe was never in Colchis or Thrace, and that she was styled the sister of Medea, merely on account of the similarity of their characters; that they both were called daughters of the Sun, because they understood the properties of simples; and that their pretended enchantments were only a poetical mode of describing the effect of their beauty, which drew many suitors after them, who lost themselves in the dissipation of a voluptuous life. Indeed, Strabo says, and very judiciously, as it would seem, that Homer having heard persons mention the expedition of Jason to Colchis, and hearing the stories of Medea and Circe, he took occasion to say, from the resemblance of their characters, that they were sisters.

According to some authors, Scylla was the daughter of Phorcys and Hecate; but as other writers say, of Typhon. Homer describes her in the following terms:—'She had a voice like that of a young whelp; no man, not even a God, could behold her without horror. She had twelve feet, six long necks, and at the end of each a monstrous head, whose mouth was provided with a triple row of teeth.' Another ancient writer says, that these heads were those of an insect, a dog, a lion, a whale, a Gorgon, and a human being. Virgil has in a great measure followed the description given by Homer. Between Messina and Reggio there is a narrow strait, where high crags project into the sea on each side. The part on the Sicilian side was called Charybdis, and that on the Italian shore was named Scylla. This spot has ever been famous for its dangerous whirlpools, and the extreme difficulty of its navigation. Several rapid currents meeting there, and the tide running through the strait with great impetuosity, the sea sends forth a dismal noise, not unlike that of the howling or barking of dogs, as Virgil has expressed it, in the words, 'Multis circum latrantibus undis.'

Palæphatus and Fusebius, not satisfied with the story being based on such simple facts, assert that Scylla was a ship that belonged to certain Etrurian pirates, who used to infest the coasts of Sicily, and that it had the figure of a woman carved on its head, whose lower parts were surrounded with dogs. According to these writers, Ulysses escaped them; and then, using the privileges of a traveller, told the story to the credulous Phæacians in the marvellous terms in which Homer has related it. Bochart, however, says that the two names were derived from the Phœnician language, in which 'Scol,' the root of Scylla, signified 'a ruin,' and Charybdis, 'a gulf.'

FABLE II [XIV.75-100]

Dido entertains Æneas in her palace, and falls in love with him. He afterwards abandons her, on which she stabs herself in despair. Jupiter transforms the Cercopes into apes; and the islands which they inhabit are afterwards called 'Pithecusæ,' from the Greek word signifying 'an ape.'

After the Trojan ships, with their oars, had passed by her and the ravening Charybdis; when now they had approached near the Ausonian shores, they were carried back by the winds[5] to the Libyan coasts. The Sidonian Dido, she who was doomed not easily to endure the loss of her Phrygian husband, received Æneas, both in her home and her affection; on the pile, too, erected under the pretext of sacred rites, she fell upon the sword; and, herself deceived, she deceived all. Again, flying from the newly erected walls of the sandy regions, and being carried back to the seat of Eryx and the attached Acestes, he performs sacrifice, and pays honour[6] to the tomb of his father. He now loosens from shore the ships which Iris, the minister of Juno, has almost burned; and passes by the realms of the son of Hippotas, and the regions that smoke with the heated sulphur, and leaves behind him the rocks of the Sirens,[7] daughters of Acheloüs; and the ship, deprived of its pilot,[8] coasts along Inarime[9] and Prochyta,[10] and Pithecusæ, situate on a barren hill, so called from the name of its inhabitants.

For the father of the Gods, once abhorring the frauds and perjuries of the Cercopians, and the crimes of the fraudulent race, changed these men into ugly animals; that these same beings might be able to appear unlike men, and yet like them. He both contracted their limbs, and flattened their noses; bent back from their foreheads; and he furrowed their faces with the wrinkles of old age. And he sent them into this spot, with the whole of their bodies covered with long yellow hair. Moreover, he first took away from them the use of language, and of their tongues, made for dreadful perjury; he only allowed them to be able to complain with a harsh jabbering.

[Footnote 5: By the winds.—Ver. 77. The storm in which Æneas is cast upon the shores of Africa forms the subject of part of the first Book of the Æneid.]

[Footnote 6: And pays honour.—Ver. 84. The annual games which Æneas instituted at the tomb of his father, in Sicily, are fully described in the fifth Book of the Æneid.]

[Footnote 7: The Sirens.—Ver. 87. The Sirens were said to have been the daughters of the river Acheloüs. Their names are Parthenope, Lysia, and Leucosia.]

[Footnote 8: Deprived of its pilot.—Ver. 88. This was Palinurus, who, when asleep, fell overboard, and was drowned. See the end of the fifth Book of the Æneid.]

[Footnote 9: Inarime.—Ver. 89. This was an island not far from the coast of Campania, which was also called Ischia and Ænaria. The word 'Inarime' is thought to have been coined by Virgil, from the expression of Homer, εἶν Ἀρίμοις, when speaking of it, as that writer is the first who is found to use it, and is followed by Ovid, Lucan, and others. Strabo tells us, that 'aremus' was the Etrurian name for an ape; if so, the name of this spot may account for the name of Pithecusæ, the adjoining islands, if the tradition here related by the Poet really existed. Pliny the Elder, however, says that Pithecusæ were so called from πίθος, an earthern cask, or vessel, as there were many potteries there.]

[Footnote 10: Prochyta.—Ver. 89. This island was said to have been torn away from the isle of Inarime by an earthquake; for which reason it received its name from the Greek verb προχέω, which means 'to pour forth.']

EXPLANATION

Although Ovid passes over the particulars of the visit of Æneas to Dido, and only mentions her death incidentally, we may give a few words to a story which has been rendered memorable by the beautiful poem of Virgil. Elisa, or Dido, was the daughter of Belus, king of Tyre. According to Justin, at his death he left his crown to his son Pygmalion jointly with Dido, who was a woman of extraordinary beauty. She was afterwards married to her uncle Sicharbas, who is called Sichæus by Virgil. Being priest of Hercules, an office next in rank to that of king, he was possessed of immense treasures, which the known avarice of Pygmalion caused him to conceal in the earth. Pygmalion having caused him to be assassinated, at which Dido first expressed great resentment, she afterwards pretended a reconciliation, the better to cover the design which she had formed to escape from the kingdom.

Having secured the cooperation of several of the discontented Tyrians, she requested permission to visit Tyre, and to leave her melancholy retreat, where every thing contributed to increase her misery by recalling the remembrance of her deceased husband. Hoping to seize her treasures, Pygmalion granted her request. Putting her wealth on board ship, she mixed some bags filled with sand among those that contained gold, for the purpose of deceiving those whom the king had sent to observe her and to escort her to Tyre. When out at sea, she threw the bags overboard, to appease the spirit of her husband, as she pretended, by sacrificing those treasures that had cost him his life. Then addressing the officers that accompanied her, she assured them that they would meet with but a bad reception from the king for having permitted so much wealth to be wasted, and that it would be more advantageous for them to fly from his resentment. The officers embarking in her design, after they had taken on board some Tyrian nobles, who were privy to the plan, she offered sacrifice to Hercules, and again set sail. Landing in Cyprus, they carried off eighty young women, who were married to her companions. On discovering her flight, Pygmalion at first intended to pursue her; but the intreaties of his mother, and the remonstrances of the priests, caused him to abandon his design.

Having arrived on the coast of Africa, Dido bargained with the inhabitants of the coast for as much ground as she could encompass with a bull's hide. This being granted, she cut the hide into as many thongs as enclosed ground sufficient to build a fort upon; which was in consequence called 'Byrsa.' In making the foundation, an ox's head was dug up, which being supposed to portend slavery to the city, if built there, they removed to another spot, where, in digging, they found a horse's head, which was considered to be a more favourable omen. The story of the citadel being named from the bull's hide was very probably invented by the Greeks; who, finding in the Phœnician narrative of the foundation of Carthage, the citadel mentioned by the Tyrian name of 'Bostra,' which had that signification, and fancying, from its resemblance to their word βυρσὰ, that it was derived from it, invented the fable of the hide.

Being pressed by Iarbas, king of Mauritania, to marry him, she asked for three months to come to a determination. The time expiring, she ordered a sacrifice to be made as an expiation to her husband's shade, and caused a pile to be erected, avowedly for the purpose of burning all that belonged to him. Ascending it, she pretended to expedite the sacrifice, and then despatched herself with a poniard. Virgil, wishing to deduce the hatred of the Romans and Carthaginians from the very time of Æneas, invented the story of the visit of Æneas to Dido; though he was perhaps guilty of a great anachronism in so doing, as the taking of Troy most probably preceded the foundation of Carthage by at least two centuries. Ovid has also related her story at length in the third book of the Fasti, and has followed Virgil's account of the treacherous conduct of Æneas, while he represents Iarbas as capturing her city after her death, and driving her sister Anna into exile. In the Phœnician language the word 'Dido' signified 'the bold woman,' and it is probable that Elisa only received that name after her death. Bochart has taken considerable pains to prove that she was the aunt of Jezebel, the famous, or rather infamous, wife of King Ahab.

The Poet then proceeds to say that Æneas saw the islands of the Cercopians on his way, whom Jupiter had transformed into apes. Æschines and Suidas say that there were two notorious robbers, inhabitants of an island adjacent to Sicily, named Candulus and Atlas, who committed outrages on all who approached the island. Being about to insult Jupiter himself, he transformed them into apes, from which circumstance the island received its name of Pithecusa. Sabinus says that they were called Cercopes, because in their treachery they were like monkeys, who fawn with their tails, when they design nothing but mischief. Zenobius places the Cercopes in Libya; and says that they were changed into rocks, for having offered to fight with Hercules.

Apollo is enamoured of the Sibyl, and, to engage her affection, offers her as many years as she can grasp grains of sand. She forgets to ask that she may always continue in the bloom of youth, and consequently becomes gray and decrepit.

After he has passed by these, and has left the walls of Parthenope[11] on the right hand, on the left side he approaches the tomb of the tuneful son of Æolus[12]; and he enters the shores of Cumæ, regions abounding in the sedge of the swamp, and the cavern of the long-lived Sibyl[13], and entreats her, that through Avernus, he may visit the shade of his father. But she raises her countenance, a long time fixed on the ground; and at length, inspired by the influence of the God, she says, "Thou dost request a great thing, O hero, most renowned by thy achievements, whose right hand has been proved by the sword, whose affection has been proved by the flames. Yet, Trojan, lay aside all apprehension, thou shalt obtain thy request; and under my guidance thou shalt visit the abodes of Elysium, the most distant realms of the universe, and the beloved shade of thy parent. To virtue, no path is inaccessible."

Thus she spoke, and she pointed out a branch refulgent with gold, in the woods of the Juno of Avernus[14], and commanded him to pluck it from its stem. Æneas obeyed; and he beheld the power of the dread Orcus, and his own ancestors, and the aged ghost of the magnanimous Anchises; he learned, too, the ordinances of those regions, and what dangers would have to be undergone by him in his future wars. Tracing back thence his weary steps along the path, he beguiled his labour in discourse with his Cumæan guide. And while he was pursuing his frightful journey along darkening shades, he said, "Whether thou art a Goddess personally, or whether thou art but a woman most favoured by the Deities, to me shalt thou always be equal to a Divinity; I will confess, too, that I exist through thy kindness, who hast willed that I should visit the abodes of death, and that I should escape those abodes of death when beheld by me. For this kindness, when I have emerged into the breezes of the air, I will erect a temple to thee, and I will give thee the honours of frankincense."

The prophetess looks upon him, and, with heaving sighs, she says, "Neither am I a Goddess, nor do thou honour a human being with the tribute of the holy frankincense. And, that thou mayst not err in ignorance, life eternal and without end was offered me, had my virginity but yielded to Phœbus, in love with me. But while he was hoping for this, while he was desiring to bribe me beforehand with gifts, he said: 'Maiden of Cumæ, choose whatever thou mayst wish, thou shalt gain thy wish.' I, pointing to a heap of collected dust, inconsiderately asked that as many birth-days might be my lot, as the dust contained particles. It escaped me to desire as well, at the same time, years vigorous with youth. But yet he offered me these, and eternal youth, had I submitted to his desires. Having rejected the offers of Phœbus, I remain unmarried. But now my more vigorous years have passed by, and crazy old age approaches with its trembling step, and this must I long endure.

"For thou beholdest me, having now lived seven ages; it remains for me to equal the number of particles of the dust; yet to behold three hundred harvests, and three hundred vintages. The time will come, when length of days will make me diminutive from a person so large; and when my limbs, wasted by old age, will be reduced to the most trifling weight. Then I shall not seem to have once been beloved, nor once to have pleased a God. Even Phœbus himself will, perhaps, not recognize me; or, perhaps, he will deny that he loved me. To that degree shall I be said to be changed; and though perceived by none, I shall still be recognized by my voice. My voice the Destinies will leave me."

[Footnote 11: Parthenope.—Ver. 101. The city of Naples, or Neapolis, was called Parthenope from the Siren of that name, who was said to have been buried there.]

[Footnote 12: Son of Æolus.—Ver. 103. Misenus, the trumpeter, was said to have been the son of Æolus. From him the promontory Misenum received its name.]

[Footnote 13: Long-lived Sibyl.—Ver. 104. The Sibyls were said by some to have their name from the fact of their revealing the will of the Deities, as in the Æolian dialect, Σιὸς was 'a God,' and βουλὴ was the Greek for 'will.' According to other writers, they were so called from Σίου βύλλη, 'full of the Deity.']

[Footnote 14: Juno of Avernus.—Ver. 114. The Infernal, or Avernian Juno, is a title sometimes given by the poets to Proserpine.]

EXPLANATION

The early fathers of the church, and particularly Justin, in their works in defence of Christianity, made use of the Sibylline verses of the ancients. The Emperor Constantine, too, in his harangue before the Nicene Council, quoted them, as redounding to the advantage of Christianity; although he then stated that many persons did not believe that the Sibyls were the authors of them. St. Augustin, too, employs several of their alleged predictions to enforce the truths of the Christian religion.

Sebastian Castalio has warmly maintained the truth of the oracles contained in these verses, though he admits that they have been very much interpolated. Other writers, however, having carefully examined them, have pronounced them to be spurious, and so many pious frauds; which, perhaps, may be pronounced to be the general opinion at the present day. We will, however, shortly enquire how many Sibyls of antiquity there were, and when they lived; whether any of their works were ever promulgated for the perusal of the public, and whether the verses which still exist under their name have any ground to be considered genuine.

There is no doubt but that in ancient times there existed certain women, who, led by a frenzied enthusiasm, uttered obscure sentences, which passed for predictions with the credulous people who went to consult them. Virgil and Ovid represent Æneas as going to the cave of the Cumæan Sibyl, to learn from her the success of the wars he should be engaged in. Plato, Strabo, Plutarch, Pliny, Solinus, and Pausanias, with many other writers, have mentioned the Sibyls; and it would be absurd, with Faustus Socinus, to affirm that no Sibyls ever existed. Indeed, Plato and other authors of antiquity go so far as to say, that by their productions they were essentially the benefactors of mankind. Some mention but one Sibyl, who was born either at Babylon or at Erythræ, in Phrygia. Diodorus Siculus mentions one only, and assigns Delphi as her locality, calling her by the name of Daphne. Strabo and Stephanus Byzantinus mention two, the one of Gergæ, a little town near Troy, and the other of Mermessus, in the same country. Solinus reckons three; the Delphian, named Herophile, the Erythræan, and the Cumæan. According to Varro, their number amounted to ten, whose names, in the order of time which Pausanias assigns them, were as follows:

The first and the most ancient was the Delphian, who lived before the Trojan war. The second was the Erythræan, who was said to have been the first composer of acrostic verses, and who also lived before the Trojan war. The third was the Cumæan, who was mentioned by Nævius in his book on the first Punic war, and by Piso in his annals. She is the Sibyl spoken of in the Æneid, and her name was Deïphobe. The fourth was the Samian, called Pitho, though Eusebius calls her Herophile, and he makes her to have lived about the time of Numa Pompilius. The fifth, whose name was Amalthea, or Demophile, lived at Cumæ, in Asia Minor. The sixth was the Hellespontine Sibyl, born at Mermessus, near Troy. The seventh was the Libyan, mentioned by Euripides. Some suppose that she was the first who had the name of Sibyl, which was given to her by the people of Africa. The eighth was the Persian or Babylonian Sibyl, whom Suidas names Sambetha. The ninth was the Phrygian, who delivered her oracles at Ancyra, in Phrygia. The tenth was the Tiburtine, who was called Albunea, and prophesied near Tibur, or Tivoli, on the banks of the Anio. In the present story Ovid evidently intends to represent these various Sibyls as being the same person; and to account for her prolonged existence, by representing that Apollo had granted her a life to last for many ages.

Several ages before the Christian era, the Romans had a collection of verses, which were commonly attributed to the Sibyls. These they often consulted; and in the time of Tarquinius Superbus, two officers were appointed for the purpose of keeping the Sibylline books, whose business it was to look in them on the occasion of any public calamity, in order to see whether it had been foretold and to make their report to the Senate. The books were kept in a stone chest, beneath the temple of Jupiter Capitolinus. These Duumvirs continued until the year of Rome 388, when eight others being added, they formed the College of the Decemvirs. About eighty-three years before the Christian era five other keepers of these books were added, who thus formed the body called the Quindecimvirs.

Dionysius of Halicarnassus, Aulus Gellius, Servius, and many other writers, state the following as the origin of the Sibylline books. An aged woman presented to Tarquinius Superbus three books that contained the oracles of the Sibyls, and demanded a large sum for them. The king refusing to buy them, she went and burned them; and returning, asked the same price for the remaining six, as she had done for the original number. Being again repulsed, she burnt three more, and coming back again, demanded the original price for the three that remained. Astonished at the circumstance, the king bought the books. Pliny and Solinus vary the story a little, in saying that the woman at first presented but three books, and that she destroyed two of them.

It is generally supposed, that on the burning of the Capitol, about eighty-three years before the Christian era, the Sibylline books of Tarquinius Superbus were destroyed in the flames. To repair the loss, the Romans despatched officers to various cities of Italy, and even to Asia and Africa, to collect whatever they could find, under the name of Sibylline oracles. P. Gabinius, M. Ottacilius, and L. Valerius brought back a large collection, of which the greater part was rejected, and the rest committed to the care of the Quindecimvirs. Augustus ordered a second revision of them; and, after a severe scrutiny, those which were deemed to be genuine, were deposited in a box, under a statue of Apollo Palatinus. Tiberius again had them examined, and some portion of them was then rejected. Finally, about the year A.D. 399, Stilcho, according to Rutilius Numatianus, or rather, the Emperor Honorius himself, ordered them to be burnt.

The so-called collection of Sibylline verses which now exists is generally looked upon as spurious; or if any part is genuine, it bears so small a proportion to the fictitious portion, that it has shared in the condemnation. Indeed, their very distinctness stamps them as forgeries; for they speak of the mysteries of Christianity in undisguised language, and the names of our Saviour and the Virgin Mary occur as openly as they do in the Holy Scriptures.

It is a singular assertion of St. Jerome, that the gift of prophecy was a reward to the Sibyls for their chastity. If such was the condition, we have a right to consider that the Deities were very partial in the distribution of their rewards, and in withholding them from the multitudes who, we are bound in charity to believe, were as deserving as the Sibyls themselves of the gift of vaticination.

FABLE IV [XIV.154-247]

Æneas arrives at Caieta, in Italy. Achæmenides, an Ithacan, who is on board his ship, meets his former companion Macareus there; and relates to him his escape from being devoured by Polyphemus. Macareus afterwards tells him how Ulysses had received winds from Æolus in a hide, and by that means had a prosperous voyage; till, on the bag being opened by the sailors in their curiosity, the winds rushed out, and raised a storm that drove them back to Æolia, and afterwards upon the coast of the Læstrygons.

While the Sibyl was relating such things as these, during the steep ascent, the Trojan Æneas emerged from the Stygian abodes to the Eubœan city,[15] and the sacrifice being performed, after the usual manner, he approached the shores that not yet bore the name of his nurse;[16] here, too, Macareus of Neritos, the companion of the experienced Ulysses, had rested, after the prolonged weariness of his toils. He recognized Achæmenides, once deserted in the midst of the crags of Ætna; and astonished that, thus unexpectedly found again, he was yet alive, he said, "What chance, or what God, Achæmenides, preserves thee? why is a barbarian[17] vessel carrying thee, a Greek? What land is sought by thy bark?"

No longer ragged in his clothing, but now his own master,[18] and wearing clothes tacked together with no thorns, Achæmenides says, "Again may I behold Polyphemus, and those jaws streaming with human blood, if my home and Ithaca be more delightful to me than this bark; if I venerate Æneas any less than my own father. And, though I were to do everything possible, I could never be sufficiently grateful. 'Tis he that has caused that I speak, and breathe, and behold the heavens and the luminary of the sun; and can I be ungrateful, and forgetful of this? 'Tis through him that this life of mine did not fall into the jaws of the Cyclop; and though I were, even now, to leave the light of life, I should either be buried in a tomb, or, at least, not in that paunch of his. What were my feelings at that moment (unless, indeed, terror deprived me of all sense and feeling), when, left behind, I saw you making for the open sea? I wished to shout aloud, but I was fearful of betraying myself to the enemy; the shouts of Ulysses were very nearly causing[19] the destruction of even your ship. I beheld him when, having torn up a mountain, he hurled the immense rock in the midst of the waves; again I beheld him hurling huge stones, with his giant arms, just as though impelled by the powers of the engine of war. And, forgetful that I was not in it, I was now struck with horror lest the waves or the stones might overwhelm the ship.

"But when your flight had saved you from a cruel death, he, indeed, roaring with rage, paced about all Ætna, and groped out the woods with his hands, and, deprived of his eye, stumbled against the rocks; and stretching out his arms, stained with gore, into the sea, he cursed the Grecian race, and he said, 'Oh! that any accident would bring back Ulysses to me, or any one of his companions, against whom my anger might find vent, whose entrails I might devour, whose living limbs I might mangle with my right hand, whose blood might drench my throat, whose crushed members might quiver beneath my teeth: how insignificant, or how trifling, then, would be the loss of my sight, that has been taken from me!' This, and more, he said in his rage. Ghastly horror took possession of me, as I beheld his features, streaming even yet with blood, and the ruthless hands, and the round space deprived of the eye, and his limbs, and his beard matted with human blood. Death was before my eyes, and yet that was the least of my woes. I imagined that[20] now he was about to seize hold of me, and that now he was on the very point of swallowing my vitals within his own; in my mind was fixed the impress of that time when I beheld two bodies of my companions three or four times dashed against the ground. Throwing himself on the top of them, just like a shaggy lion, he stowed away their entrails, their flesh, their bones with the white marrow, and their quivering limbs, in his ravenous paunch. A trembling seized me; in my alarm I stood without blood in my features, as I beheld him both chewing and belching out his bloody banquet from his mouth, and vomiting pieces mingled with wine; and I fancied that such a doom was in readiness for wretched me.

"Concealing myself for many a day, and trembling at every sound, and both fearing death and yet desirous to die, satisfying hunger with acorns, and with grass mixed with leaves, alone, destitute, desponding, abandoned to death and destruction, after a length of time, I beheld a ship not far off; by signs I prayed for deliverance, and I ran down to the shore; I prevailed; and a Trojan ship received me, a Greek. Do thou too, dearest of my companions, relate thy adventures, and those of thy chief, and of the company, which, together with thee, entrusted themselves to the ocean."

The other relates how that Æolus rules over the Etrurian seas; Æolus, the grandson of Hippotas, who confines the winds in their prison, which the Dulichean chief had received, shut up in a leather bag, a wondrous gift; how, with a favouring breeze, he had proceeded for nine days, and had beheld the land he was bound for; and how, when the first morning after the ninth had arrived, his companions, influenced by envy and a desire for booty, supposing it to be gold, had cut the fastenings of the winds; and how, through these, the ship had gone back along the waves through which it had just come, and had returned to the harbour of the Æolian king.

"Thence," said he, "we came to the ancient city[21] of Lamus, the Læstrygon. Antiphates was reigning in that land. I was sent to him, two in number accompanying me; and with difficulty was safety procured by me and one companion, by flight; the third of us stained the accursed jaws of the Læstrygon with his blood. Antiphates pursued us as we fled, and called together his followers; they flocked together, and, without intermission, they showered both stones and beams, and they overwhelmed men, and ships, too, did they overwhelm; yet one, which carried us and Ulysses himself, escaped. A part of our companions thus lost, grieving and lamenting much we arrived at those regions which thou perceivest afar hence. Look! afar hence thou mayst perceive an island,[22] that has been seen by me; and do thou, most righteous of the Trojans, thou son of a Goddess, (for, since the war is ended, thou art not, Æneas, to be called an enemy) I warn thee—avoid the shores of Circe."

[Footnote 15: Eubœan city.—Ver. 155. 'Cumæ' was said to have been founded by a colony from Chalcis, in Eubœa.]

[Footnote 16: Of his nurse.—Ver. 157. Caieta was the name of the nurse of Æneas, who was said to have been buried there by him.]

[Footnote 17: Barbarian.—Ver. 163. That is, Trojan; to the Greeks all people but themselves were βαρβαροί.]

[Footnote 18: His own master.—Ver. 166. 'Now his own master,' in contradistinction to the time when Macareus looked on himself as the devoted victim of Polyphemus.]

[Footnote 19: Nearly causing.—Ver. 181. Homer, in the Ninth Book of the Odyssey, recounts how Ulysses, after having put out the eye of Polyphemus, fled to his own ship, and when the Giant followed, called out to him, disclosing his real name; whereas, he had before told the Cyclop that his name was οὔτις, 'nobody.' By this indiscreet action, the Cyclop was able to ascertain the locality of the ship, and nearly sank it with a mass of rock which he hurled in that direction.]

[Footnote 20: I imagined that.—Ver. 203-4. 'Et jam prensurum, jam, jam mea viscera rebar In sua mersurum.' Clarke thus renders these words; 'And now I thought he would presently whip me up, and cram my bowels within his own.']

[Footnote 21: The ancient city.—Ver. 233. This city was afterwards known as Formiæ, in Campania.]

[Footnote 22: An island.—Ver. 245. Macareus here points towards the promontory of Circæum, which was supposed to have formerly been an island.]

EXPLANATION

Æolus, according to Servius and Varro, was the son of Hippotas, and about the time of the Trojan war reigned in those islands, which were formerly called 'Vulcaniæ,' but were afterwards entitled 'Æoliæ,' and are now known as the Lipari Islands. Homer mentions only one of these islands, which were seven in number. He calls it by the name of Æolia, and probably means the one which was called Lipara, and gave its name to the group, and which is now known as Strombolo. Æolus seems to have been a humane prince, who received with hospitality those who had the misfortune to be cast on his island. Diodorus Siculus says that he was especially careful to warn strangers of the shoals and dangerous places in the neighbouring seas. Pliny adds, that he applied himself to the study of the winds, by observing the direction of the smoke of the volcanos, with which the isles abounded.

Being considered as an authority on that subject, at a time when navigation was so little reduced to an art, the poets readily feigned that he was the master of the winds, and kept them pent up in caverns, under his control. The story of the winds being entrusted to Ulysses, which Ovid here copies from Homer, is merely a poetical method of saying, that Ulysses disregarded the advice of Æolus, and staying out at sea beyond the time he had been recommended, was caught in a violent tempest. It is possible that Homer may allude to some custom which prevailed among the ancients, similar to that of the Lapland witches in modern times, who pretend to sell a favourable wind, enclosed in a bag, to mariners. Homer speaks of the six sons and six daughters of Æolus; perhaps they were the twelve principal winds, upon which he had expended much pains in making accurate observations.

Bochart suggests that the isle of Lipara was called by the Phœnicians 'Nibara,' on account of its volcano, (that word signifying 'a torch,') which name was afterwards corrupted to Lipara.

FABLE V [XIV.248-319]

Achæmenides lands in the isle of Circe, and is sent to her palace with some of his companions. Giving them a favourable reception, she makes them drink of a certain liquor; and, on her touching them with a wand, they are immediately transformed into swine. Eurylochus, who has refused to drink, informs Ulysses, who immediately repairs to the palace, and obliges Circe to restore to his companions their former shape.

"We, too, having fastened our ships to the shores of Circe, remembering Antiphates and the cruel Cyclop, refused to go and enter her unknown abode. By lot were we chosen; that lot sent both me and the faithful Polytes, and Eurylochus, and Elpenor, too much addicted[23] to wine, and twice nine[24] companions, to the walls of Circe. Soon as we reached them, and stood at the threshold of her abode; a thousand wolves, and bears and lionesses mixed with the wolves, created fear through meeting them; but not one of them needed to be feared, and not one was there to make a wound on our bodies. They wagged their caressing tails in the air, and fawning, they attended our footsteps, until the female servants received us, and led us, through halls roofed with marble, to their mistress.

"She is sitting in a beautiful alcove, on her wonted throne, and clad in a splendid robe; over it she is arrayed in a garment of gold tissue. The Nereids and the Nymphs, together, who tease no fleeces with the motion of their fingers nor draw out the ductile threads, are placing the plants in due order, and arranging in baskets the flowers confusedly scattered, and the shrubs variegated in their hues. She herself prescribes the tasks that they perform; she herself is aware what is the use of every leaf; what combined virtue there is in them when mixed; and giving attention, she examines each herb as weighed.[25] When she beheld us, having given and received a salutation, she gladdened her countenance, and granted every thing to our wishes. And without delay, she ordered the grains of parched barley to be mingled, and honey, and the strength of wine, and curds with pressed milk. Secretly, she added drugs to be concealed beneath this sweetness. We received the cups presented by her sacred right hand. Soon as, in our thirst, we quaffed them with parching mouth, and the ruthless Goddess, with her wand, touched the extremity of our hair (I am both ashamed, and yet I will tell of it), I began to grow rough with bristles, and no longer to be able to speak; and, instead of words, to utter a harsh noise, and to grovel on the ground with all my face. I felt, too, my mouth receive a hard skin, with its crooked snout, and my neck swell with muscles; and with the member with which, the moment before, I had received the cup, with the same did I impress my footsteps.

"With the rest who had suffered the same treatment (so powerful are enchanted potions) I was shut up in a pig-sty; and we perceived that Eurylochus, alone, had not the form of a swine; he, alone, escaped the proffered draught. And had he not escaped it, I should even, at this moment, have still been one of the bristle-clad animals; nor would Ulysses, having been informed by him of so direful a disaster, have come to Circe as our avenger. The Cyllenian peace-bearer had given him a white flower; the Gods above call it 'Moly;'[26] it is supported by a black root. Protected by that, and at the same time by the instruction of the inhabitants of heaven, he entered the dwelling of Circe, and being invited to the treacherous draughts, he repelled her, while endeavouring to stroke his hair with her wand, and prevented her, in her terror, with his drawn sword. Upon that, her promise was given, and right hands were exchanged; and, being received into her couch, he required the bodies of his companions as his marriage gift.

"We are then sprinkled with the more favouring juices of harmless plants, and are smitten on the head with a blow from her inverted wand; and charms are repeated, the converse of the charms that had been uttered. The longer she chaunts them, the more erect are we raised from the ground; and the bristles fall off, and the fissure leaves our cloven feet; our shoulders return; our arms become attached[27] to their upper parts. In tears, we embrace him also in tears; and we cling to the neck of our chief; nor do we utter any words before those that testify that we are grateful.

"The space of a year detained us there; and, as I was present for such a length of time, I saw many things; and many things I heard with my ears. This, too, among many other things I heard, which one of the four handmaids appointed for such rites, privately informed me of. For while Circe was passing her time apart with my chief, she pointed out to me a youthful statue made of snow-white marble, carrying a woodpecker on its head, erected in the hallowed temple, and bedecked with many a chaplet. When I asked, and desired to know who he was, and why he was venerated in the sacred temple, and why he carried that bird; she said:—'Listen, Macareus, learn hence, too, what is the power of my mistress, and give attention to what I say.'"

[Footnote 23: Too much addicted.—Ver. 252. He alludes to the fate of Elpenor, who afterwards, in a fit of intoxication, fell down stairs, and broke his neck.]

[Footnote 24: Twice nine.—Ver. 253. Homer mentions Eurylochus and twenty-two others as the number, being one more than the number here given by Ovid.]

[Footnote 25: As weighed.—Ver. 270. Of course drugs and simples would require to be weighed before being mixed in their due proportions.]

[Footnote 26: Call it 'Moly.'—Ver. 292. Homer, in the tenth Book of the Odyssey, says that this plant had a black root, and a flower like milk.]

[Footnote 27: Become attached.—Ver. 304-5. 'Subjecta lacertis Brachia sunt,' Clarke has not a very lucid translation of these words. His version is, 'Brachia are put under our lacerti.' The 'brachium' was the forearm, or part, from the wrist to the elbow; while the 'lacertus' was the muscular part, between the elbow and the shoulder.]

EXPLANATION

Ulysses having stayed some time at the court of Circe, where all were immersed in luxury and indolence, begins to reflect on the degraded state to which he is reduced, and resolutely abandons so unworthy a mode of life. This resolution is here typified by the herb moly, the symbol of wisdom. His companions, changed into swine, are emblems of the condition to which a life of sensuality reduces its votaries; while the wolves, lions, and horses show that man in such a condition fails not to exhibit the various bad propensities of the brute creation. Thus was the prodigal son, mentioned in the New Testament, reduced to a level with the brutes, 'and fain would have filled his belly with the husks that the swine did eat.'

It is not improbable that Circe was the original from which the Eastern romancer depicted the enchantress queen Labè in the story of Beder and Giauhare in the Arabian Nights' Entertainments. They were both ladies of light reputation, both fond of exercising their magical power on strangers, and in exactly the same manner: and as Ulysses successfully resisted the charms of Circe, so Beder thwarted the designs of Labè; but here the parallel ends.

Circe, being enamoured of Picus, and being unable to shake his constancy to his wife Canens, transforms him into a woodpecker, and his retinue into various kinds of animals. Canens pines away with grief at the loss of her husband, and the place where she disappears afterwards bears her name.

"'Picus, the son of Saturn, was a king in the regions of Ausonia, an admirer of horses useful in warfare. The form of this person was such as thou beholdest. Thou thyself here mayst view his comeliness, and thou mayst approve of his real form from this feigned resemblance of it. His disposition was equal to his beauty; and not yet, in his age, could he have beheld four times the Olympic contest celebrated each fifth year in the Grecian Elis. He had attracted, by his good looks, the Dryads, born in the hills of Latium; the Naiads, the fountain Deities, wooed him; Nymphs, which Albula,[28] and which the waters of Numicus, and which those of Anio, and Almo but very short[29] in its course, and the rapid Nar,[30] and Farfarus,[31] with its delightful shades, produced, and those which haunt the forest realms of the Scythian[32] Diana, and the neighbouring streams.

"'Yet, slighting all these, he was attached to one Nymph, whom, on the Palatine hill, Venilia is said once to have borne to the Ionian Janus.[33] Soon as she was ripe with marriageable years, she was presented to Laurentine Picus, preferred by her before all others; wondrous, indeed, was she in her beauty, but more wondrous still, through her skill in singing; thence she was called Canens.[34] She was wont, with her voice, to move the woods and the rocks, and to tame the wild beasts, and to stop the course of the long rivers, and to detain the fleeting birds. While she was singing her songs with her feminine voice, Picus had gone from his dwelling into the Laurentine fields, to pierce the wild boars there bred; and he was pressing the back of his spirited horse, and was carrying two javelins in his left hand, having a purple cloak fastened with yellow gold. The daughter of the Sun, too, had come into the same wood; and that she might pluck fresh plants on the fruitful hills, she had left behind the Circæan fields, so called after her own name.

"'Hidden by the shrubs, soon as she beheld the youth, she was astounded; the plants which she had gathered fell from her bosom, and a flame seemed to pervade her entire marrow. As soon as she regained her presence of mind from so powerful a shock, she was about to confess what she desired; the speed of his horse, and the surrounding guards, caused that she could not approach. 'And yet thou shalt not escape me,' she said, 'even shouldst thou be borne on the winds, if I only know myself, if all potency in herbs has not vanished, and if my charms do not deceive me.' Thus she said; and she formed the phantom of a fictitious wild boar, with no substance, and commanded it to run past the eyes of the king, and to seem to go into a forest, thick set with trees, where the wood is most dense, and where the spot is inaccessible to a horse. There is no delay; Picus, forthwith, unconsciously follows the phantom of the prey; hastily too, he leaves the reeking back of his steed, and, in pursuit of a vain hope, wanders on foot in the lofty forest. She repeats prayers to herself, and utters magical incantations, and adores strange Gods in strange verses, with which she is wont both to darken the disk of the snow-white moon, and to draw the clouds that suck up the moisture, over the head of her father. Then does the sky become lowering at the repeating of the incantation, and the ground exhales its vapours; and his companions wander along the darkened paths, and his guards are separated from the king.

"'She, having now gained a favourable place and opportunity, says, 'O, most beauteous youth! by thy eyes, which have captivated mine, and by this graceful person, which makes me, though a Goddess, to be thy suppliant, favour my passion, and receive the Sun, that beholds all things, as thy father-in-law, and do not in thy cruelty despise Circe, the daughter of Titan.' Thus she says. He roughly repels her and her entreaties: and he says, 'Whoever thou art, I am not for thee; another female holds me enthralled, and for a long space of time, I pray, may she so hold me. I will not pollute the conjugal ties with the love of a stranger, while the Fates shall preserve for me Canens, the daughter of Janus.' The daughter of Titan, having often repeated her entreaties in vain, says, 'Thou shalt not depart with impunity, nor shalt thou return to Canens; and by experience shalt thou learn what one slighted, what one in love, what a woman, can do; but that one in love, and slighted, and a woman, is Circe.'

"'Then twice did she turn herself to the West, and twice to the East; thrice did she touch the youth with her wand; three charms did she repeat. He fled; wondering that he sped more swiftly than usual, he beheld wings on his body; and indignant that he was added suddenly as a strange bird to the Latian woods, he struck the wild oaks with his hard beak, and, in his anger, inflicted wounds[35] on the long branches. His wings took the purple colour of his robe. The piece of gold that had formed a buckle, and had fastened his garment, became feathers, and his neck was encompassed with the colour of yellow gold; and nothing now remained to Picus of his former self, beyond the name.

"'In the meantime his attendants, having, often in vain, called on Picus throughout the fields, and, having found him in no direction, meet with Circe, (for now she has cleared the air, and has allowed the clouds to be dispersed by the woods and the sun); and they charge her with just accusations, and demand back their king, and are using violence, and are preparing to attack her with ruthless weapons. She scatters noxious venom and poisonous extracts; and she summons together Night, and the Gods of Night, from Erebus and from Chaos, and she invokes Hecate in magic howlings. Wondrous to tell, the woods leap from their spot; the ground utters groans, the neighbouring trees become pallid, the grass becomes moist, besprinkled with drops of blood; the stones seem to send forth harsh lowings, the dogs seem to bark, and the ground to grow loathsome with black serpents, and unsubstantial ghosts of the departed appear to flit about. The multitude trembles, astonished at these prodigies; she touches their astonished faces, as they tremble, with her enchanted wand. From the touch of this, the monstrous forms of various wild beasts come upon the young men; his own form remains to no one of them.

"'The setting Sun has now borne down upon the Tartessian shores;[36] and in vain is her husband expected, both by the eyes and the longings of Canens. Her servants and the people run about through all the woods, and carry lights to meet him. Nor is it enough for the Nymph to weep, and to tear her hair, and to beat her breast; though all this she does, she rushes forth, and, in her distraction, she wanders through the Latian fields. Six nights, and as many returning lights of the Sun, beheld her, destitute of sleep and of food, going over hills and valleys, wherever chance led her. Tiber, last of all, beheld her, worn out with weeping and wandering, and reposing her body on his cold banks. There, with tears, she poured forth words attuned, lamenting, in a low voice, her very woes, as when the swan, now about to die, sings his own funereal dirge.

"'At last, melting with grief, even to her thin marrow, she pined away, and by degrees vanished into light air. Yet the Fame of it became attached to the spot, which the ancient Muses have properly called Canens, after the name of the Nymph.' During that long year, many such things as these were told me and were seen by me. Sluggish and inactive through idleness, we were ordered again to embark on the deep, again to set our sails. The daughter of Titan had said that dangerous paths, and a protracted voyage, and the perils of the raging sea were awaiting us. I was alarmed, I confess; and having reached these shores, here I remained."

[Footnote 28: Albula.—Ver. 328. The ancient name of the river Tiber was Albula. It was so called from the whiteness of its water.]

[Footnote 29: But very short.—Ver. 329. The Almo falls in the Tiber, close to its own source, whence its present epithet.]

[Footnote 30: Rapid Nar.—Ver. 330. The 'Nar' was a river of Umbria, which fell into the Tiber.]

[Footnote 31: Farfarus.—Ver. 330. This river, flowing slowly through the valleys of the country of the Sabines, received a pleasant shade from the trees with which its banks were lined.]

[Footnote 32: Scythian.—Ver. 331. He alludes to the statue of the Goddess Diana, which, with her worship, Orestes was said to have brought from the Tauric Chersonesus, and to have established at Aricia, in Latium. See the Fasti, Book III. l. 263, and Note.]

[Footnote 33: Ionian Janus.—Ver. 334. Janus was so called because he was thought to have come from Thessaly, and to have crossed the Ionian Sea.]

[Footnote 34: Canens.—Ver. 338. This name literally means 'singing,' being the present participle of the Latin verb 'cano,' 'to sing.']

[Footnote 35: Inflicted wounds.—Ver. 392. The woodpecker is supposed to tap the bark of the tree with his beak, to ascertain, from the sound, if it is hollow, and if there are any insects beneath it.]

[Footnote 36: Tartessian shores.—Ver. 416. 'Tartessia' is here used as a general term for Western, as Tartessus was a city of the Western coast of Spain. It afterwards had the name of Carteia, and is thought to have been situated not far from the site of the present Cadiz, at the mouth of the Bætis, now called the Guadalquivir. Some suppose this name to be the same with the Tarshish of Scripture.]

EXPLANATION

When names occur in the ancient Mythology, of Oriental origin, we may conclude that they were imported into Greece and Italy from Egypt or Phœnicia; and that their stories were derived from the same sources; such as those of Adonis, Arethusa, Arachne, and Isis. Those that are derived from the Greek languages are attached to fictions of purely Greek origin, such as the fables of Daphne, Galantis, Cygnus, and the Myrmidons; and where the names are of Latin original, we may conclude that their stories originated in Italy: such, for instance, as those of Canens, Picus, Anna Perenna, Flora, Quirinus, and others.

To this rule there are certain exceptions; for both Greece and Italy occasionally appropriated each other's traditions, by substituting the names of one language for those of the other. Thus it would not be safe to affirm positively that the story of Portumnus and Matuta is of Latin origin, since Greece lays an equal claim to it under the names of Leucothoë and Palæmon, while, probably, Cadmus originally introduced it from Phœnicia, under the names of Ino and Melicerta.

Dionysius of Halicarnassus, on the authority of Cato the Censor and Asellius Sempronius, says that the original inhabitants of Italy were a Greek colony. Cato and Sempronius state that they were from Achaia, while Dionysius says that they came from Arcadia, under the command of Œnotrius. Picus is generally supposed to have been one of the aboriginal kings of Italy, who was afterwards Deified. Servius, in his Commentary on the seventh Book of the Æneid, informs us that Picus pretended to know future events, and made use of a woodpecker, which he had tamed, for the purpose of his auguries. On this ground, after his death, it was generally reported that he had been transformed into that bird, and he was ranked among the Dii Indigetes of Latium. Dying in his youth, his wife Canens retired to a solitary spot, where she ended her life, and the intensity of her grief gave rise to the fable that she had pined away into a sound.

It has been suggested that the story took its rise from the oracles of Mars among the Sabines, when a woodpecker was said to give the responses. According to Bochart, it arose from the confusion of the meaning of the Phœnician word 'picea,' which signified a 'diviner.' It is the exuberant fancy of Ovid alone which connects Picus with the story of Circe.

FABLES VII AND VIII [XIV.441-526]

Turnus having demanded succour from Diomedes against Æneas, the Grecian prince, fearing the resentment of Venus, refuses to send him assistance; and relates how some of his followers have been transformed by Venus into birds. An Apulian shepherd surprising some Nymphs, insults them, on which he is changed into a wild olive tree.

Macareus had concluded. And the nurse of Æneas, now buried in a marble urn, had this short inscription on her tomb:—"My foster-child, of proved piety, here burned me, Caieta, preserved from the Argive flames, with that fire which was my due." The fastened cable is loosened from the grassy bank, and they leave far behind the wiles and the dwelling of the Goddess, of whom so ill a report has been given, and seek the groves where the Tiber, darkened with the shade of trees, breaks into the sea with his yellow sands. Æneas, too, gains the house and the daughter of Latinus, the son of Faunus;[37] but not without warfare. A war is waged with a fierce nation, and Turnus is indignant on account of the wife that had been betrothed to him.[38] All Etruria meets in battle with Latium, and long is doubtful victory struggled for with ardent arms. Each side increases his strength with foreign forces, and many take the part of the Rutulians, many that of the Trojan side. Nor had Æneas arrived in vain at the thresholds of Evander,[39] but Venulus came in vain to the great city, of the exiled Diomedes. He, indeed, had founded a very great city under the Iapygian Daunus, and held the lands given to him in dower.

But after Venulus had executed the commands of Turnus, and had asked for aid, the Ætolian hero pleaded his resources as an excuse: that he was not wishful to commit the subjects of his father-in-law to a war, and that he had no men to arm of the nation of his own countrymen; "And that ye may not think this a pretext, although my grief be renewed at the bitter recollection, yet I will endure the recital of it. After lofty Ilion was burnt, and Pergamus had fed the Grecian flames, and the Narycian hero,[40] having ravished the virgin, distributed that vengeance upon all, which he alone merited, on account of the virgin; we were dispersed and driven by the winds over the hostile seas; we Greeks had to endure lightning, darkness, rain, and the wrath both of the heavens and of the sea, and Caphareus, the completion of our misery. And not to detain you by relating these sad events in their order, Greece might then have appeared even to Priam, worthy of a tear. Yet the care of the armed universe preserved me, rescued from the waves.

"But again was I driven from Argos, the land of my fathers; and genial Venus exacted satisfaction in vengeance for her former wound: and so great hardships did I endure on the deep ocean, so great amid arms on shore, that many a time were they pronounced happy by me, whom the storm, common to all, and Caphareus, swallowed up in the threatening[41] waves; and I wished that I had been one of them. My companions having now endured the utmost extremities, both in war and on the ocean, lost courage, and demanded an end of their wanderings. But Agmon, of impetuous temper, and then embittered as well by misfortunes, said, 'What does there remain now, ye men, for your patience to refuse to endure? What has Cytherea, (supposing her to desire it), that she can do beyond this? For so long as greater evils are dreaded, there is room for prayers; but where one's lot is the most wretched possible, fear is trampled under foot, and the extremity of misfortune is free from apprehensions. Let Venus herself hear it, if she likes; let her hate, as she does hate, all the men under the rule of Diomedes. Yet all of us despise her hate, and this our great power is bought by us at great price.'

"With such expressions does the Pleuronian[42] Agmon provoke Venus against her will, and revive her former anger. His words are approved of by a few. We, the greater number of his friends, rebuke Agmon: and as he is preparing to answer, his voice and the passage of his voice together become diminished; his hair changes into feathers; his neck newly formed, his breast and his back are covered with down; his arms assume longer feathers; and his elbows curve out into light wings. A great part of his foot receives toes; his mouth becomes stiff and hardened with horn, and has its end in a point. Lycus and Idas, and Nycteus, together with Rhetenor, and Abas, are all astounded at him; and while they are astounded, they assume a similar form; and the greater portion of my company fly off, and resound around the oars with the flapping of their wings. Shouldst thou inquire what was the form of these birds so suddenly made; although it was not that of swans, yet it was approaching to that of white swans. With difficulty, for my part, do I, the son-in-law of the Iapygian Daunus, possess these abodes and the parched fields with a very small remnant of my companions."

Thus far the grandson of Œneus. Venulus leaves the Calydonian[43] realms and the Peucetian[44] bays, and the Messapian[45] fields. In these he beholds a cavern, which, overshadowed by a dense grove, and trickling with a smooth stream, the God Pan, the half goat, occupies; but once on a time the Nymphs possessed it. An Apulian shepherd alarmed them, scared away from that spot; and, at first, he terrified them with a sudden fear; afterwards, when their presence of mind returned, and they despised him as he followed, they formed dances, moving their feet to time. The shepherd abused them; and imitating them with grotesque capers, he added rustic abuse in filthy language. Nor was he silent, before the growing tree closed his throat. But from this tree and its sap you may understand what were his manners. For the wild olive, by its bitter berries, indicates the infamy of his tongue; the coarseness of his words passed into them.

[Footnote 37: Son of Faunus.—Ver. 449. The parents of Latinus were Faunus and Marica.]

[Footnote 38: Betrothed to him.—Ver. 451. Amata, the mother of Lavinia, had promised her to Turnus, in spite of the oracle of Faunus, which had declared that she was destined for a foreign husband.]

[Footnote 39: Evander.—Ver. 456. His history is given by Ovid in the first Book of the Fasti.]

[Footnote 40: Narycian hero.—Ver. 468. Naryx, which was also called Narycium and Naryce, was a city of Locris. He alludes to the divine vengeance which punished Ajax Oïleus, who had ravished Cassandra in the temple of Minerva. For this reason the Greeks were said to have been afflicted with shipwreck, on their return after the destruction of Troy.]

[Footnote 41: Threatening.—Ver. 481. 'Importunis' is translated by Clarke, 'plaguy.' For some account of Caphareus, see the Tristia, or Lament, Book I. El. 1. l. 83. and note.]

[Footnote 42: Pleuronian.—Ver. 494. Pleuron was a town of Ætolia, adjoining to Epirus.]

[Footnote 43: Calydonian.—Ver. 512. That part of Apulia, which Diomedes received from Daunus, as a dower with his wife, was called Calydon, from the city of Calydon, in his native Ætolia.]

[Footnote 44: Peucetian.—Ver. 513. Apulia was divided by the river Aufidus into two parts, Peucetia and Daunia. Peucetia was to the East, and Daunia lay to the West. According to Antoninus Liberalis, Daunus, Iapyx, and Peucetius, the sons of Lycaon, were the first to colonize these parts.]

[Footnote 45: Messapian.—Ver. 513. Messapia was a name given to a part of Calabria, from its king Messapus, who aided Turnus against Æneas.]

EXPLANATION

Latinus having been told by an oracle that a foreign prince should come into his country and marry his daughter Lavinia, received Æneas hospitably, and formed an alliance with him, promising him his daughter in marriage; on which Turnus, who was the nephew of Amata, his wife, and to whom Lavinia was betrothed, declared war against Æneas.

The ancient historians tell us, that, on returning from the siege of Troy, Diomedes found that his throne had been usurped by Cyllabarus, who had married his wife Ægiale. Not having sufficient forces to dispossess the intruder, he sought a retreat in Italy, where he built the city of Argyripa, or Argos Hippium. Diomedes having married the daughter of Daunus, quarrelled with his father-in-law, and was killed in fight; on which his companions fled to an adjacent island, which, from his name, was called Diomedea. It was afterwards reported, that on their flight they were changed into birds, and that Venus inflicted this punishment, in consequence of Diomedes having wounded her at the siege of Troy. Of this story a confused version is here presented by Ovid, who makes the transformation to take place in the lifetime of Diomedes. It is supposed that the fact of the island being the favourite resort of swans and herons, facilitated this story of their transformation. Pliny and Solinus add to this marvellous account by stating, that these birds fawned upon all Greeks who entered the island, and fled from the people of all other nations. Ovid says that the birds resembled swans, while other writers thought them to be herons, storks, or falcons.

The ancient authors are utterly silent as to the rude shepherd who was changed into a wild olive, but the story was probably derived by Ovid from some local tradition.

FABLES IX AND X [XIV.527-608]

Turnus sets fire to the fleet of Æneas: but Cybele transforms the ships into sea Nymphs. After the death of Turnus, his capital, Ardea, is burnt, and a bird arises out of the flames. Venus obtains of Jupiter that her son, after so many heroic deeds, shall be received into the number of the Gods.

When the ambassador had returned thence, bringing word that the Ætolian arms had been refused them, the Rutulians carried on the warfare prepared for, without their forces; and much blood was shed on either side. Lo! Turnus bears the devouring torches against the ships, fabrics of pine; and those, whom the waves have spared, are now in dread of fire. And now the flames were burning the pitch and the wax, and the other elements of flame, and were mounting the lofty mast to the sails, and the benches of the curved ships were smoking; when the holy Mother of the Gods, remembering that these pines were cut down on the heights of Ida, filled the air with the tinkling of the clashing cymbal, and with the noise of the blown boxwood pipe. Borne through the yielding air by her harnessed lions, she said: "Turnus, in vain dost thou hurl the flames with thy sacrilegious right hand; I will save the ships, and the devouring flames shall not, with my permission, burn a portion, and the very limbs of my groves."

As the Goddess speaks, it thunders; and following the thunder, heavy showers fall, together with bounding hailstones; the brothers, sons of Astræus, arouse both the air and the swelling waves with sudden conflicts, and rush to the battle. The genial Mother, using the strength of one of these, first bursts the hempen cables of the Phrygian fleet, and carries the ships headlong, and buries them beneath the ocean. Their hardness being now softened, and their wood being changed into flesh, the crooked sterns are changed into the features of the head; the oars taper off in fingers and swimming feet; that which has been so before, is still the side; and the keel, laid below in the middle of the ship, is changed, for the purposes of the back bone. The cordage becomes soft hair, the yards become arms. Their colour is azure, as it was before. As Naiads of the ocean, with their virgin sports they agitate those waves, which before they dreaded; and, born on the rugged mountains, they inhabit the flowing sea; their origin influences them not. And yet, not forgetting how many dangers they endured on the boisterous ocean, often do they give a helping hand to the tossed ships; unless any one is carrying men of the Grecian race.

Still keeping in mind the Phrygian catastrophe, they hated the Pelasgians; and, with joyful countenances, they looked upon the fragments of the ship of him of Neritos; and with pleasure did they see the ship of Alcinoüs[46] become hard upon the breakers, and stone growing over the wood.

There is a hope that, the fleet having received life in the form of sea Nymphs, the Rutulian may desist from the war through fear, on account of this prodigy. He persists, however, and each side has its own Deities;[47] and they have courage, equal to the Gods. And now they do not seek kingdoms as a dower, nor the sceptre of a father-in-law, nor thee, virgin Lavinia, but only to conquer; and they wage the war through shame at desisting. At length, Venus sees the arms of her son victorious, and Turnus falls; Ardea falls, which, while Turnus lived, was called 'the mighty.' After ruthless flames consumed it, and its houses sank down amid the heated embers, a bird, then known for the first time, flew aloft from the midst of the heap, and beat the ashes with the flapping of its wings. The voice, the leanness, the paleness, and every thing that befits a captured city, and the very name of the city, remain in that bird; and Ardea itself is bewailed by the beating of its wings.

And now the merit of Æneas had obliged all the Deities, and Juno herself, to put an end to their former resentment; when, the power of the rising Iülus being now well established, the hero, the son of Cytherea, was ripe for heaven, Venus, too, had solicited the Gods above; and hanging round the neck of her parent had said: "My father, who hast never proved unkind to me at any time, I beseech thee now to be most indulgent to me; and to grant, dearest father, to my Æneas, who, born of my blood, has made thee a grandsire, a godhead, even though of the lowest class; so that thou only grant him one. It is enough to have once beheld the unsightly realms, enough to have once passed over the Stygian streams." The Gods assented; nor did his royal wife keep her countenance unmoved; but, with pleased countenance, she nodded assent. Then her father said; "You are worthy of the gift of heaven; both thou who askest, and he, for whom thou askest: receive, my daughter, what thou dost desire." Thus he decrees. She rejoices, and gives thanks to her parent; and, borne by her harnessed doves through the light air, she arrives at the Laurentine shores; where Numicius,[48] covered with reeds, winds to the neighbouring sea with the waters of his stream. Him she bids to wash off from Æneas whatever is subject to death, and to bear it beneath the ocean in his silent course.

The horned river performed the commands of Venus; and with his waters washed away from Æneas whatever was mortal, and sprinkled him. His superior essence remained. His mother anointed his body thus purified with divine odours, and touched his face with ambrosia, mingled with sweet nectar, and made him a God. Him the people of Quirinus, called Indiges,[49] and endowed with a temple and with altars.

[Footnote 46: Ship of Alcinoüs.—Ver. 565. Alcinoüs, the king of the Phæacians, having saved Ulysses from shipwreck, gave him a ship in which to return to Ithaca. Neptune, to revenge the injuries of his son Polyphemus, changed the ship into a rock.]

[Footnote 47: Its own Deities.—Ver. 568. The Trojans were aided by Venus, while Juno favoured the Rutulians.]

[Footnote 48: Numicius.—Ver. 599. Livy, in the first Book of his History, seems to say that Æneas lost his life in a battle, fought near the Numicius, a river of Latium. He is generally supposed to have been drowned there.]

[Footnote 49: Indiges.—Ver. 608. Cicero says, that 'those, who for their merits were reckoned in the number of the Gods, and who formerly living on earth, and afterwards lived among the Gods (in Diis agerent), were called Indigetes;' thus implying that the word 'Indiges' came from 'in Diis ago;' 'to live among the Gods.' This seems a rather far-fetched derivation. The true meaning of the word seems to be 'native,' or 'indigenous;' and it applies to a person Deified, and considered as a tutelary Deity of his native country. Most probably, it is derived from 'in,' or 'indu,' the old Latin form of 'in,' and γείνω (for γίνομαι), 'to be born.' Some would derive the word from 'in,' negative, and 'ago,' to speak, as signifying Deities, whose names were not be mentioned.]

EXPLANATION

It is asserted by some writers, that when the ships of Æneas were set on fire by Turnus, a tempest arose, which extinguished the flames; on which circumstance the story here related by Ovid was founded. Perhaps Virgil was the author of the fiction, as he is the first known to have related it, and is closely followed by Ovid in the account of the delivery of the ships.

The story of the heron arising out of the flames of Ardea seems to be founded on a very simple fact. It is merely a poetical method of accounting for the Latin name of that bird, which was very plentiful in the vicinity of the city of Ardea, and, perhaps, thence derived its name of 'ardea.' The story may have been the more readily suggested to the punning mind of Ovid, from the resemblance of the Latin verb 'ardeo,' signifying 'to burn,' to that name.

Some of the ancient authors say, that after killing Turnus and marrying Lavinia, Æneas was killed in battle with Mezentius, after a reign of three years, leaving his wife pregnant with a son, afterwards known by the name of Sylvius. His body not being found after the battle, it was given out that his Goddess mother had translated him to heaven, and he was thenceforth honoured by the name of Jupiter Indiges.

FABLE XI [XIV.609-697]

Vertumnus, enamoured of Pomona, assumes several shapes for the purpose of gaining her favour; and having transformed himself into an old woman, succeeds in effecting his object.

From that time Alba and the Latin state were under the sway of Ascanius with the two names;[50] Sylvius[51] succeeded him; sprung of whom, Latinus had a renewed name, together with the ancient sceptre. Alba succeeded the illustrious Latinus; Epitos sprang from him; and next to him were Capetus, and Capys; but Capys was the first of these. Tiberinus received the sovereignty after them; and, drowned in the waves of the Etrurian river, he gave his name to the stream. By him Remulus and the fierce Acrota were begotten; Remulus, who was the elder, an imitator of the lightnings, perished by the stroke[52] of a thunder-bolt. Acrota, more moderate than his brother in his views, handed down the sceptre to the valiant Aventinus, who lies buried on the same mount over which he had reigned; and to that mountain he gave his name. And now Proca held sway over the Palatine nation.

Under this king Pomona lived; than her, no one among the Hamadryads of Latium more skilfully tended her gardens, and no one was more attentive to the produce of the trees; thence she derives her name. She cares not for woods, or streams; but she loves the country, and the boughs that bear the thriving fruit. Her right hand is not weighed down with a javelin, but with a curved pruning-knife, with which, at one time she crops the too luxuriant shoots, and reduces the branches that straggle without order; at another time, she is engrafting the sucker in the divided bark, and is so finding nourishment for a stranger nursling. Nor does she suffer them to endure thirst; she waters, too, the winding fibres of the twisting root with the flowing waters. This is her delight, this her pursuit; and no desire has she for love. But fearing the violence of the rustics, she closes her orchard within a wall, and both forbids and flies from the approach of males.

What did not the Satyrs do, a youthful crew expert at the dance, and the Pans with their brows wreathed with pine, and Sylvanus, ever more youthful than his years, and the God who scares the thieves either with his pruning-hook or with his groin, in order that they might gain her? But yet Vertumnus exceeded even these in his love, nor was he more fortunate than the rest. O! how often did he carry the ears of corn in a basket, under the guise of a hardy reaper; and he was the very picture of a reaper! Many a time, having his temples bound with fresh bay, he would appear to have been turning over the mowed grass. He often bore a whip in his sturdy hand, so that you would have sworn that he had that instant been unyoking the wearied oxen. A pruning-knife being given him, he was a woodman, and the pruner of the vine. Now he was carrying a ladder, and you would suppose he was going to gather fruit. Sometimes he was a soldier, with a sword, and sometimes a fisherman, taking up the rod; in fact, by means of many a shape, he often obtained access for himself, that he might enjoy the pleasure of gazing on her beauty.

He, too, having bound his brows with a coloured cap,[53] leaning on a stick, with white hair placed around his temples, assumed the shape of an old woman, and entered the well-cultivated gardens, and admired the fruit; and he said, "So much better off art thou!" and then he gave her, thus commended, a few kisses, such as no real old woman ever could have given; and stooping, seated himself upon the grass, looking up at the branches bending under the load of autumn. There was an elm opposite, widely spread with swelling grapes; after he had praised it, together with the vine united to it, he said, "Aye, but if this trunk stood unwedded,[54] without the vine, it would have nothing to attract beyond its leaves; this vine, too, while it finds rest against the elm, joined to it, if it were not united to it, would lie prostrate on the ground; and yet thou art not influenced by the example of this tree, and thou dost avoid marriage, and dost not care to be united. I only wish that thou wouldst desire it: Helen would not then be wooed by more suitors, nor she who caused the battles of the Lapithæ, nor the wife of Ulysses, so bold against the cowards. Even now, while thou dost avoid them courting thee, and dost turn away in disgust, a thousand suitors desire thee; both Demigod and Gods, and the Deities which inhabit the mountains of Alba.

"But thou, if thou art wise, and if thou dost wish to make a good match, and to listen to an old woman, (who loves thee more than them all, and more than thou dost believe) despise a common alliance, and choose for thyself Vertumnus, as the partner of thy couch; and take me as a surety for him. He is not better known, even to himself, than he is to me. He is not wandering about, straying here and there, throughout all the world; these spots only does he frequent; and he does not, like a great part of thy wooers, fall in love with her whom he sees last. Thou wilt be his first and his last love, and to thee alone does he devote his life. Besides, he is young, he has naturally the gift of gracefulness, he can readily change himself into every shape, and he will become whatever he shall be bidden, even shouldst thou bid him be everything. And besides, have you not both the same tastes? Is not he the first to have the fruits which are thy delight? and does he not hold thy gifts in his joyous right hand? But now he neither longs for the fruit plucked from the tree, nor the herbs that the garden produces, with their pleasant juices, nor anything else, but thyself. Have pity on his passion! and fancy that he who wooes thee is here present, pleading with my lips; fear, too, the avenging Deities, and the Idalian Goddess, who abhors cruel hearts, and the vengeful anger of her of Rhamnus.[55]

"And that thou mayst the more stand in awe of them, (for old age has given me the opportunity of knowing many things) I will relate some facts very well known throughout all Cyprus, by which thou mayst the more easily be persuaded and relent."

[Footnote 50: The two names.—Ver. 609. The other name of Ascanius was Iülus. Alba Longa was built by Ascanius.]

[Footnote 51: Sylvius.—Ver. 610. See the lists of the Alban kings, as given by Ovid, Livy, Dionysius of Halicarnassus, and Eusebius, compared in the notes to the Translation of the Fasti, Book IV. line 43.]

[Footnote 52: By the stroke.—Ver. 618. Possibly both Remulus (if there ever was such a person) and Tullus Hostilius may have fallen victims to some electrical experiments which they were making; this may have given rise to the story that they had been struck with lightning for imitating the prerogative of Jupiter.]

[Footnote 53: A coloured cap.—Ver. 654. 'Pictâ redimitus tempora mitrâ,' is rendered by Clarke, 'Having his temples wrapped up in a painted bonnet.' The 'mitra,' which was worn on the head by females, was a broad cloth band of various colours. The use of it was derived from the Eastern nations, and, probably, it was very similar to our turban. It was much used by the Phrygians, and in later times among the Greeks and Romans. It is supposed that it was worn in a broad fillet round the head, and was tied under the chin with bands. When Clodius went disguised in female apparel to the rites of Bona Dea, he wore a 'mitra.']

[Footnote 54: Stood unwedded.—Ver. 663. Ovid probably derived this notion from the language of the Roman husbandmen. Columella and other writers on agricultural matters often make mention of a 'maritus ulmus,' and a 'nupta vitis,' in contradistinction to those trees which stood by themselves.]

[Footnote 55: Her of Rhamnus.—Ver. 694. See Book III. l. 406.]

EXPLANATION

Among the Deities borrowed by the Romans from the people of Etruria, were Vertumnus and Pomona, who presided over gardens and fruits. Propertius represents Vertumnus as rejoicing at having left Tusculum for the Roman Forum. According to Varro and Festus, the Romans offered sacrifices to these Deities, and they had their respective temples and altars at Rome, the priest of Pomona being called 'Flamen Pomonalis.' It is probable that this story originated in the fancy of the Poet.

The name of Vertumnus, from 'verto,' 'to change,' perhaps relates to the vicissitudes of the seasons; and if this story refers to any tradition, its meaning may have been, that in his taking various forms, to please Pomona, the change of seasons requisite for bringing the fruits to ripeness was symbolized. It is possible that in the disguises of a labourer, a reaper, and an old woman, the Poet may intend to pourtray the spring, the harvest, and the winter.

There was a market at Rome, near the temple of this God, who was regarded as one of the tutelary Deities of the traders. Horace alludes to his temple which was in the Vicus Tuscus, or Etrurian Street, which led to the Circus Maximus. According to some authors, he was an ancient king of Etruria, who paid great attention to his gardens, and, after his death, was considered to have the tutelage of them.

FABLES XII AND XIII [XIV.698-851]

Vertumnus relates to Pomona how Anaxarete was changed into a rock after her disdain of his advances had forced her lover Iphis to hang himself. After the death of Amulius and Numitor, Romulus builds Rome, and becomes the first king of it. Tatius declares war against him, and is favoured by Juno, while Venus protects the Romans. Romulus and Hersilia are added to the number of the Deities, under the names of Quirinus and Ora.

Iphis, born of an humble family, had beheld the noble Anaxarete, sprung from the race of the ancient Teucer;[56] he had seen her, and had felt the flame in all his bones; and struggling a long time, when he could not subdue his passion by reason, he came suppliantly to her doors. And now having confessed to her nurse his unfortunate passion, he besought her, by the hopes she reposed in her nursling, not to be hard-hearted to him; and at another time, complimenting each of the numerous servants, he besought their kind interest with an anxious voice. He often gave his words to be borne on the flattering tablets;

sometimes he fastened garlands, wet with the dew of his tears, upon the door-posts, and laid his tender side upon the hard threshold, and uttered reproaches against the obdurate bolt.

She, more deaf than the sea, swelling when the Constellation of the Kids is setting, and harder than the iron which the Norican fire[57] refines, and than the rock which in its native state is yet held fast by the firm roots, despises, and laughs at him; and to her cruel deeds, in her pride, she adds boastful words, and deprives her lover of even hope. Iphis, unable to endure this prolonged pain, endured his torments no longer; and before her doors he spoke these words as his last: "Thou art the conquerer, Anaxarete; and no more annoyances wilt thou have to bear from me. Prepare the joyous triumph, invoke the God Pæan, and crown thyself with the shining laurel. For thou art the conqueror, and of my own will I die; do thou, woman of iron, rejoice. At least, thou wilt be obliged to commend something in me, and there will be one point in which I shall be pleasing to thee, and thou wilt confess my merits. Yet remember that my affection for thee has not ended sooner than my life; and that at the same moment I am about to be deprived of a twofold light. And report shall not come to thee as the messenger of my death; I myself will come, doubt it not; and I myself will be seen in person, that thou mayst satiate thy cruel eyes with my lifeless body. But if, ye Gods above, you take cognizance of the fortunes of mortals, be mindful of me; beyond this, my tongue is unable to pray; and cause me to be remembered in times far distant; and give those hours to Fame which you have taken away from my existence."

Thus he said; and raising his swimming eyes and his pallid arms to the door-posts, so often adorned by him with wreaths, when he had fastened a noose at the end of a halter upon the door; he said,—"Are these the garlands that delight thee, cruel and unnatural woman?" And he placed his head within it; but even then he was turned towards her; and he hung a hapless burden, by his strangled throat. The door, struck by the motion of his feet as they quivered, seemed to utter a sound, as of one groaning much, and flying open, it discovered the deed; the servants cried aloud, and after lifting him up in vain, they carried him to the house of his mother (for his father was dead). She received him into her bosom; and embracing the cold limbs of her child, after she had uttered the words that are natural to wretched mothers, and had performed the usual actions of wretched mothers, she was preceding[58] the tearful funeral through the midst of the city, and was carrying his ghastly corpse on the bier, to be committed to the flames.

By chance, her house was near the road where the mournful procession was passing, and the sound of lamentation came to the ears of the hardhearted Anaxarete, whom now an avenging Deity pursued. Moved, however, she said:—"Let us behold these sad obsequies;" and she ascended to an upper room[59] with wide windows. And scarce had she well seen Iphis laid out on the bier, when her eyes became stiffened, and a paleness coming on, the warm blood fled from her body. And as she endeavoured to turn her steps back again, she stood fixed there; and as she endeavoured to turn away her face, this too she was unable to do; and by degrees the stone, which already existed in her cruel breast, took possession of her limbs.

"And, that thou mayst not think this a fiction, Salamis still keeps the statue under the form of the maiden; it has also a temple under the name of 'Venus, the looker-out.' Remembering these things, O Nymph, lay aside this prolonged disdain, and unite thyself to one who loves thee. Then, may neither cold in the spring nip thy fruit in the bud, nor may the rude winds strike them off in blossom." When the God, fitted for every shape, had in vain uttered these words, he returned to his youthful form,[60] and took off from himself the garb of the old woman. And such did he appear to her, as, when the form of the sun, in all his brilliancy, has dispelled the opposing clouds, and has shone forth, no cloud intercepting his rays. And he now purposed violence, but there was no need for force, and the Nymph was captivated by the form of the God, and was sensible of a reciprocal wound.

Next, the soldiery of the wicked Amulius held sway over the realms of Ausonia; and by the aid of his grandsons, the aged Numitor gained the kingdom that he had lost; and on the festival of Pales, the walls of the City were founded. Tatius and the Sabine fathers waged war; and then, the way to the citadel being laid open, by a just retribution, Tarpeia lost her life, the arms being heaped upon her. On this, they, sprung from the town of Cures, just like silent wolves, suppressed their voices with their lips, and fell upon the bodies now overpowered by sleep, and rushed to the gates, which the son of Ilia had shut with a strong bolt. But Juno, the daughter of Saturn, herself opened one, and made not a sound at the turning of the hinge. Venus alone perceived that the bars of the gate had fallen down; and she would have shut it, were it not, that it is never allowed for a Deity to annul the acts of the other Gods. The Naiads of Ausonia occupied a spot near the temple of Janus, a place besprinkled by a cold fountain; of these she implored aid. Nor did the Nymphs resist, the Goddess making so fair a request; and they gave vent to the springs and the streams of the fountain. But not yet were the paths closed to the open temple of Janus, and the water had not stopped the way. They placed sulphur, with its faint blue light, beneath the plenteous fountain, and they applied fire to the hollowed channels, with smoking pitch.

By these and other violent means, the vapour penetrated to the very sources of the fountain; and you, ye waters, which, so lately, were able to rival the coldness of the Alps, yielded not in heat to the flames themselves. The two door-posts smoked with the flaming spray; and the gate, which was in vain left open for the fierce Sabines, was rendered impassable by this new-made fountain, until the warlike soldiers had assumed their arms. After Romulus had readily led them onward, and the Roman ground was covered with Sabine bodies, and was covered with its own people, and the accursed sword had mingled the blood of the son-in-law with the gore of the father-in-law; they determined that the war should end in peace, and that they would not contend with weapons to the last extremity, and that Tatius should share in the sovereignty.

Tatius was now dead, and thou, Romulus, wast giving laws in common to both peoples; when Mavors,[61] his helmet laid aside, in such words as these addressed the Parent of both Gods and men: "The time is now come, O father, (since the Roman state is established on a strong foundation, and is no longer dependent on the guardianship of but one), for thee to give the reward which was promised to me, and to thy grandson so deserving of it, and, removed from earth, to admit him to heaven. Thou saidst to me once, a council of the Gods being present, (for I remember it, and with grateful mind I remarked the affectionate speech), he shall be one, whom thou shalt raise to the azure heaven. Let the tenor of thy words be now performed."

The all-powerful God nodded in assent, and he obscured the air with thick clouds, and alarmed the City with thunder and lightning. Gradivus knew that this was a signal given to him for the promised removal; and, leaning on his lance, he boldly mounted behind his steeds, laden with the blood-stained pole of the chariot, and urged them on with the lash of the whip; and descending along the steep air, he stood on the summit of the hill of the woody Palatium; and he took away the son of Ilia, that moment giving out his royal ordinances to his own Quirites. His mortal body glided through the yielding air; just as the leaden plummet, discharged from the broad sling, is wont to dissolve itself[62] in mid air. A beauteous appearance succeeded, one more suitable to the lofty couches[63] of heaven, and a form, such as that of Quirinus arrayed in his regal robe. His wife was lamenting him as lost; when the royal Juno commanded Iris to descend to Hersilia, along her bending path; and thus to convey to the bereft wife her commands:—

"O matron, the especial glory of the Latian and of the Sabine race; thou woman, most worthy to have been before the wife of a hero so great, and now of Quirinus; cease thy weeping, and if thou hast a wish to see thy husband, under my guidance repair to the grove which flourishes on the hill of Quirinus, and overshadows the temple of the Roman king." Iris obeys, and gliding down to earth along her tinted bow, she addressed Hersilia in the words enjoined. She, with a modest countenance, hardly raising her eyes, replies, "O Goddess, (for though it is not in my power to say who thou art, yet, still it is clear that thou art a Goddess), lead me, O lead me on, and present to me the features of my husband. If the Fates should but allow me to be enabled once to behold these, I will confess that I have beheld Heaven."

There was no delay; with the virgin daughter of Thaumas she ascended the hill of Romulus. There, a star falling from the skies, fell upon the earth; the hair of Hersilia set on fire from the blaze of this, ascended with the star to the skies. The founder of the Roman city received her with his well-known hands; and, together with her body, he changed her former name; and he called her Ora; which Goddess is still united to Quirmus.

[Footnote 56: Ancient Teucer.—Ver. 698. When Teucer returned home after the Trojan war, his father Telamon banished him, for not having revenged the death of his brother Ajax, which was imputed to Ulysses, as having been the occasion of it, by depriving him of the armour of Achilles. Thus exiled, he fled to Cyprus, where he founded the city of Salamis.]

[Footnote 57: Norican fire.—Ver. 712. Noricum was a district of Germany, between the Danube and the Alps. It is still famous for its excellent steel; the goodness of which, Pliny attributes partly to the superior quality of the ore, and partly to the temperature of the climate.]

[Footnote 58: She was preceding.—Ver. 746. It was customary for the relations, both male and female, to attend the body to the tomb or the funeral pile. Among the Greeks, the male relatives walked in front of the body, preceded by the head mourners, while the female relations walked behind. Among the Romans, all the relations walked behind the corpse; the males having their heads veiled, and the females with their heads bare and hair dishevelled, contrary to the usual practice of each sex.]

[Footnote 59: An upper room.—Ver. 752. Anaxarete went to an upper room, to look out into the street, as the apartments on the ground floor were rarely lighted with windows. The principal apartments on the ground floor received their light from above, and the smaller rooms there, usually derived their light from the larger ones; while on the other hand, the rooms on the upper floor were usually lighted with windows. The conduct of Anaxarete reminds us of that of Marcella, the hardhearted shepherdess, which so aroused the indignation of the amiable, but unfortunate, Don Quixotte.]

[Footnote 60: His youthful form.—Ver. 766-7. 'In juvenem rediit: et anilia demit Instrumenta sibi.' These words are thus translated by Clarke: 'He returned into a young fellow, and takes off his old woman's accoutrements from him.' We hear of the accoutrements of a cavalry officer much more frequently than we do those of an old woman.]

[Footnote 61: Mavors.—Ver. 806. Mavors, which is often used by the poets as a name of Mars, probably gave rise to the latter name as a contracted form of it.]

[Footnote 62: To dissolve itself.—Ver. 826. Not only, as we have already remarked, was it a notion among the ancients that the leaden plummet thrown from the sling grew red hot; but they occasionally *went still further, and asserted that, from the rapidity of the motion, it melted and disappeared altogether. See note to Book II. l. 727.]*

[Footnote 63: Lofty couches.—Ver. 827. The 'pulvinaria' were the cushions, or couches, placed in the temples of the Gods, for the use of the Divinities; which probably their priests (like their brethren who administered to Bel) did not omit to enjoy. At the festivals of the 'lectisternia,' the statues of the Gods were placed upon these cushions. The images of the Deities in the Roman Circus, were also placed on a 'pulvinar.']

EXPLANATION

We are not informed that the story of Iphis, hanging himself for love of Anaxarete, is based upon any actual occurrence, though probably it was, as Salamis is mentioned as the scene of it. The transformation of Anaxarete into a stone, seems only to be the usual metaphor employed by the poets to denote extreme insensibility.

Following the example of Homer, who represents the Gods as divided into the favourers of the Greeks and of the Trojans, he represents the Sabines as entering Rome, while Juno opens the gates for them; on which the Nymphs of the spot pour forth streams of flame, which oblige them to return. He tells the same story in the first Book of the Fasti, where Janus is introduced as taking credit to himself for doing what the Nymphs are here said to have effected.

As Dionysius of Halicarnassus gives some account of these transactions, on the authority of the ancient Roman historians, it will be sufficient here to give the substance thereof. Jealous of the increasing power of Romulus, the Sabines collected an army, and marched to attack his city. A virgin named Tarpeia, whose father commanded the guard, perceiving the golden bracelets which the Sabines wore on their arms, offered Tatius to open the gate to him, if he would give her these jewels. This condition being assented to, the enemy was admitted into the town; and Tarpeia, who is said by some writers only to have intended to disarm the Sabines, by demanding their bucklers, which she pretended were included in the original agreement, was killed on the spot, by the violence of the blows; Tatius having ordered that they should be thrown on her head.

The same historian says, that opinions were divided as to the death of Romulus, and that many writers had written, that as he was haranguing his army, the sky became overcast, and a thick darkness coming on, it was followed by a violent tempest, in which he disappeared; on which it was believed that Mars had taken him up to heaven. Others assert that he was killed by the citizens, for having sent back the hostages of the Veientes without their consent, and for assuming an air of superiority, which their lawless spirits could ill brook. For these reasons, his officers assassinated him, and cut his body in pieces; each of them carrying off some portion, that it might be privately interred. According to Livy, great consternation was the consequence of his death; and the people beginning to suspect that the senators had committed the crime, Julius Proculus asserted that Romulus had appeared to him, and assured him of the fact of his having been Deified. His speech on the occasion is given by Livy, and Ovid relates the same story in the second Book of the Fasti. On this, the Roman people paid him divine honours as a God, under the name of Quirinus, one of the epithets of Mars. He had a chief priest, who was called 'Flamen Quirinalis.'

His wife, Hersilia, also had divine honours paid to her, jointly with him, under the name of Ora, or 'Horta.' According to Plutarch, she had the latter name from the exhortation which she had given to the youths to distinguish themselves by courage.

BOOK THE FIFTEENTH

FABLE I [XV.1-59]

Myscelos is warned, in a dream, to leave Argos, and to settle in Italy. When on the point of departing, he is seized under a law which forbids the Argives to leave the city without the permission of the magistrates. Being brought up for judgment, through a miracle he is acquitted. He retires to Italy, where he builds the city of Crotona.

Meanwhile, one is being sought who can bear a weight of such magnitude, and can succeed a king so great. Fame, the harbinger of truth, destines the illustrious Numa for the sovereign power. He does not deem it sufficient to be acquainted with the ceremonials of the Sabine nation; in his expansive mind he conceives greater views, and inquires into the nature of things. 'Twas love of this pursuit, his country and cares left behind, that caused him to penetrate to the city of the stranger Hercules. To him, making the inquiry what founder it was that had erected a Grecian city on the Italian shores, one of the more aged natives, who was not unacquainted with the history of the past, thus replied:

"The son of Jove, enriched with the oxen of Iberia, is said to have reached the Lacinian shores,[1] from the ocean, after a prosperous voyage, and, while his herd was straying along the soft pastures, himself to have entered the abode of the great Croton, no inhospitable dwelling, and to have rested in repose after his prolonged labours, and to have said thus at departing: 'In the time of thy grandsons this shall be the site of a city;' and his promise was fulfilled. For there was a certain Myscelos, the son of Alemon, an Argive, most favoured by the Gods in those times. Lying upon him, as he is overwhelmed with the drowsiness of sleep, the club-bearer, Hercules, addresses him: 'Come, now, desert thy native abodes; go, and repair to the pebbly streams of the distant Æsar.'[2] And he utters threats, many and fearful, if he does not obey: after that, at once both sleep and the God depart. The son of Alemon arises, and ponders his recent vision in his thoughtful mind; and for a long time his opinions are divided among themselves. The Deity orders him to depart; the laws forbid his going; and death has been awarded as the punishment of him who attempts to leave his country.

"The brilliant Sun had now hidden his shining head in the ocean, and darkest Night had put forth her starry face, when the same God seemed to be present, and to give the same commands, and to utter threats, more numerous and more severe, if he does not obey. He was alarmed; and now he was also preparing to transfer his country's home to a new settlement, when a rumour arose in the city, and he was accused of holding the laws in contempt. And, when the accusation had first been made, and his crime was evident, proved without a witness, the accused, in neglected garb, raising his face and his hands towards the Gods above, says, 'Oh thou! for whom the twice six labours have created the privilege of the heavens, aid me, I pray; for thou wast the cause of my offence.' It was the ancient custom, by means of white and black pebbles, with the one to condemn the accused, with the other to acquit them of the charge; and on this occasion thus was the sad sentence passed, and every black pebble was cast into the ruthless urn. Soon as it, being inverted, poured forth the pebbles to be counted, the colour of them all was changed from black to white, and the sentence, changed to a favourable one by the aid of Hercules, acquitted the son of Alemon.

"He gives thanks to the parent, the son of Amphitryon,[3] and with favouring gales sails over the Ionian sea, and passes by the Lacedæmonian Tarentum,[4] and Sybaris, and the Salentine Neæthus,[5] and the bay of Thurium,[6] and Temesa, and the fields of Iapyx;[7] and having with difficulty coasted along the spots which skirt these shores, he finds the destined mouth of the river Æsar; and, not far thence, a mound, beneath which the ground was covering the sacred bones of Croton. And there, on the appointed land, did he found his walls, and he transferred the name of him that was there entombed to his city. By established tradition, it was known that such was the original of that place, and of the city built on the Italian coasts."

[Footnote 1: Lacinian shores.—Ver. 13. Lacinium was a promontory of Italy, not far from Crotona.]

[Footnote 2: Distant Æsar.—Ver. 23. The Æsar was a little stream of Calabria, which flowed into the sea, near the city of Crotona.]

[Footnote 3: Son of Amphitryon.—Ver. 49. Hercules was the putative son of Amphitryon, king of Thebes, who was the husband of his mother Alcmena.]

[Footnote 4: Tarentum.—Ver. 50. Tarentum was a famous city of Calabria, said to have been founded by Taras, the son of Neptune. It was afterwards enlarged by Phalanthus, a Lacedæmonian, whence its present epithet.]

[Footnote 5: Neæthus.—Ver. 51. This was a river of the Salentine territory, near Crotona.]

[Footnote 6: Thurium.—Ver. 52. Thurium was a city of Calabria, which received its name from a fountain in its vicinity. It was also called Thuria and Thurion.]

[Footnote 7: Fields of Iapyx.—Ver. 52. Iapygia was a name which Calabria received from Iapyx, the son of Dædalus. There was also a city of Calabria, named Iapygia, and a promontory, called Iapygium.]

EXPLANATION

To the story here told of Micylus, or Myscelus, as most of the ancient writers call him, another one was superadded. Suidas, on the authority of the Scholiast of Aristophanes, says that Myscelus, having consulted the oracle, concerning the colony which he was about to lead into a foreign country, was told that he must settle at the place where he should meet with rain in a clear sky, ἐξ αἰθρίας. His faith surmounting the apparent impossibility of having both fair and foul weather at the same moment, he obeyed the oracle, and put to sea; and, after experiencing many dangers, he landed in Italy. Being full of uncertainty where to fix his colony, he was reduced to great distress; on which his wife, whose name was Aithrias, with the view of comforting him, embraced him, and bedewed his face with her tears. He immediately adopted the presage, and understood the spot where he then was to be the site of his intended city.

Strabo says that Myscelus, who was so called from the smallness of his legs, designing to found a colony in a foreign land, arrived on the coast of Italy. Observing that the spot which the oracle had pointed out enjoyed a healthy climate, though the soil was not so fertile as in the adjacent plains, he went once more to consult the oracle; but was answered that he must not refuse what was offered him; an answer which was afterwards turned into a proverb. On this, he founded the city of Crotona, and another colony founded the city of Sybaris on the spot which he had preferred; a place which afterwards became infamous for its voluptuousness and profligacy.

FABLES II AND III [XV.60-478]

Pythagoras comes to the city of Crotona, and teaches the principles of his philosophy. His reputation draws Numa Pompilius to hear his discourses; on which he expounds his principles, and, more especially, enlarges on the transmigration of the soul, and the practice of eating animal food.

There was a man, a Samian by birth; but he had fled from both Samos and its rulers,[8] and, through hatred of tyranny, he was a voluntary exile. He too, mentally, held converse with the Gods, although far distant in the region of the heavens; and what nature refused to human vision, he viewed with the eyes of his mind. And when he had examined all things with his mind, and with watchful study, he gave them to be learned by the public; and he sought the crowds of people as they sat in silence, and wondered at the revealed origin of the vast universe, and the cause of things, and what nature meant, and what was God; whence came the snow, what was the cause of lightning; whether it was Jupiter, or whether the winds that thundered when the cloud was rent asunder; what it was that shook the earth; by what laws the stars took their course; and whatever besides lay concealed from mortals.

He, too, was the first to forbid animals to be served up at table, and he was the first that opened his lips, learned indeed, but still not obtaining credit, in such words as these: "Forbear, mortals, to pollute your bodies with such abominable food. There is the corn; there are the apples that bear down the branches by their weight, and there are the grapes swelling upon the vines; there are the herbs that are pleasant; there are some that can become tender, and be softened by the action of fire. The flowing milk, too, is not denied you, nor honey redolent of the bloom of the thyme. The lavish Earth yields her riches, and her agreable food, and affords dainties without slaughter and bloodshed. The beasts satisfy their hunger with flesh; and yet not all of them; for the horse, and the sheep, and the herds subsist on grass. But those whose disposition is cruel and fierce, the Armenian tigers, and the raging lions, and the bears together with the wolves, revel in their diet with blood. Alas! what a crime is it, for entrails to be buried in entrails, and for one ravening body to grow fat on other carcases crammed into it; and for one living creature to exist through the death of another living creature! And does, forsooth! amid so great an abundance, which the earth, that best of mothers, produces, nothing delight you but to gnaw with savage teeth the sad produce of your wounds, and to revive the habits of the Cyclops? And can you not appease the hunger of a voracious and ill-regulated stomach unless you first destroy another? But that age of old, to which we have given the name of 'Golden,' was blest in the produce of the trees, and in the herbs which the earth produces, and it did not pollute the mouth with blood.

"Then, both did the birds move their wings in safety in the air, and the hare without fear wander in the midst of the fields; then its own credulity had not suspended the fish from the hook; every place was without treachery, and in dread of no injury, and was full of peace. Afterwards, some one, no good adviser[9] (whoever among mortals he might have been), envied this simple food, and engulphed in his greedy paunch victuals made from a carcase; 'twas he that opened the path to wickedness; and I can believe that the steel, since stained with blood, first grew warm from the slaughter of wild beasts. And that had been sufficient. I confess that the bodies of animals that seek our destruction are put to death with no breach of the sacred laws; but, although they might be put to death, yet they were not to be eaten as well. Then this wickedness proceeded still further; and the swine is believed to have deserved death as the first victim, because it grubbed up the seeds with its turned-up snout, and cut short the hopes of the year. Having gnawed the vine, the goat was led[10] for slaughter to the altars of the avenging Bacchus. Their own faults were the ruin of the two. But why have you deserved this, ye sheep? a harmless breed, and born for the service of man; who carry the nectar in your full udders; who afford your wool as soft coverings for us, and who assist us more by your life than by your death. Why have the oxen deserved this, an animal without guile and deceit, innocent, harmless, born to endure labour? In fact, the man is ungrateful, and not worthy of the gifts of the harvest, who could, just after taking off the weight of the curving plough, slaughter the tiller of his fields; who could strike, with the axe, that neck worn bare with labour, through which he had so oft turned up the hard ground, and had afforded so many a harvest.

"And it is not enough for such wickedness to be committed; they have imputed to the Gods themselves this abomination; and they believe that a Deity in the heavens can rejoice in the slaughter of the laborious ox. A victim free from a blemish, and most beauteous in form (for 'tis being sightly that brings destruction), adorned with garlands and gold, is placed upon the altars, and, in its ignorance, it hears one praying, and sees the corn, which it has helped to produce, placed on its forehead between its horns; and, felled, it stains with its blood the knives perhaps before seen by it in the limpid water. Immediately, they examine the entrails snatched from its throbbing breast, and in them they seek out the intentions of the Deities. Whence comes it that men have so great a hankering for forbidden food? Do you presume to feed on flesh, O race of mortals? Do it not, I beseech you; and give attention to my exhortations. And when you shall be presenting the limbs of slaughtered oxen to your palates, know and consider that you are devouring your tillers of the ground. And since a God impels me to speak, I will duly obey the God that so prompts me to speak; and I will pronounce my own Delphic warnings, and disclose the heavens themselves; and I will reveal the oracles of the Divine will. I will sing of wondrous things, never investigated by the intellects of the ancients, and things which have long lain concealed. It delights me to range among the lofty stars; it delights me, having left the earth and this sluggish spot far behind, to be borne amid the clouds, and to be supported on the shoulders of the mighty Atlas; and to look down from afar on minds wandering in uncertainty, and devoid of reason; and so to advise them alarmed and dreading extinction, and to unfold the range of things ordained by fate.

"O race! stricken by the alarms of icy death, why do you dread Styx? why the shades, why empty names, the stock subjects of the poets, and the atonements of an imaginary world? Whether the funeral pile consumes your bodies with flames, or old age with gradual dissolution, believe that they cannot suffer any injury. Souls are not subject to death; and having left their former abode, they ever inhabit new dwellings, and, there received, live on.

"I, myself, for I remember it, in the days of the Trojan war, was Euphorbus,[11] the son of Panthoüs, in whose opposing breast once was planted the heavy spear of the younger son of Atreus. I lately recognised the shield, once the burden of my left arm, in the temple of Juno, at Argos, the realm of Abas. All things are ever changing; nothing perishes. The soul wanders about and comes from that spot to this, from this to that, and takes possession of any limbs whatever; it both passes from the beasts to human bodies, and so does our soul into the beasts; and in no lapse of time does it perish. And as the pliable wax is moulded into new forms, and no longer abides as it was before, nor preserves the same shape, but yet is still the same wax, so I tell you that the soul is ever the same, but passes into different forms. Therefore, that natural affection may not be vanquished by the craving of the appetite, cease, I warn you, to expel the souls of your kindred from their bodies by this dreadful slaughter; and let not blood be nourished with blood.

"And, since I am now borne over the wide ocean, and I have given my full sails to the winds, there is nothing in all the world that continues in the same state. All things are flowing onward,[12] and every shape is assumed in a fleeting course. Even time itself glides on with a constant progress, no otherwise than a river. For neither can the river, nor the fleeting hour stop in its course; but, as wave is impelled by wave, and the one before is pressed on by that which follows, and itself presses on that before it; so do the moments similarly fly on, and similarly do they follow, and they are ever renewed. For the moment which was before, is past; and that which was not, now exists; and every minute is replaced. You see, too, the night emerge and proceed onward to the dawn, and this brilliant light of the day succeed the dark night. Nor is there the same appearance in the heavens, when all things in their weariness lie in the midst of repose, and when Lucifer is coming forth on his white steed; and, again, there is another appearance, when Aurora, the daughter of Pallas, preceding the day, tints the world about to be delivered to Phœbus. The disk itself of that God, when it is rising from beneath the earth, is of ruddy colour in the morning, and when it is hiding beneath the earth it is of a ruddy colour. At its height it is of brilliant whiteness, because there the nature of the æther is purer, and far away, he avoids all infection from the earth. Nor can there ever be the same or a similar appearance of the nocturnal Diana; and always that of the present day is less than on the morrow, if she is on the increase; but greater if she is contracting her orb.

"And further. Do you not see the year, affording a resemblance of our life, assume four different appearances? for, in early Spring, it is mild, and like a nursling, and greatly resembling the age of youth. Then, the blade is shooting, and void of strength, it swells, and is flaccid, and delights the husbandman in his expectations. Then, all things are in blossom, and the genial meadow smiles with the tints of its flowers; and not as yet is there any vigour in the leaves. The year now waxing stronger, after the Spring, passes into the Summer; and in its youth it becomes robust. And indeed no season is there more vigorous, or more fruitful, or which glows with greater warmth. Autumn follows, the ardour of youth now removed, ripe, and placed between youth and old age, moderate in his temperature, with a few white hairs sprinkled over his temples. Then comes aged Winter, repulsive with his tremulous steps, either stript of his locks, or white with those which he has.

"Our own bodies too are changing always and without any intermission, and to-morrow we shall not be what we were or what we now are. The time was, when only as embryos, and the earliest hope of human beings, we lived in the womb of the mother. Nature applied her skilful hands, and willed not that our bodies should be tortured by being shut up within the entrails of the distended parent, and brought us forth from our dwelling into the vacant air. Brought to light, the infant lies without any strength; soon, like a quadruped, it uses its limbs after the manner of the brutes; and by degrees it stands upright, shaking, and with knees still unsteady, the sinews being supported by some assistance. Then he becomes strong and swift, and passes over the hours of youth; and the years of middle age, too, now past, he glides adown the steep path of declining age. This undermines and destroys the robustness of former years; and Milo,[13] now grown old, weeps when he sees the arms, which equalled those of Hercules in the massiveness of the solid muscles, hang weak and exhausted. The daughter of Tyndarus weeps, too, as she beholds in her mirror the wrinkles of old age, and enquires of herself why it is that she was twice ravished. Thou, Time, the consumer of all things, and thou, hateful Old Age, together destroy all things; and, by degrees ye consume each thing, decayed by the teeth of age, with a slow death.

"These things too, which we call elements, are not of unchanging duration; pay attention, and I will teach you what changes they undergo.

"The everlasting universe contains four elementary bodies. Two of these, namely, earth and water, are heavy, and are borne downwards by their weight; and as many are devoid of weight, and air, and fire still purer than air, nothing pressing them, seek the higher regions. Although these are separated in space, yet all things are made from them, and are resolved into them. Both the earth dissolving distils into flowing water; the water, too, evaporating, departs in the breezes and the air; its weight being removed again, the most subtle air shoots upwards into the fires of the æther on high. Thence do they return back again, and the same order is unravelled; for fire becoming gross, passes into dense air; this changes into water, and earth is formed of the water made dense. Nor does its own form remain to each; and nature, the renewer of all things, re-forms one shape from another. And, believe me, in this universe so vast, nothing perishes; but it varies and changes its appearance; and to begin to be something different from what it was before, is called being born; and to cease to be the same thing, is to be said to die. Whereas, perhaps, those things are transferred hither, and these things thither; yet, in the whole, all things ever exist.

"For my part, I cannot believe that anything lasts long under the same form. 'Twas thus, ye ages, that ye came down to the iron from the gold; 'tis thus, that thou hast so often changed the lot of various places. I have beheld that as sea, which once had been the most solid earth. I have seen land made from the sea; and far away from the ocean the sea-shells lay, and old anchors were found there on the tops of the mountains. That which was a plain, a current of water has made into a valley, and by a flood the mountain has been levelled into a plain; the ground that was swampy is parched with dry sand; and places which have endured drought, are wet with standing pools. Here nature has opened fresh springs, but there she has shut them up; and rivers have burst forth, aroused by ancient earthquakes; or, vanishing, they have subsided.

"Thus, after the Lycus[14] has been swallowed up by a chasm in the earth, it burst forth far thence, and springs up afresh at another mouth. Thus the great Erasinus[15] is at one time swallowed up, and then flowing with its stream concealed, is cast up again on the Argive plains. They say, too, that the Mysus, tired of its spring and of its former banks, now flows in another direction, as the Caicus. The Amenanus,[16] too, at one time flows, rolling along the Sicilian sands, and at another is dry, its springs being stopped up. Formerly, the water of the Anigros[17] was used for drinking; it now pours out water which you would decline to touch; since, (unless all credit must be denied to the poets), the Centaurs, the double-limbed mortals, there washed the wounds which the bow of the club-bearing Hercules had made. And what besides? Does not the Hypanis[18] too, which before was sweet, rising from the Scythian mountains, become impregnated with bitter salts? Antissa,[19] Pharos,[20] and Phœnician Tyre,[21] were once surrounded by waves; no one of these is now an island. The ancient inhabitants had Leucas[22] annexed to the continent; now the sea surrounds it. Zancle,[23] too, is said to have been united to Italy, until the sea cut off the neighbouring region, and repelled the land with its waves flowing between.

"Should you seek Helice and Buris,[24] cities of Achaia, you will find them beneath the waves, and the sailors are still wont to point out these levelled towns, with their walls buried under water.

"There is a high hill near Trœzen of Pittheus, without any trees, once a very level surface of a plain, but now a hill; for (frightful to tell) the raging power[25] of the winds, pent up in dark caverns, desiring to find some vent and having long struggled in vain to enjoy a freer air, as there was no opening in all their prison and it was not pervious to their blasts, swelled out the extended earth, just as the breath of the mouth is wont to inflate a bladder, or the hide[26] stripped from the two-horned goat. That swelling remained on the spot, and still preserves the appearance of a high hill, and has grown hard in length of time. Though many other instances may occur, either heard of by, or known to, yourselves, yet I will mention a few more. And besides, does not water, as well, both produce and receive new forms? In the middle of the day, thy waters, horned Ammon,[27] are frozen, at the rising and at the setting of the sun they are warm. On applying its waters, Athamanis[28] is said to kindle wood when the waning moon has shrunk into her smallest orb. The Ciconians have a river,[29] which when drunk of, turns the entrails into stone, and lays a covering of marble on things that are touched by it. The Crathis[30] and the Sybaris adjacent to it, in our own country, make the hair similar in hue to amber and gold.

"And, what is still more wonderful, there are some streams which are able to change, not only bodies, but even the mind. By whom has not Salmacis,[31] with its obscene waters, been heard of? Who has not heard, too, of that lake of Æthiopia,[32] of which, if any body drinks with his mouth, he either becomes mad, or falls into a sleep wondrous for its heaviness? Whoever quenches his thirst from the Clitorian spring[33] hates wine, and in his sobriety takes pleasure in pure water. Whether it is that there is a virtue in the water, the opposite of heating wine, or whether, as the natives tell us, after the son of Amithaon,[34] by his charms and his herbs, had delivered the raving daughters of Prœtus from the Furies, he threw the medicines for the mind in that stream; and a hatred of wine remained in those waters.

"The river Lyncestis[35] flows unlike that stream in its effect; for as soon as any one has drunk of it with immoderate throat, he reels, just as if he had been drinking unmixed wine. There is a place in Arcadia, (the ancients called it Pheneos,)[36] suspicious for the twofold nature of its water. Stand in dread of it at night; if drunk of in the night time, it is injurious; in the daytime, it is drunk of without any ill effects. So lakes and rivers have, some, one property, and some another. There was a time when Ortygia[37] was floating on the waves, now it is fixed. The Argo dreaded the Symplegades tossed by the assaults of the waves dashing against them; they now stand immoveable, and resist the attacks of the winds.

"Nor will Ætna, which burns with its sulphureous furnaces, always be a fiery mountain; nor yet was it always fiery. For, if the earth is an animal, and is alive, and has lungs that breathe forth flames in many a place, it may change the passages for its breathing, and oft as it is moved, may close these caverns and open others; or if the light winds are shut up in its lowermost caverns, and strike rocks against rocks, and matter that contains the elements of flame, and it takes fire at the concussion, the winds once calmed, the caverns will become cool; or, if the bituminous qualities take fire, or yellow sulphur is being dried up with a smouldering smoke, still, when the earth shall no longer give food and unctuous fuel to the flame, its energies being exhausted in length of time, and when nutriment shall be wanting to its devouring nature, it will not be able to endure hunger, and left destitute, it will desert its flames.

"The story is, that in the far Northern Pallene[38] there are persons, who are wont to have their bodies covered with light feathers, when they have nine times entered the Tritonian lake. For my part I do not believe it; but the Scythian women, as well, having their limbs sprinkled with poison, are said to employ the same arts. But if we are to give any credit[39] to things proved by experience, do you not see that whatever bodies are consumed by length of time, or by dissolving heat, are changed into small animals? Come too, bury some choice bullocks just slain, it is a thing well ascertained by experience, that flower-gathering bees are produced promiscuously from the putrefying entrails. These, after the manner of their producers, inhabit the fields, delight in toil, and labour in hope. The warlike steed,[40] buried in the ground, is the source of the hornet. If you take off the bending claws from the crab of the sea-shore, and bury the rest in the earth, a scorpion will come forth from the part so buried, and will threaten with its crooked tail.

"The silkworms, too, that are wont to cover the leaves with their white threads, a thing observable by husbandmen, change their forms into that of the deadly moth.[41] Mud contains seed that generate green frogs; and it produces them deprived of feet;[42] soon it gives them legs adapted for swimming; and that the same may be fitted for long leaps, the length of the hinder ones exceeds that of the fore legs. And it is not a cub[43] which the bear produces at the moment of birth, but a mass of flesh hardly alive. By licking, the mother forms it into limbs, and brings it into a shape, such as she herself has. Do you not see, that the offspring of the honey bees, which the hexagonal cell conceals, are produced without limbs, and that they assume both feet and wings only after a time. Unless he knew it was the case, could any one suppose it possible that the bird of Juno, which carries stars on its tail, and the eagle, the armour-bearer of Jove, and the doves of Cytherea, and all the race of birds, are produced from the middle portion of an egg? There are some who believe that human marrow changes into a serpent,[44] when the spine has putrefied in the enclosed sepulchre.

"But these which I have named derive their origin from other particulars; there is one bird which renews and reproduces itself. The Assyrians call it the Phœnix. It lives not on corn or grass, but on drops of frankincense, and the juices of the amomum. This bird, when it has completed the five ages of its life, with its talons and its crooked beak constructs for itself a nest in the branches of a holm-oak, or on the top of a quivering palm. As soon as it has strewed in this cassia and ears of sweet spikenard and bruised cinnamon with yellow myrrh, it lays itself down on it, and finishes its life in the midst of odours. They say that thence, from the body of its parent, is reproduced a little Phœnix, which is destined to live as many years. When time has given it strength, and it is able to bear the weight, it lightens the branches of the lofty tree of the burden of the nest, and dutifully carries both its own cradle and the sepulchre of its parent; and, having reached the city of Hyperion through the yielding air, it lays it down before the sacred doors in the temple of Hyperion.

"And if there is any wondrous novelty in these things, still more may we be surprised that the hyæna changes its sex,[45] and that the one which has just now, as a female, submitted to the embrace of the male, is now become a male itself. That animal, too, which feeds upon[46] the winds and the air, immediately assumes, from its contact, any colour whatever. Conquered India presented her lynxes to Bacchus crowned with clusters; and, as they tell, whatever the bladder of these discharges is changed into stone,[47] and hardens by contact with the air. So coral, too, as soon as it has come up to the air becomes hard; beneath the waves it was a soft plant.[48] "The day will fail me, and Phœbus will bathe his panting steeds in the deep sea, before I can embrace in my discourse all things that are changed into new forms. So in lapse of time, we see nations change, and these gaining strength, while those are falling. So Troy was great, both in her riches and her men, and for ten years could afford so much blood; whereas, now laid low, she only shows her ancient ruins, and, instead of her wealth, she points at the tombs of her ancestors. Sparta was famed;[49] great Mycenæ flourished; so, too, the citadel of Cecrops, and that of Amphion. Now Sparta is a contemptible spot; lofty Mycenæ is laid low. What now is Thebes, the city of Œdipus, but a mere story? What remains of Athens, the city of Pandion, but its name?

"Now, too, there is a report that Dardanian Rome is rising; which, close to the waters of Tiber that rises in the Apennines, is laying the foundations of her greatness beneath a vast structure. She then, in her growth, is changing her form, and will one day be the mistress of the boundless earth. So they say that the soothsayers, and the oracles, revealers of destiny, declare; and, so far as I recollect, Helenus, the son of Priam, said to Æneas, as he was lamenting, and in doubt as to his safety, when now the Trojan state was sinking, 'Son of a Goddess, if thou dost thyself well understand the presentiment of my mind, Troy shall not, thou being preserved, entirely fall. The flames and the sword shall afford thee a passage. Thou shalt go, and, together with thee, thou shalt bear ruined Pergamus; until a foreign soil, more friendly than thy native land, shall be the lot of Troy and thyself. Even now do I see that our Phrygian posterity are destined to build a city, so great as neither now exists, nor will exist, nor has been seen in former times. Through a long lapse of ages, other distinguished men shall make it powerful, but one born[50] of the blood of Iülus shall make it the mistress of the world. After the earth shall have enjoyed his presence, the æthereal abodes shall gain him, and heaven shall be his destination.' Remembering it, I call to mind that Helenus prophesied this to Æneas, who bore the Penates from Troy; and I rejoice that my kindred walls are rising apace, and that to such good purpose for the Phrygians the Pelasgians conquered.

"But that we may not range afar with steeds that forget to hasten to the goal; the heavens, and whatever there is beneath them, and the earth, and whatever is upon it, change their form. We too, who are a portion of the universe, (since we are not only bodies, but are fleeting souls as well, and can enter into beasts as our abode, and be hidden within the breasts of the cattle), should allow those bodies which may contain the souls of our parents, or of our brothers, or of those allied with us by some tie, or of men at all events, to be safe and unmolested; and we ought not to fill[51] our entrails with victuals fit for Thyestes. How greatly he disgraces himself, how in his impiety does he prepare himself for shedding human blood, who cuts the throat of the calf with the knife, and gives a deaf ear to its lowings! or who can kill the kid as it sends forth cries like those of a child; or who can feed upon the bird to which he himself has given food. How much is there wanting in these instances for downright criminality? A short step only is there thence to it!

"Let the bull plough, or let it owe its death to aged years; let the sheep furnish us a defence against the shivering Boreas; let the well-fed she-goats afford their udders to be pressed by the hand. Away with your nets, and your springes and snares and treacherous contrivances; deceive not the bird with the bird-limed twig; deceive not the deer with the dreaded feather foils;[52] and do not conceal the barbed hooks in the deceitful bait. If any thing is noxious, destroy it, but even then only destroy it. Let your appetites abstain from it for food, and let them consume a more befitting sustenance."

[Footnote 8: And its rulers.—Ver. 61. Pythagoras is said to have fled from the tyranny of Polycrates, the king of Samos.]

[Footnote 9: No good adviser.—Ver. 103. Clarke translates 'Non utilis auctor,' 'Some good-for-nothing introducer.']

[Footnote 10: The goat is led.—Ver 114. See the Fasti, Book I. l. 361.]

[Footnote 11: Was Euphorbus.—Ver. 161. Diogenes Laërtius, in the life of Pythagoras, says that Pythagoras affirmed, that he was, first, Æthalides; secondly, Euphorbus, which he proved by recognizing his shield hung up among the spoil in the temple of Juno, at Argos; next, Hermotimus; then, Pyrrhus and fifthly, Pythagoras.]

[Footnote 12: Flowing onward.—Ver. 178. 'Cuncta fluunt' is translated by Clarke, 'All things are in a flux.']

[Footnote 13: Milo.—Ver. 229. Milo, of Crotona, was an athlete of such strength that he was said to be able to kill a bull with a blow of his fist, and then to carry it with ease on his shoulders, and afterwards to devour it. His hands being caught within the portions of the trunk of a tree, which he was trying to cleave asunder, he became a prey to wild beasts.]

[Footnote 14: Lycus.—Ver. 273. There were several rivers of this name. The one here referred to was also called by the name of Marsyas, and flowed past the city of Laodicea, in Lydia.]

[Footnote 15: Erasinus.—Ver. 276. This was a river of Arcadia, which running out of the Stymphalian marsh, under the name of Stymphalus, disappeared in the earth, and rose again in the Argive territory, under the name of Erasinus.]

[Footnote 16: Amenanus.—Ver. 279. This was a little river of Sicily, rising in Mount Ætna, and falling into the sea near the city of Catania.]

[Footnote 17: Anigros.—Ver. 282. The Anigros, flowing from the mountain of Lapitha, in Arcadia, had waters of a fetid smell, in which no fish could exist. Pausanias thinks that this smell proceeded from the soil, and not the water. He adds, that some said that Chiron, others that Polenor, when wounded by the arrow of Hercules, washed the wound in the water of this river, which became impure from its contact with the venom of the Hydra.]

[Footnote 18: Hypanis.—Ver. 285. Now the Bog. It falls into the Black Sea.]

[Footnote 19: Antissa.—Ver. 287. This island, in the Ægean Sea, was said to have been formerly united to Lesbos.]

[Footnote 20: Pharos.—Ver. 287. According to Herodotus, this island was once a whole day's sail from the main land of Egypt. In later times, having been increased by the mud discharged by the Nile, it was united to the shore by a bridge.]

[Footnote 21: Tyre.—Ver. 288. Tyre once stood on an island, separated from the shore by a strait, seven hundred paces in width. Alexander the Great, when besieging it, united it to the main land by a causeway. This, however, does not aid the argument of Pythagoras, who intends to recount the changes wrought by nature, and not by the hand of man. Besides, it is not easy to see how Pythagoras could refer to a fact which took place several hundred years after his death.]

[Footnote 22: Leucas.—Ver. 289. The island of Leucas was formerly a peninsula, on the coast of Acarnania.]

[Footnote 23: Zancle.—Ver. 290. Under this name he means the whole of the isle of Sicily, which was supposed to have once joined the shores of Italy.]

[Footnote 24: Helice and Buris.—Ver. 293. We learn from Pliny the Elder and Orosius, that Helice and Buris, cities of Achaia at the mouth of the Corinthian gulf, were swallowed up by an earthquake, and that their remains could be seen in the sea. A similar fate attended Port Royal, in the island of Jamaica, in the year 1692. Its houses are said to be still visible beneath the waves.]

[Footnote 25: The raging power.—Ver. 299. Pausanias tells us, that in the time of Antigonus, king of Macedonia, warm waters burst from the earth, through the action of subterranean fires, near the city of Trœzen. Perhaps the 'tumulus' here mentioned sprang up at the same time.]

[Footnote 26: Or the hide.—Ver. 305. He alludes to the goat-skins, which formed the 'utres,' or leathern bottles, for wine and oil.]

[Footnote 27: Horned Ammon.—Ver. 309. The lake of Ammon, in Libya, which is here referred to, is thus described by Quintius Curtius (Book IV. c. 7)—'There is also another grove at Ammon; in the middle it contains a fountain, which they call 'the water of the Sun.' At daybreak it is tepid; at mid-day, when the heat is intense, it is ice cold. As the evening approaches, it grows warmer; at midnight, it boils and bubbles; and as the morning approaches, its midnight heat goes off.' Jupiter was worshipped in its vicinity, under the form of a ram.]

[Footnote 28: Athamanis.—Ver. 311. This wonderful fountain was said to be in Dodona, the grove sacred to Jupiter.]

[Footnote 29: Have a river.—Ver. 313. Possibly the Hebrus is here meant. The petrifying qualities of some streams is a fact well known to naturalists.]

[Footnote 30: The Crathis.—Ver. 315. Crathis and Sybaris were streams of Calabria, flowing into the sea, near Crotona. Euripides and Strabo tell the same story of the river Crathis. Pliny the Elder, in his thirty-second Book, says—'Theophrastus tells us that Crathis, a river of the Thurians, produces whiteness, whereas the Sybaris causes blackness, in sheep and cattle. Men, too, are sensible of this difference; for those who drink of the Sybaris, become more swarthy and hardy, with the hair curling; while those who drink of the Crathis become fairer, and more effeminate with the hair straight.']

[Footnote 31: Salmacis.—Ver. 319. See Book IV. l. 285.]

[Footnote 32: Lake of Æthiopia.—Ver. 320. Possibly these may be the waters of trial, mentioned by Porphyry, as being used among the Indians. He says, that, according to their influence on the person accused, when drunk of by him, he was acquitted or condemned.]

[Footnote 33: Clitorian spring.—Ver. 322. Clitorium was a town of Arcadia. Pliny the Elder, quoting from Varro, mentions the quality here referred to.]

[Footnote 34: Son of Amithaon.—Ver. 325. Melampus, the physician, the son of Amithaon, cured Mera, Euryale, Lysippe, and Iphianassa, the daughters of Prœtus, king of Argos, of madness, which Venus was said to have inflicted on them for boasting of their superior beauty. Their derangement consisted in the fancy that they were changed into cows. Melampus afterwards married Iphianassa. He was said to have employed the herb hellebore in the cure, which thence obtained the name of 'melampodium.']

[Footnote 35: Lyncestis.—Ver. 329. The Lyncesti were the people of the town of Lyncus, in Epirus. This stream flowed past that place.]

[Footnote 36: Pheneos.—Ver. 332. Pheneos was the name of a town of Arcadia, afterwards called 'Nonacris.' In its neighbourhood, according to Pausanias, was a rock, from which water oozed drop by drop, which the Greeks called 'the water of Styx.' At certain periods it was said to be fatal to men and cattle, to break vessels with which it came in contact, and to melt all metals. Ovid is the only author that mentions the difference in its qualities by day and by night.]

[Footnote 37: Ortygia.—Ver. 337. Ortygia, or Deloe, was said to have floated till it was made fast by Jupiter as a resting-place for Latona, when pregnant with Apollo and Diana. The Symplegades, or Cyanean Islands, were also said to have formerly floated.]

[Footnote 38: Far Northern Pallene.—Ver. 356. Pallene was the name of a mountain and a city of Thrace. Tritonis was a lake in the neighbourhood. Vibius Sequester says, 'When a person has nine times bathed himself in the Tritonian lake, in Thrace, he is changed into a bird.' The continuous fall of fleecy snow in that neighbourhood is supposed by some to have given rise to the story.]

[Footnote 39: Give any credit.—Ver. 361. This was a very common notion among the ancients. See the story of Aristæus and the recovery of his bees, in the Fourth Book of Virgil's Georgics, l. 281-314. It is also told by Ovid in the Fasti, Book I. l. 377.]

[Footnote 40: The warlike steed.—Ver. 368. Pliny the Elder, Nicander, and Varro state that bees and hornets are produced from the carcase of the horse. Pliny also says, that beetles are generated by the putrefying carcase of the ass.]

[Footnote 41: Deadly moth.—Ver. 374. Pliny, in the twenty-eighth Book of his History, says, 'The moth, too, that flies at the flame of the lamp, is numbered among the bad potions,' evidently alluding to their being used in philtres or incantations. There is a kind called the death's head moth; but it is so called simply from the figure of a skull, which appears very exactly represented on its body, and not on account of any noxious qualities known to be inherent in it.]

[Footnote 42: Deprived of feet.—Ver. 376. He alludes to frogs when in the tadpole state.]

[Footnote 43: Not a cub.—Ver. 379. This was long the common belief. Pliny says, speaking of the cub of the bear, 'These are white and shapeless lumps of flesh, a little bigger than mice, without eyes, and without hair; the claws, however, are prominent. These the dams by degrees reduce to shape.']

[Footnote 44: Into a serpent.—Ver. 390. Pliny tells the same story; and Antigonus (on Miracles, ch. 96) goes still further, and says, that the persons to whom this happens, after death, are able to smell the snakes while they are yet alive. The fiction, very probably, was invented with the praiseworthy object of securing freedom from molestation for the bones of the dead.]

[Footnote 45: Changes its sex.—Ver. 408. Pliny mentions it as a vulgar belief that the hyæna is male and female in alternate years. Aristotle took the pains to confute this silly notion.]

[Footnote 46: Which feeds upon.—Ver. 411. The idea that the chameleon subsists on wind and air, arose from the circumstance of its sitting with its mouth continually open, that it may catch flies and small insects, its prey. That it changes colour according to the hue of the surrounding objects, is a fact well known. It receives its name from the Greek χάμαι λέων, 'The lion on the ground.']

[Footnote 47: Changed into stone.—Ver. 415. Pliny says, that this becomes hard, and turns into gems, like the carbuncle, being of a fiery tint, and that the stone has the name of 'lyncurium.' Beckmann (Hist. Inventions) thinks that this was probably the jacinth, or hyacinth, while others suppose it to have been the tourmaline, or transparent amber.]

[Footnote 48: A soft plant.—Ver. 417. Modern improvement in knowledge has shown that coral is not a plant, but an animal substance.]

[Footnote 49: Sparta was famed.—Ver. 426-30. These lines are looked upon by many Commentators as spurious, as they are omitted in most MSS. Besides, all these cities were flourishing in the time of Pythagoras. If they are genuine, Ovid is here guilty of a series of anachronisms.]

[Footnote 50: But one born.—Ver. 447. This was Octavius, the adopted son of Julius Cæsar. According to Suetonius, he traced his descent, through his mother, from Ascanius or Iülus.]

[Footnote 51: Ought not to fill.—Ver. 462. Clarke's quaint translation is, 'And let us not cram our g—ts with Thyestian victuals.']

[Footnote 52: Feather foils.—Ver. 475. He alludes to the 'formido;' which was made of coloured feathers, and was used to scare the deer into the toils.]

EXPLANATION

The Poet having now exhausted nearly all the transformations which ancient history afforded him, proceeds to enlist in the number some of the real phenomena of nature, together with some imaginary ones. As Pythagoras was considered to have pursued metaphysical studies more deeply, perhaps, than any other of the ancient philosophers, Ovid could not have introduced a personage more fitted to discuss these subjects. Having travelled through Asia, it is supposed that Pythagoras passed into Italy, and settled at Crotona, to promulgate there the philosophical principles which he had acquired in his travels through Egypt and Asia Minor.

The Pythagorean philosophy was well-suited for the purpose of mingling its doctrines with the fabulous narratives of the Poet, as it consisted, in great part, of the doctrine of an endless series of transformations. Its main features may be reduced to two general heads; the first of which was the doctrine of the Metempsychosis, or continual transmigration of souls from one body into another. Pythagoras is supposed not to have originated this doctrine, but to have received it from the Egyptians, by whose priesthood there is little doubt that it was generally promulgated. Some writers have suggested that this transmigration was only taught by Pythagoras in a metaphorical sense; as, for instance, when he said that the souls of men were transferred to beasts, it was only to teach us that irregular passions render us brutes; on examination, however, we shall find that there is no ground to doubt that he intended his doctrines to be understood according to the literal meaning of his words; indeed, the more strongly to enforce his doctrine by a personal illustration, he was in the habit of promulgating that he remembered to have been Euphorbus, at the time of the siege of Troy, and that his soul, after several other transmigrations, had at last entered the body which it then inhabited, under the name of Pythagoras. In consequence of this doctrine, it was a favourite tenet of his followers to abstain from eating the flesh of animals, for fear of unconsciously devouring some friend or kinsman.

The second feature of this philosophy consisted in the elucidation of the changes that happen in the physical world, a long series of which is here set forth by the Poet; truth being mingled at random with fiction. While some of his facts are based upon truth, others seem to have only emanated from the fertile invention of the travellers of those days; of the latter kind are the stories of the river of Thrace, whose waters petrified those who drank of it; the fountains that kindled wood, that caused a change of sex, that created an aversion to wine, that transformed men into birds, and fables of a similar nature; such, too, are those stories which were generally believed by even the educated men of antiquity, but which the wisdom of modern times has long since shown to be utterly baseless, as, for instance, that bees grew from the entrails of the ox, and hornets from those of the horse. The principle of Pythagoras, that everything is continually changing and that nothing perishes, is true to a certain extent; but in his times, and even in those of Ovid, philosophy was not sufficiently advanced to speak with precision on the subject, and to discover the true boundary between truth and fiction.

FABLES IV, V, AND VI [XV.479-621]

Egeria, the wife of Numa, is inconsolable after his death, and is changed into a fountain. The horses of Hippolytus being frightened by a sea-monster, he is killed by being thrown from his chariot, and becomes a God, under the name of Virbius. Tages, the Diviner, arises out of a clod of earth. The lance of Romulus is changed into a cornel-tree. Cippus becomes horned, and goes into voluntary banishment, rather than his country should be deprived of its liberty by his means.

With his mind cultivated with precepts such as these and others, they say that Numa returned to his country, and, being voluntarily invited,[53] received the sovereignty of the Roman people. Blest with a Nymph for his wife, and the Muses for his guides, he taught the rites of sacrifice, and brought over to the arts of peace a race inured to savage warfare. After, full of years, he had finished his reign and his life, the Latian matrons and the people and the Senators lamented Numa at his death. But his wife, leaving the city, lay hid, concealed in the thick groves of the valley of Aricia, and by her groans and lamentations disturbed the sacred rites of Diana, brought thither by Orestes. Ah! how oft did the Nymphs of the grove and of the lake entreat her not to do so, and utter soothing words. Ah! how often did the hero, the son of Theseus, say to her as she wept, "Put an end to it; for thy lot is not the only one to be lamented. Consider the like calamities of others, thou wilt then bear thine own better. And would that an example, not my own, could lighten thy grief! yet even my own can do so."

"I suppose, in discourse it has reached thy ears that a certain Hippolytus met with his death through the credulity of his father, by the deceit of his wicked step-mother. Thou wilt wonder, and I shall hardly be able to prove it; but yet I am he. In former times, the daughter of Pasiphaë, having tempted me in vain, pretended that I wished to defile the couch of my father, a thing that she herself wished to do; and having turned the accusation against me, (whether it was more through dread of discovery, or through mortification at her repulse) she charged me. And my father expelled me, thus innocent, from the city, and as I went he uttered imprecations against my head, with ruthless prayers. I was going to Trœzen, the city of Pittheus,[54] in my flying chariot, and I was now proceeding along the shores of the Corinthian gulf, when the sea was aroused, and an enormous mass of waters seemed to bend and to grow in the form of a mountain, and to send forth a roaring noise, and to burst asunder at its very summit. Thence, the waves being divided, a horned bull was sent forth, and erect in the light air as far as his breast, he vomited forth a quantity of sea-water from his nostrils and his open mouth. The hearts of my attendants quailed; my mind remained without fear, intent only on my exile, when the fierce horses turned their necks towards the sea, and were terrified, with ears erect; and they were alarmed with dread of the monster, and precipitated the chariot over the lofty rocks. I struggled, with unavailing hand, to guide the bridle covered with white foam, and, throwing myself backwards, I pulled back the loosened reins. And, indeed, the madness of my steeds would not have exceeded that strength of mine, had not the wheel, by running against a stump, been broken and disjoined just where it turns round on the long axle-tree.

"I was hurled from my chariot; and, the reins entwined around my limbs, you might have seen my palpitating entrails dragged, my sinews fasten upon the stump, my limbs partly torn to pieces and partly left behind, being caught by various obstacles, my bones in their breaking emit a loud noise, and my exhausted breath become exhaled, and not a part in my body which you could recognize; and the whole of me formed but one continued wound. And canst thou, Nymph, or dost thou venture to compare thy misfortune to mine? I have visited, too, the realms deprived of light, and I have bathed my lacerated body in the waves of Phlegethon.[55] Nor could life have been restored me, but through the powerful remedies of the son of Apollo. After I had received it, through potent herbs and the Pæonian aid,[56] much against the will of Pluto, then Cynthia threw around me thick clouds, that I might not, by my presence, increase his anger at this favour; and that I might be safe, and be seen in security, she gave me a more aged appearance, and left me no features that could be recognized. For a long time she was doubtful whether she should give me Crete or Delos for me to possess. Delos and Crete being abandoned, she placed me here, and, at the same time, she ordered me to lay aside my name, which might have reminded me of my steeds, and she said, 'Thou, the same who wast Hippolytus, be thou now Virbius.'[57] From that time I have inhabited this grove; and, as one of the lower Gods, I lie concealed under the protection of my mistress, and to her am I devoted."[58]

But yet the misfortunes of others were not able to alleviate the grief of Egeria; and, throwing herself down at the base of the hill, she dissolved into tears; until, moved by her affection as she grieved, the sister of Phœbus formed a cool fountain from her body, and dissolved her limbs in ever-flowing waters.

But this new circumstance surprised the Nymphs; and the son of the Amazon[59] was astonished, in no other manner than as when the Etrurian ploughman beheld the fate-revealing clod in the midst of the fields move at first of its own accord and no one touching it, and afterwards assume a human form, and lose that of earth, and open its new-made mouth with the decrees of future destiny. The natives called him Tages. He was the first to teach the Etrurian nation to foretell future events.

Or, as when Romulus once saw his lance, fixed in the Palatine hill, suddenly shoot forth; which now stood there with a root newly-formed, and not with the iron point driven in; and, now no longer as a dart, but as a tree with limber twigs, it sent forth, for the admiring spectators, a shade that was not looked for.

Or, as when Cippus beheld his horns in the water of the stream, (for he did see them) and, believing that there was a false representation in the reflection, often returning his fingers to his forehead, he touched what he saw. And now, no longer condemning his own eyesight, he stood still, as he was returning victorious from the conquest of the enemy; and raising his eyes towards heaven, and his hands in the same direction, he exclaimed, "Ye Gods above! whatever is portended by this prodigy, if it is auspicious, then be it auspicious to my country and to the people of Quirinus; but if unfortunate, be it so for myself." And then he made atonement at the grassy altars built of green turf, with odoriferous fires, and presented wine in bowls, and consulted the panting entrails of slaughtered sheep what the meaning of it was. Soon as the soothsayer of the Etrurian nation had inspected them, he beheld in them the great beginnings of future events, but still not clearly. But when he raised his searching eyes from the entrails of the sheep, to the horns of Cippus, he said, "Hail, O king! for thee, Cippus, thee and thy horns shall this place and the Latian towers obey. Only do thou lay aside all delay; hasten to enter the gates wide open; thus the fates command thee. For, once received within the City, thou shalt be king, and thou shalt safely enjoy a lasting sceptre." He retreated backwards, and turning his stern visage away from the walls of the City, he exclaimed, "Far, O far away may the Gods drive such omens! Much more righteously shall I pass my life in exile, than if the Capitol were to see me a king."

Thus he says; and forthwith he convokes the people and the dignified Senate; but first, he veils his horns with laurel that betokens peace, and he stands upon a mound raised by his brave soldiers; and praying to the Gods after the ancient manner, "Behold!" says he, "one is here who will be king, if you do not expel him from the City. I will tell you who he is by a sign, and not by name. He wears horns on his forehead; the augur predicts to you, that if he enters the City, he shall give you laws as his slaves. He, indeed, was able to enter the open gates, but I have opposed him; although no one is more nearly allied with him than myself. Forbid your City to this man, ye Romans, or, if he shall deserve it, bind him with heavy fetters; or else end your fears by the death of the destined tyrant."

As the murmur which arises among the groves of the slender pine,[60] when the furious East wind whistles among them, or as that which the waves of the ocean produce, if any one hears them from afar, such is the noise of the crowd. But yet amid the confused words of the shouting multitude, one cry is distinguished, "Which is he?" And then they examine the foreheads, and seek the predicted horns. Cippus again addresses them: "Him whom you require, ye now have;" and, despite of the people, throwing the chaplet from his head, he exhibits his temples, remarkable for two horns. All cast down their eyes, and utter groans, and (who would have supposed it?) they unwillingly look upon that head famed for its merits. And no longer suffering it to be deprived of its honours, they place upon it the festive chaplet. But the nobles, Cippus, since thou art forbidden to enter the city, give thee as much land, as a mark of honour, as thou canst, with the oxen yoked to the pressed plough, make the circuit of from the rising of the sun to its setting. They carve, too, the horns, imitating their wondrous form, on the door-posts adorned with brass, there to remain for long ages.

[Footnote 53: *Voluntarily invited.*—Ver. 481. *He was living at the Sabine town of Cures, when the throne was pressed upon him by the desire of both the Roman and the Sabine nations.*]

[Footnote 54: *City of Pittheus.*—Ver. 506. *Pittheus was the son of Pelops, and the father of Æthra, the mother of Theseus; consequently he was the great-grandfather of Hippolytus.*]

[Footnote 55: *Phlegethon.*—Ver. 532. *This was said to be one of the rivers of the Infernal Regions, and to be flowing with fire and brimstone.*]

[Footnote 56: *Pæonian aid.*—Ver. 536. *Pæon was a skilful physician, mentioned by Homer, in the Fifth Book of the Iliad. Eustathius thinks that Apollo is meant under that name.*]

[Footnote 57: *Virbius.*—Ver. 544. *This name is formed from the words 'vir' and 'bis,' twice a man.*]

[Footnote 58: *Am I devoted.*—Ver. 546. *In the same relation to her as Adonis was to Venus, Ericthonius to Minerva, and Atys to Cybele.*]

[Footnote 59: Son of the Amazon.—Ver. 552. Hippolytus was the son either of the Amazon Hippolyta, or Antiope.]

[Footnote 60: Slender pine.—Ver. 603-4. The words 'succinctis pinetis' are rendered by Clarke, 'the neat pine-groves.']

EXPLANATION

Ovid, following the notion that was generally entertained of the wisdom of Numa, pretends that before he was elected to the sovereignty he went to Crotona, for the purpose of studying under Pythagoras; but he is guilty of a considerable anachronism in this instance, as Pythagoras was not born till very many years after the time of Numa. According to Livy, Pythagoras flourished in the time of Servius Tullius, the sixth Roman king, about one hundred and fifty years after Numa. Modern authors are of opinion that upwards of two hundred years intervened between the days of Numa and Pythagoras. Besides, Dionysius of Halicarnassus distinctly asserts that the city of Crotona was only built in the fourth year of the reign of Numa Pompilius.

Numa is said to have been in the habit of retiring to the Arician grove, to consult the Nymph Egeria upon the laws which he was about to promulgate for the benefit of his subjects. It is probable, that to ensure their observance the more effectually, he wished the people to believe that his enactments were compiled under the inspection of one who partook of the immortal nature, and that in so doing he followed the example of previous lawgivers. Zamolxis pretended that the laws which he gave to the Scythians were dictated to him by his attendant genius or spirit. The first Minos affirmed that Jupiter was the author of the ordinances which he gave to the people of Crete, while Lycurgus attributed his to Apollo. It is not improbable that in this they imitated the example of Moses, a tradition of whose reception of the laws on Mount Sinai they may have received from the people of Phœnicia.

Dionysius of Halicarnassus has an interesting passage relative to Numa, which throws some light upon his alleged intercourse with the Nymph Egeria. His words are—'The Romans affirm that Numa was never engaged in any warlike expedition; but that he passed his whole reign in profound peace: that his first care was to encourage piety and justice in his dominions, and to civilize his people by good and wholesome laws. His profound skill in governing made him pass for being inspired, and gave rise to many fabulous stories. Some have said that he had secret interviews with the Nymph Egeria; others, that he frequently consulted one of the Muses, and was instructed by her in the art of government. Numa was desirous to confirm the people in this opinion; but because some hesitated to believe his bare affirmation, and others went so far as to call his alleged converse with the Deities a fiction, he took an opportunity to give them such proofs of it, that the most sceptical among them should have no room left for suspicion. This he effected in the following manner. He one day invited several of the nobles to his palace, and showed them the plainness of the apartments, where no rich furniture was to be seen, nor any thing like an attempt at splendour; and how even the most ordinary necessaries were wanting for anything like a great entertainment; after which, he dismissed them with an invitation to come to sup with him on the same night. At the appointed hour his guests arrived; they were received on stately couches; the tables were decked with a variety of plate, and were loaded with the most exquisite dainties. The guests were struck with the sumptuousness and profusion of the entertainment, and considering how impossible it was for any man to have made such preparations in so short a time, were persuaded that his communication with heaven was not a fiction, and that he must have had the aid of the celestial powers to do things of a nature so extraordinary. 'But,' as the same author says, 'those who were not so ready at adopting fabulous narratives as a part of history, say that it was the policy of Numa which led him to feign a conversation with the Nymph Egeria, to make his laws respected by his people, and that he thence followed the example of the Greek sages, who adopted the same method of enforcing the authority of their laws with the people.'

The Romans were so persuaded of the fact of Numa's conferences with the Nymph Egeria, that they went into the grove of Aricia to seek her; but finding nothing but a fountain in the spot which he used to frequent, they promulgated the story of the transformation of the Nymph. St. Augustin, speaking on this subject, says that Numa made use of the waters of that fountain in the divination which was performed by the aid of water, and was called Hydromancy.

Theseus having left Ariadne in the isle of Naxos, flattered himself with the hopes of marrying her sister Phædra. Deucalion, succeeding Minos in Crete immediately after his death, sent Phædra to Athens. On arriving there, she fell in love with Hippolytus, the son of Theseus, who had been brought up at Trœzen by Pittheus. As she did not dare to request of Theseus that his son might be brought from the court of Pittheus, she built a temple to Venus near Trœzen, that she might the more frequently have the opportunity of seeing Hippolytus, and called it by the name of Hippolyteum. According to Euripides, this youth was wise, chaste, and an enemy to all voluptuousness. He spent his time in hunting and chariot racing, with other exercises which formed the pursuits of youths of high station. According to Plutarch, it was at the time when Theseus was a prisoner in Epirus, that Phædra took the opportunity of disclosing to Hippolytus the violence of her passion for him. Her declaration being but ill received, she grew desperate on his refusal to comply with her desires, and was about to commit self-destruction, when her nurse suggested the necessity of revenging the virtuous disdain of the youth.

Theseus having been liberated by Hercules, Phædra, being fearful lest the intrigue should come to his knowledge, hanged herself, having first written a letter to inform him that she could not survive an attempt which Hippolytus had made on her virtue. Plutarch, Servius and Hyginus, following Euripides, give this account of her death. But Seneca, in his Hippolytus, says that she only appeared before her husband in extreme grief, holding a sword in her hand to signify the violence which Hippolytus had offered her. On this, Theseus implored the assistance of Neptune, who sent a monster out of the sea, to frighten his horses, as he was driving along the sea-shore: on which, they took fright, and throwing him from his chariot, he was killed. It has been suggested that the true meaning of this is, that Theseus having ordered his son to come and justify himself, he made so much haste that his horses ran away with him; and his chariot being dashed over the rocks, he was killed.

Seneca also differs from the other writers, in saying that Phædra did not put herself to death till she had heard of the catastrophe of Hippolytus, on which she stabbed herself. The people of Trœzen, regretting his loss, decreed him divine honours, built a temple, and appointed a priest to offer yearly sacrifices to him. Euripides says, that the young women of Trœzen, when about to be married, cut off their hair and carried it to the temple of Hippolytus. It was also promulgated that the Gods had translated him to the heavens, where he was changed into the Constellation, called by the Latins 'Auriga,' or 'the Charioteer.' Later authors, whom Ovid here follows, added, that Æsculapius restored him to life, and that he afterwards appeared in Italy under the name of Virbius. This story was probably invented as a source of profit by the priesthood, who were desirous to find some good reason for introducing his worship into the Arician grove near Rome. This story is mentioned by Apollodorus, who quotes the author of the Naupactan verses in favour of it, and by the Scholiasts of Euripides and Pindar.

The ancient Etrurians were great adepts in the art of divination; their favourite method of exercising which was by the inspection of the entrails of beasts, and the observation of the flight of birds; and from them, as we learn from Cicero in his book on Divination, the system spread over the whole of Italy. Tages is supposed to have been the first who taught this art, and he wrote treatises upon it, which, according to Plutarch, were quoted by ancient authors. It not being known whence he came, or who were his parents, he was called, in the language of the poets, a son of the earth. Ammianus Marcellinus speaks of him as being said to have sprung out of the earth in Etruria.

Ovid next makes a passing allusion to the spear of Romulus, which, when thrown by him from the Mount Aventine towards the Capitol, sticking in the ground was converted into a tree, which immediately put forth leaves. This prodigy was taken for a presage of the future greatness of Rome: and Plutarch, in his life of Romulus, says that so long as this tree stood, the Republic flourished. It began to wither in the time of the first civil war; and Julius Cæsar having afterwards ordered a building to be erected near where it stood, the workmen cutting some of its roots in sinking the foundations, it soon after died. It is hardly probable that a cornel tree would stand in a thronged city for nearly seven hundred years; and it is, therefore, most likely, that care was taken to renovate it from time to time, by planting slips from the former tree.

The story of Genucius Cippus is one of those strange fables with which the Roman history is diversified. Valerius Maximus gives the following account of it. He says that Cippus, going one day out of Rome, suddenly found that something which resembled horns was growing out of his forehead. Surprised at an event so extraordinary, he consulted the augurs, who said that he would be chosen king, if he ever entered the city again. As the royal power was abhorred in Rome, he preferred a voluntary banishment to revisiting Rome on those terms. Struck with this heroism, the Romans erected a brazen statue with horns over the gate by which he departed, and it was afterwards called 'Porta raudusculana,' because the ancient Latin name of brass was 'raudus,' 'rodus,' or 'rudus.' The fact is, however, as Ovid represents it, that Cippus was not going out of Rome, but returning to it, when the prodigy happened; he having been to convey assistance to the Consul Valerius. The Senate also conferred certain lands on Cippus, as a reward for his patriotism. He lived about two hundred and forty years before the Christian era. Pliny the Elder considers the story of the horns of Cippus as much a fable as that of Actæon. It appears, however, that the account of the horns may have possibly been founded on fact, as excrescences resembling them have appeared on the bodies of individuals. Bayle makes mention of a girl of Palermo, who had little horns all over her body, like those of a young calf. In the Ashmolean museum at Oxford, a substance much resembling the horn of a goat is shown, which is said to have sprung from the forehead of a female named Mary Davis, whose likeness is there shown. The excrescence was most probably produced by a deranged secretion of the hair, and something of a similar nature may perhaps have befallen Genucius Cippus, which, of course, would be made the most of in those ages of superstition. Valerius Maximus, with all his credulity, does not say that they were real horns that made their appearance, but that they were 'just like horns.'

It is not improbable that the story originally was, that Cippus, on his return to Rome, dreamt that he had horns on his head, and that having consulted the augurs, and received the answer mentioned by Ovid, he preferred to suffer exile, rather than enslave his country; and that, in length of time, the more wonderful part of the story was added to it.

FABLE VII [XV.622-744]

Rome being wasted by a pestilence, the Delphian oracle is consulted; and the answer is given, that to cause it to cease Æsculapius must be brought to Rome. On this, ambassadors are sent to Epidaurus to demand the God. The people refuse to part with him; but he appears to one of the Romans in a dream, and consents to go. On his arrival at Rome the contagion ceases, and a Temple is built in his honour.

Relate, now, ye Muses, the guardian Deities of poets (for you know, and remote antiquity conceals it not from you), whence it is that the Island surrounded by the channel of the Tiber introduced the son of Coronis into the sacred rites of the City of Romulus. A dire contagion had once infected the Latian air, and the pale bodies were deformed by a consumption that dried up the blood. When, wearied with so many deaths, they found that mortal endeavours availed nothing, and that the skill of physicians had no effect, they sought the aid of heaven, and they repaired to Delphi which occupies the centre spot of the world, the oracle of Phœbus, and entreated that he would aid their distressed circumstances by a response productive of health, and put an end to the woes of a City so great. Both the spot, and the laurels, and the quivers which it has, shook at the same moment, and the tripod[61] gave this answer from the recesses of the shrine, and struck with awe their astonished breasts:—"What here thou dost seek, O Roman, thou mightst have sought in a nearer spot: and now seek it in a nearer spot; thou hast no need of Apollo to diminish thy grief, but of the son of Apollo. Go with a good omen, and invite my son."

After the prudent Senate had received the commands of the Deity, they enquired what city the youthful son of Phœbus inhabited; and they sent some to reach the coasts of Epidaurus[62] with the winds. Soon as those sent had reached them in the curving ship, they repaired to the council and the Grecian elders, and besought them to grant them the Divinity, who by his presence could put an end to the mortality of the Ausonian nation; for that so the unerring response had directed. Their opinions were divided, and differed; and some thought that aid ought not to be refused. Many refused it, and advised them not to part with their own protector, and to give up their own guardian Deity. While they were deliberating, twilight had now expelled the waning day, and the shadow of the earth had brought darkness over the world; when, in thy sleep, the saving God seemed, O Roman, to be standing before thy couch; but just as he is wont to be in his temple; and, holding a rustic staff in his left hand, he seemed to be stroking the long hair of his beard with his right, and to utter such words as these from his kindly breast—"Lay aside thy fears; I will come, and I will leave these my statues. Only observe now this serpent, which with its folds entwines around this staff, and accurately mark it with thine eyes, that thou mayst be able to know it again. Into this shall I be changed; but I shall be greater, and I shall appear to be of a size as great as that into which heavenly bodies ought to be transformed."

Forthwith, with these words, the God departs; and with his words and the God sleep departs, and genial light follows upon the departure of sleep. The following morn has now dispersed the starry fires; uncertain what to do, the nobles meet together in the sumptuous temple of the God then sought, and beseech him to indicate, by celestial tokens, in what spot he would wish to abide. Hardly have they well ceased, when the God, all glittering with gold, in the form of a serpent, with crest erect, sends forth a hissing, as a notice of his approach; and in his coming, he shakes both his statue, the altars, the doors, the marble pavement, and the gilded roof, and as far as the breast he stands erect in the midst of the temple, and rolls around his eyes that sparkle with fire. The frightened multitude is alarmed; the priest, having his chaste hair bound with a white fillet, recognizes the Deity and exclaims, "The God! Behold the God! Whoever you are that are present, be of good omen, both with your words and your feelings. Mayst thou, most beauteous one, be beheld to our advantage; and mayst thou aid the nations that perform thy sacred rites." Whoever are present, adore the Deity as bidden; and all repeat the words of the priest over again; and the descendants of Æneas give a pious omen, both with their feelings, and in their words. To these the God shows favour; and with crest erected, he gives a hiss, a sure token, repeated thrice with his vibrating tongue. Then he glides down the polished steps,[63] and turns back his head, and, about to depart, he looks back upon his ancient altars, and salutes his wonted abode and the temple that so long he has inhabited. Then, with his vast bulk, he glides along the ground covered with the strewn flowers, and coils his folds, and through the midst of the city repairs to the harbour protected by its winding quay.

Here he stops; and seeming to dismiss his train, and the dutiful attendance of the accompanying crowd, with a placid countenance, he places his body in the Ausonian ship. It is sensible of the weight of the God; and the ship now laden with the Divinity for its freight, the descendants of Æneas rejoice; and a bull having first been slain on the sea-shore, they loosen the twisted cables of the bark bedecked with garlands. A gentle breeze has now impelled the ship. The God is conspicuous aloft,[64] and pressing upon the crooked stern with his neck laid upon it, he looks down upon the azure waters; and with the gentle Zephyrs along the Ionian sea, on the sixth rising of the daughter of Pallas, he makes Italy, and is borne along the Lacinian shores, ennobled by the temple of the Goddess Juno, and the Scylacean[65] coasts. He leaves Iapygia behind, and flies from the Amphissian[66] rocks with the oars on the left side; on the right side he passes by the steep Ceraunia, and Romechium, and Caulon,[67] and Narycia, and he crosses the sea and the straits of the Sicilian Pelorus, and the abodes of the king the grandson of Hippotas, and the mines of Temesa; and then he makes for Leucosia,[68] and the rose-beds of the warm Pæstum. Then he coasts by Capreæ,[69] and the promontory of Minerva, and the hills ennobled with the Surrentine[70] vines, and the city of Hercules,[71] and Stabiæ,[72] and Parthenope made for retirement, and after it the temple of the Cumæan Sibyl. Next, the warm springs[73] are passed by, and Linternum,[74] that bears mastick trees; and then Vulturnus,[75] that carries much sand along with its tide, and Sinuessa, that abounds with snow-white snakes,[76] and the pestilential Minturnæ,[77] and she for whom[78] her foster-child erected the tomb, and the abode of Antiphates,[79] and Trachas,[80] surrounded by the marsh, and the land of Circe, and Antium,[81] with its rocky coast.

After the sailors have steered the sail-bearing ship hither (for now the sea is aroused), the Deity unfolds his coils, and gliding with many a fold and in vast coils, he enters the temple of his parent, that skirts the yellow shore. The sea now becalmed, the God of Epidaurus leaves the altars of his sire; and having enjoyed the hospitality of the Deity, thus related to him, he furrows the sands of the sea-shore with the dragging of his rattling scales, and reclining against the helm of the ship, he places his head upon the lofty stern; until he comes to Castrum,[82] and the sacred abodes of Lavinium, and the mouths of the Tiber. Hither, all the people indiscriminately, a crowd both of matrons and of men, rush to meet him; they, too, Vesta! who tend thy fires; and with joyous shouts they welcome the God. And where the swift ship is steered through the tide running out, altars being erected in a line, the frankincense crackles along the banks on either side, and perfumes the air with its smoke; the felled victim too, with its blood makes warm the knives thrust into it.

And now he has entered Rome, the sovereign of the world. The serpent rises erect, and lifts his neck that reclines against the top of the mast, and looks around for a habitation suited for himself. There is a spot, where the river flowing around, is divided into two parts; it is called "the Island." The river in the direction of each side extends its arms of equal length, the dry land lying in the middle. Hither, the serpent, son of Phœbus, betakes himself from the Latian ship; and he puts an end to the mourning, having resumed his celestial form. And thus did he come, the restorer of health, to the City.

[Footnote 61: The tripod.—Ver. 635. The tripod on which the priestess of Apollo or 'Pythia,' sat when inspired, was called 'Cortina,' from the skin, 'corium,' of the serpent Python, which, when it had been killed by Apollo was used to cover it.]

[Footnote 62: Epidaurus.—Ver. 643. There were several towns of this name. The one here mentioned was in the state of Argolis.]

[Footnote 63: Polished steps.—Ver. 685. Clarke translates 'Gradibus nitidis,' 'the neat steps.']

[Footnote 64: Is conspicuous aloft.—Ver. 697. 'Deus eminet alte.' This is rendered by Clarke, 'The God rears up to a good height.']

[Footnote 65: Scylacean.—Ver. 702. Scylace was a town on the Calabrian coast; it was said to have been founded by an Athenian colony.]

[Footnote 66: Amphissian.—Ver. 703. Amphissia was the name of a city of Locris; but that cannot be the place here alluded to on the coast of Italy. It is most probably a corrupt reading.]

[Footnote 67: Caulon.—Ver. 705. Caulon was a colony of the Achæa on the coast of Calabria. Narycia, or Naritium, or Naricia, was also a town on the Calabrian coast. The localities of Ceraunia and Romechium are not known.]

[Footnote 68: Leucosia.—Ver. 708. Leucosia was a little island off the town of Pæstum, which was in Lucania; it was famous for its mild climate, and the beauty of its roses, which are celebrated by Virgil.]

[Footnote 69: Capreæ.—Ver. 709. Capreæ was an island near the coast of Naples.]

[Footnote 70: Surrentine.—Ver. 710. Surrentum was a city of Campania, famed for its wines.]

[Footnote 71: City of Hercules.—Ver. 711. This was Herculaneum, at the foot of Vesuvius; the place which shared so disastrous a fate from the eruption of that mountain.]

[Footnote 72: Stabiæ.—Ver. 711. This was a town of Campania, which was destroyed by Sylla in the Social war. It was afterwards rebuilt.]

[Footnote 73: The warm springs.—Ver. 711. He alludes to the city of Baiæ, famed for its warm springs and baths.]

[Footnote 74: Linternum.—Ver. 714. This place was in Campania. It was famous as the place of retirement of the elder Scipio; he was buried there.]

[Footnote 75: Vulturnus.—Ver. 715. This was a river of Campania, which flowed past the city of Capua.]

[Footnote 76: Snow-white snakes.—Ver. 715. Sinuessa was a town of Campania; Heinsius very properly suggests 'columbis,' 'doves;' for 'colubris,' 'snakes.' We are told by Pliny the Elder, that Campania was famed for its doves.]

[Footnote 77: Minturnæ.—Ver. 716. This was a town of Latium; the marshes in its neighbourhood produced pestilential exhalations.]

[Footnote 78: She for whom.—Ver. 716. This was Caieta, who, being buried there by her foster-child Æneas, gave her name to the spot.]

[Footnote 79: Abode of Antiphates.—Ver. 717. Formiæ.]

[Footnote 80: Trachas.—Ver. 717. This place was also called 'Anxur.' Its present name is Terracina. Livy mentions it as lying in the marshes.]

[Footnote 81: Antium.—Ver. 718. This was the capital of the ancient Volscians.]

[Footnote 82: Castrum.—Ver. 727. This was 'Castrum Inui,' or 'the tents of Pan;' an old town of the Rutulians.]

EXPLANATION

The story here narrated by Ovid is derived from the Roman history, to which we will shortly refer for an explanation.

Under the consulate of Quintus Fabius Gurges, and Decimus Junius Brutus Scæva, Rome was ravaged by a frightful pestilence. The resources of physic having been exhausted, the Sibylline books were consulted to ascertain by what expedient the calamity might be put an end to, and they found that the plague would not cease till they had brought Æsculapius from Epidaurus to Rome. Being then engaged in war, they postponed their application to the Epidaurians for a year, at the end of which time they despatched an embassy to Epidaurus; on which a serpent was delivered to them, which the priests of the Deity assured them was the God himself. Taking it on board their ship, the delegates set sail. When near Antium, they were obliged to put in there by stress of weather, and the serpent, escaping from the ship, remained three days on shore; after which it came on board of its own accord, and they continued their voyage. On arriving at the Island of the Tiber the serpent escaped, and concealed itself amid the reeds; and as they, in their credulity, fancied that the God had chosen the place for his habitation, they built a temple there in his honour. From this period, which was about the year of Rome 462, the worship of Æsculapius was introduced in the city, and to him recourse was had in cases of disease, and especially in times of pestilence.

FABLE VIII [XV.745-879]

Julius Cæsar is assassinated in the Senate-house, and by the intercession of Venus, his ancestor, he is changed into a star. The Poet concludes his work with a compliment to Augustus, and a promise of immortality to himself.

And still, he came a stranger to our temples; Cæsar is a Deity in his own city; whom, alike distinguished both in war and peace, wars ending with triumphs, his government at home, and the rapid glory of his exploits, did not more tend to change into a new planet, and a star with brilliant train, than did his own progeny. For of all the acts of Cæsar, there is not one more ennobling than that he was the father of this our Cæsar. Was it, forsooth, a greater thing to have conquered the Britons surrounded by the ocean, and to have steered his victorious ships along the seven-mouthed streams of the Nile that bears the papyrus, and to have added to the people of Quirinus the rebellious Numidians[83] and the Cinyphian Juba, and Pontus[84] proud of the fame of Mithridates, and to have deserved many a triumph, and to have enjoyed some, than it was to have been the father of a personage so great, under whose tutelage over the world, you, ye Gods above, have shewn excessive care for the human race? That he then might not be sprung from mortal seed, 'twas fit that Julius should be made a Divinity. When the resplendent mother of Æneas was sensible of this; and when she saw that a sad death was in preparation for the Pontiff, and that the arms of the conspirators were brandished; she turned pale, and said to each of the Deities, as she met them:—

"Behold, on how vast a scale treason is plotted against me, and with how great perfidy that life is sought, which alone remains for me from the Dardanian Iülus. Shall I alone be everlastingly harassed by justified anxieties? I, whom one while the Calydonian lance of the son of Tydeus is wounding, and at another time the walls of Troy, defended in vain, are grieving? I, who have seen my son driven about in protracted wanderings, tossed on the ocean, entering the abodes of the departed, and waging war with Turnus; or, if we confess the truth, with Juno rather? But, why am I now calling to mind the ancient misfortunes of my own offspring? Present apprehensions do not allow me to remember things of former days. Against me, you behold how the impious swords are now being whetted. Avert them, I entreat; hinder this crime, and do not, by the murder of the priest, extinguish the flames of Vesta."

Such expressions as these did Venus, full of anxiety, vainly let fall throughout the heavens, and she moved the Gods above. Although they were not able to frustrate the iron decrees of the aged sisters, yet they afforded no unerring tokens of approaching woe. They say, that arms resounding amid the black clouds, and dreadful blasts of the trumpet, and clarions heard through the heavens, forewarned men of the crime. The sad face too of the sun gave a livid light to the alarmed earth. Often did torches seem to be burning in the midst of the stars; often did drops of blood fall in the showers. The azure-coloured Lucifer had his light tinted with a dark iron colour; the chariot of the moon was besprinkled with blood. The Stygian owl gave omens of ill in a thousand places; in a thousand places did the ivory statues shed tears; dirges, too, are said to have been heard, and threatening expressions in the sacred groves. No victim gave an omen of good; the entrails, too, showed that great tumults were imminent; and the extremity of the liver was found cut off among the entrails. They say, too, that in the Forum, and around the houses and the temples of the Gods, the dogs were howling by night; and that the ghosts of the departed were walking, and that the City was shaken by earthquakes. But still the warnings of the Gods could not avert treachery and the approach of Fate, and drawn swords were carried into a temple; and no other place in the whole City than the Senate-house pleased them for this crime and this atrocious murder.

But then did Cytherea beat her breast with both her hands, and attempt to hide the descendant of Æneas in a cloud, in which, long since, Paris was conveyed from the hostile son of Atreus,[85] and Æneas had escaped from the sword of Diomedes. In such words as these did her father Jove address her: "Dost thou, my daughter, unaided, attempt to change the insuperable decrees of Fate? Thou, thyself, mayst enter the abode of the three sisters, and there thou wilt behold the register of future events, wrought with vast labour, of brass and of solid iron; these, safe and destined for eternity, fear neither the thundering shock of the heavens, nor the rage of the lightnings, nor any source of destruction. There wilt thou find the destinies of thy descendants engraved in everlasting adamant. I myself have read them, and I have marked them in my mind; I will repeat them, that thou mayst not still be ignorant of the future. He (on whose account, Cytherea, thou art thus anxious), has completed his time, those years being ended which he owed to the earth. Thou, with his son, who, as the heir to his glory, will bear the burden of government devolving on him, wilt cause him, as a Deity, to reach the heavens, and to be worshipped in temples; and he, as a most valiant avenger of his murdered parent, will have us to aid him in his battles. The conquered walls of Mutina,[86] besieged under his auspices, shall sue for peace; Pharsalia shall be sensible of him, and Philippi,[87] again drenched with Emathian gore; and the name of one renowned as Great, shall be subdued in the Sicilian waves; the Egyptian dame too, the wife[88] of the Roman general, shall fall, vainly trusting in that alliance; and in vain shall she threaten, that our own Capitol shall be obedient to her Canopus.[89] Why should I recount to thee the regions of barbarism, and nations situate in either ocean? Whatever the habitable world contains, shall be his; the sea, too, shall be subject to him. Peace being granted to the earth, he will turn his attention to civil rights, and, as a most upright legislator, he will enact laws. After his own example, too, will he regulate manners; and, looking forward to the days of future time, and of his coming posterity, he will order the offspring born of his hallowed wife[90] to assume both his own name and his cares. Nor shall he, until as an aged man he shall have equalled his glories with like years,[91] arrive at the abodes of heaven and his kindred stars. Meanwhile, change this soul, snatched from the murdered body, into a beam of light, that eternally the Deified Julius may look down from his lofty abode upon our Capitol and Forum."

Hardly had he uttered these words, when the genial Venus, perceived by none, stood in the very midst of the Senate-house, and snatched the soul, just liberated from the body, away from the limbs of her own Cæsar, and, not suffering it to dissolve in air, she bore it amid the stars of heaven. And as she bore it, she perceived it assume a train of light and become inflamed; and she dropped it from her bosom. Above the moon it takes its flight, and, as a star, it glitters, carrying a flaming train with a lengthened track; and, as he beholds the illustrious deeds of his son, he confesses that they are superior to his own, and rejoices that he is surpassed by him. Although Augustus forbids his own actions to be lauded before those of his father, still Fame, in her freedom and subject to no commands, prefers him against his will; and, in this one point, she disobeys him. Thus does Atreus yield to the glories of the great Agamemnon; thus does Theseus excel Ægeus, and thus Achilles Peleus. In fine, that I may use examples that equal themselves, thus too, is Saturn inferior to Jove. Jupiter rules the abodes of heaven and the realms of the threefold world:[92] the earth is under Augustus: each of them is a father and a ruler. Ye Gods, the companions of Æneas,[93] for whom both the sword and the flames made a way; and you, ye native Deities, and thou, Quirinus, the father of the City, and thou, Gradivus, the son of the invincible Quirinus, and thou, Vesta, held sacred among the Penates of Cæsar; and, with the Vesta of Cæsar, thou, Phœbus, enshrined in thy abode, and thou, Jupiter, who aloft dost possess the Tarpeian heights, and whatever other Deities it is lawful and righteous for a Poet to invoke; late, I pray, may be that day, and protracted beyond my life, on which the person of Augustus, leaving that world which he rules, shall approach the heavens: and when gone, may he propitiously listen to those who invoke him.

And now I have completed a work, which neither the anger of Jove, nor fire, nor steel, nor consuming time will be able to destroy! Let that day, which has no power but over this body of mine, put an end to the term of my uncertain life, when it will. Yet, in my better part, I shall be raised immortal above the lofty stars, and indelible shall be my name. And wherever the Roman power is extended throughout the vanquished earth, I shall be read by the lips of nations, and (if the presages of Poets have aught of truth) throughout all ages shall I survive in fame.

[Footnote 83: Numidians.—Ver. 754. The Numidians under Syphax, together with Juba, King of Mauritania, aided Cato, Scipio, and Petreius, who had been partizans of Pompey, against Julius Cæsar, and were conquered by him.]

[Footnote 84: Pontus.—Ver. 756. Cæsar conquered Pharnaces, the son of Mithridates, king of Pontus, in one battle. It was on this occasion, according to Suetonius, that his despatch was in the words, 'Veni, Vidi, Vici,' 'I came, I saw, I conquered.']

[Footnote 85: Son of Atreus.—Ver. 805. This was Menelaüs, from whom Paris was saved by Venus. See the Iliad, book III.]

[Footnote 86: Mutina.—Ver. 823. This was a place in Cisalpine Gaul, where Augustus defeated Antony, and took his camp.]

[Footnote 87: Philippi.—Ver. 824. Pharsalia was in Thessaly, and Philippi was in Thrace. He uses a poet's license, in treating them as being the same battle-field, as they both formed part of the former kingdom of Macedonia. Pompey was defeated by Julius Cæsar at Pharsalia, while Brutus and Cassius were defeated by Augustus and Antony at Philippi. The fleet of the younger Pompey was totally destroyed off the Sicilian coast.]

[Footnote 88: The wife.—Ver. 826. Mark Antony was so infatuated as to divorce his wife, Octavia, that he might be enabled to marry Cleopatra.]

[Footnote 89: Canopus.—Ver. 828. This was a city of Egypt, situate on the Western mouth of the river Nile.]

[Footnote 90: His hallowed wife.—Ver. 836. Augustus took Livia Drusilla, while pregnant, from her husband, Tiberius Nero, and married her. He adopted her son Tiberius, and constituted him his successor.]

[Footnote 91: With like years.—Ver. 838. Julius Cæsar was slain when he was fifty-six years old. Augustus died in his seventy-sixth year.]

[Footnote 92: Threefold world.—Ver. 859. This is explained as meaning the realms of the heavens, the æther and the air; but it is difficult to guess exactly what is the Poet's meaning here.]

[Footnote 93: Companions of Æneas.—Ver. 861. He probably refers to the Penates which Æneas brought into Latium. Dionysius of Halicarnassus says that he had seen them in a temple at Rome, and that they bore the figures of two youths seated and holding spears.]

EXPLANATION

The Poet having fulfilled his promise, and having brought down his work from the beginning of the world to his own times, concludes it with the apotheosis of Julius Cæsar. He here takes an opportunity of complimenting Augustus, as being more worthy of divine honours than even his predecessor, while he promises him a long and glorious reign. Augustus, however, had not to wait for death to receive divine honours, as he enjoyed the glory of seeing himself worshipped as a Deity and adored at altars erected to him, even in his lifetime. According to Appian, he was but twenty-eight years of age when he was ranked among the tutelar Divinities by all the cities of the empire.

The Romans, who deduced their origin from Æneas, were flattered at the idea of Venus interesting herself in behalf of her posterity, and securing the honours of an apotheosis for Julius Cæsar. The historical circumstances which Ovid here refers to were the following:—After Julius Cæsar had been murdered in the Senate house, Augustus ordered public games to be instituted in his honour. We learn from Suetonius, that during their celebration a new star, or rather a comet, made its appearance, on which it was promulgated that the soul of the deified Julius had taken its place among the stars, and that Venus had procured him that honour. It was then remembered, that the light of the Sun had been unusually pallid the whole year following the death of Cæsar; this which is generally supposed to have been caused by some spots which then appeared on the disk of the sun, was ascribed to the grief of Apollo. Various persons were found to assert various prodigies. Some said that it had rained blood, others that the moon and stars had been obscured; while others, still more imaginative, asserted that beasts had uttered words, and that the dead had risen from their graves.

The sorrow of the Gods and of nature at the untimely death of Julius being thus manifested, Augustus proceeded to found a temple in his honour, established priests for his service, and erected a statue of him with a star on its forehead. He was afterwards represented in the attitude of ascending to the heavens, and wielding a sceptre in his hand. While flatterers complimented Augustus upon the care which he had taken to enrol his predecessor among the Deities, there were some, the poet Manilius being of the number, who considered that heaven was almost over-peopled by him. Augustus, however, was not the sole author of the story of the apotheosis of Julius Cæsar. The people had previously attempted to deify him, though opposed by Cicero and Dolabella. In the funeral oration which was delivered over Julius Cæsar by Antony, he spoke of him as a God, and the populace, moved by his eloquence, and struck at his blood-stained garments and his body covered with wounds, were filled with indignation against the conspirators, and were about to take the corpse to the Capitol, there to be buried; but the priests would not permit it, and had it brought back to the Forum, where it was burnt. Dio Cassius says, that the Roman people raised an altar on the spot where the body had been burnt, and endeavoured to make libations and to offer sacrifices there, as to a Divinity, but that the Consuls overthrew the altar. Suetonius says, that a pillar was also erected to him, of about twenty feet in height, with the inscription, 'parenti patriæ,' 'To the father of his country,' and that for some time persons resorted to that spot to offer sacrifices and to make vows. He adds, that he was made a Divinity by a public decree, but he does not say at what time.

Henry Thomas Riley (Translator)

Riley was born in June 1816, the only son of Henry Riley of Southwark, an ironmonger.

He was educated at Chatham House, Ramsgate, and at Charterhouse School. University was at Trinity College, Cambridge, but at the end of his first term he moved to Clare College where he was admitted on 17th December 1834 and elected a scholar on 24th January 1835.

He graduated B.A. in 1840.

Riley was called to the bar at the Inner Temple on 23rd November 1847, but early in life he worked for booksellers, editing and translating. These skills were to bring him perhaps the real jewels of his legacy with his translations of Terence, Ovid, Plautus and Lucan during the 1850's.

When the Royal Charter of April 1869 set up the Historical Manuscripts Commission he was engaged as an inspector and tasked with examining the archives of various municipal corporations, the muniments of the colleges at Oxford and Cambridge, and the documents in the registries of various bishops and chapters.

Henry Thomas Riley died at Hainault House, the Crescent, Selhurst, Croydon, on 14th April 1878, aged 61.

www.ingramcontent.com/pod-product-compliance
Lightning Source LLC
LaVergne TN
LVHW041153080426
835511LV00006B/585